OUT OF PRINT
HELD AT
LAST COPY STORE

Sustainability Unpacked

D1638612

C014692434

Sustainability Unpacked

Food, Energy and Water for Resilient Environments and Societies

Kristiina A. Vogt, Toral Patel-Weynand, Maura Shelton,
Daniel J. Vogt, John C. Gordon, Calvin T. Mukumoto,
Asep S. Suntana and Patricia A. Roads

publishing for a sustainable future

London • Washington, DC

Hampshire County Library	
C014692434	
Askews	Sep-2010
333.7	£34.99
	9781844079018

First published in 2010 by Earthscan

Copyright © Kristiina A. Vogt, Toral Patel-Weynand, Maura Shelton, Daniel J. Vogt, John C. Gordon, Calvin T. Mukumoto, Asep S. Suntana and Patricia A. Roads 2010

The moral right of the author has been asserted.

All rights reserved. No part of this publication may be reproduced, stored in a retrieval system or transmitted, in any form or by any means, electronic, mechanical, photocopying, recording or other-wise, except as expressly permitted by law, without the prior, written permission of the publisher.

Earthscan Ltd, Dunstan House, 14a St Cross Street, London EC1N 8XA, UK
Earthscan LLC, 1616 P Street, NW, Washington, DC 20036, USA

Earthscan publishes in association with the International Institute for Environment and Development

For more information on Earthscan publications, see www.earthscan.co.uk or write to earthinfo@earthscan.co.uk

ISBN: 978-1-84407-900-1 hardback
ISBN: 978-1-84407-901-8 paperback

Typeset by MapSet Ltd, Gateshead, UK

Cover design by Clifford Hayes

A catalogue record for this book is available from the British Library

Library of Congress Cataloging-in-Publication Data

Vogt, Kristiina A.
    Sustainability unpacked : food, energy and water for resilient environments and societies /
Kristiina A. Vogt…[et.al.].
        p. cm.
    ISBN 978-1-84407-900-1 (hardback) — ISBN 978-1-84407-901-8 (pbk.) 1. Sustainable living.
2. Environmental responsibility. 3. Environmental change. I. Title.
GF78.V64 2010
333.7—dc22
                                                                                                2010007997

At Earthscan we strive to minimize our environmental impacts and carbon footprint through reducing waste, recycling and offsetting our CO_2 emissions, including those created through publication of this book. For more details of our environmental policy, see www.earthscan.co.uk.

Printed and bound in the UK by TJ International,
an ISO 14001 accredited company.
The paper used is FSC certified.

Mixed Sources
Product group from well-managed
forests and other controlled sources
www.fsc.org Cert no. SGS-COC-2482
© 1996 Forest Stewardship Council

Contents

Part I: From the Beginning

Part 2: Scientific Approach to Decoding Sustainability

Part 3: The Real Country Stories

Part 4: Climate and Soils: Unavoidable Constraints to Solar Capital

Part 5: Societies Adapt to a Quagmire of Resource Choices

Cartoon illustrations by Ryan Rosendal

Authors and Contributors

Authors

KRISTIINA A. VOGT, born in Turku, Finland, is a Professor of Ecosystem Management and founder (and co-coordinator) of the Forest Systems and Bioenergy program at the University of Washington, Seattle, USA. She was one of the founders and is currently the Chair of a start-up bioenergy company, Renewol LLC, producing a mobile methanol generator to use low-quality wood and cellulosic waste. She also is the Vice-President of Bio-Energy, Interforest LLC. She obtained the Professor rank at Yale where she was appointed the Margaret K. Musser Professor of Forest Ecology. In 2000, she joined the College of Forest Resources at the University of Washington as a Dean and Professor and continues in her capacity as a Professor. She is a co-investigator on a multi-million dollar Integrative Graduate Education and Research Training (IGERT) grant funded by the National Science Foundation entitled 'Bio-resource Based Energy for Sustainable Societies'. This award supports the development of a multidisciplinary, multicultural graduate education and research programme in Bioresource-based Energy for Sustainable Societies focusing on producing PhD graduates from American Indian tribes. Her research focus can be summarized as: interdisciplinary research in organizing problem solving, developing interdisciplinary educational consortium and developing tools to solve complex interdisciplinary problems around the world in conservation, bioenergy and forestry. She has conducted research in Iceland, Malaysia, Mexico, Brazil, Belize, Indonesia and in Alaska and Puerto Rico as well as within the continental US. Professor Vogt has authored or co-authored seven books and published over 140 refereed articles including *Forests and Society. Sustainability and Life Cycles of Forests in Human Landscapes* (CABI), *Ecosystems: Balancing Science with Management* (Springer-Verlag) and *Forest Certification: Roots, Issues, Challenges and Benefits* (CRC Press). She has published on a range of topics varying from global forest carbon budgets; belowground ecology in an ecosystem context; the role of species in conservation; nutrient cycling; invasive species; restoration ecology; ecosystem-based assessments including human values and non-human constraints; and bioenergy by linking biomass to produce transportation fuels and electricity in the western US and in Indonesia. She has a BA degree in Biology from the University of Texas and obtained her MS and PhD degrees in Biology from New Mexico State University. She has an Honorary Master of Art degree from Yale University.

TORAL PATEL-WEYNAND is an Affiliate Associate Faculty at the University of Washington and an Associate of the Forest Systems and Bioenergy, UW. Before taking up her current position as a Senior Policy Adviser at the US Forest Service in Reston, Virginia, she was a biologist in the US Geological Survey, BRD/Biological Informatics group. She supervised and managed the International Biological Informatics Group and engaged in cooperation through multilateral and bilateral activities and professional meetings. She also coordinated the International Program to address gaps in conservation networks and assist in developing bilateral and regional initiatives that help link biological networks and databases to geospatial information systems to improve the predictive capability of models which aid in policy formulation and decision making. She served as co-lead on the Pacific Biodiversity Information Facility and the Ocean Biogeographic Information Network and works closely with Japan, Australia and New Zealand and Pacific Island Countries both bilaterally and in multilateral fora on biological data sharing. She also served as the US delegation lead to the United Nations Environment Programme (UNEP) on Strengthening the Scientific Base of UNEP. Prior to this, she served as technical adviser to the Department of State and as USGS liaison on Cooperation with the Rio Conventions, including the UN Convention on Biological Diversity, Convention to Combat Desertification, the Ramsar Convention on wetlands and the UN Framework Convention on Climate Change, as well as other international initiatives and organizations such as UNEP, the International Union of Forest Research Organizations/Global Forest Information Service (IUFRO/GFIS) and the Arctic Council, among others. From 2001 to 2004 she was the Senior Science Policy analyst for the US Department of State, Bureau of Oceans, Environment and Science, Office of Global Change, Washington, DC. She has a BA in Economics from Bombay University in India, a BA from Temple University in Pennsylvania, an MS (Environmental Policy and Planning) from George Washington University in Washington, DC and a PhD (Ecosystem Ecology) from Yale University. She has co-authored or edited several books including *Forests and Society: Sustainability and Life Cycles of Forests in Human Landscapes* (CABI) and *Ecosystems: Balancing Science with Management* (Springer-Verlag).

MAURA SHELTON is a Research Associate with the Forest Systems and Bioenergy Program in the School of Forest Resources, College of the Environment, at the University of Washington. She is presently a National Science Foundation IGERT Bioenergy Fellow developing geospatial techniques to determine appropriate sites from sustainable biomass removal while considering include cultural attributes. She is developing the decision tools for determining how biomass can be removed from forests without impairing their resiliency to disturbances and to maintain their provision of ecosystem services. She is also coordinating the capacity of indigenous communities in the Philippines and in Indonesia, as well as American Indian tribes, to manage their own energy systems and to determine how much forest material can be sustainably collected. She has previous experience working on capacity-building in the Philippines and in

China. She is working with an Indonesian nonprofit to develop their capacity to train villagers in the use of spatial data to assess their forest resources. She is a co-collaborator for a chapter in an upcoming book *Bio-resource Based Energy for Sustainable Societies* from Nova Science Publishers. She has previous careers in economics, financial analysis and secondary education. She holds a Bachelor and Master of Science in Economics from Baylor University and a teaching certificate from Seattle University.

DANIEL J. VOGT is Associate Professor in Soils and Ecosystem Ecology of the School of Forest Resources, College of the Environment and came to the University of Washington in July 2000 from Yale University. He is also the co-coordinator of the Forest Systems and Bioenergy program at the School of Forest Resources, University of Washington. At the School of Forestry and Environmental Studies at Yale, was a teaching faculty member in Ecosystem Ecology and Forest Soils and also the Director of the Greeley Analytical Laboratory. Professor Vogt received degrees from New Mexico State University (Biology BS, 1968; Agronomy MS, 1976) and from the University of Washington (Forest Resources PhD in 1987). He is an internationally-recognized scholar with over 50 author credits, including co-authorship of books on *Ecosystems: Balancing Science with Management* (Springer, with a Chinese translation), *Forest Certification: Roots, Issues, Challenges and Benefits* (CRC Press) and *Forests and Society: Sustainability and Life Cycles of Forests in Human Landscapes* (CABI Publishing). His research interests include studies on many different ecosystems from around the world including boreal, temperate and tropical biomes. He is also currently a senior consultant of Interforest LLC, a sustainable forestry consulting firm and a partner in a start-up bioenergy company, Renewol, which employs a mobile generator that uses low quality wood and cellulosic waste to produce methanol.

JOHN C. GORDON was Chairman of Interforest LLC, a sustainable forestry consulting firm and a founder of the Candlewood Timber Group Inc., a sustainable forestry company with forestland and operations in Argentina. He is also Pinchot Professor Emeritus of Forestry and Environmental Studies at the Yale School of Forestry and Environmental Studies, where he was Dean from 1983 to 1992 and again in 1997–98. Before that he was Head and Professor, Department of Forest Science at Oregon State University; Professor of Forestry at Iowa State University; and Principal Plant Physiologist in the Pioneering Project in Wood Formation, USDA Forest Service, Rhinelander, Wisconsin. He has a BS (Forest Management) and a PhD (Plant Physiology and Silviculture) from Iowa State University and has been a Fulbright Scholar in Finland (University of Helsinki) and India (GKVK State Agricultural University, Bangalore). His primary expertize is in the biological basis of forest productivity, the management of research and forest policy and management. He has consulting experience with public and private organizations including forest product firms, the Intertribal Timber Council, the World Bank and the United Nations Development

Programme (UNDP). He has authored, coauthored or edited over 150 papers and books, including *Environmental Leadership: Developing Effective Skills and Styles* (Island Press) and *Environmental Leadership Equals Essential Leadership* (Yale University Press), both with Joyce Berry. He has overseas experience in a variety of places, including India, Pakistan, China, Costa Rica, Brazil, Argentina, Finland and Scotland. He also is currently a partner in two start-up companies, Renewol, a bioenergy company producing a mobile methanol generator to use low quality wood and cellulosic waste and Maximum Yield Associates, which does global searches for productive forest sites and advises on increasing forest plantation yields.

CALVIN T. MUKUMOTO is currently the CEO and Chair of the Coquille Economic Development Corporation (CEDCO). CEDCO is the primary business arm of the Coquille Indian Tribe. He is also the President of Renewol LLC, a start-up company producing a mobile methanol generator to use low quality wood and cellulosic wastes and was the Chief Financial Officer for TSS Consultants. He is an experienced manager working at the senior executive level providing strategic business planning, business viability assessments, capital budget analysis, marketing, interim management, contract negotiation, project management, information systems development and turnaround management services. He has extensive experience with all components of American Indian forestry. He has served as a member of the Indian Forest Management Assessment Team (IFMAT). He served on the enterprise boards for the Quinault Indian Nation, Makah Tribal Council and the Confederated Tribes of the Warm Springs. With respect to sustainable forestry, he served on the US Board of Directors for the Forest Stewardship Council. He is currently the Vice Chair of the Oregon State Board of Forestry. When he was the Forest Resource Director for the Warm Springs Forest Products Industries in Oregon, he developed and implemented the expanded biomass plant for co-generation. He also has been a management consultant providing business management, marketing and planning services to forest products companies, American Indian Tribes and others. From 1980 to 1988 he was the Operations Manager for the Makah Tribal Council in Washington for the government of the Makah Indian Tribe. He has a BS (Forest Management) from Humboldt State University and an MBA and an Executive MBA program from the University of Washington. He also had an internship with Nissho Iwai Corporation in Japan, a forest products company.

ASEP S. SUNTANA is a Research Associate in the Forest Systems and Bioenergy program at the University of Washington and on the Board of Directors of the Indonesian Institute for Forest and Environment (RMI), Bogor, Indonesia. He has over 15 years of practical experience in institutional development, capacity building and training on sustainable forest management, forest certification, community forestry, biodiversity and environmental education in Indonesia. Since 2004, he has been working on forest systems and bio-energy programmes, particularly in linking forest management systems, biodiversity conservation, sustainable bio-energy development, carbon mitigation and sustainable rural livelihoods. In 1998 he co-founded the Indonesian Ecolabelling Institute Foundation (Yayasan Lembaga Ekolabel Indonesia or YLEI), and was also a co-founder of the RMI, in 1992. From 2000 to 2004 he was the Deputy Director of the YLEI and continued after that time as their Liaison Officer while in the US. He directed the formulation, oversaw the design and coordinated the implementation of new programmes particularly related to the community-based forest management certification system and plantation/man-made forest certification system, and developed and carried out monitoring and evaluation systems. He obtained a BS degree from the Faculty of Forestry, Bogor Agricultural University (IPB) in Indonesia and an MA degree from The Heller School for Social Policy and Management, Brandeis University in Massachusetts. He is also a PhD candidate in the College of Forest Resources at the University of Washington and was a Leadership for Environment and Development (LEAD) Fellow (LEAD International and LEAD Indonesia Program) in Indonesia, China and Canada (1998–2000). He contributed to the book *Forests and Society: Sustainability and Life Cycles of Forests in Human Landscapes* (CABI).

PATRICIA A. ROADS is the Communications Director for the Center for Adaptive Policies in Ecosystems International, a nonprofit organization originally based in Washington and now in Iceland. Prior to this, she was a Systems Analyst, Field Engineer for National Cash Register (NCR). She also was an Engineering Educational Instructor for National Cash Registers (NCR) United States Data Processing Group (USDPG) and Financial Software Product Manager for NCR USDPG followed by Operations Manager for DB&C. She has considerable experience in publishing and writing op-ed pieces for the lay and scientific media outlets on energy, use of forest materials for energy, rural community recovery efforts after disturbances and social adaptation to them. She was on the Steering Committee, a rapporteur and wrote the summary for the *Forest and Agricultural Based Bio-energy and Carbon Mitigation*, World Renewable Energy Regional Congress and Exhibition held in Indonesia in 2007. She has co-authored several publications and been an editor on publications produced by the RMI, Indonesia. She was a contributor to *Forests and Society: Sustainability and Life Cycles of Forests in Human Landscapes* (CABI) and a book co-author in the forthcoming book *Bio-resource Based Energy for Sustainable Societies* (Nova Science Publishers).

Additional Contributors to the Boxed Case Studies

TERRENCE G. BENSEL, PhD, Associate Professor and Chair, Department of Environmental Science, Allegheny College, Meadville, Pennsylvania, USA

PETE BETTINGER, Professor, Warnell School of Forestry and Natural Resources, University of Georgia, Athens, Georgia, USA

ROBERT L. EDMONDS, Professor and former Associate Dean for Research, School of Forest Resources, University of Washington, Seattle, Washington, USA

CARLOS A. GONZÁLEZ, PhD, Senior Agricultural Attaché, US Embassy, Mexico City, Foreign Agricultural Service, US Department of Agriculture, Mexico City, Mexico

MICHAEL MARCHAND, Fellow NSF Bioenergy IGERT, University of Washington, Seattle, Washington; Council Member Confederated Tribes of the Colville, Colville, Washington, USA

LLOYD L. NACKLEY, PhC, Fellow NSF Bioenergy IGERT and Research Associate, School of Forest Resources, University of Washington, Seattle, Washington, USA

PAM OVERHULSER, Timber Appraiser, Oregon Department of Revenue, Salem, Oregon, USA

GENE PECK, Associate Vice President, ARCADIS US, Middletown, Connecticut, USA

Dr BIANCA PERLA, Research Associate, School of Forest Resources, University of Washington, Seattle, Washington, USA

Dr ELIZABETH M. REMEDIO, Professor and Director, USC–CHED Zonal Research Center, University of San Carlos, Cebu City, Philippines

JASON SCULLION, Research Associate and Lecturer, School of Forest Resources and Evans School of Public Affairs, University of Washington, Seattle, Washington, USA

Dr RAGNHILDUR SIGURDARDOTTIR, PhD, Director CAPEIntl Iceland and President of Umhverfisrannsoknir ehf, Selfoss, Iceland

MIA SISCAWATI, PhC, Department of Anthropology, University of Washington, Seattle, Washington and Board Member of RMI , Bogor, Indonesia

Dr RAJESH THADANI, PhD, Director, Centre for Ecology, Development and Research (CEDAR), New Delhi, India

Dr JOHN SESSIONS, PhD, Professor, Department of Forest Engineering, Resources and Management, Oregon State University, Corvallis, Oregon, USA

Preface

Sustainability and adaptability are interdependent, essential traits of human history recorded on the Earth, which itself is dynamic. Sustainability, as a stand-alone trait or circumstance, may suggest a static condition, which, of course, is absolutely impossible in terms of the physical–chemical–biological processes that operate on and in the Earth.

Furthermore, sustainability is similar to hitting a moving target, in no small measure due to the ever-increasing population. The question must be raised: how many humans can the Earth sustain under the unavoidable constraints of climates and soils? These unavoidable constraints control the globe's productive capacity and set the boundaries for how much the human capital can be developed. It is not too early to do more than think about this pressing problem. It is time to formulate some proposals for serious consideration to achieve sustainability in practice. We hope this volume contributes towards the formulation of new proposals to sustainably produce and consume resources that also maintain societal adaptability in the face of dynamic environments and climates.

This volume addresses the survival necessities of life, in particular as they relate to humans – food, water and energy, with emphasis on their dependence on forests. It may be suggested that another necessity for survival is luck, as noted by Hsu (1986). Luck will not be discussed in our book but unpacking sustainable principles should help societies to make the necessary trade-offs to improve decision making.

When resources are considered, it is important to distinguish the two end-members – renewable, represented by biofuels and non-renewable, represented by fossil fuels. Products of both should be considered as creative wealth, as opposed to distributive wealth, represented by the monetary institutions, among others. Resource providers are producers, hopefully with responsible consideration of the ecosystems and they share that responsibility with those who are totally consumers of resources.

This book explores and decodes the interlinking and complex elements of sustainability so that resource use and human development strategies can maintain resilient environments and societies at a country level. Historical examples are used to provide insights into the characteristics of sustainability principles. These are followed by examining how 34 selected countries (advanced-, emerging- and growing-economy) have approached the sustainable acquisition of energy, food, forest materials and water for their citizens, while being part of the global economy. We shall present and compare several indices developed by international organizations (such as population levels, percentage of people living in rural areas and dependence on fossil fuels), that are being used to rank countries as to their sustainability or vulnerability to environmental and societal changes, for these 34 countries. These climatic, environmental and resource use indices will be explored for their utility in explaining how a country's resource footprints contribute to its ranking in the environmental and climatic index groupings.

Country-level index data, supplemented by data on energy, food, forests and water uses are examined to demonstrate how the elements of sustainability vary among the countries. The country-level data include:

- climatic conditions;
- forest and agriculture productivity as well as their contribution to the GDP;
- the bio-resource productive capacities of the lands;
- fossil- and non-fossil energy consumption;
- carbon dioxide (CO_2) emissions during economic development;
- the importance of bio-resources in the economy;
- food consumption;
- renewable water availabilities and sources;
- soil quality and productive capacities;
- climate risk events.

These analyses are also used to demonstrate what makes a country resilient in its consumption of the four essential resources (food, forests, water and energy) and how appropriate it is to use higher human developed countries (such as Scandinavian countries) as models of sustainability. These data demonstrate that growing-economy countries should not necessarily follow the models developed in industrialized countries for the acquisition of the four essential resources. This is mainly due to the facts that we do not have new frontiers from which to acquire additional resources; our energy supplies are diminishing; and society has to adapt to changing climates. Therefore, for emerging-economies, their resource management and acquisition options should be geared towards efficient resource uses and the adoption of appropriate new technologies that may help them avoid the errors made previously by other countries. We also make a case that the sustainable use and management of forests will be important for those countries wanting to have resilient societies and environments.

By recognizing the links and feedbacks that exist within human landscapes, we hope to suggest how human behaviour can be modified and to emphasize the trade-offs that may have to be made in resource uses. It is important that we move beyond decisions that make us feel good or provide us significant short-term economic return, but have absolutely minimal ability to maintain long-term social and environmental resiliency. We need to move beyond special-interest group decisions, driven by their personal values or even greed, to make informed decisions that allow for the human development potential to increase, without damaging the environment or human health. We hope this book will contribute to this goal.

We have developed here a comprehensive analysis that allows us to identify (1) the factors that can be managed and (2) when society needs to adapt if it wants to reach a higher human development potential. In addition, we also realize that the decoding of sustainability has to be grounded in scientific knowledge and to include the volumes of information that society has accumulated throughout its history. By simultaneously combining both a historical and a current perspective to explore resource and human development choices made by countries, it will be easier to begin to unpack the elements of what it means to be sustainable. This, we hope, is the value of a book like ours.

The authors really want to express our appreciation to Dr. John W. Shelton for his invaluable discussions, making us aware of pertinent literature, and for his editorial help that allowed us to maintain a balanced and credible discussion of fossil and renewable energy supplies for the countries included in our book. Dr. John W. Shelton is a Professor Emeritus of Geology from Oklahoma State University, and Founder and Editor of American Association of Petroleum Geologists Online Journal.

References

Hsu, K. J. (1986) *The Great Dying*, Harcourt Brace Javanovich, New York, NY

List of Figures and Tables

Figures

Tables

Part 1

FROM THE BEGINNING

Sustainability – Clues for Positive Societal and Ecosystem Change

Defining Sustainability

Sustainable practices are best understood after sustainability is defined accurately. Such a definition makes transparent the human goals and values that are integral to the term. However, defining sustainability has been challenging because of the need to include social, economic and environmental factors simultaneously. A narrowly written definition of sustainability will not be consistently interpreted in the same manner by everyone and will vary depending on the readers' backgrounds. One definition cannot and should not encompass the complexity and capture the nuances that are inherent in the word 'sustainable'. For example, the Eskimos have at least seven distinct root words for snow. Each root word describes some attribute of snow that is not revealed or communicated when one is limited to using one word. This does not mean that there is no value in this word.

The need to define sustainability broadly and the general overuse of the word 'sustainability', has made the most acceptable definition the one espoused in the Brundland Report, that is, 'management and conservation of the natural resource base and ... attainment and continued satisfaction of human needs for the present and future generations' (WCED, 1987). This definition continues to be valuable for decision makers because it identifies the overarching goals that need to be included in a sustainability assessment. This is why the same definition still needs to be espoused. The 2002 World Summit on Sustainable Development held in Johannesburg, South Africa, used similar terms when asking participating countries to 'ensure a balance between economic development, social development and environmental protections as interdependent and mutually reinforcing pillars of sustainable development' (UN, 2002).

These broad definitions require tools to ensure a balance between economic development, social development and environmental protection. Well-worded definitions provide the overarching goals wanted by society, but they are difficult to measure. This book will explore how to measure sustainability, because it has implications for how society develops both its human and its resource capitals.

Why Sustainability Needs to be Unpacked

Because we have defined sustainability, this does not automatically mean that we understand how to implement practices to achieve its goals, nor does a definition provide a 'roadmap' to show us how to pursue sustainable practices. Today, there is a need to 'decode or unpack sustainability' so that both societies and environments can retain their resiliency and still allow the development of the world's human capital while continuing to consume the globe's resources; we cannot always count on luck to survive (Hsu, 1986). Because of population growth and the lack of uninhabited regions in the world, individual human decisions have a greater impact today than in the past. Societal decisions on what resources to consume cannot be a 'cosmetic' fix because of the potential for extensive negative repercussions from unsuitable decisions. Today, decisions can increase the vulnerability of humans and ecosystems to future disturbances (e.g. climate change). In addition, when ecosystems are degraded, they are less capable of providing resources in a sustainable manner.

The emergence of several rapidly industrializing and growing-economy countries is also forcing us to decode sustainability to provide a 'roadmap' for them. The historical approaches to industrialization followed by the current highly industrialized countries will not work in today's world. History has shown us how some advancing-economy countries reached their present status by confiscating and consuming resources owned by others. Such an approach will be less successful today because of instantaneous worldwide communications, possible media exposure and, in some respects, a more global economy. Sustainable practices need to be adapted for today's reality. These emerging-economy countries will be making many critical choices for their people; these should be based on how their societies can remain adaptive and develop both their human and resource capital, in the face of climate change.

We cannot continue to compete for ownership of the few new frontiers that sporadically become available. The global communities' response to claiming new mineral deposits in the Arctic is a classic case of 'modern-day colonization'. In 2008, the melting of the ice sheets in the Arctic exposed minerals that are now more accessible because of today's technology. The magnitude of these rich mineral deposits is driving a new period of colonization and only time will tell how it ends and who will own it.

Another part of the problem in decoding sustainability is the need 'to think and function like an ecosystem'; that is, to include social, ecological and economic factors with all their interconnections and possible feedbacks into one story. Many factors need to be included that may not, at first glance, appear to be relevant to writing the resource–sustainability story. Interestingly enough, sustainability is a complex endeavour that requires the assessor to think like 'a spider spinning a web' (see Figure 1.1). Each strand of our web relates to one of the many factors that influence one resource. Webs are not 'linear', and a resource is not influenced by only one factor. The successful development of a sustainability web needs to include so many factors that sometimes the primary result of its investigation

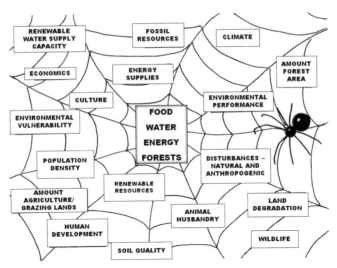

Figure 1.1 *The Sustainability Web: A conceptual figure representing some of the factors affecting human consumption of energy, food, forest materials and water*

Centre box = Essential survival needs; Satellite boxes = modifiers impacting these essential survival needs

causes 'analysis paralysis'. In this state, the assessor gets lost in trying to analyse the volumes of data and forgets what the original goals or questions may have been.

Ecosystem thinking is a relatively recent idea and one where the principles are still being developed. It began in the early 1960s when ecologists recognized that environments needed to include all the parts of the ecosystem, from the microbes to larger animals and the plants (Vogt et al, 1997). It was not until the early 1990s that social ecologists and ecosystem managers recognized that humans were part of this ecosystem and could positively or negatively impact the sustainability of natural environments. Trying to link the ecosystem and humans at a landscape level has been difficult because of the need to develop mechanistic explanations that link the actions of people with their impacts on the environment. Without such an understanding, it is almost impossible to identify the indicators that can be used to measure the efficacy of past decisions in order to improve future decision making. A lack of understanding of the repercussions and links between protecting and managing forests and people's behaviour when they are denied access to resources continues to be a problem for society. Perla and Vogt characterize how environmental degradation and loss of social resilience is a possible outcome when not all stakeholder values are included when deciding to convert a managed forest into a park (Box 1.1).

Because social and environmental problems are complex and ecosystems-based, making sustainable decisions is not easy and may require difficult trade-offs to be made. We began writing this book because of our recognition that *ecosystem thinking* is not the norm for managing natural resources and the challenge is to recognize what practice or policy is not sustainable for either humans or an ecosystem.

Box 1.1 Social and Environmental Resilience in the Skagit Watershed, Washington State, USA

Bianca S. Perla and Kristiina A. Vogt

When wilderness protection designation was given to the Skagit Watershed in north-western Washington, it impacted and altered the social and environmental resilience of people living in the upper and lower reaches of this watershed. Social and environmental resilience was impacted by *resources, diversity, memory and connection*; these factors varied with watershed location. Understanding how these factors were expressed in upper and lower portions of the watershed can be used to increase the efficacy of conservation when protected areas are established. The social and ecological landscapes that surround protected areas need to be managed if the system's resilience is a goal.

The upper Skagit Watershed, with 43 per cent forest cover, exhibits a short growing season, higher average elevations, steep slopes and poor soils, with limited job opportunities. In contrast, the lower watershed, with 8 per cent forest cover, has longer growing seasons and flat, rich, alluvial plains conducive to both farming and other industries. Lower watershed areas have consistently exhibited higher social resilience values than upper watershed areas (e.g. 9.6 per cent below poverty versus 12.7 per cent); conversely the latter has shown higher ecological resilience. In the 1960s and again in the 1980s, there was a level of community breakdown in the upper watershed as people left or started commuting downriver for jobs; these changes were associated with the designation of the protected area, decline in timber industry, closing of a cement plant and completion of the hydropower dam. Compared to downriver residents, more vulnerable upriver residents perceived more costs and fewer benefits from having a protected area designation in their landscape. The lower watershed has exhibited higher population retention rates; these residents also have higher incomes and education levels. Residents of the lower watershed have 1.7 different jobs over their lifetimes, while the average is 3.4 different jobs for the upper watershed areas.

When protected areas occur in resilient social systems, desirable consequences result; they translate into environmental benefits as well. Relationships between parks and neighbouring areas are an evolutionary process, rather than a one-time effort. Exploration of social and environmental resilience in the Skagit watershed shows that maintaining social resilience is essential to maintaining environmental resilience. This means that effective protected area managers must become increasingly responsible for understanding and promoting social resilience of park borderlands. In short, any type of conservation mandate cannot be successful if it exceeds the ability of social systems to absorb the changes imposed on them. Unstable social systems deteriorate natural systems in the long run.

In an attempt to understand the complex factors impacting human acquisition of basic survival needs, researchers have compiled many stories on resource production and consumption by different societies. It is expensive and time-consuming to collect the data needed to write these stories. They are invaluable to make sustainable decisions for the actual location where they were originally developed; however, they may be totally inappropriate for a neighbouring land. In addition, resource stories are sparse that meticulously document the ecosystem interconnections and possible feedbacks across multiple temporal and spatial scales.

Humans are especially fascinated by stories of societies that collapsed. The success of Jared Diamond's book *Collapse* (Diamond, 2005) attests to this interest. These stories about the collapse of past societies are interesting to read, but today it is more important to read stories about how and why societies did not 'collapse'. Societies that did *not* 'collapse' have done something right and their stories may provide us with a greater understanding of what factors are required to be sustainable. Unfortunately, the examples of societies that collapsed will not enable us to make adequately informed decisions so that we can avoid a similar fate, for these stories may simply illustrate a unique condition that does not pertain or is not applicable, to any other situation or area in the world. However, it is clear that most of these examples are linked to over-exploitation of a natural resource that reduced a society's capacity to survive on its own lands. For example, it is clear that during a 4,000-year period the usefulness and economic opportunities provided by Lebanon's cedar trees drove their over-exploitation. Many fierce battles were fought over the ownership of these resources. Loss of these cedar forests triggered the erosion and leaching of salt-rich sediments into the lowland agricultural areas. These sediments reduced agricultural productivity by more than one-half and decreased the capacity of these soils to feed the people dependent upon them (Jacobsen and Adams, 1958; Hillel, 1991). This general statement of over-exploitation as the cause of collapse is further confounded by the fact that several of these societies had survived for hundreds of years and were highly developed until climate change, typically, severe droughts, pushed them towards being unsustainable (Fagan, 2008).

If we look beyond the over-exploitation of a resource as the simple answer as to why a society collapsed, then we shall have a greater chance of making choices that are sustainable. Over-exploitation is only one of the many diverse factors that impinge on whether a choice is sustainable. There is a need to be able to identify why some societies collapsed while others flourished under what initially appear to have been similar ecosystem conditions. There is a need to understand the 'connections' between decisions made regarding the use of both human or natural resources and the increased societal vulnerability to their environments. These connections are not always obvious because ecosystems are complex and the repercussions of decisions may be spatially and temporally displaced from the decision itself. Also, most tools available today do not have the ability to integrate the various dynamics of the water, food, energy and forest resources needed by humans to survive.

Decoding Our Current Perceptions of Sustainability and Is There a Right Model?

History would suggest that humans have not been very capable of living within their social, environmental and economic footprints; this means that we do not have acceptable models that can be used to learn what works, to increase the possibility that a country will make sustainable choices. Traditionally, the expansion of the human footprint has been driven by the economic development activities of industrializing countries. However, several emerging and growing economies are rapidly expanding their resource footprints while pursuing opportunities to participate in the current industrialization visions made possible by carbon compounds. We contend that part of the problem of humans not living within their footprint is that humans address each problem individually and not as a linked set of problems, where a decision made for one problem will have repercussions on another human or environmental problem. Our societal approach to deal with complex environmental and social problems is typically a *disciplinary-based approach* and is symbolically addressed by using a *bandage to control a symptom* and not the *disease*. This means that a bandage solution to a complex environmental problem does not make the problem disappear. It will probably erupt again when triggered by something else. This adds multi-dimensionality to each problem and where its symptom will reflect each ecosystem's specific characteristics. This is similar to the pimples that form on the face of a person with severe acne problems. The person does not know where the next pimple will appear or what causes the pimple to form, but they are able to treat each pimple when it does appear, similar to the bandage analogy above.

Therefore, if sustainable energy production, water use and food production are to become a reality, it is urgent that we understand how to ensure that the mistakes already made by the current industrialized countries are not repeated by the developing countries and that we have a better decision making process. No social group has ownership of the 'realistic' answers. However, we can learn lessons from the struggles of many different sectors of our global society and how these groups have resolved their problems. Yet, we also should not naively believe the vision that societies more closely linked to their bio-resources (i.e. the 'back to nature' approach) are more sustainable and could, therefore, be used as a guideline for 'how to consume resources' sustainably. This would be naive and foolish. People living 'close to nature' have a tough life and it is not as idealistic as some portray. For example, forests provide fuelwood for many communities dependent upon nature for their survival; however, burning wood in cooking stoves has been labelled as the 'silent killer' of women and children when they breathe in the particulates released when wood is burned in small and confined spaces (Smith, 1994; WHO/UNDP, 2004; Bhattasali, 2006; Vogt et al, 2007).

Today, the same historical pattern (i.e. utilizing someone else's resources to power and build a country's economy) is still being repeated. The emergence of new economic powerhouses, such as China and India, that need considerable resources to industrialize, is driving competition for resource supplies at the expense of other countries (e.g. Indonesia and Angola). This duplicates the approach used by the European colonialists when they began to conquer other regions of the world and exploited someone else's resources. This is the historical industrialized model of growth. Today, this scenario is more difficult to repeat because countries with resources are less willing to let others control access to them. Historically, countries conquered lands for the bio-resource supplies they required, without providing compensation to the local inhabitants. Now countries are using the global economic markets to acquire these resources. For example, China needs oil and is acquiring a stake in oil companies in Angola, Indonesia and Nigeria (Lee and Oster, 2008) to ensure their access to the oil needed to power their industries. China is also fuelling deforestation in several locations around the world (e.g. Burma and the Russian Federation) because of their interest in having the largest global wood-processing industry and being the major exporter of finished wood products (Goodman and Finn, 2007). In fact, 'In just 10 years China had moved from being a net importer of wood products to becoming the world's leading exporter of furniture, plywood and wood flooring, sucking in vast amounts of timber from key sensitive areas' (Lovel, 2007).

In effect, China is pursuing a goal of local and regional sustainability that is destabilizing and reducing global sustainability. Its approach to being sustainable does not factor-in the impact on countries where resources are being acquired. If this approach were used, China might be making some very different choices. If we thought of the global community as a 'symphony orchestra', it might be easier to imagine how a decision made in one country can impact others. Imagine that each country's resources are musical instruments. Having each country play musical notes from different music scores will result in a cacophony of sounds that will be quite harsh to the human ear, similar to an orchestra tuning their instruments before a concert. The role of the conductor is to make sure that everyone in the 'symphony' is not only playing the same tune, but starting and stopping at the same time. However, we do not have and probably will never have a 'global conductor' empowered to force each country to play 'global notes' on their musical instrument (see Figure 1.2). If we considered that some resources (the musical instrument of each country) are located in global hotspots, it might become more apparent for the need to coordinate resource consumption globally, so that their use becomes more sustainable; that is, the 'symphony' plays a beautiful piece of music.

In the orchestra analogy one needs to replace each musical instrument with a resource or resources and include all countries as part of the orchestra. For example, the percussion instruments might be the amount of forest area existing in a country, the woodwind could be the amount of fossil fuels and the brass instruments might be the available supplies of water or food, etc (Figure 1.2). This analogy needs to be taken one step further to include the realistic capacity of each country to provide these resources; i.e. its productive capacity or sustainable supply capacity. This would move us to the idea of living within our 'solar income' rather than from our 'solar capital' (see Chapters 9 and 12).

Today, societies mostly acknowledge that human resource consumption is contributing towards environmental degradation and climate change. These

Figure 1.2 *Orchestra analogy of global sustainability*

environmental changes are increasing societal vulnerability and reducing the bio-resource supply capacity of our environments. This is the situation the Confederated Tribes of the Colville faced when the Grand Coulee dam was built on their lands and subsequently destroyed their traditional livelihood (Box 1.2). The Grand Coulee dam was built in 1942, but similar questions are still being asked today in many regions of the world. For example, Iceland is struggling to define what are acceptable trade-offs from building dams on almost every river system in Iceland to generate inexpensive electricity (Box 1.3). Similar to the Colville, the dams may impact the viability of certain fish stocks in Icelandic waters. These conflicts continue today because of the difficulty of assessing the trade-offs and documenting when human resource consumption does contribute towards environmental degradation.

Few historical examples exist to enlighten us regarding how to simultaneously reduce our energy, food, forest and water footprints. Today, we acknowledge that we need to make trade-offs when making decisions regarding the acquisition of these resources. This recognition has driven the world's interest in the science of sustainability and the development of tools to help make these decisions.

Large Datasets and Moving Beyond Irrational Human Choices

In most cases, econometric or environmental models are sufficiently robust to make rational decisions; however, they are less able to assess whether a decision sufficiently considered the multitude of complex and interdisciplinary factors that can impact ecosystems and environments. Large datasets, the best models and

Box 1.2 The Building of the Grand Coulee Dam, Washington, USA and its Consequences

Michael Marchand

Completion of the Grand Coulee Dam in 1942 represents a major renewable energy project that provided significant national benefits in the US. It is still the largest concrete structure in the world, generating 42 per cent of the power provided by eight dams located on the upper Columbia River, three of which are located in Canada. With a total generating capacity of 6809MW, Coulee Dam is the fourth largest power producer in the world.

Benefits of the Grand Coulee Dam include employment during the Depression era, electricity, irrigation and flood control. The energy provided by the dam was vital for plutonium and aluminum production during World War II. It powered the development of the current high-technology industry of the Pacific Northwest and continues to provide power to industries and households in the region. The project provided work for 10,000 construction workers. It irrigates 1400 farms with some farms located more than 160km from the dam; the total land area irrigated is about 276,000ha. The annual revenue from the dam is estimated at one thousand million US$.

However, these benefits, including hydropower, have been offset by negative consequences almost entirely borne by Native Americans; the upper Columbia River was the original homeland of the Colville Tribes. These negative impacts include loss of salmon (a main food source and trade commodity), displacement of people (i.e. entire communities were moved from the flooded area that was formerly prime farmland) and creating barriers to travel (only two small ferry boats service the more than 250km-long Roosevelt Lake). Young Native American soldiers returned home from World War II only to find that Great Kettle Falls (once truly great) had been flooded and that there were no fish; this used to be one of the great fisheries of the world and a regional trading centre. The region remains one of the poorest in the US almost 60 years after the dam was constructed. In addition to the economic hardships, there have been adverse cultural and spiritual consequences.

Grand Coulee is one of many examples of USA's development of resources whereby Native Americans were negatively impacted: oil and gas, coal, uranium, water, as well as timber resources, have similar stories. Procedures to compensate Native Americans for the damages due to the building of the Grand Coulee Dam were not resolved until the 1990s. While the region still remains economically depressed, the Colville Tribes will probably still be striving for compensation for damages well into this century. The government has agreed to pay the tribe(s) a percentage of the profits from Bonneville Power Administration dam projects based on the area flooded and the Northwest American tribes negotiated an agreement with BPA to implement nearly one thousand million US$ of dam mitigation projects to restore salmon on the river system. This negotiated settlement is hopefully a turning point.

Box 1.3 Geothermal and Hydroelectric Power versus Ecology in Iceland

Ragnhildur Sigurdardottir

In Iceland 90 per cent of the houses use geothermal water for heating, with almost all remaining houses using electricity from hydropower. These native energy resources have proved to be very economical and ecological by offering reliable, adequate, renewable energy. Geothermal energy owes its occurrence and potential to Iceland lying on the Mid-Atlantic Ridge, where magma, which lies at relatively shallow depths, is the source of volcanic eruptions. Some 20–25 high-temperature geothermal areas (e.g. 200°C at a depth of 1000m) are known in Iceland. The high temperature areas are usually of great conservation value because they normally have high colour, geologic and ecological diversity. Six or seven of those fields have already been developed; about the same number have been claimed for exploration to build new geothermal power stations. In 2008, hydropower supplied 12.4TWh of electricity, which was 75 per cent of the electrical energy production in Iceland. Although the greenhouse gas emissions from reservoirs are insignificant, the industries powered by this native energy may cause a greater impact at the country level than previously recognized.

Both energy sources are usually viewed as being green, sustainable and climate-friendly. Today, Iceland's energy is also being used to power non-Icelandic industries attracted by the inexpensive electricity provided by these native energy resources. To date, three aluminum (Al) smelters and a ferrosilicon factory consume about 80 per cent of Iceland's electricity. In 2008, 791 thousand tons/yr of Al was produced, consuming 11.4TWh of energy; this emitted considerable amounts of CO_2 and pollutants. As of 2009, at least three companies are planning to increase their Al production capacities and/or build new plants. They will be powered by geothermal and hydro-energy, thereby increasing its capacity by more than 200 per cent over a five to six year period. This will use 85–90 per cent of the electricity produced in Iceland or 23–30TWh/yr.

Recently, using renewable resources to provide inexpensive energy to global customers is being severely criticized in Iceland today because of its negative environmental externalities. Furthermore, the government now proposes a 15 per cent cut in CO_2 emissions by 2020, compared to 1990 levels. Non-Icelandic use of native energy makes it difficult for Iceland to reach their CO_2 emissions reduction goals. The production and use of geothermal energy contributes to the emissions of greenhouse and toxic gases and dissolved chemicals, in some cases hazardous to toxic. Estimated emissions from only the proposed geothermal plants in Iceland and from Al smelters are 1050–1850 thousand Gg CO_2/yr and 1950–3450 thousand Gg CO_2/yr, respectively. If the government policy to reduce CO_2 emissions is adopted, the stimulus for building energy-intensive industries may disappear well before 2020.

The proposed hydropower and geothermal capacity will harness almost every feasible river system and high-temperature field in Iceland, whether or not they contain important wildlife, commercially important fish populations, conservation landmarks or other environmental features. Areas with high conservation value also show good potential for harnessing energy. Sustainability or lack thereof, of energy production in Iceland must answer the question of whether the benefits of 50TWh/yr of non-fossil fuels are balanced by the environmental and social costs.

frameworks will not allow us to determine what choices should be made to consume, conserve, mitigate or restore the supply capacity of any resource if we do not factor in the unavoidable constraints of either the environment or the human potential to make irrational decisions when the threads of the sustainability web are not transparent. Large datasets help us to identify what problems need solutions but not how to characterize the solution options for each problem. These models provide rational decisions for a specific and clearly defined set of circumstances but are less able to identify solutions when sensitive factors were unknowingly not included in the original assessment. This can lead to irrational decisions.

History has documented many examples of human behaviour that we would characterize as bizarre today but were accepted as normal in their context and timeframe. In 1841, Charles MacKay published the *Memoirs of Extraordinary Popular Delusions and the Madness of Crowds* that recounted many examples of irrational human behaviour. For example, in many countries in Europe it was socially acceptable to poison someone slowly but not to stab the same person in the heart. The end result for the victim was death, no matter which practice was socially acceptable. Eventually, the fine art of poisoning was deemed unacceptable in England during the time of Henry VIII; it was punishable by being boiled to death (MacKay, 1841). During this period, many women were burned at the stake as witches, especially after unexplainable climatic events; killing of witches still happens today (e.g., 2008 in Tanzania) following prolonged droughts, even though the women are not burned at the stake. 'Tulipomania' is another example of a very irrational and delusional investment activity that began in 1600 and ended with many people in financial ruin. By 1634 'it was deemed a proof of bad taste in any man of fortune to be without a collection of them', that is, tulip bulbs (MacKay, 1841). At this time the dealers selling tulips were so desperate to obtain one bulb that an inferior quality bulb was bought for 'twelve acres of building-ground' and another bulb for 'a new carriage, two grey horses and a complete set of harness'.

Assuming that these types of delusional behaviour do not happen today may be itself delusional following the investment market crash of 2008–2009. When decisions are not made using a system framework that recognizes system complexity and feedbacks, it becomes easy to accept unrealistic and irrational assumptions. Krugman (2009) stated that 'economists fell back in love with the old, idealized vision of an economy in which rational individuals interact in perfect markets, this time gussied up with fancy equations.' The key words are 'rational individuals' and 'fancy equations'. He further stated that economists will have to 'acknowledge the importance of irrational and often unpredictable behaviour, face up to the often idiosyncratic imperfections of markets and accept that an elegant economic theory of everything is a long way off.'

Humans have a long history of making 'cosmetic' decisions because a superficial examination suggested that the benefits appeared to outweigh the costs. This makes it very easy to examine each problem as an independent issue without considering the implications of these decisions. Cosmetic decisions do not develop solutions to problems using the 'ecosystem' approach. An unfortunate but demonstrative example of this situation occurred in the 1770s. At this time, people began to bleach their skin using arsenic to give it a porcelain appearance (Flanders, 2009). It was the fashion those days to practise skin bleaching because porcelain skin suggested that you were of the upper class and perhaps a lady of leisure, in other words not a servant. Through the early 1800s, rubbing arsenic into the face and arms was used to improve one's complexion or treat skin diseases, even though it was used to poison vermin under the name 'ratsbane' (British History, 2007). Therefore, the potential human health effects did not seem to be important. The medical effects of large doses of arsenic have been reported in an 1984 American Medical Association publication as: hair falling out, severe nosebleeds, losing unconsciousness for several hours and having seizures, to name a few. It is hard to imagine people wanting to use arsenic to improve their complexions if they had recognized its possible adverse health effects.

These scenarios play out in our everyday life, as we consume or use products without really understanding what their repercussions are on the environment or on our bodies. Most of the time, these irrational decisions do not impact our health so they are tolerated and perhaps considered to be a cultural oddity. The senior author of this book remembers hearing her grandmother talk about a woman in Finland not answering a knock at the front door to the house without first attempting to improve the condition of her red, rough-looking hands. In Finland, no chemicals were used on the skin, but a woman would beat on dough being used to make bread because it would make her hands temporarily appear white as the blood was pushed away from the hands during this vigorous working of the dough. Such kitchen activity did not remove the toughened skin or alter the condition of the hand; it was purely a short-term cosmetic effect. A popular woman could be in the kitchen and working dough frequently during the day; yet the time was not wasted, for the family would consume a lot of bread! We need to move beyond these short-term cosmetic changes that do not resolve a problem and from those decisions for which delusion results in the false expectation of becoming rich at no cost.

We, as a global society, need to make decisions that will, in turn, allow us to make sustainable energy, food, forest and water choices that will be viable in each region of the world. For example, renewable energy resources from biomass is being promoted in the United States and in Europe to substitute for the fossil fuels used in transportation. Even if these are logical choices to pursue in the US and Europe, this practice is not realistic for China to adopt because of its need to increase forest cover for erosion control. Selection of a one-model approach or option cannot be pursued everywhere. The individual characteristics of each country should direct the development of options that are sustainable within the context of that country and its capacity to recover following resource use or disturbances. A critical take-home message is that sustainable solutions need to be developed for each country and its local contexts. It is critical for a country not to be driven to follow another country's strategy; rather, it should determine objectively what is the right solution, options or policy for it to adopt.

An ability to plan for an 'unknown future' and to approach sustainable resource consumption at the same time will require a whole array of tools. There is a need to expand the 'tool box' used to evaluate whether resource uses are going to be sustainable. Many of the sustainability indicators are currently adequate to allow a country to plan for the future use of one of its resources (energy, food or water consumption), but these same tools are not sufficient to develop a strategy that is able to minimize either the local or global negative environmental repercussions at the ecosystem level. To maintain the resiliency of the entire system, our tools need to address the complex network of factors that interconnect and feed back to impact other resources at the ecosystem level. Breaking or losing one strand in the Sustainability Web (Figure 1.1) will affect the other resources in the web.

A practical sustainability-option tool must consider the resilience of countries to natural and to human-generated disturbances. The importance of including disturbances is clearly apparent from the recent global reports of the environmental, economic and social devastation resulting from hurricanes and tropical storms. Whatever decisions are made for resource uses must factor in how well a region can recover from such a disturbance. If a sustainable ecosystem that includes people is the goal and the desired condition, resource uses should not diminish the resiliency of countries to disturbances. However, do we have the tools that will allow us to measure the resiliency of a country to resource uses and/or disturbances?

If an all-inclusive sustainable ecosystem is the goal, resource uses that diminish the resilience of countries to disturbances need to be avoided at all costs. However, a focus only on environmental indices does not adequately measure human vulnerability and ecosystem degradation because it does not factor-in people's behaviour in landscapes; Nordhaus and Shellenberger (2007) provided an extensive discussion of this topic. Most of the environmental indices created have not balanced the trade-offs that conservation or environmental values must make within the human development context. The economic and ecological trade-offs inherent to forests are discussed by Sessions et al (Box 1.4) and highlight the point that obtaining more economic benefits from a forest will reduce its ecological benefits. These are generally not complementary and therefore impacts sustainability decisions. In fact, it has been the pattern to displace people from environments that had conservation value because of the perception that the two were mutually incompatible and that environmental values should have priority over the people who inhabited these lands (Dowie, 2005).

To ensure that societies are not deluded into making a cosmetic fix or what appears on the surface to be good decisions, it is worth exploring what choices are available for them with respect to their four essential resource needs. It is revealing to evaluate the choices that a country did make when facing similar problems, such as reduced supplies of oil. We need to move beyond the quick fixes or decisions that are ineffective in assessing the mix of business, resources, culture and economics that are found in a sustainability web.

Box 1.4 Sustainability into Forest Planning for the Western United States

John Sessions, Pam Overhulser and Pete Bettinger

Three scenarios of sustainability for a hypothetical forest in the western US are considered: (1) sustainability of timber production; (2) sustainability of multiple values; and (3) sustainability of ecosystems of interest. The common thread is that as the measures of sustainability increase within a forest plan, the economic value declines while the ecological value increases. These cases represent the state-of-the-art in sustainability modelling within the region. An examination of alternative scenarios helps forest managers think about the trade-offs more clearly, even though the modelling process is a simplification of reality and complex biological and economic processes are reduced to functional relationships that are tractable within a planning system.

In North America, concerns over timber depletion in the early 20th century forced land managers to consider ways to maintain a stable timber supply; yet as the understanding of the linkage between timber production and other natural resources grew, the issue of sustainability shifted from timber production to multiple resource values, then to ecosystem integrity. Each of the sustainability concepts continues to be used by various landowners in some form or fashion. Sustainability of timber production is guided by the need to balance the growth of a forest with the harvest levels; sustainability of multiple uses is represented by the yield that a forest can produce continuously, as well as maintenance of physiographic conditions and habitat conditions for certain wildlife species. Sustainability of ecosystems and social values are represented by complex goals that create healthy, diverse, productive forests, with a mosaic of stand structures and their associated ecological processes. The categories of stand structures used in this study are regeneration, closed single canopy, understorey, layered and older forest structure.

The hypothetical forest landscape covers over 55,000ha and is represented by 558 strata that include three main cover types (Douglas fir, western hemlock and hardwoods); three site index classes; five size classes; and three differential growth rates affected by Swiss needle cast. In comparison to scenario (3), scenarios (1) and (2) produce about 30 per cent more harvest volume per year over the 150-year planning horizon and about 50–67 per cent as many layered forests. Scenario (2) produces about 5 per cent less volume per year than scenario (1). Although each of the three scenarios would provide a sustainable harvest volume over the long run, the relative differences between them is the cost of incorporating other measures of sustainability in the long-term forest plans. The first two sustainability scenarios both exhibit about a 30 per cent decline in standing inventory from the initial condition through the first analysis period. Scenario 3 also shows a slight decline in standing inventory; however, this scenario facilitates the development of inventory stocks over time.

Using Human Development Ranking to Understand Large Datasets

Resource consumption decisions, which need to be sustainable, fundamentally alter how resources are consumed. Decisions have to be structured in an ecosystem framework and have to include other factors that at first glance may not appear to be relevant to the resource itself. Unpacking sustainability also suggests that we need to become better managers of our 'solar capital' (i.e. fossil carbon) and 'solar income' (non-fossil carbon materials) that power and glue societies together in an ecosystem. Only by managing our solar-derived materials are we going to be able to continue to consume bio-resources and make the trade-offs that minimize our negative environmental footprint. Furthermore, the 'human capital' of a country is an important element of any sustainability assessment and it has been included in our data collection. To organize our data analyses, we used the United Nations Development Program Human Development Index (HDI) to group countries by their resource capital and social capital stories.

For our assessment, indices and data were collated for 34 countries. Countries were originally selected using several criteria: whether it was or was not an oil producer and/or exporter; the amount of forest biomass and wastes (i.e. woodfuel) that was used as its primary energy source; the amount of forest cover; and its ranking in the human development index. The countries and how they ranked in these four primary categories are provided in Table 1.1.

The HDI was used to group countries by their 'social or human capital' and to organize our comparisons. This index focuses attention on the social development potential of people living in a country, based on their education levels, life expectancy and the role of women in the economy (HDI, 2007/2008). Because the HDI addresses the potential for a country to develop its social capital, it is a useful index to further compare whether there are any patterns in resource consumption that change in a similar manner by socioeconomic groupings. The HDI has a substantial health component, as historians and political scientists have identified inequality, not only in income or wealth, but also in health and nutrition as driving forces in social, political and economic stability.

The approach used by HDI to rank countries facilitated our ability to group them into broader categories based on their social capital. Because the HDI does not include biological or environmental aspects, it can be used to make comparisons to other indices or resource data without producing connections that are autocorrelated. This index does not emphasize whether a country is ranked 70th or 155th in the list. An individual country's exact numerical ranking is less meaningful for our analyses, for it is not always clear why a country has garnered the rank it has been given. For example, the top ten countries with the highest level of human development have highly variable ecological footprints; this means that the ecological footprint has little utility when predicting patterns of human development. However, the information will allow us to identify other factors which might provide more insights into why a country has followed a particular development pathway and the impacts of its decisions.

Table 1.1 *Four categories used in our data analysis for ranking countries*

% Crude oil produced/exported	
HIGH	Angola, Congo DR, Nigeria, Norway, Sudan, United Arab Emirates (UAE), United Kingdom (UK), Yemen
MEDIUM	Australia, Canada, Indonesia, Malaysia, Mexico, Russian Federation (Russia), Venezuela
LOW	Argentina, Brazil, China, France, Germany, Netherlands, Peru, United States (US)
No crude oil production	
Bangladesh, Finland, Haiti, Iceland, India, Japan, Namibia, Nepal, Philippines, Sweden, Tanzania	
Human Development Index ranking	
Group 1 (HDI > 0.9)	Australia, Canada, Finland, France, Germany, Iceland, Japan, Netherlands, Norway, Sweden, UK, US
Group 2 (HDI = 0.8–0.9)	Argentina, Brazil, Malaysia, Mexico, Russia, UAE
Group 3 (HDI = 0.7–0.8)	China, Indonesia, Peru, Philippines, Venezuela
Group 4 (HDI = 0.6–0.7)	India, Namibia
Group 5 (HDI = 0.5–0.6)	Bangladesh, Haiti, Nepal, Sudan, Yemen
Group 6 (HDI = 0.4–0.5)	Angola, Congo DR, Nigeria, Tanzania
% total land area in forests	
HIGH (>35–67%)	Angola, Brazil, Congo DR, Finland, Indonesia, Japan, Malaysia, Peru, Russia, Sweden, Tanzania, Venezuela
MEDIUM (25–35%)	Canada, France, Germany, Mexico, Nepal, Norway, Sudan, US
MEDIUM–LOW (10–< 25%)	Argentina, Australia, China, India, Nigeria, Philippines, UK
LOW (< 10%)	Bangladesh, Haiti, Iceland, Namibia, Netherlands, UAE, Yemen
Biomass and wastes (% of total primary energy supply)	
HIGH (> 75–100%)	Congo DR, Haiti, Nepal, Nigeria, Sudan, Tanzania
MEDIUM–HIGH (> 50–75%)	Angola
MEDIUM (> 25–50%)	Bangladesh, Brazil, India, Indonesia, Philippines
LOW-MEDIUM (> 10–25%)	China, Finland, Namibia, Peru, Sweden
LOW (0–10%)	Australia, Argentina, Canada, France, Germany, Iceland, Japan, Malaysia, Mexico, Netherlands, Norway, Russia, UAE, UK, US, Venezuela, Yemen

Source: FAO, 2005; HDI, 2007/2008; IEA, 2007

Furthermore, because the country rankings for the various indices change year to year, it is important to recognize that the numbers used here are not as relevant as the trajectories of change and the relationships that are shown between the variables. For example, it is not as important to know who is ranked number one in the world because of their CO_2 emissions, but who the world's top CO_2 emitters are. The rankings do not provide insights as to whether a country is altering its behaviour and if it resulted in a changed ranking. Most data currently used to rank countries' global CO_2 emissions list the US as the number one global carbon emitter, despite the fact that these data are from 2004. In 2006, the US was displaced by China, which now has the distinction of being ranked as the number one global carbon emitter. This ranking, however, depends on what and how the data are summarized. For example, if a comparison is made using emissions per capita, the US is still ranked as the highest emitter globally (19.10Mg CO_2/cap), China no longer being ranked at the top (4.68Mg CO_2/cap in 2007) (IEA, 2009). The important point here is that both countries are large emitters of CO_2. The discussion should not focus on who within the group is the worst offender, but on the need for those ranked among the top emitters to make choices that will decrease their overall emissions.

Every country will have its own version of this story and it should not automatically emulate the processes followed by another country to develop its resource and human capital. We cannot convert Nigeria into Finland or Norway. Despite this, there are lessons to be learnt from the documented stories from the Scandinavian countries because they rank so high on most environmental and human development indices. The Scandinavian countries also need to continue to adapt if they are going to retain their high ranking, for they will be impacted to a greater extent by future climate change, as evidenced by the melting of the polar ice. Understanding how they achieved these high ranks and how they adapt to a changing climate can be very instructive and will be explored further in later chapters.

Because all these analyses are snapshots in time and are based on fragmentary data, it is important to use them to explore for patterns of change. Despite their fragmentary nature, they can provide insights as to whether a country is making choices that place it on a trajectory to develop its sustainability capital. This information is especially useful when resource and human capital fluctuations can be detected subsequent to disturbances in view of the unavoidable constraints particular to each country. This will allow each country to begin to develop a portfolio of options that reduce its risk of making unsustainable choices, as it factors-in its characteristics and capacity to recover following resource use or disturbances. As noted above, a critical take-home message is that sustainable solutions need to be developed for each country and within its local contexts.

References

Bhattasali, A. (2006) 'A silent killer of rural women', *BBC*, Calcutta, India, http://news.bbc.co.uk/2/hi/south_asia/4308983, accessed 7 July 2008

British History (2007) 'Arsenic', www.british-history.ac.uk/report.aspx?compid=58689, accessed 12 January 2009

Diamond, J. (2005) *Collapse: How Societies Choose to Fail or Succeed*, Viking Books, New York, NY

Dowie, M. (2005) 'Conservation refugees: when protecting nature means kicking people out', *Orion Magazine*, www.orionmagazine.org/index.php/articles/article/161, accessed 30 May 2008

Fagan, B. (2008) *The Great Warming. Climate Change and the Rise and Fall of Civilizations*, Bloomsbury Press, New York, NY

FAO (2005) 'Global Forest Resources Assessment 2005', Food and Agriculture Organization, Rome, Italy

Flanders, J. (2009) 'They broke it', *The New York Times,* 10 January 2009, pA17

Goodman, P. S. and Finn, P. (2007) 'Corruption stains timber trade. Forests destroyed in China's race to feed global wood-processing industry', *Washington Post Foreign Service,* 1 April 2007, pA01

HDI (2007/2008) 'Human Development Index', http://hDrundp.org/en/statistics, accessed 1 October 2008

Hillel, D. J. (1991) *Out of the Earth. Civilization and the Life of the Soil,* The Free Press, New York, NY

Hsu, K. J. (1986) *The Great Dying,* Harcourt Brace Jovanovich, New York, NY

IEA (2007) *2007 Key World Energy Statistics,* International Energy Agency, http://tonto.eia.doe.gov/country/country_energy_data.cfm?fips=AO, accessed 1 September 2008

IEA (2009) *CO$_2$ emissions from fuel combustion,* Highlights, 2009 edition, www.iea.org/Textbase/stats, accessed 2 June 2009

Jacobsen, T. and Adams, R. M. (1958) 'Salt and silt in ancient Mesopotamian agriculture', *Science,* vol 128, pp1251–1258

Krugman, P. (2009) 'How did economists get it so wrong?' *The New York Times Magazine,* 6 September 2009, pp36–43

Lee, H. Y. and Oster, S. (2008) 'China energy firms seek to broaden reach —-Cnooc, Ltd. and China Petrochemical Sinopec join to purchase stake in an Angolan oil field', *The Wall Street Journal Asia,* 2 October 2008

Lovell, J. (2007) 'World must seek change in China timber trade – report', *Reuters News Service,* 10 May 2007, www.planetark.com/dailynewsstory.cfm/newsid/41814/story.htm, accessed 10 January 2009

MacKay, C. (1841) *Extraordinary Popular Delusions and the Madness of Crowds,* MetroBooks, Friedman/Fairfax Publishers, New York, NY

Nordhaus, T. and Shellenberger, M. (2007) *Break Through. From the Death of Environmentalism to the Politics of Possibility,* Houghton Mifflin Company, Boston, MA and New York, NY

Smith, K. R. (1994) 'Health, energy and greenhouse-gas impacts of biomass combustion in household stoves', *Energy for Sustainable Development 1994,* vol 1, no 4, pp23–29

UN (2002) United Nations Johannesburg Summit, www.un.org/jsummit/html/basic_info/basicinfo.html, accessed 21 May 2009

Vogt, K. A., Honea, J. M., Vogt, D. J., Edmonds, R. L., Patel-Weynand, T., Sigurdardottir, R. and Andreu, M. G. (2007) *Forests and Society. Sustainability and Life Cycles of Forests in Human Landscapes,* CABI International, Wallingford, UK

WCED (1987) *Our Common Future,* World Commission on Environment and Development, United Nations, New York, NY

WHO/UNDP (2004) 'Indoor air pollution – the killer in the kitchen', Joint Statement WHO/UNDP, Geneva, www.who.int/mediacentre/news/statements/2004/statement5/en/index.html, accessed 10 December 2008

2

Learning From the PAST: Why Societies Collapsed or Survived

It is very useful to start decoding sustainability by examining how, throughout history, humans have managed to satisfy their four basic needs: energy, food, forest materials and water. Historical accounts also document how a scarcity of one or more of these four basic human needs will make it difficult for a group of people to survive at a specific location. In addition, these accounts also show how resources needed for human survival are connected and how a decrease in one resource will reverberate and impact the availability of the other three. This brief overview will also enlighten the reader as to why some societies collapse and why others have survived for more than a thousand years. At particular points in their history, the societies that collapsed obviously made some wrong choices while acquiring their survival needs. On the other side, there are lessons to be learnt from those societies which have survived from several hundred to over a thousand years. We shall use a historical approach to demonstrate how humans have survived in different landscapes and which factors contribute to increasing their survival rates or had the opposite effect.

Why People Live Where They Do

Looking at the geography of a country where people live is very revealing and helps us to decode sustainability. It packages the choices made in the context of geographic constraints. It identifies some of the constraints that each country faces in pursuing bio-resource solutions to economic, social and environmental problems that affect their sustainability. Geography helps identify regions of the world where climatic constraints, combined with the land's biotic potential, either limit or create advantages for human survival (de Blij, 2005). Some geographic locations are able to support resilient societies and environments, whereas others severely limit human survival. These geographic constraints help to identify where people's consumptive footprints for energy, food, forests and water will need to extend beyond their borders, if they are to continue on a trajectory to develop their human capital.

Geography also tells us that there are areas in the world where it will be difficult for a country to reduce its environmental footprint because the 'stage or the land' where people live is not capable of producing or providing some of their basic needs. It also tells us that some countries have considerable advantages for promoting the development of their human capital, while others are not as fortunate. Sustainable development for these latter countries may be an elusive and problematic goal. In some cases, climatic or environmental constraints may be so strong that it will not be economically feasible to alter the environments to increase resource supplies, whereas in other cases, the practices that can enable the higher production of a resource may create unacceptable environmental problems. In these circumstances, sustainable development will be a difficult goal to pursue without some major technological breakthrough that can counteract any unacceptable environmental damage.

To decipher geographic limits to human survival, it helps first to discuss where it is relatively easy for humans to live.

Where is it easier for humans to live within their footprints?

A country's climatic zone can be used roughly to index the many constraints that make it either easier or more difficult for humans to make choices to live within their country's resource footprints. Where it has been easier for humans to live and to survive are coincident with the area of the world most altered historically due to land-uses (Hannah et al, 1995). The most human-altered environments are found in the temperate climatic zones.

Not all temperate regions are equally suitable for humans to live in. Areas where temperate broadleaf forests grow well have been altered significantly (~82 per cent) by humans. These forests have more nutrient-rich soils and therefore plant productive capacities are higher. These soils also produce an abundance of the many bio-resources that humans need to survive. Therefore, resource supplies are more secure. In contrast, the coniferous forests in the temperate zone have only been altered approximately 12 per cent by humans; these regions have nutrient-poor soils where trees grow quite well but where agricultural production is poor. Consequently, food security will be low in areas where coniferous trees grow well.

The temperate climatic zones with nutrient-rich soils are ideal habitats for humans. Most human needs can be obtained from these lands without dramatically increasing the human resource consumptive footprint. Thus, even though humans have altered these landscapes most dramatically, the climatic and abiotic soil conditions found associated with these forests can support a higher intensity of management while still contributing towards social and environmental resilience. The potential for harvesting resources from the same land-base at frequent and at shorter timescales means that humans in these areas can harvest a greater total amount of bio-resources. It is not a coincidence that most of today's highly developed human societies are found in these climatic zones (e.g. North Asia, the Scandinavian countries, the US and Western Europe).

In general, the temperate regions of the world are characterized by having more productive soils and more predictable amounts of rainfall (Vogt et al, 2007).

Table 2.1 *Land area distribution types for the US and the world*

	United States	World
Forests, woodlands	29	33
Pastures, rangelands	26	23
Agriculture	20	10
Desert	14	32
Built land	7	2

Note: Units = % of total in 1999 for the world data, 2005 for the US except for built land which are 2001 data; the high variance in the published numbers means that the totals do not equal 100%.
Source: FAO, 2008; Alig et al, 2009

It is notable that North Asia, east of the Urals, has 40 per cent of its soils with no major constraints to agriculture (FAO, 2000). This same study reported that North America has 27 per cent of its soils with no major constraints to production of the 'solar income'; that is, productivity of food crops or trees. The conditions in these regions are in direct contrast to the situation found in North Africa and the Near East, where only 9 per cent of the lands do not have some major constraint limiting agricultural production. This means that local food security for both North Africa and the Near East will be a challenge.

Some countries are fortunate enough to have fewer limitations for growing food locally; consequently, food supplies are secure. This is the situation for the United States. The Food and Agriculture Organization (FAO) estimated that the US had twice as much land in productive agricultural lands as the global average (see Table 2.1). Therefore, land conversion into agriculture production is less commonly reported in the media, as sufficient land area is available to grow crops. Many of the wet tropical regions of the world have a lower proportion of their total land area in productive soils that can be used to produce food. In these countries, it is not uncommon to read about forests being converted into agriculture or to grow biofuel crops.

Other than its vulnerability to climate change, it is easier for people living in the US to maintain their social and environmental resiliency because of their high 'solar income' or plant-productive potential compared to other regions of the world. A comparison of the differences in plant-productive potential can be gleaned from a comparison of the annual growth rate of forests in the temperate and tropical climatic zones. The temperate regions have aboveground forest productivity that can be as high as $26.\text{Mg ha}^{-1} \text{ yr}^{-1}$, compared to 14.9Mg ha^{-1} yr^{-1} in the subtropical region and $12.6\text{Mg ha}^{-1} \text{ yr}^{-1}$ in the tropics (Vogt et al, 1997). In forests, this 'solar income' is important because it determines the supply capacity and the frequency with which a forest can provide ecosystem services to humans and still maintain the healthy functioning of the ecosystem itself. The lower productivity in the tropical areas reflects the greater soil constraints found at these latitudes. In fact, tropical grasslands have only been 5 per cent altered by humans; tropical grasslands grow on highly leached soils where food crops are difficult to grow. Grasses grow well in these environments and humans are dependent on viable livestock management systems to meet their survival needs.

However, food security is not the only metric that will determine where people will live most comfortably in the world, because disturbances or climate change can periodically or cyclically, reduce a land's productive capacity (see Chapter 7). Even though the present-day US has productive soils and, therefore, high 'solar income'– that is, secure food production – these are vulnerable to disturbances and climate change. Weather events (e.g. hurricanes, tornadoes and lightning strikes) reduce social resilience in parts of the US.

Norway also appears to be an ideal country for humans to live and is ranked as one of the most sustainable countries globally. Its people have successfully made decisions to provide a high socioeconomic status for themselves. They also have an abundance of fossil and non-fossil resources to develop their human capital. Norway, which produces and exports a significant quantity of oil to global markets, produces over 98 per cent of its electricity using hydropower – a locally available and 'carbon neutral' process. However, Norway is vulnerable to droughts and then has to shift from hydropower to fossil fuels to produce its electricity. Inasmuch as fossil fuels are the dominant emitters of Greenhouse Gases (GHG) globally, Norway emits more GHG during droughts. This drought vulnerability reduces Norway's capacity continually to produce 'green' electricity and to meet its goal to reduce GHG emissions. Norway's high dependency on hydropower for its economic development means that it is highly vulnerable to changes in precipitation and, therefore, to climate change (PreventionWeb, 2005). Thus, during non-drought years, Norway is one of the most sustainable countries in the world. Unfortunately, if droughts occur frequently or are prolonged, this classification could change.

In general, the temperate climatic zones have fewer constraints that would decrease the development of a country's socioeconomic capital (e.g. fossil and renewable energy supplies are plentiful; soil productive capacity is high; and, therefore, food supplies are more secure). In addition to their moderate climates and fewer soil constraints to plant production, they also have fewer human health problems compared to tropical countries. The main problem that moderate climate countries face is weather events that would decrease a country's social and natural resilience. However, these countries are less vulnerable and are more buffered against climate change or disturbances because their resource and human capital are sufficiently high and well developed.

Where is it difficult for humans to live within their footprints?

One-third of the total terrestrial land area is difficult for humans to live in because bio-resource supplies (e.g. energy, food, forest and water) are scarce. Humans are dependent on gathering resources or growing 'solar income' on the remaining two-thirds of the terrestrial landscape. The one-third of the terrestrial landscape less suitable for human survival is mostly deserts and/or the coldest regions of the world. Even though people are found living in these less suitable habitats (e.g.

Eskimos and Laplanders), they were never able to develop large permanent settlements because of resource scarcities.

In the colder and drier regions of the world, humans have primarily survived by being nomadic and dependent upon domesticated animals or following and culling migrating animal herds for food. Historically these areas did not support large population densities because bio-resource supplies were inadequate to feed a larger group of people. Agricultural production is limited in these regions because of the low temperatures and low soil nutrient supply capacity which reduce plant growth rates. Plants do grow well during a two to three month period each year, but this means that food supplies are scarce during the remaining months. Sufficient food would need to be produced during the short growing season and stored for the remainder of the year. In addition, because some communities are frequently isolated during the winter months, sufficient food supplies have to be stored for these months. This inability to grow food during most of the year has forced people to adapt by being nomadic. These people spend a considerable amount of time searching for food, energy for heating or cooking and water. Today, increases in the human population densities and the establishment of political boundaries has eliminated the traditional strategies pursued by nomadic people that allowed them to adapt to their environments; traditionally livestock rearing was practised by nomadic people who moved from regions experiencing droughts to those areas capable of supporting them (Allan and Warren, 1993).

The most difficult areas for humans to live have been the arid deserts. Deserts are found globally where water availability is limited. The Sahara desert is the world's largest desert and crosses 11 countries; it comprises 8 per cent of the global terrestrial area. The Sahara began to form some 4000 years BCE (Allan and Warren, 1993). Few plants are able to survive and most people who have lived in these areas were nomadic (Allan and Warren, 1993). Agricultural production is limited in deserts because of the low rainfall and the low productive capacity of the soils. Desert soils are nutrient-limited and contain higher salt concentrations that can be toxic to most plants.

When larger population densities were found in arid regions, the social structures were based on strong trade routes that allowed people to obtain bio-resources from areas beyond their territorial boundaries (Fagan, 2008). An example of this would be the Anasazi in the US southwest. Despite living in a desert, the American Indians who lived on these lands developed impressive social and economic infrastructures. They irrigated lands for food production and imported timber to construct their houses. The demise of the Anasazi was the result of prolonged droughts that began in 1130 CE and reduced food production. This forced most of the Anasazi to migrate to other territories because they could not grow enough food. The interesting point related to the Anasazi is how well people were able to live in arid environments during the non-drought periods. Unfortunately, climate change, such as droughts, causes these areas to frequently become drier and less capable of supporting the larger human population densities that develop during high rainfall periods (Fagan, 2008).

Humans have attempted to engineer solutions to provide water during droughts, a normal event in deserts. Since the 19th and 20th centuries, humans have engineered large-scale irrigation systems to transfer water from water-rich areas to those with inadequate water, primarily the desert. Transferring significant quantities of water from water-rich regions has its hazards, for this can result in the loss of environmental resiliency in the water-rich region. Allan and Warren (1993) discussed how the former Soviet Union transferred significant quantities of water from its more water-rich northern regions to the more arid regions in the south, noting that 'the consequences for the Aral Sea have been disastrous and the livelihoods of local people and the local ecology have been ruined.' Poor water management has also increased the deposition of salts on the surface; this further decreases the soil's productive capacity.

In the Sahara, recurring droughts resulted in widespread famines in the 1970s and 1980s. Today, these same regions of Africa are experiencing droughts that are impairing food production and contributing to widespread poverty, malnutrition and poor human development. In addition, as land ownership in this region has become formalized by the development of political boundaries (de Blij, 2005), the nomadic lifestyle of many desert people has been lost, along with their knowledge for surviving in the dynamic environment where resource supplies are available only in pulses. Many former nomadic tribes were moved into permanent settlements. This situation contributed towards the over-consumption of resources at one location that caused environmental degradation and the loss of livelihood options for most nomads.

Climate change has also been implicated in the increase of total land area classified as desert. Such a trend will further decrease the total land area suitable for human survival. This increased desertification trend has been documented for the African Sahara (de Blij, 2005). However, deserts continue to be attractive areas for people to harvest resources and humans will, therefore, continue to engineer these environments to increase their quality of life.

Today, deserts attract global attention because of their large mineral and oil deposits. Even though deserts still cannot support large human population densities, cities are being built there to provide the housing and transportation infrastructures needed by a large workforce collecting these resources. Global economies need desert resources (e.g. crude oil) to power, maintain or build their industrial infrastructures. The global economies have provided the revenue that stimulated the growth of human population densities in the deserts; however, people living there are almost totally dependent on importing food and water.

The sustainability of these desert areas is 'artificially' maintained. Because these societies are dependent upon extracting resources to maintain their socio-economic development, they are vulnerable to the energy or mineral resource choices made by the rest of the world. They will be less resilient to climate change because they are already expending considerable financial resources towards the maintenance of this 'artificial' infrastructure. This was the situation faced by Dubai during last year's global economic crisis in 2009. When the economic crisis stimulated countries to consume less crude oil, Dubai, of necessity, severely curtailed its infrastructure development projects. Therefore, Dubai is less buffered to global changes in the consumption of at least one resource, oil, which the United Arab Emirates (UAE) has used to build the 'artificial' lifestyle of Dubai.

Similar to the coldest and driest regions of the world, some of the wettest and hottest areas (i.e. wet tropics) are also difficult places for people to live comfortably. It is a paradox that areas with high plant and animal biodiversities are not optimal locations for humans to survive by harvesting food from the natural landscapes. These regions of the world are dominated by plants with sophisticated chemical defensive mechanisms they employ to keep insects and animals from eating their tissues. These defensive chemicals make most of the tropical forest plants unpalatable for human consumption and force people to live by eating a few root crops (Vogt et al, 2007). It is also difficult to practise agriculture here because the soils in these areas have a low productive capacity. Wet tropical forests soils are characteristically low in nutrients and high in chemicals toxic to plant growth (aluminum [Al]; see Chapter 4). A period of over 1000 years of high rainfall common to these climatic zones has leached much of the original nutrients from the soils (Sanchez, 1976). Humans are adapted to these environments, but they survive at smaller population densities because of the difficulty of growing enough food. Shifting agriculture is a farming practice that adapted crop growth to soil constraints; farmers needed to move their fields every few years to different locations because of soil fertility losses resulting from continuous farming. Farmers took advantage of the nutrient-capture ability of trees to produce the pulse of 'fertilizer' needed to grow their crops. Forests that regrew in former agricultural fields were burned to release a pulse of nutrients in the form of ash to the crops that were immediately planted in the field.

The question of where it is difficult for humans to survive has become less important today because of the extent to which humans have been successful at engineering their environments. Half of the global population lives in highly altered environments where humans have learned to eliminate or modify the ecosystem constraints that restrict their survival. Despite this situation, this continues to be an important question to ask today because half of the global population, without the same access to fossil carbons and bio-resources, need to alter their environments to improve their living conditions.

It is important to discuss briefly the role of carbon in facilitating human survival and in determining what human lifestyle choices are available. The development of the carbon economy has allowed humans to increase their densities in areas that were originally difficult for them to survive. Carbon (both fossil and non-fossil materials) provided the energy that fuelled the engines of industrialization and allowed the many technological marvels of today to be developed and built. Non-fossil carbon (forest materials) fuelled the European conquest of much of the world between 1200 and 1700 CE. Forest materials built the ships and heated the foundries that made guns and cannons. Subsequently, the fossil carbon drove and accelerated the industrialization of these new global military and economic powers.

Fossil carbon accelerated the rate at which humans altered their environ-ments and it continues to be the most important material sustaining global economies. Fossil carbon provides the energy used to drive vehicles, to fly aeroplanes and to heat or cool houses. It is used to produce chemical fertilizers that increase food production and then to protect plants – in the form of pesti-cides – against animals that would reduce a crop's yield. It is almost impossible to list all of the uses and products derived from fossil carbon today. Fossil carbon has become an important part of almost every aspect of society from the carpets we walk upon to the medicines we take when unhealthy, to the clothes we wear on our backs. Because fossil fuel-based carbon drives our economies and permeates every aspect of a human life, as well as producing negative environmental impacts, there is a need to understood how humans became dependent upon it and the similarities between fossil carbon and the compounds that we call 'carbon neutral', such as forest materials, wind, solar and geothermal.

Industrialization Fuelled by Carbon

Today, carbon compounds have become universally accepted materials essential for powering and maintaining every aspect of our industrialized economies; but, when combusted, severe environmental problems can result. These environmental impacts, global in scope, mean that decisions made in relation to our carbon economies impact our neighbours. They have also generated debates because there is no consensus on the magnitude of their impacts on altering climates. If one accepts that our carbon economies are changing climates, mitigation will be costly and our knowledge is not at the level where scientists can guarantee that the benefits will surpass the costs faced by society. However, there is general accept-ance that mitigation is needed due to the increased vulnerability of societies to the repercussions of changing climates. Shifting to the use of renewable energy sources is under way today – at least, it is in its infancy. The rationale for substitut-ing or supplementing fossil-energy sources with carbon-neutral and renewable materials (e.g. biomass) is based on the fact that they can mitigate the impacts occurring from the combustion of fossil fuels. These carbon-neutral compounds are still complex carbon molecules, albeit not having as high number of carbon molecules linked together as found in fossil fuels. This shift does not move us away from being a carbon economy but simply shifts some of our carbon consumption to renewable resources and to carbon-based fuels capable of mitigating the impacts of combusting fossil fuels.

How did we get to the point where carbon (e.g. fossil fuels) has become the fuel powering almost every aspect of human life and the driver controlling the policy decisions made by countries throughout the world? Many wars have been and still continue to be fought over this complex carbon molecule, as they have been over water. It is worthwhile briefly to examine when fossil fuels were first recognized by humans for their utility. Today, we discuss petrodollars, carbon credits, carbon debits, carbon caps and carbon trade-offs the same way that we discuss dollars, roubles, marks and Euros.

History helps us understand why carbon has become so important to global societies. It summarizes the connections, discoveries and inventions that placed human societies on a trajectory to becoming a 'carbon dependent' society. Part of the answer lies in the earth's development itself and also partly in the way humans have used the earth's resources, including fossil fuels. There are three primary forms of fossil fuels: coal, oil and natural gas. The manner in which fossil fuels were formed explains why these carbon sources are not renewable or carbon neutral and why their combustion alters global carbon cycles.

The chemical composition of fossil fuels means that they can be used to produce energy very efficiently. Therefore, they are still the preferred energy source for most industrial applications. Future scarcity of fossil fuels and increased competition for these supplies has become a global concern. Consequently, similar compounds are being developed to replace them. Ongoing research is attempting to form similar complex carbon molecules in a decadal timescale. Technology is also being developed today that can take CO_2 and convert it into complex molecules similar to oil in chemical composition. This process is not very efficient today and also is very energy-intensive so that the benefits derived are currently not cost-effective. The problem with this approach is that it still does not address the fact that considerable amounts of CO_2 are emitted when these fuels are consumed. This technology does not sequester carbon, just emits it, so that the human impacts on the carbon cycle are not mitigated.

A brief overview of how our societies became dependent upon fossil fuels for almost every aspect of a human life is revealing. It shows that human societies will have a difficult time shifting towards a carbon-free society. This is also a goal that society may want to reconsider and will be further discussed in Chapter 10. The history of how societies became dependent upon on carbon also reveals a story of human adaptation and ingenuity.

A history of how society became dependent on 'artificial' products made from fossil carbon

Fossil fuels have been consumed by human societies for centuries. Since they were first used, humans transformed them into multiple products to improve their livelihoods, from illumination and heating to sham medicines. Humans have not always been dependent upon fossil carbon to produce products and to power their economies. For example, societies were not very dependent on fossil fuels to achieve a higher standard of living before 1700 CE. During this time, forests and other forms of plant biomass provided energy. This is in sharp contrast to when industrialization began, in the mid-1700s, to transform completely 'a world of stone and wood, powered by animals, wind and water ... entirely new, forged of steel and iron and powered by steam, coal and oil' (Weightman, 2009). These changes occurred over a 150-year timescale. This industrialization period began to dominate most aspects of societal development because fossil fuel, primarily coal, was used to power the new machines that were built. People also used 'newly acquired techniques of smelting iron with purified coal or "coke" instead of charcoal, a fuel which was becoming prohibitively expensive' (Weightman, 2009). It also was driven by new processes for textiles that were developed in Britain and resulted in 'spies everywhere in eighteenth-century Britain ... to unearth the secrets of Britain's industrial success'; spies coming from France were especially common (Weightman, 2009).

Industrialization was not a global phenomenon because half of the world did not participate in and benefit from it. For example, the less industrially developed countries garnered few benefits of industrialization even though many of the resources were collected from within their borders. An exception to this trend was the present day US. The European colonialists who emigrated to North America benefited from the many inventions and skills that were developed in Britain. There was an influx of skilled artisans from Britain to North America (Weightman, 2009). British engineers helped build canals and railways in the present-day US and stimulated the industrialization of the American colonies. According to Weightman (2009), American industrialization was remarkable because the first 50 years used wood from the forests for energy, as coal had not been discovered by the immigrants in North America.

Interestingly, the countries that were originally industrialized and became wealthy are beginning to shift their infrastructures to poorer countries because of their cheaper labour (see Chapter 11, Valuing Labour as a Resource). This is driving the industrialization of these countries, but also producing the accompanying environmental impacts that are part of industrialization in countries other than where the drivers of industrialization originate.

Societies shift from using renewable carbon to fossil carbon will be briefly described next. Society is making a full circle related to what carbon source is being utilized, starting with woodfuel, transitioning to coal and eventually oil and now including liquid fuels from biomass. Today, consumption of renewable carbon is fashionable in industrialized countries but not in the form consumed by agrarian societies of the past.

Agrarian societies are dependent on renewable carbon

The first series of agricultural advancements occurred in the Middle East. Archaeological data indicates that seven or eight locations worldwide independently domesticated both plants and animals during this period. The earliest documents supporting these development date back to approximately 10,000 BCE in the Middle East. Agriculture developed in these separate locations because of many factors; primary among these is geography and the availability of plants for domestication. A region east of the Mediterranean Sea, the 'Fertile Crescent', was ideal for agriculture. It had a climate that was characterized by a long dry season with brief periods of rain. This made it ideal for growing small plants with large seeds, such as wheat and barley, with higher protein contents. The 'Fertile Crescent' had a large area of varied geographical features and altitudes which made agriculture more successful for the former hunter-gatherers.

During this period, humans first switched from being nomadic hunter-gathers to settling in communities where agriculture was developed. Today, there is speculation among anthropologists that the development of agrarian societies was started by women. Prior to this period, human roles were very gender-specific; males hunted animals for their meat and hides while females gathered edible plants, nuts and berries. Knowledge about the edible foods that they gathered was passed from mother to daughter, building a storehouse of information over the centuries. Applying this storehouse of plant knowledge, as surmised, may have been the first steps to becoming an agrarian society.

This move from being hunter-gathers to living in villages and growing their produce in one place enabled humans to produce surplus food. With extra food available, population densities increased and this enabled the development of more complex labour diversifications, global trade routes, centralized political administration with laws governing behaviour and the promotion of education among more individuals. The domestication of animals (used for food, clothing and ploughing or towing) provided these communities with a large advantage that allowed their cultures and economies to develop.

Living in one locality also enabled people to acquire more personal possessions and the ownership of land became vital. Once trade was established and surplus food was either traded or stored to provide a reserve for periods of low food supplies, population densities could grow. The increased free time that the citizens of these communities enjoyed enabled artisans to develop technologies that created either art or weapons. Increased population densities also produced the need to develop new vocations; professional soldiers, for example, could protect the possessions of village and town dwellers.

During this period, wood was the primary source of heating, illumination and cooking; wood was also used in construction and in powering the industries that developed. Nevertheless, coal was already beginning to replace wood for many of these tasks.

The 'carbonization' of society and the importance of coal

Even though industrialization is typically traced back to the middle of the 18th century and to Britain, where it flourished, China had developed technologies to utilize fossil carbon in the form of coal and oil, some 2000 years before Europe (see Table 2.2). There is some difference of opinion as to why Britain and not countries such as China, led global industrialization.

Coal was the primary fuel used to power European industrialization that began in the mid-1700s. The high energy value of coal made it ideally suited for these purposes because it provides a higher heating value than is possible from burning wood for energy. Industrialization coincided with the designing and building of the machines and tools capable of being powered by fossil fuels (see Table 2.3). If these two activities had not occurred simultaneously in Britain, the Industrial Revolution would not have become a reality then. Machines were developed that allowed mass production of many products, such as textiles, for a growing population living in several European countries.

Table 2.2 *Timeline for China to develop fossil carbon technology*

500 BCE	Chinese in the state of Wu have developed iron smelting and extensively mine coal as a power source
100 BCE	Chinese metallurgists combine wrought iron and cast iron to forge steel
347 CE	The Chinese, using bits attached to bamboo poles, drilled oil wells up to 800 feet deep

It is noteworthy that oil was not the dominant fossil fuel powering these developments. The invention of coke to smelt iron ore was an especially important development in Britain and was so important that many spies from other countries attempted to steal the recipe to make coke (Weightman, 2009). This development allowed Britain to smelt iron much more cheaply, for it was not dependent on producing charcoal from wood but was able to use coal, a material abundantly available in Britain. This provided Britain with a significant advantage and many countries bought their iron supplies from Britain.

The development of the automobile also coincided with technology to build engines capable of being powered by fossil fuels. Automobiles became a common fixture when the technology for converting fossil fuels into a form capable of powering cars became a reality. The concept of automobiles was designed more than 500 years before they became a popular mode of transportation and can be traced back to 1335 CE and a wind-driven vehicle designed by Guido da Vigevano. Later, drawings by Leonardo da Vinci presented a facsimile of a motorized vehicle that was a clockwork-driven tricycle with a differential mechanism between the rear wheels. Historical records showed that a steam-powered vehicle was designed and built by a Catholic priest, Father Ferdinand Verbiest, for the Chinese Emperor Chien Lung in 1678 CE. Unfortunately, no details are available regarding the vehicle design. Numerous inventors improved on the steam-powered engines, but it was Nicholas Joseph Cugnot who designed the first vehicle that moved under its own power. This vehicle was constructed by M. Brezin in 1769 and a full-scale replica is on display in Paris at the Conservatoire des Arts et Métiers.

The building of our fossil-carbon economy demonstrates well how human development is dependent on a series of connected factors. Innovation is critical, but it has to occur at the 'right time'. It is this ability to innovate that has moved global economies forward and allowed our society to pursue the 'good life'. Fossil fuel did not support the development of society until 1849, because it was dependent upon the development of technology by Dr Abraham Gesnerin, which laid the foundation for the modern petroleum industry. He converted 'raw sludge of fossil remains into kerosene and other fuels' (Weightman, 2009). This innovation is what allowed the further development of the many other technological gadgets and products of industrialized societies. Oil became the harbinger of a highly advanced-economy society that would have been impossible without innovation and inventions in oil conversion. Oil, the cornerstone of industrialization, made fossil carbon the 'backbone' of global societies. The chemical industry

Table 2.3 *Timeline of industrialization and building machines using fossil fuels*

1708	Jethro Tull's mechanical seed drill enables large-scale row plantings for easier cultivation
1709	Abraham Darby uses coke to smelt iron ore, eliminating use of wood/charcoal as a fuel
1712	Thomas Newcomen develops the steam engine
1730	Joseph Foljambe produces Europe's first commercially successful iron ploughs
1733	John Kay invents the flying shuttle
1764	James Hargreaves invents the spinning jenny that weaves the warp in cloth
1769	James Watt patents improvements on the Newcomen steam engine
1769	Arkwright develops a water-powered frame which automates the weft in cloth
1779	Crompton builds the first steam-powered mills that fully automate the weaving process
1785	Edward Cartwright patents a power loom
1786	Arkwright uses Watt's steam engine to power a cotton mill
1793	Eli Whitney patents the cotton gin that cleans raw cotton
1801	Robert Trevithick demonstrates the steam locomotive
1807	Robert Fulton's *Clermont* is the first successful steamboat
1821	Faraday demonstrates electromagnetic rotation, the principle behind the electric motor
1830	Liverpool and Manchester railway begins first regular commercial rail service
1831	Faraday discovers electromagnetic current; generators/electric engines can be built
1846	Pneumatic tyre patented
1856	Henry Bessemer develops the Bessemer converter
1859	Gaston Plante invents the electric battery
1860	Etienne Lenoir demonstrates the first successful gasoline engine
1865	Nicholas and Joseph Cugnot construct the steam-powered tractor
1866	The Siemens brothers improve steelmaking by creating the open-hearth furnace
1867	Siegfried Markus invents the ignition device
1876	Nikolaus Otto invents the internal combustion engine
1883	Gottlieb Daimler invents the modern petrol-powered engine
1884	Charles Algernon Parsons invents the steam turbine
1885	Benz develops the first automobile to use an internal-combustion engine; Gottlieb Daimler invented the gasoline-powered motorcycle
1887	Paul Heroult invented an electric steel furnace; Nikola Tesla invented the induction motor
1888	John Boyd Dunlop develops the first practical pneumatic tyre
1889	Mikhail Dolivo-Dobrovolsky transmits electric power
1892	Rudolf Diesel patents the diesel engine
1900	The first Zeppelin is built by Count Ferdinand von Zeppelin
1903	Orville and Wilbur Wright make the first successful aeroplane flight
1908	Henry Ford mass-produces the Model T

flourished during this time and developed a multitude of products from oil that stimulated the making of our 'synthetic' carbon world.

Oil made our 'synthetic' world possible

Today petroleum is processed to create several types of fuel and petrochemical feedstocks for plastic-type products, but the early refineries were only interested in one thing: kerosene. Kerosene was used to replace whale oil to illuminate homes and businesses. Originally, gasoline was considered an unwanted byproduct of oil processing to obtain kerosene. When it was first used, crude oil was processed in coal/oil refineries, but by the early 1860s there were approximately 20 petroleum refineries in a small area of Pennsylvania, USA, alone. Before this, petroleum seeping into water wells was primarily considered a nuisance, except by a few enterprising individuals who bottled the liquid as medicines. This medicine was sold throughout the world as a cure for everything from headaches and boils to snake bites, hence the terms 'snake oil' and 'snake oil salesman'.

The first record of drilling for oil occurred in China in 347 CE (see Table 2.4). The next evidence of oil mining dates to 1264 in present-day Poland, but it was not until the mid-19th century that the first oil well, probably in present-day Azerbaijan (near Baku), was drilled. The Drake well, drilled in 1859 in western Pennsylvania, was the birthplace of the oil and gas industry. Utilization of kerosene produced a petroleum industry boom period, but the first petroleum industry recession also occurred when Thomas Edison developed and produced the electric light bulb in 1878. Post-1900, the importance of oil in driving the growth of global economies began to be more apparent. In fact, World War I was the first motorized war, in which oil played a decisive role in the war effort.

Despite the roots of industrialization or the 'carbonization' of our society in the mid-1700s, fossil fuel consumption really flourished just prior to and after World War I. During the late 1800s and early 1900s, the production of chemicals from fossil fuels evolved and became quite sophisticated. The chemical industry was formed and flourished. This industry allowed the production of dyes, synthetic drugs and the manufacture of explosives (Weightman, 2009). What was astonishing about the chemical industry is that a multitude of products were made artificially, beginning the journey along the road for societal dependence on carbon-based products for almost every aspect of human existence. This new 'synthetic' world reduced human dependence on natural resources as the raw materials to produce products.

Of these three fossil fuels, petroleum seems to have had the most impact on the world's politics, imagination and wallets. Oil allowed the development of suburbia when people could easily drive to and from the city. Oil has also produced international conflicts and controlled how countries interacted in the political sphere. Global economies fluctuate, based on oil prices; these attest to oil's importance as part of the economic fabric of people's everyday life. Today, we watch the changes in oil prices on the global markets because it affects the quality of our life and our ability to drive vehicles.

Table 2.4 *Timeline of oil use in industrialization*

347	The Chinese, using bits attached to bamboo poles, drilled oil wells up to 800ft deep
1264	Marco Polo witnessed and reported the mining of seep oil in Baku (part of medieval Persia)
1500	Seep oil was collected in the Carpathian Mountains of Poland
1735	French oil sands are mined at the Pechelbronn fields of Alsace
1815	In the United States oil is extracted as an undesirable by-product from brine wells in Pennsylvania
1848	On the Aspheron Peninsula of Asia, the *first* modern oil well was drilled by F. N. Semyenov
1849	Dr Abraham Gesner distilled kerosene from oil, which replaces whale oil
1850	Petrol (gasoline) refining first done
1854	The first oil well in Europe is drilled in Bobrka, Poland
1858	The first oil well in North America is drilled in Ontario, Canada
1859	The first major oil well field in the United States, located in Titusville, Pennsylvania
1876	Robert and Ludwig Nobel modernize the oilfields in Baku, Azerbaijan and transport the oil across the Caspian Sea to Russia in the world's first oil tanker, the *Zoroaster*
1878	Thomas Edison developed the electric light bulb and caused the world's first petroleum industry recession
1896	Henry L. Williams built a pier 300ft into the waters off Santa Barbara, CA, to create the first platform for oil drilling and the first offshore oilfield
1914–1918	World War I becomes the first motorized war with oil playing a decisive factor; the first military aeroplanes were used by the Italians in 1915; the first tanks were used by the British and French in 1916
1923	Geologists use seismology to search for new oilfields
1938	Large oilfields are discovered in Kuwait and Saudi Arabia
1939–1945	Oil is the most important fuel in World War II; Germany lacks oil and relies heavily on synthetic oil
1951	Al-Ghawar in Saudi Arabia starts production and is the world's largest oilfield
1960	Organization of Petroleum Exporting Countries (OPEC) is founded
1973	OPEC raises prices, Arab members place embargo on US shipments so oil crisis occurs in West
1986	The international oil market collapses (from US$32 to US$10 a barrel) due to over-supply
2008	Oil reaches US$147 a barrel

Since the early development of gasoline-powered vehicles, automobiles have been considered an expression of an individual's personality, style and affluence. Advertising campaigns from the early 1900s onwards have led us to believe that we have gained 'freedom to explore our world', that is, if we owned an automobile.

Table 2.5 *Timeline of major environmental impacts of oil consumption*

1979	The Pemex-owned *Ixtoc-1* drilling platform in the Gulf of Mexico spewed oil that not only burned for months, but also polluted coastlines 600 miles away
1986	The international oil market collapses (from US$32 to US$10 a barrel) due to over-supply
1988	Worst offshore oil disaster occurs in North Sea on the *Piper Alpha* drilling platform, killing 167 people in the fire
1989	The *Exxon Valdez* oil tanker runs aground, dumping oil on protected Alaskan coastline
1991	Iraq sets fire to the oil wells of Kuwait during the Gulf War
2001	The world's largest offshore oil platform (*P-36*) sinks off the coast of Brazil

We 'decorate' our vehicles with all types of accessories from fuel injection to DVD/CD players and GPS systems that help us get to our destinations faster while still entertaining us. They can be bought in a wide range of styles and a rainbow of colours. If the manufacturer is unable to satisfy our desires for what we expect from a vehicle, there are companies that specialize in doing nothing more than customizing them to meet our demands. Our means of transportation defines us to both ourselves and the rest of the people who live in our world.

The late 1970s was also the time when it was first recognized that oil consumption might contribute to environmental degradation (see Table 2.5). Today one of our biggest challenges will be whether we can mitigate the environmental impacts that result from our dependence on oil. These environmental impacts appear to be one of the main factors determining whether the human society can live sustainably on this earth.

The Norm: Transboundary Consumption of Someone Else's Resources

Sustainability is a term that had little meaning in the past because resources appeared abundant. There is a long history of human societies living under an illusion of sustainability because access to bio-resource supplies appeared to be infinitely abundant; this suggested that a scarcity of resources did not need to be considered. Most resource supplies were available within one's own territorial boundaries or they could be obtained by exploiting someone else's resources or by trading for them. Profitable trade routes developed to transport resources to be consumed by people living in another part of the world. If the resources were not available, some countries acquired them by conquering other people and exploiting their resources. This has been the very successful past history of many western European countries. The idea of resource scarcity did not enter people's minds, because you either had sufficient funds to buy the resources you needed or you could acquire them in some other way.

There are many historical accounts of bio-resource exploitation by people who did not have ownership rights to them. Controlling access to resources has been an effective weapon of war, especially when armies were able to surround towns or fortifications and prevent those in the area under siege from obtaining the water and/or food they needed to survive. History is replete with examples of the more powerful members of society fighting to control access to energy, food, forests and water supplies that belonged to someone else. This drove unsustainable practices in the regions that were exploited, but powered the engines of development of the more powerful members of society who lived elsewhere. This recurring story is not just part of historical accounts; it is a continuing phenomenon today.

Forest materials were a common resource exploited by global societies for their own benefit with little concern for the people who owned or lived in these forests. The first recorded epic, *The Epic of Gilgamesh*, described the over-exploitation of the cedar forests in present-day Lebanon by a ruler who did not own the forests. This mythological story describes how Huwawa, the Mesopotamian Forest God who protected these cedar forests, was killed by the warrior-king Gilgamesh for control of the trees. Subsequent to killing Huwawa, the warrior-king cut down the forests. and cedar forests became remnant patches in this region of the world. Today, these old-growth cedar forests are a majestic image found in paintings, but not something that can be a physical experience for most people.

The European history of colonization of North America began an intensive period of global exploration and colonization (from 1200 to 1700) to control access to and acquire, bio-resources, such as timber (Figure 2.1; Vogt et al, 2007). European countries controlled the wood supplies in these newly colonized areas and gave little thought to the indigenous communities living and surviving in the same landscapes. Ships built from wood gave the European colonizers naval supremacy and control of global trade routes. Furthermore, timber provided military superiority to a country controlling wood supplies, for wood was used to construct fortifications and make weapons such as cannons and rifles. The countries of Europe would not have become military and economic powerhouses if they had been restricted to using local resources, because local supplies were insufficient to feed their rapid rates of consumption.

In addition to the over-exploitation of global forest materials, access to and control of renewable water supplies has also triggered human conflict and warfare. Controlling or denying others access to water supplies that they needed to survive is an effective weapon of war. Gleick (2008) summarized the various drivers of water conflicts around the world. What is amazing is that water conflicts can be documented dating back to 3000 BCE. During 5000 years of human history, a total of 186 major water conflicts were recorded all over the world (see Table 2.6). This may not seem to be significant, at first glance, but no region of the world was immune to having experienced a major water conflict. When one summarizes the drivers of the water conflict, most of them were caused by military reasons followed by development disputes and finally terrorism.

Figure 2.1 *Caricature of European countries harvesting trees in North America*

Human consumption of resources produced and owned by someone else was common in the past and continues to be an issue today (EIA, 2007a). This has been driven by the fact that resources are not distributed evenly around the world. For example, 80 per cent of the global uranium supplies are on indigenous-owned lands (Dowie, 2009). This means that, if there is going to be harvesting of this ore for nuclear power production, indigenous communities will need to be the suppliers of this resource. When these ores were originally collected from American Indian lands, the indigenous communities had little choice in whether uranium was to be mined on their lands. Many Native Americans died because they had no understanding of what the impacts of uranium were on human health; for example, waste uranium debris was used by the Navajos to build their houses (Vogt et al, 2010). Of the four human survival needs (energy, food, forests and water), forests and water have extensive histories of warfare or over-exploitation by those more powerful and able to control their access to these resources, even when they did not own them.

Table 2.6 *Causes of water conflicts from 3000 BCE to 2008 CE*

Political	Religious	Military tool	Development dispute	Terrorism
7%	3%	52%	34%	31%

Note: units show percentage of total conflicts, mentioning each cause
Source: Gleick, 2008

Human History: A Search for Food Security

Getting enough food, a recurring problem faced by humans, continues to plague our society, but at the same time we have pursued creative solutions to overcome it. According to Richard Wrangham (2009), the early pre-agricultural humans would have starved if they had been confined to eating raw food. He suggests that 'Cooking increases the share of food digested in the stomach and small intestine, where it can be absorbed, from 50 per cent to 95 per cent according to work done on people fitted for medical reasons with collection bags at the end of their small intestines.' If this hypothesis is correct, more than 200,000 years ago our human ancestors learned to obtain more food value by eating cooked food. This still did not solve the food-security problem for humans because food supplies were still inadequate and unpredictable.

This lack of food security had negative effects on human health and has resulted in some novel survival adaptations by humans. Some cultures adapted to food shortages by travelling with migrating animals that provided them 'mobile food' on the hoof; many animals migrate when food supplies diminish (see Chapter 3). This adaptation occurred in environments where cycles of food availability were common, usually the colder and hotter regions of the world.

When humans did not migrate, a few groups evolved sophisticated metabolic adaptations to store food within their bodies to subsist during the periods when food supplies were limited. For example, the human body adapted to cycles of insufficient food by storing 'calories in times of plenty to sustain them during droughts and crop failures' (Brody, 1991). Societies living in arid regions of the world were especially adept at surviving these unpredictable cycles of food supplies by efficiently converting calories to body fat that was then burned for energy when food was less available.

A 'feast-and-famine cycle' adaptation by humans may have worked in the past, but it does not provide food security today. It is also an extremely poor adaptation for a community when these people are conquered by others and introduced to foods to which they are no longer physiologically adapted. Australian aborigines, some Pacific Islanders and several American Indian tribes living in the southwest US are not adapted to the rich and high-carbohydrate foods that were introduced by the European colonizers (Brody, 1991). These groups face a variety of health problems today because their bodies are not adapted to digest high-carbohydrate foods that are now available all the time.

Most humans, however, have not evolved sophisticated physiological or migratory approaches to deal with cycles of low food availability. These adaptations are not realistic when there is a need to feed a larger population. More than 4000 years ago, non-migrating members of the human population began to improve the growth and yields of food plants and to manage soils to increase crop yields (Hillel, 1991).

The European colonialists to North America were fortunate in finding many agricultural plants growing in North America that did not exist on the European continent (Maier et al, 2003). These agricultural plants have become accepted food items in Europe today and most people do not know that they originated in the Americas. The European diet was quite bland without the agricultural crops that were taken back by the early European colonialists. The Americas provided Italy with its first tomatoes, France its string beans, Ireland its potato; tobacco, chocolate and raspberries also originated in the Americas. Today, tomatoes are the staple of Italian cooking and it is hard to imagine the Irish or many of the Scandinavian countries living without potatoes.

The Europeans benefited culinarily from their travels to the Americas. Documents show that Native Americans cultivated over 300 plants that were taken to Europe and quickly became the staple food in these countries. These new food crops allowed population densities to increase in Europe. Maier et al (2003) noted that the 'spread of American crops increased the earth's capacity to feed ever larger numbers of people by allowing a more efficient and productive use of the land'. A few of the plants that became common food items and prospered under a variety of growth conditions are maize (corn) which was more productive than rice or wheat; the potato which produces more food per hectare of land than wheat and grew well even at high latitudes; the sweet potato, which is high-yielding on dry and poor soils; and manioc or tapioca which flourished in tropical regions of the world where wheat did not grow well (Maier et al, 2003). It may be that the most important export from the Americas was food crops capable of feeding a growing population.

Despite the sophisticated agricultural systems that developed over time, food security and food safety for the global community has been an elusive goal throughout much of human history. It is not a simple problem of just needing to grow more food crops or distributing it to locations where it is needed. Most of human history has been a battle with other animals and fungi who also covet the same food grown by humans. In addition, the problem of food storage and handling is just as relevant today as it was in the past. Humans continue to lose a significant portion of their food supplies to animals and micro-organisms or have their food contaminated with chemicals or organisms that make people sick or can kill them. In fact, food health issues, which continue to be an important global concern today, are used to justify trade embargos. The European Union ban on the importation of US beef describes well how politics have become an important part of food safety and used to control access to country markets (Box 2.1). Outbreaks of foot and mouth disease, mad cow disease and the Ebola virus attest to the continuing and significant food safety issues that society faces.

A brief summary of the role of food in human societies is useful to show the difficulties that humans have faced in obtaining sufficient quantities of healthy food and in developing methods to store it. The past informs us of the continuing challenges that we still face in relation to food and how we still have not resolved our historical problems regarding its equitable distribution. Food has played and continues to play an important social and cultural role for humans. Since the 20th century, food has increasingly become a source of contention when its production has negative environmental externalities (e.g. chemical addition into streams due to herbicides, pesticides or fertilizers) or when it competes with other human

Box 2.1 The Politics of Food Safety

Carlos A. González

Beef is a great example to illustrate the politics involved in marketing food globally. Although beef is produced in all parts of the globe, production methods vary greatly. Many developing nations raise cattle primarily for local consumption, whereas a smaller number of nations maintain larger-scale operations in order to supply beef to the world market. Of the 57 beef-exporting countries, the US and the European Union (EU) will be examined here since they are the two largest beef and veal producers. In total, more than 58 million Mg of beef and veal are produced annually around the world. This production level continues to increase, as has the use of growth-stimulating and quality-enhancing hormones and feed additives. Some have argued that these changes could increase the risks faced by consumers as inappropriate drug use, even at a single farm or plant, may now affect beef consumers worldwide. Different hormones and hormone combinations are used in beef and veal production, depending on the desired result as well as the age, breed and type of cattle being treated; they may be natural, synthetic or xenobiotic (plant-derived). In essence, the US and other exporting nations practise a resource-intensive system of beef production, resulting in higher-grade beef and decreasing its production time. As a result, higher priced beef is produced in shorter periods of time.

EU dislike of hormone use in beef production dates back to the 1970s. These attitudes intensified after the discovery in 1977 of breast enlargement in school children in Milan, Italy and, more importantly, the detection in 1980 of hormone residues in Italian baby food made from veal produced in France. Primarily due to these episodes, consumer organizations began successfully boycotting veal.

The broad question is how countries can balance the desire for trade with the need to ensure the safety of their consumers. The General Agreement on Tariffs and Trade (GATT), the precursor to the World Trade Organization (WTO), created a safety-net to ensure that countries could protect their consumers while still honouring their trade commitments. The WTO currently numbers 153 countries with economies that account for approximately 97 per cent of world trade. The GATT and the Application of Sanitary and Phytosanitary Measures (SPS) Agreement, in particular, sought to ensure that countries abided by certain sanitary measures to ensure food safety and to eliminate unjustified trade barriers.

The US challenged the EU ban on hormone-treated meat on the grounds that it was not based on science and was instead a disguised trade barrier. In the first test of the SPS Agreement, both countries quarreled before the WTO. The ban, which was not fully implemented until 1989, was countered by the US imposing US$100 million import duties on a list of EU products. This issue went before the WTO in 1996 and was 'settled' in 1998, but not to the satisfaction of the EU. Authorized groups before and after the 'settlement' studied the question, yet in general their reports were not accepted by the EU which continued to place roadblocks on meaningful action and decisions. The issue itself remained unresolved to anyone's satisfaction until May 2009, when both sides agreed to a guaranteed, duty-free quota for hormone-free US beef exports to the EU.

needs (e.g. renewable water for agriculture, electricity production or salmon in streams).

Food and social status

Throughout human history and even today, food security has been inequitable. In the same landscape, you can find people who are malnourished and lack food security living next to people who do not appear to have any problem acquiring an abundance of food and even over-consuming it. Unfortunately, human history suggests that there always has been an imbalance with more people lacking food security compared with those who have secure food supplies.

Historically, food security was linked to one's economic status. Few peasants were ever overweight, while many more leaders appeared to be extremely well fed. This disparity in who was able to access food supplies contributed to our linking of a person's social status with how well fed one was, whether a person was thin or obese. Therefore, the easiest way to show your status in society was to overeat until you became obese or corpulent. You did not have much status by being thin. During the 16th and 17th centuries in Europe, being portly demonstrated your high status in society, as well as making the statement that you could afford to feed your family. This did not say anything about the quality and nutrition value of the food, nor did it say anything about how healthy you were or how long you would live.

This historical idea, that you had a higher social status if you were obese, is not accepted in most parts of the world today. The prevalence of obese people is now considered to be a serious problem in industrialized societies. The idea of being thin and not obese, is acceptable because of the negative health problems, such as diabetes, resulting from obesity. This does not mean that the link has disappeared between being plump or well fed and your economic status. In some places, for example southern Nigeria, there are special facilities where women go to be 'fattened up' prior to their weddings since larger women are more desirable as marriage partners (Lamb, 2001).

Questions regarding what food items humans should eat and how much food should be eaten continue to be debated in the literature. However, the negative aspects of eating too much has gained greater acceptance in the advanced-economy countries. Food intake has also been linked to one's longevity; the less you eat, the longer you will live. Research conducted 20 years ago suggested that if humans reduced their food intake to almost starvation levels; they would live longer (Gertner, 2009). Incidentally, this research was conducted on rats, that lived longer when their food intake was reduced.

When eight individuals enclosed themselves in *BIO2* in the Arizona desert in the US for two years to see if humans could survive in smaller enclosed systems, they used a computer programme daily to regulate their food intake in order to follow a 'low intake' diet. The experiment had to be terminated before any insights could be made as to the efficacy of this diet because the altered chemistry of the enclosed atmosphere (such as higher CO_2 levels and lower O_2 levels) was potentially dangerous to the 'biospherians'. Some have provided evidence that a calorie-restricted diet will decrease human 'secondary ageing' processes (Gertner, 2009); secondary-ageing processes are cancer, diabetes and cardiovascular disease. Others have suggested that this diet is too similar to anorexia and that people following this diet will face future health problems where the functioning of their internal organs is significantly impaired at later stages in their lives.

Eating less food and having intake levels close to starvation does not address the psychological impacts of insufficient food consumption. The *BIO2* biospherians were more irritable when they had less food to eat. How a human's psychological framework affects the length of one's life was not discussed by the researchers studying the *BIO2*. What is amazing about the proposed idea of eating food close to a starvation level is that historically people eating less food were considered to be the peasants and the higher social status people were more obese. If peasants had not had such hard and stressful lives, would they have lived longer because of their diets?

The important role that food has played in our social interactions transcends cultural and social groups. It was not just important in defining social status, but it was also used to forge and solidify social and political contracts. If you 'broke bread' with a person, it was typically bad manners to kill them because you had accepted them into your social group by your offer of bread. Even today, heads of states receive a ceremonial loaf of bread as a token of friendship when visiting some of the former Soviet bloc countries such as Ukraine.

Humans have a long history of searching for and acquiring sufficient food to feed their populations. Controlling the supply capacity for food was essential for social and economic development. When food supplies diminish, social and economic development is affected because people spend more time gathering food. It is very difficult to think about technological developments or new products when there is not enough food to eat. A lack of food or food that is nutritiously imbalanced, is linked to poor health. Unhealthy people are less capable of working; this then reduces the human development potential of the community. Military leaders have recognized these connections for a long time and have blocked access to food as an important weapon of war. Starving the opposition works.

Many of the growing-economy countries have more than half of their population involved in food production but still do not have food security (see Chapter 9). One might think that industrialized countries do not have food-security issues because of their ability to grow an abundance of food, but this is not the case. The industrialized countries have about two per cent of their population involved in food production and use highly mechanized production systems based on chemical fertilizer applications to high-yield crops. Much food is produced by only a few farmers in the industrialized countries and excess food production is possible. Despite being able to grow a surplus, food security and safety continue to be an issue for these countries. Society is still attempting to deal with how to store food without losing its nutritional value or losing it because it spoils.

Food preservation for food security

Maintaining food supplies and having it available when needed have been a problem throughout human history, but became especially grim when humans moved into cities. Unless a city person had extended-family members who remained on the farm and were willing to supply them with food, city residents became reliant on a rural food production system over which they had little knowledge or control and where there was no guarantee that food would continue to be delivered to city markets (Fagan, 2008). They were especially vulnerable to any climatic event, such as droughts or a pest outbreak that reduced crop yields.

Food security was not just a matter of working out how to distribute or transport food from a farm to where it was needed in the city. A considerable portion of the food that was produced in farms never made it to people's dinner tables. Making food supplies secure hinged on developing the knowledge to store food. Probably more than half of the food was lost to vermin or other animals that ate it or the food became unpalatable and spoiled due to microbes that produced chemicals (e.g. aflatoxins or botulism) that either killed people or made them extremely ill. The need to develop better systems for storing food became very urgent. For over a thousand years, people have lost a large portion of their food to fungi, insects and rodents.

This lack of food security was even more dire when people travelled or went on long sea voyages. It was not uncommon for people travelling by ship to lack nutritious foods that included adequate vitamin C (vitamin C deficiencies result in the formation of livid spots on the skin, spongy and bleeding gums and loosening of the teeth) or vitamin D (vitamin D deficiencies cause rickets, the symptoms being weak muscles, skeletal deformities such as bowed legs and knock-knees) or they had to eat food that was inedible because it was contaminated by microbes or chemicals (see Box 2.2). There was a reason that sea voyagers drank a lot of beer or mead – it did not spoil and probably kept the sailors' minds occupied during long sea voyages; as a result, there were probably fewer mutinies.

Box 2.2 Past food problems for sea voyages

There are accounts of ships sailing to new lands, whose crews commonly endured starvation and scurvy. The life of a sailor was difficult in the 1800s. The best documented case is that of Sir John Franklin, an English sea captain charting the Northwest Passage in the Canadian Arctic in 1819–1822 CE (*National Geographic Magazine*, 1990). His ship was frozen in ice for two years, during which time his sailors did not have enough food to eat, were suffering from lead poisoning and had to resort to eating lichen and their leather boots to survive. Higher lead levels were found in tissue samples collected from the sailors who died during this expedition. The food poisoning resulted from the sailors eating food preserved in cans whose lids had been sealed using lead solder. This story is especially gruesome, since there is evidence that one sailor was murdered, and there might have been cannibalism. According to Inuit witnesses who saw the sailors, it appeared they suffered from scurvy.

Food shortages were especially problematic during military campaigns. Large armies needed to collect food from the lands they were conquering in order to feed their soldiers. There were limits to how much food could be stolen by a conquering country from people living on the lands they wanted to control. Stealing or taking food grown by local people could increase their resistance to the invading army, so that an army could face multiple fighting fronts. In addition, it was not a good idea to starve the people who you were conquering since you needed their labour to continue to produce food or to work in your industries. This military need was what finally provided the stimulus to fund the development of food preservation methodologies. Napoleon I of France recognized this dilemma and in 1795 offered a monetary award to anyone who developed an easy and safe manner to preserve food (Swedberg and Swedberg, 1985). He wanted to have pre-prepared and secure food supplies available to the travelling army during its campaigns.

In 1809, 14 years after this award money had been offered, Nicholas Appert of France received 12,000 francs from Napoleon for a food preservation process he developed using glass bottles sterilized using boiling water. Despite the importance of his invention, glass bottles were heavy and not easy to transport and were therefore not a good solution for storing food for a travelling army. To overcome these problems, food began to be preserved in tin or steel containers. Originally, soldiers had to use bayonets to open the tin cans – again not a very good solution for a massive army on the move. Food canned in tins was first marketed in England in 1812 and the first commercial cannery was established in the same year (Busch, 1981). This method of preserving food was not yet perfected, since lead solder was used to seal the tin cans and people suffered from lead poisoning. Despite this problem, canned food became popular and everything from oysters to fruits and vegetables, as well as meats, was stored in cans.

Once this technology was developed, it began to be easier to store food and feed the rapidly urbanizing population that was becoming common in an industrializing Europe in the mid-1800s. Developments in energy technologies coincided with more efficient food preservation methods and probably allowed more people to work in industry instead of worrying about whether their food was safe to eat or where they would get their next meal.

Industrialization did not solve the food security problems during the 19th and 20th centuries. This was especially problematic during periods of widespread conflict and wars. In response to shortages of canned food during World War I, the British government began issuing cigarettes and – supposedly – amphetamines, to suppress the appetites of soldiers. During the 1939 Finnish–Russian war, the senior author's father talked about how Finnish soldiers were sent out to fight and given a bag of raw potatoes to take along as food. So, not only were you expected to fight, but you were not well fed either. A bag of potatoes is not going to last too long and many of the potatoes were already wrinkled and old. Once you had eaten your commissioned bag of potatoes, you were dependent on people living in the countryside being willing to share their food with you. This can be a tricky proposition during a war and probably resulted in many hungry soldiers.

The Finnish–Russian war also occurred during one of this region's coldest and snowiest winters in history. This fact also limited the ability of soldiers to find food in the forests where much of the fighting occurred.

The 20th century was a time where the science of growing food flourished in the industrialized world. Financial investments were made to improve agricultural production techniques to increase crop yields. The Green Revolution was an attempt to feed more people using chemical fertilizers and from selected genetic plant varieties that grew under less than ideal conditions and food production did keep pace with population growth because of these developments. One might assume that the Green Revolution has finally resolved the food security problem that societies have historically faced. This has not happened: the human population still faces malnutrition and starvation. The Green Revolution also introduced new problems for society because chemical fertilizers/herbicides were over-used to increase crop yields and caused soil contamination.

Restaurants and our perceptions of food security

Food security or a lack of security, exemplifies the disparity that exists in who accesses or controls resource supplies in the world. The globe is split into two apparent worlds: one dominated by those who have been able to *over-develop* their human capital using global resources and the other dominated by those where the human capital is *under-developed*. This latter group is unable to develop their human capital using global resources and survives at a subsistence level. Subsistence survivors do not typically eat in restaurants and do not worry about which food choices to eat at home. They contrast sharply with the other half of the global population which frequently eats in restaurants. This latter group is more isolated from the day-to-day problems of finding enough food to eat or knowing what practices will allow crops to grow under drought-prone conditions. People living in this world of abundance are not familiar with food scarcity and base their global ideas related to food production from the images they see on television. Restaurants usually do not run out of food and food scarcity is a concept but not a reality for them. It will not trigger reflexes such as 'adapt, mitigate or die' because of food shortages due to droughts.

Humans have struggled with acquiring sufficient food to feed their populations for thousands of years. Today, the over-developed part of the world is struggling with over-consumption of food as a health problem. The roots for this change can be traced to the development of restaurants. Restaurants were not formally 'invented' until the 1760s and 1770s, when they functioned as public rooms where local people could acquire bouillon or wine as a health food (if one was 'restoring lost strength to a sickly or tired individual') in pre-revolutionary France (Spang, 2000). Restaurants allowed the middle-class or the common person to enter a food establishment easily and to buy prepared food; this was no longer a place frequented by wealthy people. This began to change the eating habits of large sectors of the population in the rapidly industrializing regions of the world. Communal eating arrangements have existed throughout human history, but not the facilities where total strangers could eat food, pay a fixed price for it and then travel somewhere else. An ordinary person going to restaurants several times a week did not become a common tradition until after World War II. The father of one of the authors remembers having lunch served to students at school in Texas and it being a real treat to eat at a cafeteria on Sunday with his aunt and uncle in Fort Worth, Texas. There were hamburger joints, drugstores and variety stores that served relatively affordable food for a single worker to have for lunch.

Restaurants formalized the process for humans to satisfy their biological need for food at any time of the day that the restaurants were open for business. Correspondingly, the only constraint to satisfying one's hunger was to have the financial resources to buy the food. Restaurants started the process of isolating people from knowing how to grow food or understanding the impacts of droughts on food production. Today, we publish cookbooks on how to prepare hundreds of different cuisines and we have television stations that only broadcast shows telling us how to cook. We also have encyclopaedias to inform the reader on the scientific basis of cooking and the particulars of ingredients needed to produce a diversity of dishes for all ethnicities. Because food ingredients are grown on different continents from where they are consumed, the climatic and geographic constraints are no longer relevant or understood by the food consumer. For example, cardamom is a basic ingredient in Finnish bread-making but it is a seed produced by a plant that does not grow in Finland but in the tropics. It has become part of the Finnish culture even though there is no traditional or historical basis for it.

Restaurants give a false perception that food is plentiful. In the more economically advanced countries, the most important decision during a day may be the need to decide whether you want Chinese, Japanese, Mexican or Thai food. There is no inkling of whether the restaurant has adequate ground meat or cheese at the establishment to produce the food you want to buy. Each person focuses more on deciphering the menu and selecting a preferred item to eat that day. This disconnect between food production and the factors that constrain food supplies is exemplified by the enormous amounts of money people pay for one food item (Box 2.3).

The link and anecdotal evidence between what you eat and your health has been known for a long time even though society has been less able to ensure that food consumption is always nutritious. When restaurants were invented, they combined cooking and medicine to provide potential customers a system to improve their health and were called 'maisons de santé' or 'private infirmaries' (Spang, 2000). Today restaurants are not typically thought of as locations to become healthy. In industrialized countries the high percentage of overweight adults and children attests to society continuing to focus on eating too much. This occurs even when the other half of the world faces malnutrition and inadequate food supplies. Food security has been an issue that society has dealt with for as long as we have human records and it continues today. The Green Revolution was going to solve global food insecurity problems, but climate and soil limitations precluded this.

Box 2.3 Examples of expensive food items

In Japan, the craving for certain species of fish, such as the bluefin tuna used to prepare sushi, means that they are being over-fished, and quotas for fishing tuna are in place (Harden, 2007). The extent of the monetary cost to satisfy one's food cravings is the fact that one bluefin tuna 'sold at Tsukijli market for $173,600, because of its size, quality and, it is said, a fierce bidding war' (Harden, 2007).

Saffron, used to produce luxurious desserts, is expensive (especially the Persian variety grown mainly in Iran). From a low of US$200 an ounce, prices fluctuate with 'international politics, unpredictable weather and ornery customs officers' (Snyder, 2009). There is a reason for its high price. It takes 75,000 crocus flowers to produce a pound of saffron, and the flower part must be hand-picked before the sun goes down during a short month, typically October. Eating small quantities of raw saffron has no health impact, however in greater amounts it can cause loss of liver function, but in small quantities has no health impact.

A Long Human History of Poor Health

It is very revealing to read the book written by Steckel and Rose (2002) where they documented the strong environmental links between food quality or its nutritional value and human health. Their data on human skeletons from the western hemisphere (many from cemetery excavations) spanned the period from 5000 BCE to the late 19th century, and seven basic indicators of human health were summarized.

Their examination of over 13,000 skeletons and data derived from using the seven health indicators suggested a strong connection between a society's political development and its agricultural practices. Steckel and Rose (2002) wrote that 'life became … nasty, brutish and short' for the typical person when human societies began to develop with the rise of agriculture, government and urbanization. The healthiest groups of people were the hunter-gatherer societies and those who continued to live in 'dispersed settlements'. This contrasted sharply with the health issues faced by people living together in a larger community. The Maya civilization, for example, was plagued with a high incidence of chronic stressors especially during periods of social disruption. The impacts of social disruption were recorded in skeletons as a continual decrease in the average stature of adults.

The difficulties of acquiring sufficient food and the adverse effects on health of poor nutrition was further aggravated by major events such as the European colonization of North and South America. It is clear that there was not enough food to provide for the thousands of additional people now expecting to live off the resources available in the conquered countries. Many of the European colonizers who established sugar plantations in the newly conquered lands in the Caribbean recognized their inability to provide sufficient food to feed their workers. They imported food plants (e.g. breadfruit) to feed their labourers. Breadfruit is a high-carbohydrate fruit that would efficiently feed a large group of people; a diet primarily based on breadfruit, however, is not very healthy and changed the diets of the conquered people.

These changing food habits are still impacting the indigenous communities today. For example, 'As many as half the Pima and Tohono O'odham (formerly Papago) Indians in the United States now develop diabetes by the age of 35, an incidence 15 times higher than for Americans as a whole' (Brody, 1991). Today, attempts are being made to reintroduce the consumption of the edible parts of plants that were an element of the diet for indigenous cultures in the past. In the southwest US, there is a drive to consume plants such mesquite, cactus, nuts of oak trees and a 'hominy-type corn' that has little sugar but is mainly comprised of starch.

The most horrendous impact of the European colonizers in the lands they conquered was the spread of new diseases to regions of the world that had not previously experienced them. The native populations had little resistance to these introduced diseases. This introduction occurred at a time when the native communities were already struggling with malnutrition and insufficient supplies of food. Steckel and Rose (2002) wrote how in the present day Ecuador, the Spanish Conquest was a very traumatic event in the history of the natives, since it introduced Old World diseases to a population that was not getting enough food. Their listing of the major disease outbreaks that occurred in Ecuador is revealing and explains the high mortality of native populations subsequent to the arrival of the European colonizers.

> Age at death; Arthritis; Dental health; Infections; Osteoporosis; Stature; Trauma
>
> 1524–1527 smallpox epidemic; 1531–1533 measles, possibly plague; 1546 plague, possibly typhus; 1558 smallpox, measles, possibly influenza; 1585–1591 smallpox, measles, possibly mumps; 1604 unidentified epidemic; 1606 diphtheria; 1611 measles, and typhus; 1612 scarlet fever, measles, typhus; 1614 typhus, diphtheria; 1618 measles, dysentery; 1634 typhus; 1644–1645 German measles, diphtheria; 1648–1649 smallpox, German measles; 1667 typhus; 1676–1677 smallpox; 1680 plague; 1683 plague.

The European colonizers, however, cannot be blamed for all of the poor health problems detected in bone records of people who lived in the western hemisphere. These skeletons showed that signs of biological stress in childhood and of degeneration of joints and in teeth had already increased several millennia before Columbus arrived on the North American shores. Many of these signs of poor health resulted from populations moving into less healthy ecological environments during the pursuit of food. According to Steckel and Rose (2002), the pre-Columbian Native Americans were among both the healthiest and the least healthy groups to live in the western hemisphere before the 20th century. Even though the pre-Columbian Native Americans suffered from poor health prior to the arrival of the Europeans, European colonialists aggravated the health problems further by their introduction of new diseases and the reduced food security that decreased their resistance to these diseases.

Accidental Reductions in Human Resource Uses

Contrary to what is commonly written in the literature, most examples of societal over-exploitation of their resources and their subsequent collapse were probably accidental events. They were not premeditated plans designed by conquering countries to cause societies to collapse or made with the knowledge that resource supplies would be unsustainable and eventually limit human survival. During this time, bio-resource supplies appeared to be endlessly abundant since it was so easy to procure them, albeit mostly in someone else's backyard. The idea that resource consumption could feed back negatively on our environment and therefore jeopardize human survival is recognized today, but these links were not as obvious in the past.

Even though there may not be consensus on what factors can cause societal collapse, there are many lessons that can be learned from exploring these accidental reductions in the human survival potential and the role of resource uses in these reductions. Most of the accidental reductions in human survival potential were due to a loss of essential bio-resource supplies. This resource could have been any one or more of the four basic human needs; energy, food, forest materials or water. However, on occasion there have been grand plans that were conceived and implemented in such a way that the disastrous outcome should have been apparent on hindsight to an outside observer. The following is an example of this outcome.

When the Ford Motor Company decided to build rubber plantations in the Brazilian Amazon, this dream was driven by the fact that the US had been importing rubber and concerns existed that rubber supplies would limit the growth of the emerging auto industry (Grandin, 2009). This stimulated the US auto manufacturers to think about growing their own rubber trees so they would not be dependent on the British, who monopolized the rubber trade at this time. In 1927, Ford bought land in the Amazon to grow his own rubber trees. This venture was started without really understanding the different environment that the Amazon possessed. The town built by Ford in the Amazon was a copy of a typical Michigan mill town. This town was designed to incorporate the novel industrial processes (e.g. an assembly line) that Ford had refined in Michigan and to introduce American capitalism principles into a jungle setting (Grandin, 2009). 'Ford built Cape Cod-style shingled houses for his Brazilian workers and urged them to tend flower and vegetable gardens and eat wholewheat bread and unpolished rice ... complete with 'electric lights, telephones, washing machines, victrolas and electric refrigerators' (Grandin, 2009).

Anyone who has visited the Amazon region would immediately recognize how inappropriate it was to transfer this American vision into a region of the world where even today many people still do not have electricity and survive at a subsistence level. The idea of eating wholewheat bread in an environment where only a few root crops grow well ignored the constraints of the acidic and high Al soils for crop production. Even today, local people talk about the houses that were built by Ford where the windows opened outwards (an unfamiliar design in the region) and where fire hydrants were installed along the main streets of the town even though they were not hooked to water supplies. When the venture collapsed in 1945, Ford had invested millions of dollars into a project that had not been well thought out. He could not have foreseen that the rubber trees would be attacked by diseases. A better understanding of the local context would have better prepared this venture to face the significant constraints that exist in starting businesses in tropical forests where little existing infrastructure is present and where the transportation costs would be prohibitive. There had been considerable problems in satisfying the resource needs of the workers.

Another story regarding the collapse of a society astounds us, when we understand how it created its own problem. The story of Easter Island describes a society that collapsed because it was unable to extend its food footprint beyond the island boundaries. According to Diamond (2005) the social collapse in Easter Island followed its decision to build large statues for religious purposes, causing over-exploitation of the trees growing on the island. This resulted in an inability to acquire food beyond their territorial lands, because trees were needed to build the wooden boats and the wooden harpoons used to fish for the common dolphin, the staple food item. Islanders were limited to surviving on food available on the land and its margins. It is recorded that cannibalism occurred on Easter Island once food became scarce. In 1774, Captain Cook wrote that the inhabitants were 'small, lean, timid and miserable' (Diamond, 2005). Another way of looking at this story is to view it as a case where the people became restricted to living off the land and were unable to extend their food footprint beyond the island boundaries. This would be a very different story if the communities had not over-exploited their forests and continued to be able to fish.

Cuba is another example of a country where the resource footprint was diminished and altered dramatically in 1959 as a result of politics. Cuba did not collapse as a result, but its resource footprint decreased significantly. In 1959, Fidel Castro took power in Cuba and isolated Cuba from its previous economic partners for ideological and political reasons. Once Cuba had adopted communism, the US further increased Cuba's isolation by imposing an economic embargo and restricting Cuban Americans living in the US from sending money to their relatives on the island. This is a story of how Cuba appeared to be able to survive on its own, but in reality was unable to survive without the millions of dollars of aid and energy that it received from the former Soviet Union and more recently from Venezuela. Once this aid was less available, Cuba was forced to provide for its peoples' food and energy needs from its own resources. Today, Cuba still has over 20,000 locations that provide free lunch daily to anyone who needs it, at a reported cost to the Cuban government of US$350,000,000 annually.

Unfortunately for Cuba, it is geographically located in an area that is climatically vulnerable and where the soils are not highly productive (soils can sustainably grow a few root crops, trees and grasses). Cuba is commonly impacted by hurricanes and the devastation of these weather events directly impacts its food production. In 2008, Cuba was directly hit by three hurricanes which caused food shortages and reduced farm production by at least a third (Avila, 2009). Cuba still faces many challenges to living within its food, forest, water and energy footprints.

Recent decades have produced many cases of reduced resource consumption footprints. Unfortunately, these were unplanned reductions that have caused considerable social disruption and forced people to make choices that are not very environmentally sustainable. In these situations, people are just attempting to survive under conditions where internal conflict, wars or politically driven ideology are reducing their survival potential. Frequently, dictators are making decisions that enrich their coffers without considering the plight of their people who find it increasingly difficult to obtain the resources needed to survive. Since the international community has few tools to influence these dictators, they impose trade embargoes which further isolate a country's population from being able to acquire essential resources.

These forced reductions in the human footprint for food, water, forest materials or energy have typically been disastrous for the general people but not the 'local elites'. This is the situation occurring in Zimbabwe today. Zimbabwe's problems began when the government began to confiscate farms owned by the descendants of the European colonialists who originally developed the productive agricultural infrastructure. From all accounts, the people who now own these farms were those in political power and have little interest or the skills to farm the land. Food production has suffered and food shortages are common. The end result is that the citizens of Zimbabwe who are not connected to the government have no food security. They are also experiencing several major health outbreaks (such as cholera) that the existing health system has been unable to control. In desperation, many citizens of Zimbabwe have been escaping to South Africa.

In countries facing civil war and where it is dangerous to grow food crops, human options for survival become limited. People in the lower social strata flee into forests because they appear to provide safe havens and food (e.g. wildlife that can be hunted). This increases the pressures on forests to provide food, water and energy. Conservation efforts, such as those that were undertaken in the past no longer occur, as species that were conserved become the food that allows people to survive. The fighting in eastern Congo occurred in the same location where a 'third of the world's last 700 wild mountain gorillas' are found (Gettleman, 2008). The Rwandan wars of the 1990s also forced people to flee into the forests. These people had little access to clean renewable water and disease outbreaks were common as humans had more contact with disease vectors (Vogt et al, 2007). The poorer people are those whose resource footprints are reduced, while the local elites continue to use resources at the same levels or increase their own bio-resource footprints.

Island countries are especially vulnerable when facing a potential decrease in food imports. Many island countries have developed population densities beyond what an island is capable of feeding from within its lands and many import food. If such countries face a blockage or reduced importation of food, they are unable to grow sufficient food to feed their people. In 1991, worries about being able to continue to import food occurred on the island of Puerto Rico when the US led a multinational military force to liberate Kuwait. Puerto Ricans felt that the US would be too preoccupied with the war effort to continue to ship food to them and many panicked, buying all the food in the stores so that shelves were emptied. Very quickly, stores ran out of food even though there never was a real concern that food export to Puerto Rico would stop.

Our historical assessments of why societies collapsed suffer from the fragmented and partial database that we use to conduct these retrospective analyses. The key factors essential for deciphering an applicable story may not exist. For example, the collapse of Easter Island, as noted above, has been attributed to over-exploitation of forest resources so that the islanders were unable to build boats to travel beyond the island boundaries for food. Pollen records have documented the existence of a diverse vegetative community on Easter Island and indicate the time at which particular trees species were no longer producing pollen (Diamond, 2005). However, what if this was not the reason for the collapse that occurred on Easter Island? What if Easter Island was impacted by weather events that decreased its rainfall during this time? The loss of forests could be explained by lower precipitation levels because, despite the environment, forests need a minimum amount of rainfall to grow. We do not know what the 'real' story is for Easter Island, but we can hypothesize several factors that caused its demise.

Shipley (2000) summarized this quandary when he described an example of trying to determine whether rain was the causal factor for mud to be formed. In this example, the link between the existence of mud and rainfall appears to be quite clear. We can hypothesize that mud in one's backyard means that it rained recently. However, what if we knew that it had not rained during the period of time that this mud supposedly formed? Shipley (2000) concluded 'knowing that it has not rained but there is mud in the front yard gives you information on the existence of other causes of mud'. The environmental indices are similar to the 'mud' example because having an incomplete knowledge base makes it difficult to identify which factor is most sensitive to changes in our environment. There is a need to develop tools that allow us to detect associations or connections that most accurately describe each story being written.

We will use indices (presented in the next chapter) to glean greater insights to the choices a country makes. Indices rank countries against a variety of metrics which can be used to determine how sustainable are the choices they make. Following this assessment, individual country stories will be further examined using country databases on energy, food, forests and water (see Chapters 4–6).

References

Alig, R. J., Stewart, S., Wear, D. N., Stein, S. M. and Nowak, D. (2009) 'Conversion to developed uses', Forest Encyclopedia Network, www.forestencyclopedia.net/p/p3118, accessed 20 July 2009

Allan, T. and Warren, A. (1993) *Deserts. The encroaching wilderness,* a World Conservation Atlas, Oxford University Press, New York

Avila, O. (2009) '2009 is Cuba's 'year of living dangerously', *The Seattle Times,* 1 January 2009, News A3

Brody, J. E. (1991) 'To preserve their health and heritage, Arizona Indians reclaim ancient foods', *New York Times,* 21 May 1991, http://query.nytimes.com/gst/fullpage.html?res=9D0CEFD71F31F932A15756C0A967958260&sec=health&spon=&pagewanted=all, accessed 13 March 2009

Busch, J. (1981) 'An introduction to the tin can', *Historical Archaeology,* vol 15, pp95–104

de Blij, H. (2005) *Why Geography Matters. Three Challenges Facing America. Climate Change, The Rise of China and Global Terrorism,* Oxford University Press, Oxford

Diamond, J. (2005) *Collapse: How Societies Choose to Fail or Survive,* Penguin, New York, NY

Dowie, M. (2009) 'Nuclear caribou. On the front lines of the new uranium rush with the Inuit of Nunavut', *Orion Magazine,* January/February 2009

EIA (2007) EIA, International Energy Outlook China, www.eia.doe.gov/emeu/cabs/China/Oil.html, accessed 20 January 2009[QA30]

Fagan, B. (2008). *The Great Warming. Climate Change and the Rise and Fall of Civilizations,* Bloomsbury Press, New York, NY

FAO (2000) 'World Soil Resources Report 90. Land Resource Potential and Constraints at Regional and Country Levels', Land and Water Resource Division, UN FAO, Rome, Italy

FAO (2008) 'World Resources Report', www.fao.org/docrep/011/ai476e/ai476e01.htm, 22 July 2009

Gertner, J. (2009) 'The Calorie-Restriction Experiment. Eating much, much less helped rats live longer. Will it work on humans?', *The New Times Magazine,* 11 October 2009, pp56–62, 82

Gettleman, J. (2008) 'Gorillas' home becomes war zone', *The Seattle Times,* 18 November 2008, pA17

Gleick, P. H. (2008) 'Water conflict chronology', Pacific Institute for Studies in Development, Environment and Security database on Water and Conflict (Water Brief) 11 October 2008, www.worldwater.org/conflictchronology.pdf, accessed 11 November 2008

Grandin, G. (2009) *FORDLANDIA. The Rise and Fall of Henry Ford's Forgotten Jungle City,* Metropolitan Books, Henry Holt and Company, New York, NY

Hannah, L., Carr, J. L. and Landerani, A. (1995) 'Human disturbance and natural habitat: a biome level analysis of a global dataset', *Biodiversity and Conservation,* vol 4, pp128–155

Harden, B. (2007) 'Japan's sacred bluefin, loved too much', *Washington Post Foreign Service,* 11 November 2007, pA01

Hillel, D. J. (1991) *Out of the Earth. Civilization and the Life of the Soil,* The Free Press, New York, NY

Lamb, C. (2001) 'Fat farm; Like many women, Arit Asuquo is worried about her weight. No matter how hard she tries she just can't pile on enough pounds. For in her village in

Nigeria, if you want to find love and marriage you've got to be obese. That's why she's gone to the fattening room', *The Mirror*, 31 July 2001

Maier, P., Smith, M. R., Keyssar, A. and Kevles, D. J. (2003) *Inventing America. A History of the United States*, W. W. Norton & Co, New York, NY and London

National Geographic Magazine (1990) 'Franklin Saga Deaths: A Mystery Solved?', *National Geographic Magazine*, vol 178, no 3, September 1990

PreventionWeb (2005) 'Europe: precipitation deficit as drought potential indication', Jan 2005, *European Spatial Planning Observation Network (ESPON)*, www.preventionweb.net/english/professional/maps/v.php?id=3824, accessed 9 December 2008

Sanchez, P. A. (1976) *Properties and Management of Soils in the Tropics*, Wiley, New York, NY

Shipley, B. (2000) *Cause and Correlation in Biology. A User's Guide to Path Analysis, Structural Equations and Causal Inference*, Cambridge University Press, Cambridge

Snyder, W. R. (2009) 'An uncommon thread', *The Wall Street Journal Magazine*, vol 5, p49

Spang, R. L. (2000) *The Invention of the Restaurant. Paris and Modern Gastronomic Culture*, Harvard University Press, Cambridge, MA

Steckel, R. H. and Rose, J. C. (2002) *The Backbone of History. Health and Nutrition in the Western Hemisphere*, Cambridge University Press, Cambridge

Swedberg, R. W. and Swedberg, H. (1985) *Tins 'n' Bins*, Wallace-Homestead, Lombard, IL

Vogt, K. A, Gordon, J., Wargo, J., Vogt, D., Asbjornsen, H., Palmiotto, P. A., Clark, H., O'Hara, J., Keeton, W. S., Patel-Weynand, T. and Witten, E. (1997) *Ecosystems: Balancing Science with Management*, Springer-Verlag, New York, NY

Vogt, K. A., Honea, J. M., Vogt, D. J., Edmonds, R. L., Patel-Weynand, T., Sigurdardottir, R. and Andreu, M. G. (2007) *Forests and Society. Sustainability and Life Cycles of Forests in Human Landscapes*, CAB International, Wallingford, UK

Vogt, K. A., Vogt, D. J., Shelton, M., Colonnese, T., Stefan, L., Cawston, R., Scullion, J., Marchand, M., Hagmann, R. K., Tulee, M., Nackley, L., Geary, T. C., House, T. A., Candelaria, S., Nwaneshiudu, I., Lee, A. M., Kahn, E., James, L. L., Rigdon, S. J., Theobald, R. M. and Lai, L. Y. (2010) 'Bio-resource Based Energy for Sustainable Societies' in W. H. Lee and V. G. Cho (eds), *Handbook of Sustainable Energy*, Nova Science Publishers Inc, Hauppauge, NY

Weightman, G. (2009) *The Industrial Revolutionaries. The Making of the Modern World 1776–1914*, Grove Press, New York, NY

World Bank (2007) *Growth and CO_2 emissions: How do different countries fare?*, Environment Department, The World Bank, October 2007, Washington, DC

Wrangham, R. (2009) 'What's cooking?', *Economist*, 19 February 2009

WRI (2009) 'EarthTrends Searchable Database Results', World Resources Institute http://earthtrends.wri.org, accessed 3 July 2009

Part 2

SCIENTIFIC APPROACH TO DECODING SUSTAINABILITY

3

TODAY: Decoding Country Resource Stories

Even though most case studies accurately document the complex set of factors that need to be included when making resource decisions, ecosystem complexity makes it impossible for a decision maker to automatically transfer these results to an entirely different location. Because each country's resource and environment stories are unique, scientists have begun to summarize large quantities of data in the form of indices. These indices generally include some aspect of what is commonly summarized in a sustainability definition. They are designed to rank countries based on how environmental and sustainable are their production and consumption of resources and how a country's economic, social and educational development potentials are impacted by its choices. Indices rank countries in relationship to one another, to determine how a country is performing for a particular metric.

To decode what it means to be sustainable, we shall begin this exploration by comparing several country-level indices (summarized in Table 3.1). These selected indices rank the 34 selected countries included in our list by their environmental performance, severity of land degradation, security of food production, environmental resiliency, risk to climate change/weather events, water footprint and sustainability of fossil fuel supplies.

Indices and How they Characterize Sustainable Choices

Indices rank environmental/ecological metrics well

A brief comparison of nine indices and whether they were generally changing in a similar fashion to one another is revealing (see Table 3.1). Few connections are found among the indices, even though our scientific understanding would have led us to expect them to change in similar ways. The HDI, hunger index International Food Policy Research Institute Global Hunger Index (IFPRI GH)

Table 3.1 *Comparison of nine indices for 34 countries*

HDI Group	Country	HDI Rank	EPI	TEF	LDS	EVI	GGCR	FFS	WF	IFPRI GH
1	Iceland	1	H	..	H	V	H	L	L	L
	Norway	2	H	M	L	V	H	H	L	L
	Australia	3	H	M	L	AR	M	L	H	L
	Canada	4	H	M	L	AR	M	L	H	L
	Sweden	6	H	M	M	V	M	L	M	L
	Japan	8	H	M	L	EV	M	L	H	L
	Netherlands	9	H	M	M	EV	M	L	M	L
	France	10	H	M	M	HV	L	L	H	L
	Finland	11	H	M	L	V	H	L	M	L
	US	12	H	H	M	V	L	L	H	L
	UK	16	M	M	L	EV	M	L	H	L
	Germany	22	H	M	M	HV	L	L	H	L
2	Argentina	38	H	L	M	V	M	L	H	L
	UAE	39	L	H	H	V	H	H	..	..
	Mexico	52	M	L	M	V	L	L	H	L
	Malaysia	63	H	L	H	V	M	L	H	L
	Russia	67	H	M	L	V	L	L	H	L
	Brazil	70	H	L	M	V	M	L	H	L
3	Venezuela	74	M	L	L	V	L	H	M	M
	China	81	L	L	M	HV	L	L	H	M
	Peru	87	H	L	H	V	L	..	M	M
	Philippines	90	L	L	L	EV	L	L	H	M
	Indonesia	107	M	L	M	HV	L	L	H	M
4	Namibia	125	H	L	L	R	H	..	L	M-
	India	128	L	L	M	EV	L	L	H	H
5	Bangladesh	140	L	L	M	HV	L	L	H	H
	Nepal	142	M	L	M	V	L	..	M	H
	Haiti	146	L	L	H	HV	L	..	L	H
	Sudan	147	L	L	M	V	M	..	H	H
	Yemen	153	L	L	M	V	H	H	M	H
6	Nigeria	158	L	L	H	HV	M	..	H	M
	Tanzania	159	M	L	M	AR	M	..	H	H
	Angola	162	L	L	L	AR	H	..	M	H
	Congo DR	168	L	L	L	AR	M	..	H	H

Note: data are from 2003, 2004 or 2005

- Environmental Performance Index [EPI] (EPI, 2008)
- Human Development Index [HDI] values and its sub-categories: Human Development Education Index, Human Poverty Index rank (HDI, 2007/2008)
- Total Ecological Footprint [TEF] (global ha/person), Total Biocapacity (global ha/person), and Ecological deficit (–) or reserve (+) (global ha/person) (Ecological Footprint and Biocapacity, 2006)
- Environmental Vulnerability Index [EVI] (EVI, 2004)
- Global Climate Risk Index average values for decade 1997–2006 of weather-related events [GGCR] (Germanwatch Global Climate Risk, 2008)
- Fossil Fuel Sustainability Index [FFS] (Ediger et al, 2007)
- Land degradation severity ranking [LDS] (FAO, 2000)
- Water Footprint per capita [WF] (m³/capita/year) (Chapagain and Hoekstra, 2004; Photius, 2008)
- IFPRI Global Hunger Index [IFPRI GH] (Wiesmann, 2006)

and the environmental EPI appear to be the most connected of the indices compared. When indices are ranked by their human development potential, rankings are also clustered at the extreme ends of the groupings, suggesting that the countries in the middle of the HDI ranking are not changing in a similar manner to one another.

A comparison of these indices reinforces the commonly held view that advanced-economy countries are more environmentally aware, have medium to high ecological footprints and have lower hunger rates than less developed countries (Table 3.1). For example, Angola and the Congo DR are ranked the lowest of all the countries in the EPI ranking and they have some of the highest hunger rates, but low ecological footprints. These two rankings are understandable, because people in these countries are more worried about surviving than protecting animals targeted for conservation or thinking about the effects their actions have on the environment. Their priority is to get enough food to survive, even if it means eating the mountain gorilla or elephant living in a protected area. Knowing these relationships, however, it is less clear how resource decisions can be altered so that a country can make more sustainable choices without further degrading its environments.

Nine indices were statistically compared to identify which have utility to characterize whether or not a country is making sustainable resource choices. These comparisons reinforce the broad patterns that are apparent from including all the indices in one table and highlighting the outliers. Except for the links found between the human development, environmental/ecological and hunger indices, the remaining indices are not very useful in helping us to characterize the socio-economic and environmental decisions being made by a country (see Table 3.2).

The IFPRI Global Hunger Index ranking of a country is able to explain 88 per cent of the variations in a country's HDI ranking (Table 3.2). This strong correlation would be expected because life expectancy is a factor used to calculate the HDI rank and hunger decreases one's life expectancy. This relationship characterizes what we already know: severe hunger may be found in growing-economy countries and few hunger problems are found in advanced-economy countries throughout the world. The latter countries do not have to make resource decisions that factor-in hunger alleviation. This ranking does not mean that hunger problems do not exist in there, but that a smaller fraction (< 5 per cent) of the population do not have enough food to eat. In contrast, countries ranked lower by HDI (except for Namibia and Nigeria) have a higher Global Hunger Index ranking, with one-fifth to one-half of their population not having food security.

Other than hunger, ecological and environmental indices (e.g. EPI, TEF and EVI) explain about one-half of a country's human development ranking (Table 3.2). However, a closer examination of the fluctuations in a country's HDI and EPI indices suggest that only the countries at the extreme ends of the HDI groupings vary in a similar pattern to one another (Figure 3.1); this results in a clustering of the indices data which may explain the higher correlation coefficient found for this comparison. For example, the higher HDI-ranked countries (except for the UK) are ranked as having a higher environmental performance in

Table 3.2 *Statistical comparisons of nine indices for 34 countries*

Y variable	X variable	R^2
EPI	HDI – Education [POSITIVE]	0.53
	HDI – Poverty [NEGATIVE]	0.48
	Total Biocapacity (global ha/person) [POSITIVE]	0.59
	IFPRI Global Hunger Index [NEGATIVE]	0.36
HDI	Environmental Performance Index [POSITIVE]	0.52
	Total Ecological Footprint (global ha/person) [POSITIVE]	0.56
	IFPRI Global Hunger Index [NEGATIVE]	0.88
TEF	HDI – Education [POSITIVE]	0.42
	HDI – Poverty [NEGATIVE]	0.40
	Water Footprint per capita (m³/cap/yr) [POSITIVE]	0.33
	IFPRI Global Hunger Index [NEGATIVE]	0.58
EVI	Ecological deficit (-), reserve (+) (global ha/person) [POSITIVE - Deficit]	0.28

Note: EPI = Environmental Performance Index; HDI = Human Development Index; TEF = Total Ecological Footprint (global ha/person); EVI = [direction of relationship]; R^2 = Correlation coefficients between all the indices; Relationships where the explanatory power was low are not included here

comparison to the countries grouped in the middle to lower ends of the HDI ranks. This graph also shows that there is no relationship between HDI and EPI rankings for countries grouped in the middle of the HDI scale. Therefore, the environmental performance index is not a sensitive to a country's HDI rank for most of the countries included in our list.

There is a strong correlation between the ability of people to survive in their landscape, as measured by their total ecological footprint and how high they are ranked on the human development side ($R^2 = 0.56$; Table 3.2). The TEF encompasses the bio-resource extractive area available to humans to collect resources (i.e. cropland, grazing land, fishing ground and forest – timber, pulp and paper) and also includes three other footprints more characteristic of human infrastructures (i.e. carbon, nuclear and built-up land). Both the EVI and EPI are highly correlated to some aspect of the ecological footprint; over half ($R^2 = 0.59$) of the variance in the EPI is explained by the Total Biocapacity (global ha/person), while a smaller fraction ($R^2 = 0.28$) of the EVI is explained by the Ecological deficit (−) or reserve (+) (global ha/person) of a country.

The TEF, Total Biocapacity and Ecological Reserve provide insight to whether a country will be able to use its land-base to maintain or develop its human capital (see Table 3.3). For example, several of the high HDI-ranked countries (e.g. Australia, Canada, Sweden and Finland) are outliers because each has a high TEF, but also they have a high Total Biocapacity as well as high Ecological Reserve. This suggests these four countries will have fewer land-base limits to maintaining their human development potential and will be able to grow food and use their forests to satisfy their societal needs. This comparison, based on available land area, does not

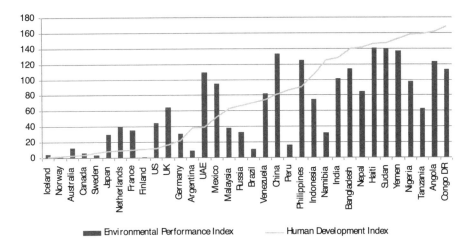

Figure 3.1 *HDI and EPI for 2005; $R^2 = 0.52$*
[HDI & EPI rank of 1 is the highest rank]

however address the quality of the soil or the constraints soils introduce to achieve the land's productive capacity (see Chapter 8).

The US and Norway also have large amounts of land area available per capita for bio-resource production even though the amount available is only half of that found in the outlier countries just mentioned (i.e. Australia, Canada, Sweden and Finland) (Table 3.3). The Total Biocapacity calculated for the US and Norway is still higher than that for the remaining countries included in our assessment, with the exception of Argentina, Russia and Brazil. Unlike Norway, the US has little Ecological Reserve that can be added to produce bio-resources.

It is striking to note that half of the countries ranked in the highest HDI group have ecological deficits; this suggests that they have an insufficient amount of land available to produce additional bio-resources (Table 3.3). These countries are also exceeding their available Total Biocapacity. This index suggests that the UK, for example, cannot maintain its human development ranking and reduce its high ecological footprint from its own lands, because of its low total biocapacity and low ecological reserve. Three other countries (Germany, Japan and the Netherlands) already have smaller TEF compared to the remaining countries in the high HDI group, but all face high ecological deficits. In fact, the medium ecological footprint rank for these three countries may reflect the fact that they have a low biocapacity and a low ecological reserve and, therefore, cannot increase the amount of land they use to produce bio-resources. Despite the results of these comparisons and the dismal results they produce, these countries have successfully managed their agricultural production and soils to maintain the productive capacity of their land (see Chapter 8), something that cannot be detected from a footprint analysis.

In comparison to the highest HDI group of countries, most of the emerging-economy and lower ranked-HDI countries have smaller ecological footprints,

Table 3.3 *Ecological footprint groupings for 34 countries*

TEF group	Total Ecological Footprint (global ha/capita)	Total Biocapacity (global ha/capita)	Ecological Reserve (global ha/capita)
High	Australia, Canada, Finland, France, Norway, Sweden, UAE, UK, US	Australia, Brazil, Canada, Finland, Sweden	Angola, Argentina, Australia, Brazil, Canada, Finland, Namibia, Peru, Russia, Sweden
Medium	Germany, Japan, Netherlands, Russia	Angola, Argentina, France, Malaysia, Namibia, Norway, Peru, Russia, US, Venezuela	Congo DR, Indonesia, Malaysia, Norway, Sudan, Tanzania, Venezuela
Low	Angola, Argentina, Bangladesh, Brazil, China, Congo DR, Haiti, India, Indonesia, Malaysia, Mexico, Namibia, Nepal, Nigeria, Peru, Philippines, Sudan, Tanzania, Venezuela, Yemen	Bangladesh, China, Congo DR, Germany, Haiti, India, Indonesia, Japan, Mexico, Nepal, Netherlands, Nigeria, Philippines, Sudan, Tanzania, UAE, UK, Yemen	Bangladesh, China, France, Germany, Haiti, India, Japan, Mexico, Nepal, Netherlands, Nigeria, Philippines, UAE, UK, US, Yemen

Note: Grouping criteria
Total Ecological Footprint; High = values > 5.6 , Medium = values between 4.4 and 4.5, Low = values < 2.6;
Total Biocapacity; High = values > 9.6, Medium = values between 2.4 and 6.9, Low = values < 1.8;
Ecological reserve; High = values > 2.4, Medium = values between 0 and 1.5, Low = deficits or negative values;
Iceland was not included in the Ecological Footprint and Biocapacity 2006 data;
UAE = United Arab Emirates, UK = United Kingdom, US = United States

compared to the higher ranked HDI group of countries (Table 3.3). In fact, countries ranked in the lowest HDI group have very small TEF. One might conclude from this trend that countries with high ecological footprints should decrease their total footprints and those that are lower in the HDI rankings should be able to increase their ecological footprints. This conclusion would be erroneous. In fact several of the countries with low total ecological footprints do not have the biocapacity for growing their bio-resources and they lack ecological reserves; the countries that fit this scenario are Bangladesh, China, India, Mexico, Nepal, the Philippines and Yemen. Therefore, these countries have a limited capacity to increase the productive capacity of their land. Most of these countries also have climatic events such as droughts and low soil nutrients and/or toxic chemicals that produce unavoidable constraints that will be extremely difficult for them to mitigate (Chapters 7 and 8). For example, Argentina has a high amount of ecological reserve but has been unable to utilize these lands for bio-resource production because of the severe droughts which they experience. According to the TEF, several countries (Argentina, Brazil, China, Malaysia, Namibia, Peru and Venezuela) have the capacity to feed their people without significantly increasing their ecological footprint.

Because a high HDI is linked to a high TEF, one may conclude that as emerging-economy countries transition towards higher levels of human development, economic activities will stimulate an increase in land area used to provide bio-resources. This footprint, however, does not factor-in the fact that many countries are not dependent on bio-resource acquisition solely from their own lands. Most countries have actively traded bio-resources for several thousand years (Chapters 2 and 11). Food has been an especially important trade commodity. Therefore, the imported food footprint, which has been labelled 'virtual', is not included in these calculations. For that reason, a country ecological footprint may not adequately represent the 'real' resource footprint.

Human and resource capital disconnect

A comparison of the various indices reveals that a country's HDI ranking, its environmental or ecological footprints, is not related to its consumption or conservation of its resources or how vulnerable its people are to climate change. Our scientific understanding and documented resource scarcities suggest that stronger connections should have existed among all the variables just mentioned.

For example, the water footprint and/or the fossil fuel sustainability index should have shown stronger connections to the human development potential of a country. Today, providing access to renewable water supplies is one of society's most pressing problems and most growing-economy countries are unable to provide clean water to half of their populations. However, the link between water consumed per capita and a country's HDI rank or its ecological and environmental footprints could not be made for our 34 countries. A weak correlation is found between a country's Water Footprint per capita and its TEF per capita ($R^2 = 0.33$) (Table 3.2); in this relationship the amount of water consumed per capita increases positively as the ecological footprint becomes larger. This is a logical relationship; however, because only 33 per cent of the variance is explained in this comparison, it suggests other factors are more important in explaining the changes in a country's ecological footprint and the amount of water consumed per person.

The fossil fuel index did not help develop an understanding of a country's human development potential. This is partially due to the fact that it appears to be the norm for most countries *not* to have sustainable supplies of fossil energy. A country has either a low or a high fossil fuel sustainability rank and none of the 34 countries is ranked in between these two extremes. As expected, countries with a high fossil fuel sustainability rank are all oil producers (Norway, UAE, Venezuela and Yemen). This inability to separate countries into more distinctive groups of fossil fuel sustainability based on their human development potential means that this index will not provide insights into a country's energy security. Despite knowing that scarcity and competition for fossil fuels are important factors impairing the socioeconomic development of a country, the index is unable to provide a better separation of a country as to its human development potential.

Several of the growing-economy countries were not evaluated when the fossil fuel sustainability rankings were initially developed. These countries (Nigeria, Angola and Congo DR) are major oil producer countries today, but they export most of their production. These are the same countries where the majority of the population burn wood biomass as their primary energy source (see Chapter 8). Therefore, this disconnect between country-level fossil fuel production and the primary energy consumed in a country means that a fossil fuel sustainability index will not be useful to evaluate socioeconomic development potential. In addition, fossil fuel data from these countries cannot be used to assess how a lack of energy security might constrain the development of their human capital potential.

Because of the importance of land degradation in determining the productive capacity of the land and societal vulnerability to climate change, we expected land degradation to explain much of the variation in the environmental and resource consumption recorded in the country-level data. When comparing the eight indices, we see that the environmental sustainability ranking of a country has no relationship to the severity of land degradation found in that country (Table 3.2). This lack of relationship occurs despite the fact that many of the low to middle HDI-ranked countries (including the emerging-economies) are ranked as being unsustainable by the EPI scale; they also have a higher proportion of their lands classified as being severely degraded (see Chapter 8). For example, China, Indonesia, India, Mexico and Nigeria all have low environmental performance as well as medium to high severity of land degradation. This combination of factors should influence whether they are able to make environmentally sustainable decisions even though this information could not be gleaned from the indices.

One could speculate that countries lower in the HDI rankings would have a higher proportion of their lands being severely degraded and that food scarcity would explain their inability to feed their people (Table 3.2). Some countries do follow this pattern (e.g. Nigeria) but others do not (Angola and the Congo DR). These three countries have not been able to develop their human capital and are not ranked as making environmental choices. In contrast to Nigeria, arable land is not degraded in Angola and the Congo DR. The latter two countries, therefore, have the potential to use their lands to increase their food security. In contrast, Nigeria, with highly degraded soils, is unable to produce sufficient food for its people even though a large portion of the land is used for agricultural production. Therefore, land degradation reduces the options available to Nigeria to increase the productive capacity of its land. These countries have also experienced several continuous years of civil conflict that stops food production; the hunger index rankings were mostly obtained during this time. The indices, therefore, are useful as a first filter characterization of a country, for they can give rise to more specific questions and, therefore, to targeting what factors may constrain their human capital while making environmentally based decisions.

It is useful to explore in more detail what insights can be gathered by examining the connections and trends for individual countries separately by their HDI groups.

Indices and Advanced-Economy Countries

Indices suggest that the highest HDI-ranked countries (with the exception of the UK) are making environmentally sustainable decisions, despite experiencing wide extremes of fossil fuel sustainability, land degradation severity and water supply access (Table 3.1). The Scandinavian countries, for example, tend to have low to medium water footprints. In contrast, countries dominated by English-speaking people tend to have high water footprints. The water footprint ranking of each country reflects its water budget and the adaptability of each to its water supplies. As a generality, this group of countries is making the right choices related to food, for hunger is not a priority problem for any of them. These advanced-economy countries have adapted successfully to both low and high resource supplies while maintaining their socioeconomic development status.

These indices also suggest that one of the major hurdles facing most of these advanced-economy countries is their ability to acquire sufficient and secure supplies of fossil fuels to maintain their industrial development (Table 3.1). With the exception of Norway, most of the countries ranked high in the HDI index had low fossil fuel supply capacity and do not have fossil fuel consumption levels that are sustainable. This lack of fossil fuel security has the potential to impact their future economic viability and environmental performance. This helps to explain why these countries are currently focusing on developing energy technologies or acquiring energy supplies that will make their energy supplies secure.

By examining all the indices for one country at a time and ignoring the lack of connections between several of the indices that science hypothesizes should be linked, one can begin to understand the trade-offs that a country needs to make in order to develop its human capital while also being sustainable. For example, even though Canada is ranked highly by HDI and for making environmental decisions, Canada has a very high climate risk that can reduce its economic development potential. Furthermore, Canada has a high water footprint which may be difficult to maintain under a climate-change scenario characterized by more frequent droughts. A drought will increase the difficulty of making trade-offs to obtain secure resource supplies. In addition to its climate risk, Canada, in the calculated ranking, has low fossil fuel sustainability that will also impact its human development potential. It should be noted that the data used in the ranking do not consider the massive resources of Alberta tar sands as a viable fossil fuel resource. Overall, on the surface, Canada appears to be sustainable, but it faces several challenges in maintaining its position in this group.

Similarly, a comparison of indices rankings for Sweden is revealing. Sweden is ranked as being environmentally vulnerable even though it has a high EPI rank (Table 3.1). Sweden also has a high proportion of its land ranked as being severely degraded. This means that Sweden will be less able to use its land to increase its own bio-resource productive capacity. If they can continue to import bio-resources, Sweden will have less difficulty in making sustainable choices. In summary, even though Sweden appears to rank well in most of the indices, it is vulnerable to losing its high HDI or EPI rankings because its lands are severely degraded and it is ranked as being environmentally vulnerable.

At first glance, it appears that Norway is one of the few countries that will have little difficulty in continuing to consume resources and being sustainable. It is ranked high by HDI and is one of the few countries with secure supplies of fossil energy because of its existing oil and gas reserves. Furthermore, Norway has not degraded its lands nor does it consume a high amount of water per capita while developing its human capital. Norway also has a low hunger risk. Despite appearing to be making all the right choices in its resource uses, Norway does face a high climate risk that can hinder its ability to pursue sustainable solutions. All the Scandinavian countries included in our study have high climate-risk rankings so that they have to consider climate change when deciding what and how much resources to consume.

Germany, Japan, the Netherlands and the UK have all been able to develop their human capital despite being ranked as extremely vulnerable environmentally. Finland, Iceland and Norway also had high climate risks during the decade 1997–2006, but have consistently maintained their high positions in the HDI rankings. Even with the risks and vulnerabilities of these countries, they have managed to make choices that minimize the impacts of their resource consumption on their HDI and EPI rankings.

Japan is another country that has developed its human capital while making sustainable decisions. The Japanese have developed their human capital without giving up their high environmental values. They have a well-earned reputation as a country that recycles at a higher rate than any other country in the world. Therefore, it seems that Japan should not have any problem making sustainable choices. However, if one examines the four essential human needs and the choices that Japan has made to satisfy them, a very different story arises. When it comes to the sustainability of water use, Japan has a high water footprint. Nor does it not have sustainable energy production: fossil energy supplies have to be imported (100 per cent of its crude oil, 100 per cent of its coal and 96 per cent of its natural gas) to maintain its industrial activities. Despite the fact that Japan has over 60 per cent of its lands under forest cover, forests are not being used to provide energy as Japan has conserved a significant portion of its forested lands. Even though the choices made by Japan have kept it highly ranked in the human development index, two out of their four essential human needs are not sustainable.

Although the advanced-economy countries have all been successful in developing their human capital, each has made very different choices to reach these ranks. Characteristics of the highest HDI-ranked countries (Australia, Canada, Finland, France, Germany, Iceland, Japan, the Netherlands, Norway, Sweden, the UK and the US) can be summarized as:

- Characteristics of the Advanced-Economy Countries
  - *High* environment performance;
  - *Low* hunger index;
  - *Low* fossil fuel sustainability.
- Causes problem

    – Low supplies and competition for fossil fuels.
- Creates opportunities
    – Have been making environmentally sustainable decisions;
    – Few hungry people.

Indices and Emerging-Economy Countries

Countries ranked in the middle of the human development index are especially interesting to examine, for these are the 'emerging economies' and are very rapidly moving up in the human development ranking scale (Table 3.1). Eleven out of the 34 countries included in our database can be classified as emerging-economy countries, with HDI rankings between 0.7–0.9.

Most of these emerging-economy countries face shortages of fossil fuels, which historically have powered the development of today's industrialized countries. Only two are oil-producing (Venezuela and the UAE) and the remainder have low fossil fuel supplies. This would suggest that these countries need to pursue multiple options when developing their energy choices, in order to make them more secure.

We will examine four of these countries in more detail: Brazil, China, Peru and Venezuela. There is no consistent pattern to the ranking of these four emerging-economy countries by EPI. For example, China has the lowest EPI rank and is closely followed by Venezuela, which is ranked in the middle of the 145 countries compared by this index. Both Brazil and Peru have very high EPI rankings, similar to that of the high HDI-ranked countries. Nevertheless, these four emerging-economy countries share one characteristic – a consistently high amount of land ranked as being medium-to-highly degraded. For example, Peru had the highest level of soil degradation possible, while the other three are ranked in the middle of this index. All four countries, therefore, will have to consider mitigation or restoration of their lands in order to increase its productive capacity.

These four emerging-economy countries also had very different environmental vulnerabilities. China was ranked as being extremely vulnerable, whereas the other three have rankings that are similar to the advanced-economy countries. Based on these indices, both Peru and Venezuela have less need to factor in climatic events when making policy decisions related to resource consumption. These two countries are in sharp contrast to China (highest risk) and Brazil (medium risk), where climatic events need to be included when making resource decisions.

Each of these countries has a different factor that could limit its socio-economic development potential. Even though Peru has the lowest risk from climatic events, it has the most severely degraded land, compared to the other three countries. This suggests that Peru will have difficulty in using its natural-resource landscape to improve its environmental performance ranking. Similarly, China has a reduced capacity to use its land and to increase its productive capacity to collect a larger amount of bio-resource, as a significant area of that land is degraded. However, unlike Peru, China also faces a high possibility that climatic events will disrupt its economic development and has other challenges that are less relevant for Peru, such as low supplies of fossil fuels to power its economic development, in addition to being extremely vulnerable environmentally.

Of these four countries, Venezuela is fortunate to have sustainable fossil fuel supplies and a low frequency of climatic events that could disrupt its economic development activities. However, a significant proportion of its land area is severely degraded so that it will be challenging for it to improve its environmental performance while pursuing activities that require the use of its landbase. Brazil faces similar land-degradation issues but it now has sustainable supplies of fossil fuels. In contrast to Venezuela, Brazil is impacted by climatic events that can reduce its economic development potential.

Similar to the advanced-economy countries, each of these emerging-economy countries has very different constraints that will impact the choices each makes to consume resources. Summary information is provided below for Argentina, Brazil, Malaysia, Mexico, Russia and the UAE:

- Characteristics of Emerging-Economy Countries Ranked Higher in this Group
  - *Medium* environmental vulnerability;
  - *High* water footprint per capita;
  - *Low* hunger index.
- Causes problem
  - High water consumptive demand.
- Creates opportunities
  - Lack of high environmental vulnerability;
  - Few hungry people.

Summary information for China, Indonesia, Peru, the Philippines and Venezuela:

- Characteristics of Emerging-Economy Countries in the Middle of this Group
  - *Low* climate risk index for 1997–2006 weather-related events;
  - *Medium* hunger index.
- Causes Problem
  - No critical problem identified.
- Creates Opportunities
  - Low risk of weather-related events affecting society.

Indices and Growing-Economy Countries

A common characteristic of the growing-economy countries is the high number of hungry people who live there. The Global Hunger Index summarizes these countries as having either alarming or extremely alarming hunger problems (Table 3.4).

Table 3.4 *Global Hunger Index rankings for emerging- and growing-economy countries (%)*

GHI < 10: hunger less of a problem	Argentina [2.0], Russian Federation [4.0], Mexico [5.0], Brazil [9.0], Malaysia [2.0], Venezuela [17.0], Peru [13.0], China [11.0]
GHI > 10–20: a serious hunger problem	Indonesia [6.0], Namibia [22.0], Nigeria [9.0], Philippines [22.0]
GHI > 20–30: alarming hunger scores	Bangladesh [30.0], Haiti [47.0], India [21.0], Nepal [17.0], Sudan [27.0], Tanzania [44.0], Yemen [36.0]
GHI > 30: scores extremely alarming	Angola [40.0], Congo DR [71.0]

Note: Proportion of undernourished in total population averaged between 2000 and 2003. Excludes advanced-economy countries
Source: Wiesmann, 2006

According to the indices, the growing-economy countries ranked in the middle of this group need to grow food crops on lands that are already severely degraded. This situation means that it will be more difficult for them to provide secure food supplies from their lands or to use their land-base to develop their human capital. These countries contrast with the growing-economy countries at the lower end of this HDI group, where severe land degradation is less of a problem hindering the development of their human capital. However, these countries are at risk from climate events and they already have high water consumptive demand per capita.

On the positive side, the indices suggest that these growing-economy countries have been making decisions that are characterized as being environmentally sustainable. They are also ranked as having a lower environmental-vulnerability risk. This suggests that, despite having to deal with major hunger problems, these countries have fewer worries about increasing their environmental vulnerability risk while dealing with their food shortages. This assessment suggests that these countries have the resource supplies and a lower vulnerability to climatic events so that they should be able to make decisions that would increase their socioeconomic development from their own resources.

Summary information for Bangladesh, Haiti, Nepal, Sudan and Yemen:

- Characteristics of Growing-Economy Countries Ranked Higher by HDI
  - *Low* to *medium* environmental sustainability performance;
  - *Medium* to *high* severity of land degradation;
  - *High* hunger index.
- Causes problems
  - Lands are severely degraded;
  - Many hungry people.
- Creates opportunities
  - Have been mostly making decisions that are environmentally sustainable.

Summary information for Angola, Congo DR, Nigeria and Tanzania:

- Characteristics of Growing-Economy Countries Ranked Lower by HDI
    - *Low* to *medium* environmental sustainability performance;
    - *At Risk* but *lower* environmental vulnerability;
    - *Medium* to *high* climate risk index for 1997–2006 weather-related events;
    - *Medium* to *high* water footprint per capita;
    - *Medium* to *high* hunger index.
- Causes problems
    - At a high risk of death and loss of GDP from weather-related events;
    - High water consumptive demand needs to be maintained;
    - Many hungry people.
- Creates opportunities
    - Have been mostly making decisions that are environmentally sustainable;
    - Environmental vulnerability risk is lower.

Lessons Learnt From Indices

What we have learnt from indices includes:

- the values of indices are calculated from incomplete data;
- our biases are embedded in each index;
- a few parameters, rather than the entire array, may yield a reasonable partial solution;
- education and hunger are key issues in sustainability;
- conclusions from one index may be inconsistent with those of another index;
- interconnection among indices may be tenuous, but individual indices may present partial assessments;
- universal application of choices showing sustainability in one country may be unwise;
- each index is a reflection/assessment of past decisions;
- indices may act as a coarse screen for trade-offs;
- inherent limitations of any land and unavoidable constraints (soil and climate) must be recognized.

The first lesson the indices teach us is that the information integrated into them is incomplete, providing us only a 'tunnel vision' impression of the sustainability challenges that each country faces. Because the data by necessity had to be selected from a larger body of science, our values begin to influence what indicators are included in our assessments. For example, the EPI is composed of 21 elements, but it appears to be particularly sensitive to some indicators, such as land conversion. We, as a society, have decided that land conversion is not environmentally accept-able because it triggers habitat loss and has climate impacts. Those countries experiencing more land conversion (e.g. emerging- and growing-economy countries) will not be ranked as high as those countries (e.g. advanced-economy countries) where land conversion is a less frequent occurrence.

It is important that a decision maker recognizes the biases embedded in each index. Saisana and Saltelli (2008) mentioned that scientists and policymakers will not be able to verify the EPI against the true conditions that exist in a country, but they felt it should still be useful as a policymaking exercise. Their analysis of the Environmental Sustainability Index (a later version of the EPI used here) identified several biases, with two of the six categories being 'random and non-significant at the 95 per cent level,' while Environmental Health and Water, as well as Productive Natural Resources, are highly correlated to EPI. The most important point of their assessment is that a few of the 25 indicators dominate in defining the ESI score. Therefore, this index should not be used by country policymakers to decide what choices to make to become more environmental.

It may be equally important to recognize that a few parameters may provide a worthy partial solution. For example, even though the HDI and the EPI are highly correlated to one another ($R^2 = 0.52$), it appeared that much of the variance in these relationships reflected the educational status of a country (Table 3.2). The HDI Education Index, a subcategory of HDI, alone explains 53 per cent of the variance in the EPI ranking. In other words, the higher a country's education level, the higher its environmental performance. Therefore, education should become the priority if a country wants to increase its ranking by EPI. The EPI–HDI–Poverty index correlation suggests poor people are unable to make environmentally sustainable choices.

The indices support the view that the pathway for making sustainable choices is by resolving a country's environmental/ecological and/or hunger problems. Yet, focusing on these problems in isolation does not allow an understanding of their context and that to achieve solutions requires a country to make difficult choices. Indices do not recognize the unavoidable constraints that hinder resolving social problems.

Another feature of the indices is that conclusions drawn from one index may not always be scientifically consistent with another. As an example, none of the countries ranked high by HDI is rated as environmentally resilient, even though they are all ranked high by EPI (Table 3.1). In this group, Japan, the Netherlands and the UK are considered as extremely vulnerable environmentally, but they are making some of the 'right' sustainability choices that create a balance between high environmental performance and low environmental resiliency. The absence of consistent patterns among the indices is also shown by Namibia. It is ranked in the middle of the HDI scale, has a high EPI rank and is the only country in our assessment ranked as being 'environmentally resilient'. This suggests that Namibia is not reducing its environmental resiliency while consuming resources, but has not developed its human capital to levels found in more industrialized societies. For example, Namibia needs to learn how to secure their energy supplies or it will be difficult for the country to consume resources sustainably and to maintain its high environmental resiliency. These apparent discrepancies highlight how countries have been adapting and mitigating their resource consumption to fit the environmental and social constraints they face. The discrepancies can also be useful for countries to identify the trade-offs they need to make, especially in the long-term as opposed to a solution to an immediate problem (e.g. fire risk in a forest, insufficient electricity supplies or farm area to irrigate during a drought).

Each sustainability index is able to rank accurately the one parameter it was designed to measure. However, each index is less effective in showing the interconnections to the other indices. This lack of connection also suggests that each index provides a partial assessment of whether a country is making the best choices for itself. No country selected for this study is able to make sustainable choices for energy, food, forests and water at the same time.

Another reason for using the indices with care is that, if they are applied equally in some countries, the results may be misleading. For example, EPI is not sensitive to predicting the human development potential for the emerging-economy countries; consequently, that index should not be used in ranking those countries. Even if it is not used to rank countries, an index still may have utility for a country by illustrating past choices. Each index is a retrospective analysis of the results of past decisions. This information can be used to discover whether common choices were being made by countries of a particular HDI group and to reveal a meaningful story about the choices already made. Therefore, these indices should help us to identify the choices that emerging- and growing-economy countries will have to make if they want to increase their human development without having a detrimental effect on their environment.

References

Chapagain, A. K. and Hoekstra, A. Y. (2004) 'Water footprints of nations. Value of Water Research Report Series no 16', *UNESCO-IHE*, Delft, The Netherlands, www.waterfootprint.org/Reports/Report16.pdf, accessed 14 May 2009

Ecological Footprint and Biocapacity (2006) 'Edition', *Global Footprint Network 2006*, www.footprintnetwork.org/gfn_sub.php?content=national_footprints, accessed 20 February 2008

Ediger V. fi., HoflgŒr, E., Sırmeli, A. N. and Tathdil, H. (2007) 'Fossil fuel sustainability index: an application of resource management', *Energy Policy*, vol 35, pp2969–2977

EPI (2008) 'Environmental Performance Index', Yale Center for Environmental Law & Policy, New Haven, CT, http://epi.yale.edu, accessed 10 March 2008

EVI (2004) '2004 Country Score Environmental Vulnerability Index (EVI)', www.vulnerabilityindex.net/EVI_2004.htm, accessed 30 June 2008

FAO (2000) 'World Soil Resources Report 90. Land Resource Potential and Constraints at Regional and Country Levels', Land and Water Resource Division, UN FAO, Rome, Italy

Germanwatch Global Climate Risk (2008) 'Global Climate Risk Index 2008. Weather-related loss events and their impacts on countries in 2006 and in a long-term comparison', www.germanwatch.org/ccpi.htm, accessed 18 March 2008

HDI (2007/2008) 'Human Development Index', http: //hdr.Drundp.org/en/statistics/, accessed 1 October 2008

Photius (2008) 'Water footprints of nations 2004: country rankings', www.photius.com/rankings/water_footprints_country_ranks_2004.html, accessed 29 December 2008

Saisana, M. and Saltelli, A. (2008) 'Appendix F: Uncertainty and sensitivity analysis of the 2008 EPI', *2008 Environmental Performance Index*, Yale Center for Environmental Law & Policy and Center for International Earth Science Information Network (CIESIN), www.yale.edu/esi, accessed 28 January 2008

Wiesmann, D. (2006) 'A global hunger index: measurement concept, ranking of countries and trends', *FCND Discussion Paper 212*, International Food Policy Research Institute, Sustainable Solutions for Ending Hunger and Poverty, December 2006, www.ifpri.org/divs/fcnd/dp/papers/fcndp212.pdf, accessed 9 January 2009

Part 3

THE REAL COUNTRY STORIES

Global data collected by credible international organizations have produced information on every facet of a society's resource consumption and production behaviour (e.g. British Petroleum, 2007b; FAO, 2000, FAO, 2008; MEA, 2005; WRI, 2009). This data availability is wonderful, but at the same time it is a daunting task to summarize it and to use it to make sustainable decisions. It is a valuable compilation of resource production and consumption data from around the world, despite the fact that it is fragmentary and focuses on summarizing some aspects of resource consumption, but not others. Some regions of the world (e.g. the tropics) are also more poorly represented by the data because well-documented inventories do not always exist to support the published summary data (WRI, 2009). Despite these data limitations, these global datasets are important because they provide a baseline of information that can be used to understand the resource and human capital stories at the country level. This allows a country to compare itself to another when it needs to make similar choices. Sustainable decisions are more likely to be made if one can benchmark each countries available supply capacity for each resource (low, medium or high) and what are their available choices. These data contextualize the choices that countries have already made while developing their economies and while facing similar climatic and/or soil constraints. When the unavoidable constraints are included in an assessment (Chapters 7–9), it will be easier to examine whether or not societal decisions will make countries more vulnerable to their changing environments.

Volumes of data have been produced during the past 50 years. Unfortunately, there is considerable variability in the accuracy of these data and most are 'snapshots' that do not address the need for multiple models of sustainability geared to each country's mix of constraints and opportunities. Most of the country data have been collected for only one portion of human survival needs: food, water, forests or energy. Again, this approach, which resolves only a single problem, ignores the fact that solutions in one area can create problems in another. The existence of volumes of data also makes it difficult for a country to develop a portfolio of options because of the data overload. One becomes a number manager, lost in the quagmire of data that usually hampers decision making. This became very apparent when compiling the data used for this book.

As we have mentioned previously, there are four basic items required for human survival: energy, food, forest materials and water. Obtaining all four of the items that humans need to survive from a single piece of land has probably never been and probably never will be, sustainable. Every piece of land has some constraints that limit its capacity to supply these human needs. No country can barricade their borders to eliminate the rest of the world and continue to survive. Each country requires a resource of one type or another from somewhere outside their borders. However, society has been effective in managing these local constraints by either ameliorating the soil to increase food production or by importing what they needed. Today, global markets can provide the forest materials, energy or food required by any country. To one degree or another, every country is both a producer and consumer of global goods. This ability to easily replenish or substitute diminishing local supplies with resources from elsewhere make it appear that most problems a country experiences can be resolved by pursuing solutions for more narrowly defined problems; hunger, lack of jobs, economic development, conservation or drilling for oil or natural gas in a new location.

Recently the focus on mitigating and reducing societal vulnerability to global climate change is bringing many of these narrowly defined problems under the same umbrella (MEA, 2005; IPCC, 2007). This 'umbrella' approach has emphasized the fact that all these problems, which had previously been handled as separate issues, are in fact interconnected. To improve one area, they must all be addressed and resolved. Every problem will be slightly different for each location and the solution will need to be addressed at the local level, but the adverse effects of some decisions will be felt globally. Some of these global effects are the clear-cutting of forests throughout the world to grow food crops, the pollution of the world's oceans with wastes created from our daily living and the pollution of our air by industries around the world.

We will examine the considerable database that can help us to understand the choices that each country has made. This will help us to identify the factors influencing resource decisions and the resulting environmental and social externalities, in a country context.

4

Fossil Energy Endowments and Externalities

Today, the fuel supplies used to produce energy face increasing scrutiny by society and have been inextricably linked to their environmental externalities, climate change and greenhouse gas (GHG) emissions. By linking energy consumption to environmental externalities, societies have explicitly linked energy supplies to food, forest material and water securities. When energy supplies become insecure, the impact ricochets through every aspect of human society. Similarly, insecure supplies of water, forest materials and food will also reverberate in the energy sector. Today, energy choices have to pass the litmus test of not altering climates; that is, not increasing GHG and specifically CO_2 emissions and not increasing the vulnerability of people by reducing their suplies of resources.

Next, we shall examine the links between CO_2 emissions, fossil fuel combustion and forest use for energy production to demonstrate how countries make choices to maintain their carbon economies. This will end with an examination of the dual roles of forests in mitigating CO_2 emissions, for example by sequestering carbon as a living forest and producing biofuels.

CO_2 Emissions Link to Energy

CO_2 emissions and total fossil fuel consumption

The search for secure supplies of energy, food, the collection of forest materials and water has repercussions on the amount of CO_2 emitted by a country. Of the four human needs introduced at the beginning of this book, energy production from fossil-based materials is most strongly linked to impacting climates, because GHG is emitted during its combustion. Carbon dioxide is an important greenhouse gas linked to global warming. Fossil fuel combustion accounts for about 70 per cent of the annual emissions of global CO_2 while land-use changes account for the remaining 30 per cent. The primary land-use activity implicated in CO_2

Table 4.1 *Correlations between* CO_2 *emissions/capita and several country characteristics*

Y variable	X variable	R^2
CO_2 emission/ capita	Gross National Income	0.18
	HDI value	0.44
	Electricity consumption/capita	0.42
	Energy use (kg of oil equivalent per capita)	0.70
	Biomass & wastes, percentage of total primary energy consumed	0.32

emissions is deforestation due to agriculture. Therefore, CO_2 emissions are linked to energy production and land-use changes associated with forests.

Strong correlations between CO_2 emissions and fossil fuels have been well documented. Our data show the same relationships (Table 4.1). Energy consumption from fossil fuels (including cement production) explain more of the variation in CO_2 emissions per capita than any of the other indicators included in our database; 70 per cent of the variance in CO_2 emissions is explained by oil consumption per capita (kilogram of oil equivalent per capita).

What is also apparent for these analyses is that the Gross National Income (GNI) is poorly linked to the amount of CO_2 emitted per capita (Figure 4.1); 38 per cent of the variation in GNI was explained by the amount of CO_2 emissions per capita. This begins to highlight that it is not a simple connection between economic development and the amount of CO_2 emitted by a country. The reasons for this lack of correlation will be discussed later.

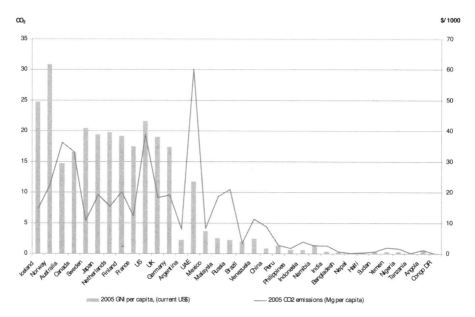

Figure 4.1 *Gross National Income and* CO_2 *emissions per capita*

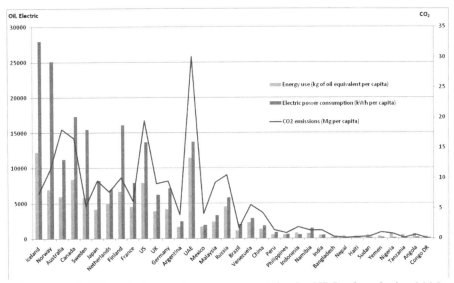

Figure 4.2 *CO_2 emissions and energy consumption by HDI values during 2005*

Note: Highest HDI rank on left and lowest on right

Of the 34 countries studied, four countries (Australia, Canada, US and the UAE) have distinctly higher CO_2 emissions per capita from fossil fuel combustion (Figure 4.2). With a lower population density, total CO_2 emissions in the UAE are lower compared to most other countries; however, when converted to a per capita basis, the UAE appears to emit higher amounts of CO_2. All four countries derive about a third of their primary energy from oil and 40–82 per cent of their remaining energy from coal or natural gas. Therefore, these four countries mainly consume fossil-based energies for their industrial development. If they continue to combust fossil fuel supplies using past technologies, they will continue to emit high levels of CO_2.

Other than Canada and the UAE, the four Scandinavian countries consume much higher amounts of electricity; Iceland had the highest electric consumption per capita compared to the other 34 countries. This is due to the Icelandic government promoting the delivery of inexpensive energy infrastructures (i.e. hydroelectric dams and geothermal sources) to attract foreign companies to establish their businesses in Iceland, as such companies need high amounts of inexpensive electricity. The hydroelectric dams (despite emitting low amounts of CO_2 once constructed), along with the harnessing of geothermal energy, and its fishing vessels (i.e. fossil fuels used in navigation) account for most of Iceland's high CO_2 emissions. Therefore, the high energy consumption and the high CO_2 emissions in Iceland are not occurring because of domestic consumption patterns. Iceland has selected to increase its employment opportunities by using its ability to produce inexpensive energy (see Box 1.2 and Chapter 10).

The higher energy use in the UAE, characterized by a low population density (39 people/km²), also suggests that this high energy consumption is significantly higher than what would be expected of a country located in this climatic zone (see Chapter 10). However, the UAE has pursued a policy of developing its human infrastructure to build an economy that draws on significant water (requiring desalination) and energy resources. This infrastructure maintains economic development at the global scale (for example, banking). Much energy is spent worldwide on heating; this is not relevant for the UAE, where the minimum temperature is above 20°C. The UAE needs to cool its built environment, however, which requires considerable more energy than if they had to heat the buildings (to lower a room temperature by 1°C by air conditioning requires more energy than to raise the temperature 1°C by heating). The UAE already had air-conditioned, refrigerated swimming pools in the 1980s.

Electricity consumption is also strongly correlated to CO_2 emissions, but it explains the lower percentage (42 per cent) of the variance in CO_2 emissions compared to oil consumption (Figure 4.2). Forest biomass and wastes used to produce energy explains an even lower percentage of the CO_2 emitted by a country; 32 per cent of the variance in CO_2 levels is explained by the amount of forest biomass and wastes consumed as a percentage of the total primary energy. This latter fact is interesting because 30 per cent is the number typically mentioned as the proportion of total CO_2 emissions due to deforestation. Therefore, if a society wants to alter its CO_2 emissions, it needs to make decisions that reduce its fossil fuel consumption and not forest-material use in producing energy.

CO_2 emissions and gasoline consumption

The production and consumption of energy and the concomitant emissions of CO_2 from consuming this energy consistently explain about 40 per cent of the variance in the human development potential for the 34 countries. A similar level of predictive power is produced whether the HDI value is compared to patterns of oil consumption, electricity production or the consumption of transportation fuels. Therefore, this suggests that the human development potential is correlated to energy consumption itself and not to types of materials used to produce the energy. For example, the consumption of motor gasoline per capita explains 40 per cent of the variance in the HDI value of a country, and the total CO_2 emissions per capita explains a similar percentage of a country's HDI value (R^2 = 0.44).

Land-use change and CO_2 emissions from land-use activities are not related to any of the human development indicators collected for the 34 countries. This inability to detect changes in the other indicators in relationship to land-use changes contrasts with the several trends found for energy consumption or CO_2 emissions from energy consumption and HDI indicators. For example, CO_2 emissions per capita due to gasoline consumption explain at least 40 per cent of the amount of CO_2 emitted at a country level (R^2 = 0.40) (Figure 4.3); motor gasoline data were converted to kg of carbon (C) emitted using the conversion factor of 1l of gasoline having 0.73 kg C (ORNL, 2009).

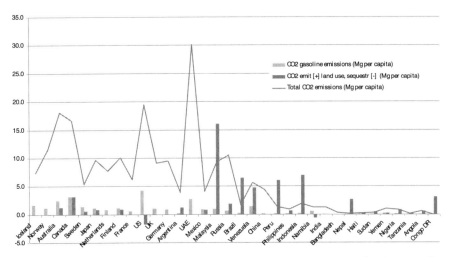

Figure 4.3 *Total CO_2 emissions from fossil fuels and cement production, gasoline consumption and from land-use for 2005*

Source: World Bank, 2007; IEA, 2009; WRI, 2009

In the highest HDI-ranked countries, the emissions of CO_2 from using gasoline to power automobiles contributed from 10 to 27 per cent of the total CO_2 emissions recorded (Table 4.2). Surprisingly, the HDI ranking of a country is not sensitive to the total CO_2 emissions during gasoline consumption; in most societies, transportation appears to be responsible for a similar percentage of the total CO_2 emissions irrespective of a society's human development potential. On average 15 per cent of the total CO_2 emissions is due to gasoline consumption for all the countries included here. Nine countries have gasoline consumption contributing over 20 per cent of the total CO_2 emitted during a year (Haiti,

Table 4.2 *Total CO_2 emissions from fossil fuel and gasoline consumption by HDI groups*

HDI ranking groups	Total CO_2 emissions from fossil fuel consumption (Mg/capita)	CO_2 emissions per capita from gasoline (Mg/capita)	CO_2 emissions from gasoline (% of total)
1	5.4–19.5	0.60–4.34	10–27
2	1.7–30.1	0.24–2.73	6–23
3	0.9–5.6	0.10–1.45	3–26
4	1.3	0.03–0.59	2–45
5	0.1–1.0	0.01–0.22	8–22
6	0.1–0.8	0.01–0.18	13–22

Note: HDI = Human Development Index [Group 1 = HDI > 0.9; Group 2 = 0.8–0.9; Group 3 = 0.7–0.8; Group 4 = 0.6–0.7; Group 5 = 0.5–0.6; Group 6 = 0.4–0.5]; total fossil fuel consumption includes cement production; data for 2005
Source: World Bank, 2007; WRI, 2009

Iceland, Mexico, Namibia, Nigeria, Sweden, US, Venezuela and Yemen). It is notable that these countries were not confined to the higher HDI-ranked group.

A few of the emerging-economy countries in our list of 34 have little of their total CO_2 being emitted during the consumption of gasoline. Argentina and Russia have six per cent of their CO_2 emissions resulting from transportation while China has only 3 per cent and India 2 per cent. The latter two have lower CO_2 emissions from the transportation sector because automobile ownership is lower compared to other countries included in our list. This trend is rapidly changing today, however, with both countries developing their own car manufacturing facilities and buying international automobile manufacturing facilities.

Societies and Fossil Energy Options

The pursuit and delivery of energy today has to satisfy many more environmental and social goals. For example, society expects that energy should be linked to providing economic solutions for rural communities, should have few environmental externalities and should not impact forests, food production or our water supplies. In most countries, energy is uniquely positioned to reach several of these goals because a diversity of energy options can be selected. If diversifying one's energy portfolio to include environmental production of energy produces these benefits, why have our energy resource options not changed dramatically during recent decades? Why are these 'green' energy technologies not being developed at a more rapid rate? This will be discussed later.

Most societies have diverse fossil fuel energy portfolios that include locally available supplies balanced by the imports they need. Although oil is only part of the mix in some countries, globally it is currently the most important fossil fuel because it is easily used for transportation and is a viable source for all other energy products and services. However, it has been a major cause of political tensions, rising to conflicts; large-scale political graft; and, supplementing coal, major environmental problems.

Diverse fossil energy portfolios the norm

The fossil fuels countries consume include all the available forms of fossil energy (i.e. oil, coal and natural gas). What is noticeable in Figure 4.4 is the diversity of energy fuels that countries consume and their lack of dependence on one primary energy supply. Most of the countries included in our assessment, based on 2005 data, derive 20–60 per cent of their total energy from oil. Natural gas is the next most important fossil-based energy consumed by these countries; however, most countries obtain less than 20 per cent of their primary energy from natural gas. All those on our list consume some oil or coal, but eight countries did not use natural gas to produce energy. The take-home message from this data analysis is that most countries, even with some diversity in their energy portfolio, are currently largely dependent upon oil. The scene is changing, but even by 2030, oil is projected to be the primary energy fuel.

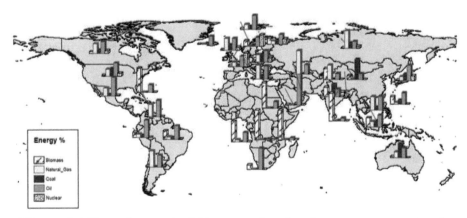

Figure 4.4 *Natural gas, coal, oil, biomass and nuclear (in percentage ranges) as the primary energy supply in 2005*

Source: IEA, 2009

Only four of the 34 countries have primary energy supplies in one fossil fuel type. As of 2005, Yemen was almost 100 per cent dependent on oil to satisfy its energy demand; in Namibia, 67 per cent is derived from oil; the UAE, surprisingly, is very dependent on natural gas (72 per cent) rather than oil as its primary energy source; and China depends on coal for 63 per cent of its primary energy.

Most countries do not have secure supplies of fossil fuels. Based on the calculations made by Ediger et al (2007), only Norway and Venezuela were ranked as having a high sustainability for continued consumption of fossil fuels (mainly oil). Both countries did not need to import oil; in fact they are large exporters. The calculations made by Ediger et al (2007) suggest that all the remaining countries on our list are ranked low in sustainable fossil fuel consumption and need to import fossil fuels. In a broad view, dependence on imports reflects (1) the irregular global distribution of the three fossil fuels; (2) the much broader utility of oil and the preference for its use over coal; and (3) governmental regulations.

Some countries (e.g. Finland and Sweden) have never had secure fossil fuel supplies because they lack large fossil fuel reserves. These countries have diversified their energy portfolios to include a significant amount of renewable energy sources to compensate for their lack of in-country fossil reserves.

A few of these countries have not needed to import oil because of their own supplies (e.g. Argentina, Mexico and Nigeria). These countries have diversified their energy portfolios less actively because of their existing oil reserves. Even they, however, do not have secure supplies of fossil fuels to produce their energy.

Three African countries in our list (Angola, Congo DR and Nigeria) export almost all of the oil that they produce. However, they are not making choices related to energy that will increase the development of their countries human capital. Most of the people living in these countries have limited energy choices and are dependent upon their forests for woodfuel (Figure 4.5).

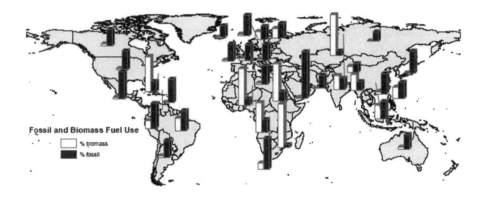

Figure 4.5 *Wood biomass/wastes and fossil fuels as energy in 2005*

Note: HDI ranking of a country and the amount of wood biomass and wastes consumed as the primary energy supply – $R^2 = 0.61$; Comparison of the amount of wood biomass and wastes used as the primary energy supply to the total amount of fossil fuels consumed as the primary energy supply – $R^2 = 0.74$. Source: IEA, 2009

Energy security after becoming a net importer of oil

The energy choices countries have made after their oil supplies have become less secure, that is, to import oil to meet their energy demands, are revealing. Many have pursued strategies to increase their energy security after they were unable to produce enough oil to satisfy the in-country demand. The US faced the need to import significant amounts of oil in the 1960s, China in 1993 and Indonesia in 2004. Each country has taken a different pathway towards energy security that was partially driven by the amount of forest area existing in-country and how much CO_2 they were emitting during their combustion of fossil fuels.

The US began to import significant amounts (and percentages) of oil in the late 1960s and has continued its reliance on fossil energy production. US-based companies have continued to invest in exploration for oil reserves globally, even with the threat of nationalization and their reduced net interests in companies controlling global reserves. The US has been in the fortunate situation that it has not dramatically increased its CO_2 emissions during the last decade, mainly because of its forests. About a third of US land is in forests that are now expanding, after agricultural abandonment. This, along with the relatively low price of oil, has resulted in less urgency for the implementation of policies to mitigate CO_2 emissions during energy combustion and it has been difficult to increase the amount of renewable energies included in the country's energy portfolio. The continued focus on consuming fossil fuels means that the US has been less effective at mitigating CO_2 emissions from its combustion of energy.

In May 2008, the National Geographic Society released a ranking of how green consumers were in 14 countries and this ranked the US low in making green choices (National Geographic, 2008). Based on this ranking, Brazil, along with India, ranked first with 60.0 points followed by China (56.1 points), Mexico

(54.3), Russia (52.4), Germany (50.2), Japan (49.1), France (48.7), Canada (48.5) and the US being the least sustainable with 44.9 points. This survey suggests that people in the US were the least likely to choose a green option when making choices in housing, transportation, food and consumer goods. Brazil ranked so well in this survey because each household building is small; few homes are heated or cooled; and on-demand water heaters are installed in many homes (Wong, 2008). It will be interesting to observe if Brazil will continue to maintain its ranking with its recent offshore discovery of super-giant oilfields.

Because consumers in the US have low energy costs, the public has had less incentive to change its energy choices. Prices paid by end-users in different countries for a litre of gasoline range widely. In 2008, OECD/IEA published the average end-use prices to selective industrialized countries for gasoline (OECD/IEA, 2008). In January of that year, the US consumers paid US$0.81/litre for gasoline and because of subsidies were not buying motor vehicle fuels based on its real costs; this is quite apparent when comparing US consumer costs for a litre of gasoline to what the French (US$2.00), Germans (US$2.07) and Spanish (US$1.58) pay. Therefore, providing estimates of how much gasoline is consumed and how much a country is capable of producing itself does not reflect the costs in that country to buy that product. All the countries noted above must import crude oil but the final price paid by the customer in the US is only half of what is being paid in the European countries (British Petroleum, 2007).

In common with the US, Indonesia has a considerable amount of land in forests, but unlike the US, is losing forests at a rapid rate. It has been more difficult for Indonesia to mitigate its CO_2 emissions using its forests because the high defor-estation rates have increased its emissions significantly during the past few years. Indonesia became an oil importing country in 2004; it experienced a 48 per cent increase in CO_2 emissions between 1994 and 2004 (EIA, 2007b). Indonesia also has one of the highest rates of illegal logging, which is being driven by the demand for its products by emerging- and advanced-economy countries. It also has the delicate task of mitigating CO_2 emissions while managing to reduce its forest conversion into palm oil plantations. Indonesia is exploring the adoption of technologies that can provide environmentally produced biofuels (e.g. biodiesel and ethanol).

In 1993–94, China became a net importer of oil (IEA, 2009), which funda-mentally changed its need to search for oil supplies in other parts of the world. China and India are emerging as two of the largest economies in the world and both need significant amounts of energy to maintain their high rates of economic development. Much of the development is being powered by fossil energy. China has pursued several strategies to continue to maintain its economic growth.

China recently had a dramatic increase in the amount of CO_2 emitted during its consumption of fossil energy while industrializing (a 68 per cent increase between 1994 and 2004). It does not have the forest area to sequester carbon being emitted, especially from coal combustion; it has been using its vast coal deposits to fuel its economy while buying interests in fossil fuel companies and/or projects in other countries to control its access to these resources. Because China does not have sufficient forest area to pursue renewable energy supplies, as is possible in the US and Indonesia, it is pursuing other options.

These include clean coal technologies and using coal to produce transportation fuels. For example, China is actively using methanol produced from coal as an alternative transportation fuel (BBJ, 2009). In fact in 2007, China was ranked as number one in the world in its use of a blend of methanol with gasoline. It has coordinated modification of its car-manufacturing enterprises with the use of methanol as a transportation fuel. 'Taxi and bus fleets operate using high methanol blends (M-85–M-100) and retail pumps sell low-level blends (M-15 or less) in many parts of the country' (BBJ, 2009).

Although China is using coal to produce methanol as a viable option, it still needs to explore other options that allow it to substitute more environmental solutions to meet its energy needs. As noted above, one strategy adopted is to buy interests in companies exploring for and producing oil, in order to establish and maintain its supply channels, as well as becoming a power-broker in petro-politics. In 2005, Angola became China's largest supplier of oil. In return China is helping to fund the infrastructure development needed by Angola to develop its economy and economic infrastructure. There is currently little incentive for Angola to reduce the 'corruption and lack of transparency in public finance' (EIA, 2007a) because Chinese demand for oil will maintain the status of the local elite in Angola which already dominates its economic infrastructure.

Angola joined the Organization of Petroleum Exporting Countries (OPEC) in January 2007, after finding significant reserves of oil (EIA, 2007a). Today, Angola is the third largest crude oil producer in Africa, after Nigeria and Libya. Like Nigeria, it is located in Sub-Saharan Africa, a region of the world with significant poverty and low human development. Less than 20 per cent of the Angolan population have access to electricity. Angola is rebuilding its economic and social infrastructures that were 'destroyed by a 27-year civil war that came to an end in 2002' (EIA, 2007a).

Angola should be sensitive to the repercussions China has faced in the process of empowering its economic development infrastructure and providing better livelihoods for its population. If Angola cannot improve the livelihood of its population, the pressures will increase on using the forests that currently comprise almost half of the land area (47.4 per cent in 2005) (FAO, 2006). The loss of forests, which provide the survival needs of many of the rural communities in Angola, has already been increasing. FAO (2006) reported that between 1990 and 2005 the average annual change in forest area was 0.2 per cent and 0.5 per cent between 2000 and 2005. According to FAO statistics, 76 per cent of the energy used by Angolans is woodfuel collected from forests.

The industrialized world model for economic development has been based on the use of fossil fuels to power its industries. How long this can continue without climate change impacting economic development is not clear. Projections concerning supply and demand suggest that a number of the oil-producing countries have less than 20 years of proven reserves to supply oil to global markets. If these projections are reasonably accurate, it is no longer a viable long-term option for many countries to continue using fossil fuels to maintain the economic engine of their development efforts. Ultimately countries will begin to make choices to adopt alternative energy supplies. Non-fossil-based energies can contribute towards diversifying countries' energy portfolios.

How much fossil fuel is imported by a country has little to do with its human development ranking or environmental performance, but it does define how easily a country can reduce its carbon footprint or how dependent it is on acquiring these resources. If a country is very dependent on acquiring resources from outside its boundary, it becomes vulnerable to global politics. One has only to watch the global problems that have come from the rise in the price of oil, or to watch how energy is used as a political weapon. The conflicts between Ukraine and Russia on natural gas deliveries that reduced gas deliveries to Europe during the winter of 2008 provide an example.

Today, non-fossil-based energies either provide a small fraction of a country's energy (i.e. in the more highly advanced-economy countries) or are the primary energy consumed (i.e. burning wood for energy in the growing-economy countries) (see Chapter 5). In some cases, forests provide environmental options for countries to produce 'green' energy, whereas in other cases people's dependence upon forests to provide for their survival needs limits their ability to pursue a diversified energy portfolio from forests.

Energy Production Is Water Demanding

It is clear that when a society makes energy choices it is also impacting other resources needed by humans to survive. For example, when food crops are used to produce biofuels, this results in a competition for that resource and has resulted in food scarcities in some parts of the world. A shift away from fossil-energy carriers towards CO_2-neutral sources, such as biomass, places increased pressure on freshwater resources. Currently, agriculture requires approximately 86 per cent of the world's freshwater (Hoekstra and Chapagain, 2007). Energy and water systems are interrelated because each energy carrier has a certain water requirement. This is a link that society frequently does not make because water use in agriculture is obvious, but the energy link to water is not as clear.

A traditional Life Cycle Assessment (LCA) of water use determines the total amount of water used by the production system from cradle to grave. The principles for determining whether water quantity is sustainable are that (1) the water sources or LCA inputs are renewable and sustainable; and (2) the volume of water released or LCA outputs are returned to humans or ecosystems for further use downstream. These are important principles to take into account when assessing sustainability of water supplies; however, an LCA does not distinguish the source or state of the water at the end of production. Therefore, using only the total input of water is not adequate to assess water resources from a sustainability perspective.

Table 4.3 *Water footprints of energy supplies (m³/Gigajoule)*

Primary energy carrier	Global average water footprint
Fossil-based energies	
Natural gas	0.11
Coal	0.16
Crude oil	1.06
Renewable energy	
Wind	0
Solar/geothermal	0.27
Hydropower	22
Biomass	70 (range 10–250)

Source: Gerbens-Leenes et al, 2009

The water footprint (Hoekstra and Hung, 2002) was developed to calculate the water needs for consumer products. This tool contrasts with the LCA calculation of water since the water footprint distinguishes the source and the quality of the water, particularly as it relates to the changes in freshwater availability for human health, ecosystem quality, groundwater use (depletion) and land-use changes (infiltration and runoff) that affect ecosystem quality. This water footprint can also be used to assess the water footprint per unit of energy from biomass and compare it with other energy carriers. The global water footprints of our primary energy supplies are summarized in Table 4.3.

The water-footprint data presented are based on rough estimates of freshwater requirement in crop production. The water footprint itself includes three types of virtual water: green, blue and grey. Virtual water is the amount required to produce a certain product. The term 'virtual' is used because the amount of water contained in the final product is very small compared to the quantity that went into its entire production cycle. This virtual water has been separated into three categories that describe water flows typically not included in an LCA. Green virtual water is the rainwater that evaporated during plant growth. Blue virtual water is the irrigated water that evaporated during plant growth. The grey virtual water is the water that is polluted during the process of producing the final product.

In Table 4.3, the water footprint calculation for biomass was based on several factors: the mixture of plant species (e.g. trees, bio-energy and food crops), the agricultural production systems practised and climate (Gerbens-Leenes et al, 2009). It is clear that biomass water usage must be included in any analysis attempting to determine the type of bioenergy to produce and which species to select to produce bioenergy. Even though the water footprint provides a better estimate of total water use in the production process, it does not currently assess the scarcity and opportunity cost of water when producing energy. This can easily be remedied by including more information in the calculation. For example, when considering fuels for transportation, the footprint of bio-ethanol is smaller than the water footprint of biodiesel (Gerbens-Leenes et al, 2009). The water footprint calculation should also be expanded to consider what portions of biomass are used to produce energy. For instance, it may be more water efficient to use the total biomass (leaves and stems) to generate electricity, than to use only a portion of the crop (sugar, starch or oil) to produce a biofuel.

Societies are vulnerable to climate change (e.g. droughts) because water availability is such an important part of renewable energy supplies. If a society is dependent on hydropower for its electricity, it is vulnerable to altered climates that reduce annual precipitation rates sufficiently to cause drought conditions. This occurred in Norway, where severe droughts reduced electricity production using hydropower, as the turbines could be damaged by low water levels (ESPON, 2009). Venezuela faced this situation in January 2010, when electricity delivery was interrupted to homes and businesses for four hours every day, for the same reason. Insufficient rainfall also affects the ability of trees or other crops dependent on it to grow and this in turn reduces the amount of biomass available for conversion to biofuels.

Other issues arise when hydropower is used to produce energy (Vogt et al, 2010). When the energy return ratio is used to select an energy source and the technology to produce electricity, hydropower is the ideal electricity production system. However, hydropower has environmental constraints and is vulnerable to climatic events that may reduce its efficacy as a continuous source of energy. For example, the atmospheric warming observed over the last few decades has been linked to changes in the large-scale hydrological cycles that reduce the amount of water flowing in river systems. Other recorded changes have included shifts in the amplitude and timing of runoff in glacier- and snowmelt-driven rivers which is correlated to the doubling in the amount of 'very dry' land area since the 1970s and the frequency of 'heavy precipitation' events that some areas are experiencing (Bates et al, 2008). Disturbances to limited freshwater supplies have perilous social consequences and have been linked to crop failures, famines, wars and wholesale collapse of civilizations and ecosystems (Diamond, 2005; Pearce, 2006). The potential of altered hydrologic cycles needs to be highlighted when considering the adoption of alternative energy sources that are intended to mitigate climate change.

At the local level, biofuel production is being linked to alterations of the water cycle because of the species being planted to produce this biomass. The same plant characteristics that make them ideal for biofuel production are also those that make them a high risk for becoming invasive (Raghu et al, 2006; Barney and DiTomaso, 2008). Grasses are being recommended for planting in many areas to produce biofuels because of their high productivity. They are, however, highly adapted to many different environments and have become invasive in these landscapes as described by Nackley (Box 4.1). In water-limited regions, grasses have been known to alter hydrological cycles (Calder et al, 2001). These plant species have also been shown to decrease water supplies and therefore threaten native biodiversity (Firbank et al, 2008; Groom et al, 2008). Furthermore, the potential for invasiveness may be increased by the disturbance cycles associated

Box 4.1 Ecosystems and Invasive Grasses

Lloyd Nackley

Grasses are now touted as the preferred plant to replace agricultural crops in the production of biofuels. They have high growth rates and several crops could be grown each year. These high growth rates improve the economics of producing biofuels. Therefore, anyone introducing grasses into new environments to produce biofuels needs to evaluate the risk that it will become invasive in each location. Most North American ecosystems, from the arctic to arid and even aquatic areas, have already been invaded by species that alter the environment sufficiently that native species become less competitive. They are known to 'engineer' natural cycles to the detriment of native biological communities.

Invasive grasses can dramatically alter native plant community structure and ecosystem processes, such as fire frequency, nutrient cycling and water circulation. Grasses constitute a major group of invasive plants that pose a threat to the continued delivery of ecosystem services on which societies depend. Grasses are well adapted to exploit the expected effects of global climate change, including growing under a wide range of temperatures and light levels, extended drought periods and higher CO_2 levels. Based on limited studies, invasive plants consistently show positive growth responses to CO_2 enrichment, especially 'cool season' grasses; temperate grasslands are thought to be among the most responsive ecosystems to increased CO_2 concentration.

Grasses successfully out-compete other plants by their ability to alter disturbance cycles as well as their ability to reduce the availability of scarce resource supplies that native plants depend upon. Grasses are well known to alter ecosystem fire-cycle frequencies and intensities which effectively eliminate native plants from surviving in the same habitat. The ability of grasses to alter the hydrologic cycle in areas that they invade suggests that they will be able to invade areas experiencing droughts or that are being influenced by climate change. Similar to other exotic and highly invasive plants, grasses (e.g. hybrid *Spartina* spp.) alter the hydrology of the areas that they invade. Riparian vegetation primarily influences three distinct hydrological processes: flow regulation, water uptake and storage and water quality. Commonly, tall perennial grasses quickly colonize scoured floodplains, achieving dominance along riverbanks and even in some estuaries. Invasive species can strongly alter the water balance in riparian areas by their exceptional efficiency in consuming water. Lowered water tables in many riparian zones of the southwestern US have been attributed to these plant invasions. When large stands of these invasive plants form, they can significantly increase water loss from underground aquifers and eventually reduce biological productivity.

Invasive plants have been well documented as a major component of global environmental change and have the capacity to degrade ecosystem goods and services. Integration of invasive plant management and water-resource management is essential in light of the future challenges facing the delivery of ecosystem services. These in turn must include, as equally essential, social considerations to ensure social and ecological resilience in the context of prudent environment and health policies. This is a challenge that society will have to face in the very near future because of the search for plants that are productive and can be used to produce biofuels. Grasses satisfy the latter goals but also have other attributes that would caution against introducing them in new habitats so that invasive species are not introduced.

with climate change, which may provide these already efficient competitors an advantage over stressed native species. The impacts of invasive crops on hydrological cycles, already altered by climate change, must be considered when making decisions related to using plants to produce energy.

Any dramatic increase in bio-energy production could alter future water and land requirements if it begins to compete with food-production capacities. Under current production levels, it has been estimated that additional water would be needed to meet the water demand of bio-energy crops (Burke and Kuylenstierna, 2009). This discussion highlights how energy, food and water supplies are closely linked to one another and how a decision to increase the consumption of one of these resources means that the consumption of another resource needs to decrease.

References

Barney, J. N. and DiTomaso, J. M. (2008) 'Nonnative species and bioenergy: are we culti-vating the next invader?' *Bioscience*, vol 58, pp64–70

Bates, B. C., Kundzewicz, Z. W., Wu, S. and Palutikof, J. P. (eds) (2008) 'Climate Change and Water', *Technical Paper of the Intergovernmental Panel on Climate Change*, Geneva, Switzerland

BBJ (2009) 'China leads in methanol fuel blending', www.bbj.hu/main/news_35709_energy:+china+leads+world+in+methanol+fuel+blending.html, accessed 30 January 2009

British Petroleum (2007) 'BP Statistical Review of World Energy June 2007', www.bp.com/statisticalreview, accessed 10 September 2008

Burke, J. and Kuylenstierna, J. (2009) 'The Water Variable: producing enough food in a climate insecure world', Co-operative Programme on Water and Climate, www.indiaenvironmentportal.org.in/files/Producing per cent20Enough per cent20 Food.pdf, accessed 30 May 2009

Calder, I. R. and Dye, P. (2001) 'Hydrological impacts of invasive alien plants', *Land Use Water Resoures*, vol 1, pp1–12

Diamond, J. (2005) *Collapse: How Societies Choose to Fail or Survive*, Penguin, New York, NY

Ediger V. fi., HoflgŒr, E., Sırmeli, A. N. and Tathdil, H. (2007) 'Fossil fuel sustainability index: an application of resource management', *Energy Policy*, vol 35, pp2969–2977

EIA (2007a) EIA, International Energy Outlook China, www.eia.doe.gov/emeu/cabs/China/oil.html, accessed 20 January 2009

EIA (2007b) Energy information administration, international energy annual short-term outlook, http://tonto.eia.doe.gov/country/country_energy_data.cfm?fips=AO, accessed 1 September 2008

ESPON (2009) 'Droughts. European spatial planning observation network', www.gsf.fi/projects/espon/Droughts.htm, accessed 6 June 2009

FAO (2000) 'World Soil Resources Report 90. Land Resource Potential and Constraints at Regional and Country Levels', UN FAO, Rome, Italy

FAO (2006) 'Global Forest Resources Assessment 2005', UN FAO, Rome, Italy

FAO (2008) 'World Resources Report', www.fao.org/docrep/011/ai476e/ai476e01.htm, 22 July 2009

Firbank, L. G., Petit, S., Smart, S., Blain, A. and Fuller, R. J. (2008) 'Assessing the impacts of agricultural intensification on biodiversity: a British perspective', *Philosophical Transactions of the Royal Society Biological Sciences*, vol 363, pp777–787

Gerbens-Leenes, P. W., Hoeskstra, A. Y. and van der Meer, T. (2009) 'The water footprint of energy from biomass: a quantitative assessment and consequences of an increasing share of bio-energy in energy supply', *Ecological Economics*, vol 68, pp1052–1060

Groom, M. J., Gray, E. M. and Townsend, P. A. (2008) 'Biofuels and biodiversity: principles for creating better policies for biofuel production', *Conservation Biology*, vol 22, pp602–609

Hoekstra, A. Y. and Chapagain, A. K. (2007) 'Water footprints of nations: water use by people as a function of their consumption patterns', *Water Resource Management*, vol 21, pp35–48

Hoekstra, A. Y. and Hung, P. Q. (2002) 'Virtual water trade: a quantification of virtual water flows between nations in relation to international crop trade', *Value of Water Research Report Series*, no 11, UNESCO-IHE, Delft, The Netherlands, www.waterfoot-print.org, accessed 20 January 2009

IEA (2009) *IEA Energy Statistics, 2007 Key World Energy Statistics*, International Energy Agency, www.iea.org/Textbase/stats/electricitydata.asp?COUNTRY_CODE=, accessed 2 June 2009

IPCC (2007) 'Summary for Policymakers', in M. L. Parry, O. F. Canziani, J. P. Palutikof, P. J. van der Linden and C. E. Hanson (eds), *Climate Change 2007: Impacts, Adaptation and Vulnerability. Contribution of Working Group II to the Fourth Assessment Report of the Intergovernmental Panel on Climate Change*, Cambridge University Press, Cambridge

MEA (2005) *Millennium Ecosystem Assessment: Ecosystems and Human Well-Being Synthesis. Findings of the Condition and Trends Working Group of the Millennium Ecosystem Assessment*, Island Press, Washington, DC

National Geographic (2008) 'Greendex 2008: Consumer Choice and the Environment – a Worldwide Tracking Survey', pp1–103

OECD/IEA (2008) 'End-user petroleum product prices and average crude oil import costs', 2 December 2008

ORNL (2009) http://bioenergy.ornl.gov/papers/misc/energy_conv.html, accessed 3 July 2009

Pearce, F. (2006) *When the Rivers Run Dry: Water, the Defining Crisis of the Twenty-first Century*, Beacon Press, Boston, MA

Raghu, S., Anderson, R. C., Daehler, C. C., Davis, A. S., Wiedenmann, R. N., Simberloff, D. and Mack, R. N. (2006) 'Adding biofuels to the invasive species fire?' *Science*, vol 313, pp1742–1742

Vogt, K. A., Vogt, D. J., Shelton, M., Colonnese, T., Stefan, L., Cawston, R., Scullion, J., Marchand, M., Hagmann, R. K., Tulee, M., Nackley, L., Geary, T. C., House, T. A., Candelaria, S., Nwaneshiudu, I., Lee, A. M., Kahn, E., James, L. L., Rigdon, S. J., Theobald, R. M. and Lai, L. X. (2010) 'Bio-resource Based Energy for Sustainable Societies', in W. H. Lee and V. G. Cho (eds), *Handbook of Sustainable Energy*, Nova Science Publishers Inc, Hauppauge, NY

Wong, Q. (2008) 'Americans rated least green', *Seattle Times*, 8 May 2008

World Bank (2007) *Growth and CO_2 emissions: How do different countries fare?*, Environment Department, The World Bank, Washington, DC

WRI (2009) 'EarthTrends Searchable Database Results', World Resources Institute http://earthtrends.wri.org, accessed 3 July 2009

5

Forests – The Backbone and Circulatory System for Human Societies

The history of forest use and conservation reflects the ability of people living adjacent to forests to adapt to changes occurring in their environments. Forests have been an integral part of social development throughout history and have buffered societies from cyclic and unpredictable environmental and climatic changes. Forests have been important not only because they allow societies to collect materials that can be used to generate heat to cook with or to keep a person warm, but because they provide a home to many other animals and plants, as well as providing important services for human beings, such as fresh air and clean water. Forests also influence global climates, as evidenced by the Amazon controlling rainfall patterns in other parts of the world.

Even though one-third of the 34 countries in our list still have from 20 to 40 per cent of their land in forests, forests are not being used in the most efficient and environmental manner to provide resources to all members of society today. For example, forests are mostly used for subsistence survival in the growing-economy world. Timber is also exported from these same forests to markets (legal and illegal) in the industrialized world. Because most of the subsistence economies face shortages of wood for cooking or heating, continuing to export timber from forests that satisfy traditional energy uses is not a compatible use.

Forests are now being drawn upon to provide resources for local communities that are dependent upon them for their subsistence survival, as well as to satisfy conservation and climate-mitigation goals. The view of advanced-economy countries is that forests are a 'global carbon and conservation commons', even if they belong to someone else. However, when the advanced-economy world goal is to protect forests for their conservation- or ecosystem-service benefits, this strategy does not consider the survival needs of people who live in there. These people would have fewer options to develop if a forest were given protected status. This generates conflict between forest-dwellers and the global community. This has been a no-win situation for all the stakeholders because the choices being made are fundamentally incompatible with one another. Therefore, one group wins in these conflicts and it has not been the rural dwellers. Until recently, the highest

HDI countries have not been willing to pay forest owners for the ecosystem services they provide – a strategy introduced by the Indonesian President in 2008. This trend changed in early 2010 when Norway decided to provide Indonesia millions of dollars to protect its forests and decrease forest conservation to palm and oil plantations.

Subsistence survival appears to be incompatible with using forests to sequester carbon. A brief discussion of forests and what products they provide will be used to set the stage for the new ways forests create options for societies. This will be followed by an examination of the potential of countries to use their forests as carbon sequestration sites, without impacting sustainable survival of the people living in them. The section will end with a discussion of how *forests are an essential part of a global carbon economy* just as the chemistry of oil was essential for developing a global carbon economy of today.

Where do you Find Forests Today?

To understand why forests are not being used as effectively as they should be in order to develop new approaches for sustainable development, it helps to understand which countries have forests today and what products or services are being collected from them. This understanding also helps to explain the different uses being made of forests today and how these uses impact the choices available to a community living near the forest, or for those collecting resources from forests but who are not dependent on them for their survival.

There are no relationships in our list of 34 countries between population density, land area in forests and the proportion of the population living in rural areas. This suggests that population density by itself is not driving how a forest is being used, what products are collected from the forests, how degraded a forest is, or its rate of deforestation. The higher deforestation rates in Indonesia are not caused by an increase in the population density of rural communities but by non-survival-based drivers. In Indonesia, forests are being converted to palm oil plantations to provide oils to the global biodiesel markets; these plantations are being planted by larger corporations that have the financial resources to convert, manage and export the oil products to international markets.

Large population densities do not equate to high deforestation rates. Contrary to global trends, some of the countries with large areas of forest are experiencing an increase in the proportion of the total population living in rural areas (Table 5.1). For example, Finland increased its rural population from 35 per cent in 1999 to 39 per cent in 2005. This population shift occurred while Finland continues to maintain one of the highest total land area in forests (74 per cent in 2005), compared to other countries. Similarly, Japan increased its rural population from 21 per cent to 34 per cent during the same time period while being able to maintain forests on 66 per cent of its land.

Germany also has a higher number of people moving into rural areas (13 per cent in 1999, 25 per cent in 2005), but this rural population shift is not being driven by jobs in the forest industry (Table 5.1), and means that Germany will probably not experience a reduction in its 32 per cent forest cover. This is further

Table 5.1 *Groupings of countries by their total land area in forests and other wooded areas in 2005*

%	Forests	Other wooded areas	Rural population density % [n/km²]
> 80–100	—	—	20 [202]
> 60–80	9, 16, 17, 28,	—	4 [1078], 8 [25], 12 [295], 14 [333], 19 [2], 31 [42], 34 [39]
> 40–60	1, 5, 8, 15, 24, 26, 31, 33	3	1 [13], 7 [136], 15 [116], 22 [153], 27 [17]
> 20–40	3, 6, 7, 10, 11, 14, 18, 20, 23, 25, 27, 32	2, 8	9 [16], 10 [110], 11 [231], 17 [78], 18 [52], 23 [14], 24 [21], 25 [295], 26 [8], 29 [49]
> 0.1–20	2, 4, 12, 13, 19, 21, 22, 29, 30, 34	6, 7, 9, 10, 13, 14, 18, 19, 20,22, 23, 24, 25, 26, 28, 31, 33, 34	2 [14], 3 [3], 5 [22], 6 [3], 13 [3], 16 [338], 21 [393], 28 [20], 30 [247], 32 [31], 33 [39]
0	—	1, 4, 5, 11, 12, 15, 16, 17, 21, 27, 29, 30, 32	—

Note: a) Country numbers in boxes: 1 – Angola; 2 – Argentina; 3 – Australia; 4 – Bangladesh; 5 – Brazil; 6 – Canada; 7 – China; 8 - Congo DR, 9 – Finland; 10 – France; 11 – Germany; 12 – Haiti; 13 – Iceland; 14 – India; 15 – Indonesia; 16 – Japan; 17 – Malaysia; 18 – Mexico; 19 – Namibia; 20 – Nepal; 21 – Netherlands; 22 – Nigeria; 23 – Norway; 24 – Peru; 25 – Philippines; 26 - Russian Federation; 27 – Sudan; 28 – Sweden; 29 – United Arab Emirates; 30 – United Kingdom; 31 – United Republic of Tanzania; 32 – United States; 33 – Venezuela; 34 – Yemen
Source: FAO, 2000, 2006; WHO, 2007; World Bank, 2007

evidenced by the fact that Germany had a 0.2 per cent increase in its forest cover from 1990 to 2005. This may not be the same situation for three other countries (Angola, Russia and Namibia) with about one-third to one-half of their land areas forested. They are also seeing a major shift of their population back into rural areas. Between 1990 and 2005, Russia showed no change in forest cover, but Angola and Namibia were losing forest cover (–0.2 per cent and 0.8, respectively) during the same time period. As all three of these countries have a larger proportion of their workforce in forestry compared to the other 34 countries, they will face more challenges in maintaining their forest cover because of the increased pressures on consuming forest resources that this population shift will stimulate.

Three other countries (Indonesia, Japan and Malaysia) stand out from the group of 34 because high percentages of their land area in forests, and they also have high population densities (116, 338 and 78/km², respectively). Indonesia, with a –1.7 per cent deforestation rate between 1990 and 2005 and Malaysia (–0.4 per cent rate) are experiencing high deforestation rates that suggest the forests may be less able to provide the resources needed by their populations in the future. Both countries need to convert forest materials into higher energy materials (i.e. biofuels, Vogt et al, 2008) instead of continuing to burn woodfuel because their current consumptive patterns are not sustainable.

In contrast to Indonesia and Malaysia, Japan has not been experiencing any deforestation and has given protected status to about one-sixth of its total forest area. Japan does not have to manage its forests, but the high forest cover creates opportunities for the production of energy – for instance liquid fuels – from them. Forests can provide Japan with socioeconomic opportunities that cannot be derived from food and water because they face severe domestic shortages of these resources.

At the other extreme, three of the 34 (Bangladesh, Haiti and the UK) had less than 12 per cent of their land area forested in 2005, but still had very high population densities (1078, 295 and 247/km^2, respectively) (Table 5.1). These countries will face many challenges in utilizing their forests to create new options for sustainable development because they do not have sufficient forest biomass to provide social buffering. Unlike Bangladesh and Haiti, the UK has given most of its forests protected status, which effectively excludes them from contributing to its economic development activities.

Several countries in our list (Bangladesh, Haiti, Namibia, Nigeria and Yemen) have high proportions of their populations (52–75 per cent) living in rural areas, and need to satisfy their bio-resource demands from these same locations. As these countries have little forest remaining, few socioeconomic opportunities can be delivered from their forests today.

Even though forest bio-resources are mainly discussed here, several countries have wooded areas comprising a portion of their landscape (Table 5.1). Australia is a good example of a country with most of its woody biomass found in its wooded landscape and not in forests. These wooded landscapes, although they may comprise less than 20 per cent of the total landscape of a country, have considerable woody biomass that could be used to produce energy using new technologies.

Energy Choices and Satisfying Human Survival Needs

Today, countries that mainly use their forests to produce energy are more vulnerable to the impacts of climate change than those that have made the shift to consuming predominantly fossil fuels. This vulnerability from using forest materials for energy is mainly due to the impact of climate change on reducing the rate of tree growth, and therefore the amount of energy materials a forest can sustainably supply. Furthermore, if there is less rainfall in an area, there is a strong potential for a vegetative community to shift from forest to grassland. Any loss of forest would directly impact the security of energy supplies for those people dependent on burning forest materials for energy. Because most of the countries that use forest materials for energy are growing-economy countries, they will be more vulnerable to climate change that decreases forest productivity.

The type of materials used to produce energy clearly varies as a function of a country's HDI ranking (Table 5.2). Those countries ranked higher in the HDI mainly consume fossil-based fuels to produce energy, while those ranked lower in the HDI mainly use wood biomass and wastes for their energy (Figure 5.1). There

Table 5.2 *Primary energy supplies from renewable resources in 2005*

%	Biomass and wastes	Nuclear	Hydro, solar, wind and geothermal power
> 80–100	8, 20, 31	- -	- -
> 60–80	1, 12, 22, 27	- -	13
> 40–60	- -	10	- -
> 20–40	4, 5, 14, 15, 25	28	23, 25
> 0.1–20	2, 3, 6, 7, 9, 10, 11, 13, 16, 17, 18, 19, 21, 23, 24, 26, 28, 30, 32, 33, 34	2, 5, 6, 7, 9, 11, 14, 16, 18, 21, 26, 30, 32	1, 2, 3, 4, 5, 6, 7, 8, 9, 10, 11, 12, 14, 15, 16, 17, 18, 19, 20, 21, 22, 24, 26, 27, 28, 30, 31, 32, 33
0	29	1, 3, 4, 8, 12, 13, 15, 17, 19, 20, 22, 23, 24, 25, 27, 29, 31, 33, 34	29, 34

Note: Country numbers in boxes: 1 – Angola; 2 – Argentina; 3 – Australia; 4 – Bangladesh; 5 – Brazil; 6 – Canada; 7 – China; 8 – Congo DR, 9 – Finland; 10 – France; 11 – Germany; 12 – Haiti; 13 – Iceland; 14 – India; 15 – Indonesia; 16 – Japan; 17 – Malaysia; 18 – Mexico; 19 – Namibia; 20 – Nepal; 21 – Netherlands; 22 – Nigeria; 23 – Norway; 24 – Peru; 25 – Philippines; 26 – Russian Federation; 27 – Sudan; 28 – Sweden; 29 – United Arab Emirates; 30 – United Kingdom; 31 – United Republic of Tanzania; 32 – United States; 33 – Venezuela; 34 – Yemen
Source: IEA, 2007

are a few exceptions to this pattern. Iceland, for example, has little forest cover and generates most of its electricity using hydroelectric dams and geothermal power. Similarly, Yemen has little forest cover or hydroelectric capacity; its energy needs are predominantly met by oil, which it has in great abundance.

Paradoxically, three out of the four lowest HDI-ranked countries are major oil producers, but their residents are mainly dependent upon forest materials to produce their energy. Of all the 34 countries, the highest user of biomass/wastes for energy production is Nigeria (79.8 per cent in 1990; 78.0 per cent in 2005), followed by the Congo DR (84.0 per cent in 1990; 92.5 per cent in 2005). Angola also consumes mostly biomass/wastes for energy (68.8 per cent in 1990; 63.8 per cent in 2005). Unfortunately, energy production from forests consists of burning wood biomass – a practice which increases human health risks (WHO/UNDP, 2004; WHO, 2007). The fact that both Nigeria and Angola are major oil-producing countries suggests that much of the oil income is not being used to improve the livelihoods of the majority of their people. The energy choices made in Nigeria and Angola result in both fossil fuel combustion and deforestation, contributing to the total CO_2 emissions recorded in each; the total CO_2 emissions are still low for both countries compared to the emissions of the industrialized countries (see Chapter 4).

Of the major fuels consumed by society, oil and biomass/wastes are most strongly related to the human development potential of a country (Table 5.3). The total fossil fuel consumption (oil, natural gas and coal) explains a small fraction ($R^2 = 0.27$) of the variations in the human development index ranking. In

Table 5.3 *Correlations between energy and other resource indicators*

Y variable	X variable	R^2
HDI ranking	Total fossil fuel consumption as primary energy	0.27
	Energy use (kg of oil equivalent per capita)	0.54
	Biomass & wastes, % of primary energy consumed	0.61
Energy use:	Agriculture imports in dollars/capita	0.52
kg of oil	Water footprint per capita (m^3/capita/year)	0.21
equivalent	Share of home budget spent on food (%)	0.58
per capita		
Biomass/	Total fossil fuel consumption as primary energy	0.74
wastes:		
% of primary		
energy		
consumed		

contrast, oil consumption explains 54 per cent, while biomass/wastes explain 61 per cent of the variance. This shows that it is not total fossil fuels that impact a country's ranking in the human development index, but the amount of oil and/or forest biomass that is used to produce energy. We have already seen that the higher the human development ranking of a country, the more fossil fuels are consumed in energy production. In contrast, the lower human development countries use mostly forest biomass for energy and little, if any, fossil fuel. Therefore, the human development index ranking is sensitive to the material used to produce energy.

There also seems to be an inverse relationship between how much oil is used to produce energy and family income spent on food. This suggests that when people need to use more of the family income for food purchases, food security has priority over energy security. It appears easier for a country to develop more options for its energy production than for food security. Purchasing oil to produce energy is more expensive compared to the other alternatives, such as the collection and burning of forest or shrub materials; these latter materials frequently can be collected freely, except for the labour costs.

Our data show that, where forest biomass and wastes are the primary energy supply for a country, the amount of the home budget spent on food increases ($R^2 = 0.58$). When oil is consumed as a country's primary source of energy, lack of food security typically has not been an issue. Oil-consuming countries have been able to import most of their food items when local production was insufficient to meet the demand. For our group of 34, 52 per cent of the variance in energy use (kilograms of oil equivalent per capita) is explained by the amount of US$ spent per capita to import agricultural products; the higher the HDI, the more money is spent on importing agricultural products (see Chapter 10). This relationship also shows that when oil is the primary energy supply, families spend less of their total home budget on food purchases.

Table 5.4 *Percentage of available forest area and of forest biomass consumed as the primary energy source*

Potential for using forests to provide social/environmental resiliency (% forest of total land area)	Countries within each category [% biomass used as primary energy]
HIGH POTENTIAL (> 40%)	Japan [1], Malaysia [1], Russia [1], Venezuela [1] Finland [2], Peru [2], Sweden [2] Brazil [3], Indonesia [3] Angola [7] Congo DR [10]
GOOD POTENTIAL (20–40%)	Australia [1], Canada [1], France [1], Germany [1], Mexico [1], Norway [1], US [1] India [3], Philippines [3] Sudan [8] Nepal [9] Tanzania [10]
NONE (< 20%)	Argentina [1], Iceland [1], Netherlands [1], UAE [1], UK [1], Yemen [1] China [2], Namibia [2] Bangladesh [4] Haiti [8], Nigeria [8]

Note: Country distribution ranking for how much biomass is used as the primary energy: 1 = < 10%; 2 = 10–20%; 3 = > 20–30%; 4 = > 30–40%; 5 = > 40–50%; 6 = > 50–60%; 7 = > 60–70%; 8 = > 70–80%; 9 = > 80–90%; 10 = > 90–100%

The importance of climate driving many aspects of human development has already been mentioned. In the past, climate stimulated people to migrate to other lands when resource supplies diminished. Today, we recognize the importance of climate change in controlling human acquisition of resources, and the fact that humans do not have the luxury of moving to alleviate these constraints. Water and energy issues are commonly discussed today in the lay literature, because both control the capacity of humans to continue to live at the comfort level to which they have become accustomed. Both issues also determine whether many of the emerging-economy countries will be able to adopt the lifestyles common to many industrialized countries.

It is worth briefly discussing the trade-offs that need to be made in relation to energy consumption, and the conflicts that have resulted in pursuing conservation and sustainable development goals globally. These conflicts will determine whether energy consumption will be sustainable.

Forests and Fossil Energies: Incompatible in a Conservation and Sustainable Development World?

Maintaining forest cover and the development of a country's human capital are incompatible goals because of the competitive and conflicted expectations societies have for forests. Today, most of the growing-economy countries and many of the emerging-economies are dependent on forests to provide most of their energy. Therefore, protecting forests in order to achieve environmental goals has not been very practical.

Except for the advanced-economy countries located in the northern latitudes, those with abundant supplies of fossil fuels (e.g. major oil exporters) and significant forest areas have not been able to balance their use of forests to produce energy with the development of their human capital (e.g. Angola, Congo DR and Nigeria). Countries with abundant fossil fuels and forests should face fewer challenges to achieve their development goals. However, people living in these countries continue to collect woodfuel from forests and burn this or convert it into charcoal to power their industries. Linking energy production to sustainable development has not been an option in these countries. Government instability and continuing civil conflicts mean that the abundant fossil reserves and forest resources are not being used effectively to develop their human capital. This can be summarized as follows: rich and multiple energy supplies exist in the same landscape as some of the poorest people in the world, and where energy and food supplies are insecure. People living in these politically unstable countries have few energy choices even though they should be able to select their preferred energy from a portfolio of options.

Except for the growing-economy countries that are completely dependent on renewable supplies, few countries consume renewable energy supplies as a major portion of their primary energy; typically less than 20 per cent of the total energy consumed by a country is renewable (Table 5.4). For example, Venezuela uses few, if any, renewable resources to generate energy (0.9 per cent in 2005), and nationalization of its energy industries resulted in reduced investments in renewable energy projects. Government policies have also encouraged and increased energy consumption; the 2007 time-zone change by half an hour has also resulted in higher electricity consumption rates because it requires electricity to be delivered for a longer time period each day (Romero, 2009). Despite having some of the largest reserves of fossil energy, the declining energy infrastructure is causing problems in Venezuela today and blackouts are not uncommon (see previous discussion on hydroelectric power and water demand).

Some advanced-economy countries use wood to produce energy but these are exceptions to the norm; they are mostly higher-latitude Scandinavian countries. When forests are used to produce energy, it is mostly inefficient and unsustainable (e.g. as firewood) (Table 5.4). As countries with high forest cover, Finland and Sweden have been most effective in developing the energy potential of their forests and using forests to develop their human capital; in 2005, Sweden produced 17.2 per cent of its energy from biomass/wastes, while Finland used

Box 5.1 Climate Change and Forest, Their Pests and Pathogens

Robert L. Edmonds

Past climate changes strongly influenced human activities. Climate also strongly influences plant pests and diseases, and thus humans, indirectly. In the 1850s a cool, wet period in Ireland increased potato late blight, resulting in a potato famine and migration of many Irish people to North America. Since 1900 human activities have increased the rate of global warming, with undoubted influence on forests, their natural plants and other ecosystems, as well as insects and diseases. In addition, humans have moved plants, animals, insects and disease organisms around the world, especially since the 1800s. Some of these have become invasive and have changed ecosystems through competition with native plants, as well as causing extensive tree mortality. The most notable in North America are chestnut blight, Dutch elm disease, white pine blister rust, gypsy moth and, most recently, sudden oak death.

In the Pacific Northwest US, both low-elevation and high-elevation forests will experience significant changes due to global warming. The widespread forest mortality currently occurring in the western US has in fact been related to regional warming and increases in water deficits. Many of the forest diebacks occurring throughout the world have also been related to climate change or unusual weather conditions. In the 20th century a number of diebacks, declines and blights were noted in North American hardwood forests. Conifer forests were similarly afflicted from Alaska to the southeastern US. This is occurring at a time when societies expect a wide variety of ecosystem services and commodities from forests, and when they have to be healthier than many are at present.

Disease-causing organisms and insects, because of their short life cycles, are able to adapt more quickly to climate change than trees, and might pose a more serious threat to forest health than global-change effects on vegetation alone. Forest pathogens including bacteria, phytoplasmas, fungi, fungus-like organisms, parasitic plants and nematodes are strongly influenced by weather and climate. For example, it appears that recent atmospheric warming, precipitation changes and weather extremes are already influencing forest diseases in western North American forests. Forests that are already stressed by high tree densities, pathogens, bark beetles, or climatic conditions such as drought, may not survive additional climatic stress. Climate strongly affects insects because many components of their life cycles are influenced by temperature and moisture. For example, defoliators and bark beetles have caused the majority of insect problems in forests, and elevated temperatures can speed up reproductive cycles and reduce cold-induced mortality. Drought can also influence outbreak dynamics by weakening trees and making them more susceptible to attack.

19.6 per cent of these materials for energy; in May 2010, Sweden had increased its total energy consumption from biomass to 32%. In contrast, in 2005 most of the other countries were too dependent on combusting woodfuel for energy, or did not include forests as part of their sustainable development activities.

Several of the higher HDI-ranked countries (e.g. Australia, Canada, France, Germany, Norway and the US) use little forest material to produce energy (< 10 per cent), despite the vulnerability of their forests to disturbance agents (e.g. fires or insects); these countries mainly use fossil fuels to produce energy. These countries face the fact that climate change will exacerbate the vulnerability of forests to pests and pathogens, as described in Box 5.1. Therefore, these countries need to manage their forests to mitigate the climate-change impacts even though currently this is not one of their high priorities. The situation in the former countries contrasts with those having significant forest areas and with 50 per cent to almost 100 per cent of their energy derived from burning wood (e.g. Angola and Congo DR). The latter have no choice but to manage their forests to decrease their vulnerability to climate change. Furthermore, the high deforestation rates have reduced the forest area sufficiently in some countries (e.g. Haiti and Nigeria) that current uses of the remnant forests for energy are over-exploitive.

Today we expect forests to provide multiple benefits to society and to accommodate multiple goals of a diverse stakeholder community, including many who do not live in the forest or are not dependent upon the forest for their survival. These external stakeholders frequently wanted to exclude indigenous people from living on their customary lands because they were perceived to cause negative repercussions on the ecosystem that had acquired other environmental values by the international community. We have caricaturized this as evicting a duck from a body of water because it competes with a species designated as endangered and the habitat is restricted for conservation (Figure 5.1). This idea appears farfetched, but it has been frequently supported by government policies because of the incentives provided by international communities. People have been evicted from a forest designated as a 'global commons' because of its important role in

Figure 5.1 *Caricature representing the international community restricting who can access or live in an area identified to have conservation value*

Table 5.5 *Grouping of countries into categories based on realistic uses of their forests*

Categories of forest use	Countries
Forests unable to provide products because high percentage of forest has protected status	Germany, Iceland, Netherlands, UK, US, Venezuela
Forests capable of providing more opportunities than it currently provides	Argentina, Australia, Brazil, Finland, France, Indonesia, Japan, Malaysia, Mexico, Norway, Peru, Philippines, Russia, Sweden, US, Venezuela
Forests mostly provide woodfuel for energy today; sufficient forest cover exists today, but higher deforestation rates expected in the future	Angola, Congo DR
Forests historically over-exploited and forest cover is insufficient to provide for resource demand	Bangladesh, China, Haiti, Iceland, India, Namibia, Nepal, Netherlands, Nigeria, Sudan, Tanzania, UK
Forests need to be urgently managed because of forest health issues	Canada, China, India, Nepal, US

Note: A country may appear in more than one category; no data on insects, disease, and/or fire for Australia, Congo DR, Haiti, Nigeria, Sudan, Tanzania, Yemen; therefore inability to determine forest health risk

climate mitigation or as a home for a diversity of species. Today, the international community has been finding it more difficult to treat forests as a global commons. For example, Russia and the Congo DR have great potentials to sequester carbon in their forests and thereby help the global community to reduce atmospheric CO_2 levels (Table 5.4). However, these two countries have no interest in adopting practices that preclude them from using their forests for their own purposes. The advanced-economy countries, for the most part, have pursued one-dimensional solutions to forests that preclude the survival of people dependent upon the same forests.

The manner in which we use forests is changing all the time. This reflects the continuing importance of forests to humans and how forests create options for them. The potential uses of forest are constrained by many factors (Table 5.5). Many countries have less forest area available to provide resources and ecosystem services today because forests were over-exploited in the past and their future uses will not be sustainable. Today, half of the global population is still dependent on forests for the traditional products they provided society several thousand years ago (woodfuel for cooking and heat). Many countries (e.g. Bangladesh, China, Haiti, Iceland, the Netherlands, Nigeria and the UK) have such low forest cover that they urgently need to plant trees to restore their forests to some semblance of what existed historically. At the same time, some countries (e.g. Canada, China, India, Nepal and the US) urgently need to manage their forests because forest health issues are jeopardizing intact forest cover. These unhealthy forests are ideal candidates for the production of energy using new technologies.

What is also obvious from comparisons of the country-level data is that where fossil fuels are a significant part of a country's domestic energy production, these countries use little biomass or biomass wastes as part of their primary energy supplies. Countries where fossil fuels are the primary energy supply are Argentina, Canada, China, France, Germany, Japan, Malaysia, Mexico, Norway, Russia, US and Venezuela. As of 2005, many of the emerging-economy countries (Brazil, India and Indonesia) and growing-economy countries (Angola, Congo DR and Nigeria) are very dependent on woodfuel to provide their energy. Angola (> 60 per cent woodfuel use) and Nigeria (~ 80 per cent) are striking in their dependence on woodfuel to produce their energy, because both are oil-exporting countries and both use only ~ 20–30 per cent of their oil production domestically.

The trade-offs between forests and energy were highlighted by Wunder (2003) who linked deforestation rates to oil; forests in oil-exporting, tropical countries tend to face fewer pressures to convert or degrade them by over-exploitation. When oil revenues are high, the pressures to convert and degrade forests decrease. Venezuela is a good example of a country that follows the pattern suggested by Wunder (2003) because it has secure oil supplies, uses little of its forests for energy and protects a sizeable portion of its forests. This relationship does not hold where and when oil is not being used for domestic consumption and for development of a country's human capital. For example, oil revenues have little impact on deforestation rates in Angola, Congo DR and Nigeria.

Fossil fuels are still the preferred energy of choice in most emerging-economy countries, even when these supplies are less secure. This pattern was apparent in our database as many of the emerging-economy countries are shifting from using forest materials to fossil fuels for energy. Both Brazil and Peru are using less forest biomass for energy even though they have sizeable tracts of forest. Similarly, Indonesia has been decreasing its use of biomass/wastes to produce energy (43.6 per cent of the energy was produced from wood in 1990, and in 2005 this had decreased to 28.5 per cent).

Two other countries are using less forest material to produce energy, but they have severely over-exploited their forests in the past and current uses are not sustainable. For example, India produced 41.7 per cent of its energy from biomass/wastes in 1990; this decreased to 29.4 per cent in 2005. China has followed a similar track, with 23.2 per cent of its 1990 energy coming from biomass/wastes and 13.0 per cent in 2005. As their wood use for energy is mainly in combustion, decreasing wood use in energy is healthier for humans and more desirable environmentally. Most of these decisions are a result of countries switching to more fossil fuels to develop their economies.

Some countries (e.g. Namibia) also have the potential to use invasive woody shrubs to produce energy by employing new technologies that convert these materials into higher energy products. Today, Namibia has to import most of its oil and is dependent on South Africa to provide one-half of its electricity. This situation is not ideal, for South Africa is unable to guarantee secure supplies of electricity to Namibia – it stopped providing electricity to Namibia in 2008 when it was unable to satisfy its own needs because of droughts. Therefore, Namibia has the challenge of managing its invasive woody shrubs and also producing energy domestically. The invasive shrubs would create opportunities for Namibia if they were converted to liquid fuels. This strategy would allow Namibia to achieve its conservation goals through energy production, because these shrubs need to be eradicated; they reduce cheetah habitat and are a poor food choice for cattle.

CO_2 Emissions, Land-use Changes and Forest Sequestration of Carbon

The global community has been paying particular attention to forest uses in some regions. As noted above, because of the global impact of climate change and loss of biodiversity, forests are being viewed as a 'global commons', where people living outside a country are demanding ownership rights to decide what should happen within the borders of another country. This is not, however, the view held by the country that owns the forests. Despite the different views of forest ownership, global communities are negotiating acceptable solutions to deforestation and the use of forests to sequester carbon. Countries with large tracts of forests are most impacted by decisions made by the international community. For example, Brazil has 20.6 per cent of the global forest carbon; the Congo DR has 9.7 per cent of the total; Russia has 13.5 per cent; and the US has 7.9 per cent. These four countries own about 52 per cent of the total carbon contained in forests worldwide. It is notable that three of these countries (Brazil, Congo DR and Russia) are frequently mentioned in the media because of their high deforestation rates and where the global communities want to be part of the process for selecting choices to be made in these forests. The other country, including the US are not being closely scrutinized by the global communities on how they are managing their forests, because these forests are recovering in extent after agricultural abandonment.

The remaining countries included in our database own less than 2.5 per cent of the global forest carbon. Having a smaller portion of the global forest does not mean that the international community ignores what activities are occurring in a country's forest. When a country owns forests with high biodiversity, the global community is very cognizant of land-use activities that might negatively impact that biodiversity. For example, Indonesia has about 2.5 per cent of the global forest carbon, but its high deforestation rate and illegal logging brings it to the attention of the global community because it has a very high biodiversity. Several years ago, Indonesia was ranked as being a significant emitter of CO_2 as a result of its high deforestation rates and the burning of forests when they were converted into palm oil plantations.

Despite the connection between CO_2 emissions and land-use changes, no significant correlations are produced between these variables for our 34 countries. In fact, the quantity of CO_2 emissions resulting from land-use change has little or no relationship to a country's HDI value. This contrasts with the relationship found for the amount of CO_2 emitted per capita due to gasoline consumption and a country's HDI value ($R^2 = 0.40$) (Figure 4.2).

Table 5.6 *Total forest carbon budgets and CO_2 emissions from land-use change and fossil fuel combustion*

HDI Rank group		Total CO_2 emissions [−] (Mg CO_2/ capita)	Total CO_2 emissions from land use (% of total)	C stocks in forests (living biomass) (Mg C/capita)	C stocks in forest production (Mg C/ capita/yr)	Total C emitted balanced by annual forest production (%)
1	Iceland	−7.4	0	5.0	0.2	10
	Norway	−11.3	0	74.5	3.0	98
	Australia	−19.4	7	408.8	16.4	312
	Canada	−19.8	16	313.2	12.5	234
	Sweden	−6.0	10	129.7	5.2	320
	Japan	−10.4	8	14.8	0.6	21
	Netherlands	−7.7	0	1.5	0.1	3
	Finland	−11.0	8	155.4	6.2	209
	France	−6.2	0	19.1	0.8	46
	US	−17.7	0	64.0	2.6	53
	UK	−9.1	0	1.9	0.1	3
	Germany	−9.5	0	15.8	0.6	25
2	Argentina	−5.2	24	62.2	2.5	132
	UAE	−30.1	0	4.0	0.2	2
	Mexico	−4.9	17	14.5	0.6	44
	Malaysia	−25.4	63	136.8	5.5	80
	Russia	−12.4	16	225.0	9.0	269
	Brazil	−8.2	79	264.1	10.6	477
3	Venezuela	−10.4	46	217.0	8.7	309
	China	−4.3	0	4.7	0.2	16
	Peru	−7.5	81	293.0	11.7	579
	Philippines	−1.6	42	11.5	0.5	77
	Indonesia	−8.8	78	26.7	1.1	32
4	Namibia	−0.7	0	114.3	4.6	320
	India	−1.3	2	2.1	0.1	24
5	Bangladesh	−0.3	..	0.2	0.0	10
	Nepal	−2.8	96	17.9	0.7	95
	Haiti	−0.4	49	0.9	0.0	33
	Sudan	−0.8	61	41.5	1.7	384
	Yemen	−1.2	14	2.4	0.1	30
6	Nigeria	−1.6	49	9.9	0.4	70
	Tanzania	−0.3	68	58.6	2.3	197
	Angola	−1.2	51	300.0	12.0	1532
	Congo DR	−3.1	100	394.5	15.8	1169

Note: units given as CO_2 and C; data for 2005
HDI = Human Development Index [Group 1 = HDI > 0.9; Group 2 = 0.8–0.9; Group 3 = 0.7–0.8; Group 4 = 0.6–0.7; Group 5 = 0.5–0.6; Group 6 = 0.4–0.5] a conservative estimate of annual forest production = 4 per cent NPP
Source: FAO, 2006; WRI, 2009

The total CO_2 emissions emitted during land-use changes are given in Table 5.6. These data show that the highest HDI-ranked countries were emitting most of their CO_2 during fossil fuel combustion; land use contributed little to the total. The remaining countries (except for China, India, Namibia and UAE) have land uses contributing significantly towards the total CO_2 emissions recorded at the country level. In contrast, growing-economy countries have land-use changes contributing most of the CO_2 emitted by each country. These calculations highlight how countries characterized as having high deforestation rates (e.g. Brazil, Indonesia, Malaysia, Nepal and Peru) have consistently had more than half to almost all of their CO_2 emitted during land-use changes and not during their combustion of fossil fuels.

Another pattern noticeable in Table 5.6 is that few of the CO_2 emissions are linked to land-use changes occurring in both the advanced-economy and also the emerging-economy countries, such as China and India. However, many of the growing-economy countries located in the tropical regions of the world, have significant portions of their CO_2 emissions resulting from land-use changes. The deforestation rates in these countries are being driven by the highest HDI-ranked countries that consume timber products produced in the former, or, in the case of China, are developing a global finished wood-products industry (AFPA, 2004; Goodman and Finn, 2007; Laurance, 2008). The more recent driver of deforestation is the conversion of tropical forests into sugar-cane fields, soy fields or palm oil plantations. These plantings are being used to supply ethanol as a gasoline supplement or to grow plants from which oils can be extracted to produce biodiesel. Again, the consumers of the ethanol and plant oils live in the highest HDI-ranked countries or the advanced-economy countries (Friel, 2002).

The amount of annual forest production that could mitigate the CO_2 emitted annually in each country is revealing (Table 5.6). As expected, the amount of carbon stock in a forest determined whether the annual growth in a forest would be able to balance the total CO_2 emitted during fossil fuel combustion and from land-use ($R^2 = 0.54$); the higher the amount of carbon stored in a forest, the higher the percentage of total CO_2 emissions that could be sequestered by a growing forest. The potential for annual forest growth to mitigate the entire CO_2 emitted during 2005 was found for almost one-half of the 34 countries. The advanced-economy and emerging-economy countries need to store a minimum of 62.2Mg C in their forests to completely mitigate the CO_2 they emit annually. Several of these countries (Argentina, Australia, Brazil, Canada, Finland, Russia and Sweden) could mitigate two to four times more CO_2 than they are emitting during fossil fuel combustion and land-use change (Table 5.6).

Similarly, a minimum of 17.9Mg C stored in a forest would allow the growing-economy and lower HDI-ranked countries to mitigate all of the CO_2 they emit annually. As of 2005, these countries emitted a lower amount of CO_2 compared to the higher HDI-ranked countries; therefore, they need less forest area to mitigate their emissions (Table 5.6). Several countries (Angola, Congo DR, Namibia, Peru, Sudan and Tanzania) have the potential to mitigate CO_2 at an emissions level from 3 to 15 times higher because of their larger forest areas. The potential annual growth of their forests provides these countries with an ability to use their forests to mitigate their CO_2 emissions, as well as to contribute towards reducing global emissions. The use of this additional sequestration potential to mitigate CO_2 emissions occurring outside of the country will be determined by the willingness of higher HDI countries to pay for this service. There is no benefit for these countries to provide these sequestration services if there is no monetary return, because too many of the residents of these countries are still dependent on forests for their energy. Sequestration services would prevent these forests from being used to provide the woodfuel that is so essential for energy production.

A few countries will not be able to utilize the growth of their forests effectively to mitigate their current rates of CO_2 emissions. This is partially due to their low existing forest carbon stocks. For example, the following countries have less than 10Mg C per capita of living biomass in their forests: Bangladesh, China, Haiti, Iceland, India, the Netherlands, Nigeria, UK, the UAE and Yemen. Some of these countries are not ideal locations for forests to grow anyway because of their geographic location and climates (e.g. the UAE and Yemen). They will not be able to grow forests unless climate change increases their rainfall. A few countries (e.g. China, India and Nigeria) have historically over-exploited their forests for woodfuel. They also face severe challenges in re-establishing their forest cover when wood supplies are inadequate to provide for their current energy needs. In order to meet current energy demands, these countries need to increase the energy value of the materials they harvest. Consequently, they are good candidates for the adoption of second- and third-generation energy supplies.

France, Germany and the US are able to mitigate approximately 25–50% of their total CO_2 emissions using the current annual growth of their forests. These three countries also face very high climate risk (e.g. hurricanes or storms) that will limit the management of forests to sequester carbon. Therefore, the challenge is to manage forests for their carbon-mitigation potential while factoring-in the climatic risks that have the potential to reduce forest cover. Weather events will produce more challenges for France and Germany because they have lower carbon stocks in their forests (< 20Mg C per capita). With the US having 64Mg C per capita in forests, it will be less challenging for this country to use its forests to mitigate its CO_2 emissions. Weather-related events such as hurricanes can also create opportunities for countries, as there will be periodic production of biomass debris that can be used to produce liquid fuels or electricity (Kotra, 2008).

The globalization and trade in resources, as well as the ecosystem services forests provide, determine what negative environmental externalities exist in forests. It is apparent that not all countries are going to be able to use their forests to improve the livelihoods of their people and to provide the global communities the desired ecosystem services from these same forests. For example, Indonesia is attempting to create solutions to several environmental problems as well as deal with its looming energy shortages. According to the 2005 International Energy Report, Indonesia had reached a turning point in energy security in 2004. Instead of being self-sufficient and exporting oil to other countries, Indonesia became an oil importer. In an effort to wean itself from a dependence on fossil fuels, it has become one of the major producers of crude palm oil (for both cooking oil and biodiesel) and is satisfying not only its own transportation fuel needs but also those of others, including the European Union (EU). Indonesia is very dependent on maintaining this supply of transportation fuels because biodiesel currently accounts for half of its fuel consumption and also provides the country with additional revenue.

Recently, the EU decided that the biodiesel being produced by Indonesia is not produced in a sustainable manner. It indicated that the reason for this decision is based on the fact that forests are being replaced by palm oil plantations. This conclusion by the EU has important implications for Indonesia, for it sets the criteria being used to determine whether the EU will buy oils produced in Indonesia. In its Renewable Energy Directive, the EU decided only to import fuels that fulfilled their minimum-sustainability requirements and that contributed towards national targets and qualified for national incentives. Currently these criteria apply to both biofuels used in transportation and to other uses for these oils. The criteria that Indonesia needs to satisfy include how much the oils mitigate the GHG impact; land-use/carbon stock requirements; biodiversity; and environmental requirements for agriculture.

China's story contrasts with what is happening in Indonesia; the former is a country that faced the need to import fossil fuels in 2004 and now is at a turning point of shifting from being an oil exporter to becoming a net oil importer (EIA, 2009) to power its economy. China also provides a cautionary note on what decisions Indonesia might want to make in relation to its acquisition of energy. Unlike China, Indonesia has oil, abundant forests and is a hotspot of biodiversity. It also faces some of the highest deforestation rates in the world. Illegal timber harvesting in Indonesia is also feeding into countries such as China. Indonesia needs to implement a sustainable livelihood and energy strategy for over 17,508 islands while conserving its biodiversity (ranked 2nd highest globally) and reducing its emissions of CO_2 (recently ranked as the third highest emitter of CO_2 by WWF). At first glance it might appear that there are no lessons from China that could be used for making informed decisions in Indonesia. Despite having abundant forest resources, the high deforestation rates and conversion of forest lands to palm oil plantations, Indonesia could in the future face the same problems as China today: abundant oil, yet needing to import it.

Indonesia does not appear to be making the same choices made by China and is actively searching for alternative energy solutions to fossil fuels. This might suggest that lessons learnt in China might not be relevant for Indonesia, but the issues Indonesia faces today are similar to those that China already faced in 1994, when it had to import oil, and in 1998, when deforestation led to floods and loss of lives (reflecting decreased social and environmental resilience). Examining the approach taken by China to acquire energy, to control their CO_2 emissions while protecting and increasing their forest cover, is informative. The strategy pursued has resulted in China increasing its global energy and bio-resource footprint because it has stimulated unsustainable practices in other countries. These are not strategies that should be emulated by Indonesia. Choices need to be understood and made in the context of the environmental and resource constraints for each country. It is important to identify when and where forests can provide multiple resources and ecosystem services. Without such knowledge, unsustainable decisions will continue to be made.

Climate-change mitigation is possible by either sequestering C in forest biomass or using forest materials to produce 'carbon neutral' energy substitutes for fossil fuels. Despite this potential, many forests are sequestering less carbon today and are emitting more C into the atmosphere following frequent forest fires (Vogt et al, 2008; Vogt et al, 2009). In the western US, afforestation projects and the use of forests to sequester carbon are threatened by the abundance of over-stocked forests with high fire risk that are an artefact of historical land uses (USFS, 2003). In this region, there is between 10.2 and 15.8Mg/ha of biomass which has a high fire risk. As the fire risk is high, these forests will sequester less carbon in their biomass. Sustainably collected wood is an untapped source of energy that can be used to mitigate CO_2 emissions (IPCC, 2003) when supplementing or substituting for, fossil fuels, while at the same time reducing the risks of forest fires that emit large amounts of CO_2.

Liquid Fuels from Forests to Mitigate CO_2 Emissions

The common link between forests and oil is the carbon molecule. Oil is comprised of carbon molecules that generally formed millions of years ago, and forests are

Figure 5.2 *Caricature of using methanol, a wood alcohol, to power a computer to call for help after a car accident*

carbon molecules accumulating in tree biomass over several hundred-year timescales. Crude oil has been used to produce a multitude of products that affect every facet of our lives. Debates about shifting from oil have been difficult because oil is used to make so many products that it is an integral part of almost every aspect of society. It would be hard to imagine what a non-carbon world would look like. Similarly, forest materials can also be converted into a multitude of products to support human activities. For example, wood materials have been used for over 350 years to make methanol, a one-carbon-atom alcohol which can be used to supplement or substitute for gasoline. One future vision held by some is that non-food biomass such as wood materials will be used to produce methanol to power many of our small appliances using fuel cells. Such a vision suggests that 'tree energy' could be used after a car disaster to communicate the problem and help people recover when energy delivery ceases, as depicted in Figure 5.2. At the same time, forests are unique, since they provide society–ecosystem services essential for human survival and provide habitats for many other animals. Conversely, fossil carbon cannot provide these services, nor is it renewable within a human lifespan. Forests have multiple functions when trees are alive, and also when they are no longer living.

Technology to transform biomass into useful liquid or gas products has existed for centuries. For example, gasifiers were used to transform wood into an automobile fuel during World War II, and the same technologies were also used to convert coal and natural gas into liquid fuels (Mousdale, 2008). Most of these technologies were not very efficient, economical, nor very climate-friendly until quite recently. Even though the technology to convert wood into liquid fuels has existed for more than 50 years, wood is still mainly combusted to produce energy. Several factors exclude trees from becoming the feedstock to produce liquid fuels, such as: (1) competing uses of wood for timber, a high-value global market product; and (2) solid fossil fuels can be converted less expensively into liquid fuels.

Forest, as well as agricultural, biomass is receiving much attention today for its potential to produce liquid fuels. The justification for producing and substituting biodiesel for 'petro'-diesel, a fossil fuel, is twofold: (1) it will decrease the amount of GHG released during fossil fuel combustion by the transportation sector; and (2) it will decrease a country's dependency upon foreign sources of oil. Certain energy sectors are receiving more attention than others because of the potential for non-fossil resources to substitute for the energy consumed by these industries. For example, over half of the total GHG emitted in the US in 1998 was from two energy-consuming sectors: electricity utilities (32 per cent of the total) and transportation (26 per cent). Substituting or supplementing for these energy demands, therefore, has the greatest potential to mitigate CO_2 emissions. The chemistry of forest materials allows them to be converted to products that can substitute for fossil fuel-powered energies.

The huge potential of biomass to produce the multiple products that society consumes daily is highlighted by how one process, biomass gasification, can serve as the entry point for a wide collection of chemical feedstocks that are all

Table 5.7 *Potential products produced from gasifying biomass to methanol*

Acetic acid (CH₃COOH) – an important acid in the food industry and a major precursor in the production of some plastics and fibres	**Ethylene** – used in plastics and as organic intermediates
Formaldehyde (CH₂O) – used to produce resins, textiles, cosmetics and fungicides	**Formic acid (HCOOH)** – a preservative
Methyl esters of organic and inorganic acids – used as solvents and methylation reagents in the production of explosives and insecticides	**Methyl halides** – solvents, organic intermediates and propellants
Methylamines – pharmaceutical precursors	**Trimethylphospine** – used to prepare pharmaceuticals, vitamins, fine chemicals, fragrances

Source: Mousdale, 2008

presently provided by petroleum (Mousdale, 2008). In this example, Mousdale documented the many materials and products that can be produced from just one product – methanol – a liquid fuel produced from forest materials or natural gas (Table 5.7).

The distinction between fossil carbon (i.e. solar capital) and renewable carbon (i.e. solar income) is less well understood by society, which is not familiar with all the carbon-based products that it consumes. There has been little consideration that our world would be a very different place if we eliminated carbon from fossil fuels as a feedstock for a wide number of products. Societal dependence on fossil carbon supplies not only will continue, but even now the emerging-economies are rapidly moving towards becoming fossil carbon-based economies. At the same time, countries are attempting to mitigate their CO_2 emissions, using renewable resources. A brief discussion will follow to demonstrate why forests can so easily replace products produced today from fossil fuels, especially oil.

Environmental challenges to biofuels

Using the full potential of biomass to generate energy and offset GHG emissions requires producing goods capable of substituting or supplementing for the fossil fuels consumed by certain industrial sectors of society (two-thirds of the methanol is produced from natural gas today, but could as easily be produced from forest or agricultural wastes). There are several ways of converting agricultural and forest biomass or wastes to bioliquids; however, some biomass materials are more efficiently and economically converted either to ethanol or to methanol because of their chemical composition. For example, wood biomass is not an ideal material to convert to ethanol until new technology emerges that can convert cellulosic wastes to sugar compounds. The efficiency and economics of conversion are important factors to consider, because the amount of CO_2 emission avoided depends on how much energy and fossil fuel is needed to produce the product compared to its energy content. The recently high efficiencies of conversion of wood biomass to methanol, and the need to thin forest to reduce its fire risk, makes it worth exploring the various ways that bio-methanol can further mitigate climate change (Vogt et al, 2009).

Today, technological developments in the conversion of biomass to other products have occurred because of the need to mitigate climate change. Done properly, it will provide greater environmental benefits than if the biomass is untouched or is discarded as waste. The biomass-driven strategy does not require extensive tree felling, but the collection of waste materials or small-sized stems and limbs of trees. There are many reasons that justify the removal of biomass materials from our landscapes. The risk from not removing the excess biomass and marginal wood is high because it contributes to forest fires and insect problems that plague forests in many regions of the world. The only current alternatives to this are prescribed burning within forests or the continued transportation of biomass wastes to landfills. If carbon-bearing material is buried, it reduces the atmospheric CO_2 – at least until other C-bearing products (e.g. methane) escape. If it decays, there is a slow return of CO_2 to the atmosphere with less (relative short-term) environmental gain relative to CO_2 than if it is buried. Neither of these options is good for the environment or public health. Even forests in the wildland–urban interfaces need to be managed to remove wood material that increases the risk of catastrophic fires (and later floods) to these areas. Biomass materials also have to be removed from our landscapes to provide conservation habitat and to eliminate woody invasive species, such as Scot's broom (*Cystisus scoparius*), from native habitats, or to restore the habitat qualities of highly altered forest environments.

The decrease in supplies of readily accessible fossil fuels is stimulating a global search for substitute alternative energy supplies. It has also resulted in countries setting targets for how much of their energy should be from renewable sources. European governments have set a goal of obtaining 10 per cent of their transportation fuels from biofuels by 2020. The US has set a target of replacing 30 per cent of its petroleum-based transportation fuels with liquid fuels generated from biomass. These targets suggest that an increasing proportion of the world's energy mix will be derived from biofuels. At first, this transition from fossil fuels to biofuels was lauded as the best means of eliminating the problems of greenhouse gases, climate change and dwindling fossil fuel supplies. Recently, however, countries have become more cautious in pursuing these goals and questioning the acceptability of the repercussions to both the environment and society resulting from the present methods of generating biofuels.

What went wrong, and why are the biofuel targets being questioned before their possible potential has been adequately tested? This critical re-evaluation of the benefits and costs of developing renewable energy sources is primarily being driven by the social and environmental concerns resulting from the use of food crops to produce energy, which has destabilized global markets for both food and energy. It is a complex story of the preferential use of agricultural crops to produce biofuels and the further degradation of forested areas by their conversion to grow these crops.

Biofuels have become embroiled in global discussions of energy security, food security and sustainable development instead of being widely lauded for their environmental benefits. This has slowed the progress of adopting them. Several countries and groupings, especially the EU, are reconsidering how rapidly they want to move toward adopting biofuels because of unresolved social and environmental concerns. They are also demanding verification that biofuel production is sustainable. Most of these concerns have focused on determining the following:

- Whether agricultural crops reduce carbon emissions when used to produce ethanol;
- How much energy is expended to grow and harvest a crop compared to the amount of energy produced;
- The land-use changes required to plant enough crops for both food and energy (e.g. previously forested areas converted to agricultural fields) and if that can be done without creating additional problems with soil erosion and water pollution;
- How much higher will food prices rise globally if crops are also used in the production of biofuels;
- Which food crops will no longer be available, as farmers switch to growing the more profitable crops used for biofuels.

To date, using food crops to produce biofuels has resulted in food shortages and higher food prices. The ultimate effect in international markets is food insecurities at local and regional scales. A recent World Bank report indicated that three-quarters of the total increases in global food prices were due to the diversion of food crops to produce biofuels. The civil unrest that occurred in 2008 in Mexico resulted from corn grown there being sold to the US instead of being consumed in Mexico as tortillas. This export was due to the higher prices being paid by the US for industries producing ethanol from corn.

If biofuels are to continue as a part of the solution to global energy shortages, the ongoing discussions must be refocused urgently so that they are effectively able to contribute towards improving the social, environmental and energy security on both the local and global scales. The first shift in this dialogue has to be to broaden the types of biomasses used to produce biofuels. A focus primarily on agricultural crops ignores the fact that all biomass types should be considered as the starting material. This is clear when one considers that even if all the corn and soya bean crops in the US were diverted from the food supply chain and were used to produce biofuels, they would replace only about 12 per cent of the gasoline and 6 per cent of the diesel consumed annually in the US. It is clear that just focusing on agricultural crops to produce biofuels in the US is a high risk option with an inadequate substitution ratio, when compared with the amount of gasoline already consumed. In addition, the amount of gasoline and energy required each year continues to increase. Despite this scenario, the US policy continues to emphasize using corn and soya beans to produce biofuels. As other countries develop their industries and increase their populations, they too will require more energy to maintain their positions in the global markets. Without energy, their economic systems will stagnate and perhaps crumble. A prime example of this is the current problem with energy production in Indonesia.

Regrettably, the current focus appears to be on adopting one biomass type for all regions of the world; for example, grasses have now become the plant of choice. There are several reasons in the media explaining why grasses are ideal: they grow rapidly and produce twice the amount of biomass annually compared to many other plants, and lower amounts of fossil fuels are needed to grow most grass species; therefore, carbon emissions are lower than those resulting from use of standard crops. Unfortunately, there are several negative attributes of the grasses proposed for use in the production of biofuels. Many are known to be invasive and their rapid growth is indicative of a well adapted plant that has a high probability of outcompeting native plants in the latter's own habitat. Land-use conversions are not diminished by growing grasses because they still need to be planted in new areas. In addition, not all areas of the globe requiring biofuels can grow these grasses. The key points are that all sustainable biomass sources should be used and the biomass source selected should be locally available.

The world's fossil fuel emissions of carbon increased by more than 20 per cent between 1990 and 2004, as did the proportion of fossil fuels used in the world's energy mix. There is an urgency to move towards new energy-production approaches that are able to mitigate carbon emissions while being socially responsible. Current practices have not been successful in shifting a greater proportion of our energy mix to renewable energy sources or in decreasing carbon emissions into the atmosphere during energy production or consumption. Changing these trends will require that we optimize our use of biofuels, but only by using biomass that has been determined to have the fewest possible social and environmental repercussions. In addition, the biomass that will work best in one area of the world will not necessarily work everywhere. Each location may need to determine its own unique biomass type in order to eliminate its own unique social and environmental problems. For example, in the western US (Vogt et al, 2008) total state carbon emissions can be reduced by 22.8–80.7 per cent when bio-methanol is substituted for gasoline. When forest fire risk is high and where most of the energy produced is from fuelwood (as in growing-economy countries), converting that wood to bio-methanol for the production of electricity is an attractive alternative. In Indonesia, using bio-methanol from forest materials to produce electricity and as a gasoline substitute has the potential to reduce total carbon emissions by 9–38 per cent and 8–35 per cent, respectively (Suntana et al, 2009).

Forest energy and sustainability from distributed energy production

Forests are ideally suited to provide distributed energy, but they are mostly being used in co-generation facilities that are large and centralized. This approach to producing energy from forest materials is expensive and cost-prohibitive in some local areas. Electricity is not the desired product in places where infrastructure limits and inadequacy deny the incorporation of the electricity into the power grid. In this situation it might be important to identify several different types of energy products for a locale so that a move to energy production from renewable resources does not stall. For example, Indonesia needs motor vehicle or motorcycle fuels as a higher priority than the production of electricity. In such a case, it makes sense to satisfy that need instead of just assuming that electricity generation is the ideal energy product.

With that in mind, what are the other approaches to produce energy products? Globally, forest and agricultural biomass wastes and materials have rapidly become accepted as one of the most suitable sources to convert to liquid fuels for energy production. Based on an economic analysis alone, investors are primarily funding the construction of large-scale biomass conversion facilities around the world. At this time it is important to question whether the building of large-scale infrastructures is the appropriate solution universally. Is this type of fixed site for production of biofuels sustainable? Is it beneficial to shift from these large stationary structures to small-scale mobile biomass conversion units to produce liquid fuels? Even though using biomass to produce biofuels is initially more economical at the large centralized facility scale, it is not appropriate or feasible at all locations. Many large-scale facilities have negative impacts on the environment and climate, as well as on humans. Most of the negative impacts of large-scale facilities result from their huge and centralized daily requirement for biomass, and the resultant use of fossil fuels or land conversion to obtain a sufficient biomass supply. The adoption of a distributed network of small-scale mobile facilities can be designed to eliminate a large portion of these negative environmental and climate impacts. In addition, recent technological breakthroughs in energy production make their implementation more economical.

Recently the building of several large-scale facilities has been placed on hold or have been cancelled because they were unable to acquire the investments needed. This halt was due to both global environmental concerns and food-security issues. If the use of biomass to produce energy is such a good idea, why are some proposed facilities being cancelled? The economics of scale drives the profitability of building a biomass-energy system because it determines the cost outlay to supply each infrastructure and the viability of the supply capacity existing in the local or regional area to feed the biomass demands of a large-scale facility. In general, the supply availability and cost of having to transport biomass from distances greater than 160km (~100miles) become prohibitive when transporting low-bulk-density materials, such as biomass. There is no guarantee that the supply will be available and the environmental costs increase significantly as the transportation distances increase. CHOREN Industries in Germany was very aware of this when it described what would be the ideal conditions to produce SunDiesel® from agricultural and forest biomasses. Its stated need is for an adequate local supply of biomass, a good transport infrastructure (railway, roads and shipping) and an integrated network with existing chemical plant/refineries. A key issue here is an adequate supply of biomass. This is a major issue to keep in mind when considering the location of a large facility or infrastructure to convert biomass to either biofuels or energy.

The economic and environmental costs of transportation must be considered as a major factor in determining whether a product will be produced or if it will supply a small niche market. In January 2008, *The New York Times* published an article on all of the sum total environmental costs (the amount of CO_2 emitted) per bottle of red wine cultivated in California and then sold in New York City markets. Of the total environmental costs, 56 per cent was due strictly to transportation. Wine has a high market value so that the transportation costs can be transferred to the buyer. However, this is not the case for biomass or its wastes, which are used to produce energy. Untransformed biomass has a high density and therefore costs more to transport. Biomass becomes valuable when it is converted into a liquid fuel that is transported to the marketplace, rather than transporting the biomass itself. These bio-liquid fuels have been competitive in global markets when compared to the subsidized fossil fuel energy supplies currently used worldwide.

There are cases where transportation costs and supply capacity are not an issue. For example, if biomass has already been transported to a facility because it is being converted to other high-end-market products (e.g. wood products, paper), transportation costs do not need to be factored into feasibility studies. In fact, under these circumstances, the biomass wastes can be burned in a boiler to make steam and then used to drive turbines to produce electricity without incurring significantly more costs. Sweden has been updating its existing pulp and papermill infrastructures with new technology that converts dry pulp waste into an alcohol (methanol) to supply emerging markets in transportation fuel mixtures. This has resulted in the addition of new products generated by pulp mills, utilizing wastes which were previously burnt or sent to landfills.

However, because most locations interested in using biomass for energy do not have existing infrastructures, such as the mills mentioned above, the transportation costs of moving biomass to a newly constructed facility can become expensive and cost-prohibitive. Furthermore, co-generation will probably not increase the use of biomass to produce energy, for the cost of building a new plant to produce these other products can be over US$100 million. Currently, producing energy using a similar type of technology is not worth pursuing because the energy generated from the biomass is converted at a low efficiency rate (about 20 per cent) and the economic trade-offs work for the 20–50MW range but not at smaller or even larger ranges.

What is driving the building of large-scale facilities? Economic analyses consistently report that only large-scale facilities will be economical to build. These analyses have focused investors on funding large-scale facilities and avoiding the building of smaller scale or mobile facilities as they were not deemed economically feasible. Such an approach fails to consider the characteristics of biomass that make it extremely difficult and expensive to transport to a large-scale conversion facility located more than 160km from its supply source. Facilities such as SunDiesel in Germany are being located in areas where the cost of transportation is not relevant because it has been determined that sufficient biomass exists at that location. Unfortunately, that condition may change due to factors not considered, or unknown at this time.

Recently, the idea of mobile and small-scale facilities to convert biomass has received much more attention because of its ability to deal with the dispersed nature of most biomass supplies and to provide local–regional areas with liquid fuels. In December 2007, Stephen Trimble articulated a wider vision for Boeing Aerospace. A single, huge repository of biofuel feedstock to supply fuel to airlines was replaced with a distributed network of many smaller feedstocks to produce fuel locally; the feedstocks selected being those most appropriate for an area because of its geography and climate. Stephen Trimble compared this shift in vision as being similar to personal computers replacing mainframe computers as the dominant mode of interactivity and information exchange more than 20 years ago. This change could revolutionize the production of energy.

This vision of having a distributed network of feedstocks to produce biofuels would eliminate the supply–availability problems and the high costs that large-scale facilities experience. With the advent of small-scale, mobile facilities, the types of biomass that can be converted to biofuels increase, improving the economics of the facilities. The biomass particular to each location can be used, instead of attempting or needing to grow a larger amount of biomass per given land area, or focusing on the use of traditional food crops to produce the desired biofuels.

Scaling down facilities is by itself insufficient to improve the economics of converting biomass to liquid fuels. If the conversion of biomass continues to occur at the same efficiency as that which has occurred in the past (10–20 per cent), biomass conversion to biofuels will be a niche market in some localized regions where few other options exist for energy production. However, with the technology available today, efficiencies of conversion are higher and closer to a 50 per cent rate which makes smaller facilities very economical. The technological developments in the conversion as well as the development of fuel cells have brought down the barriers to the use of biomass for energy production.

Small-scale facilities become economical when all the costs – external and internal – are included in an economic analysis. The externalities are the factors that will determine whether society will accept biofuel production and the ultimate costs of adopting biofuels. These externalities include:

1   Energy security;
2   Higher paying jobs and new markets;
3   Climate-change mitigation;
4   Maintaining environmental/ecosystem services and human health;

5   Reduction in fire risk;
6   National and regional regulations.

Today we should shift from trying to implement a single, universal solution to our energy problems and include the other factors that are important to society when they decide what energy options to adopt. The building of centralized facilities to convert biomass to liquid fuels is a model that needs to be implemented in those areas where it is appropriate and the supply chain is adequate and economical (e.g. pulp mills). This model, however, is not appropriate in areas with no previously existing large-scale infrastructure or where the transportation distances make it too expensive or uneconomical. This model is also not appropriate where the existing power lines to transport the produced energy are not in place.

Because of technological breakthroughs in fuel cells and their use in small appliances, the conversion of biomass to liquid fuels is worth pursuing at the small scale. One of the liquid fuels, methanol, is already being used by several companies (e.g. Toshiba, Casio, IdaTech, Protonex and MTI Micro) to power fuel cells as replacement systems for batteries, as critical backup power units in telecommunications and for utilities, to produce electricity and transportation fuels. One fuel cartridge is designed to charge an average cellphone battery over eight times. This would allow average users to power their cellphone for about one month. Such technology would dramatically improve the livelihoods of people living in areas where it is too expensive to install and maintain large electrical distribution infrastructures.

Biofuel markets have to be green to be economical. Small-scale and mobile biofuel facilities can avoid the environmental impacts that may result from large-scale facilities. If we do not adopt different models for energy production and adapt to the cultural context of a region, the use of biomass to produce liquid biofuels will be hampered. It is urgent that we expand our models of energy production beyond the large-scale facilities that are so dominant today. Brazil has very effectively leveraged its production of ethanol from sugar cane and supplies many global markets (such as Sweden, Indonesia and China). This solution works for Brazil, but it is a model that cannot and should not be emulated around the world. There are many environmental repercussions (e.g. climate change, land-use conversion, etc.) to maintaining large-scale biofuel production facilities, and these are becoming less acceptable globally. As noted above, a good example is Europe, which is buying only those biofuels that can be certified as not increasing CO_2 emissions and not resulting in land transformations that are considered detrimental to the environment.

Forest Uses have Negative Environmental Repercussions Elsewhere

When using forests for human development we need to deal with the fact that historical collection of forest materials has not always been environmentally or

Figure 5.3 *Caricature of the link between deforestation in Siberia and the loss of corridors for woodpeckers to migrate to Finland's protected forests*

socially sustainable. For the most part, recognition of the unsustainable uses of forests becomes apparent subsequent to an environmental disaster. Many examples exist where an environmental decision made by one or two consumer countries may negatively feedback on the environment of the producer country. For example, Finland and China are protecting their forests but continuing to consume timber harvested from Russia (Mayer et al, 2006).

China is protecting its forests because of the widespread flooding and accelerated desertification that resulted from the high deforestation rates that occurred prior to 1998. Finland is attempting to increase the amount of protected area it has in its southern region in order to meet its conservation goals. This means that China and Finland have increased the amount of timber products they are importing from Russian forests. The only problem with this decision is that several migratory animals have an important part of their life-cycle in Russian forests. The rare, white-backed woodpecker is a focal species of late successional-stage deciduous forests and Finland is dependent on this periodic immigration from Russia to maintain the population size and the genetic diversity of this species. In fact, many of the boreal species disperse from Russia to Sweden and Norway using northern Finnish forests as a corridor. Therefore, when Russia cuts down part of this forest and exports the timber, this decision has negative repercussion on forest biodiversity in Finland and other parts of Scandinavia, because parts of the migratory corridor no longer exist. The felling of trees in Siberia is eliminating the habitat needed by some of these late-successional species and isolating them from the genetic diversity needed for healthy populations, as depicted in Figure 5.3. This shows that a localized decision to increase protected areas could have the opposite effect, a decrease in conservation success, because of choices made elsewhere.

China instituted regulations to protect its existing forests and to plant new forests for the ecosystem services (e.g. erosion control and water supplies) they provide. The Chinese government established the 1998 Natural Forest Conservation Program (NFCP) following severe deforestation which accelerated soil erosion and caused desertification and extensive flooding in large areas of China in 1998. Logging is now banned or restricted across more than half of its forests. About one-fifth of its land is forested today and China wants to increase its forest cover to about 26 per cent.

Protection of forests in China, however, has had repercussions on conservation efforts and led to illegal timber harvesting in forests outside of China. China began to import wood because local demand continued to be high (e.g. to build houses and for the production of wood products) and the low tariffs due to World Trade Organization regulations made this an inexpensive alternative for them. However, China is driving illegal timber harvesting in several parts of the world as a result of reducing harvests from their own forests. A cursory appraisal would suggest that China is being very environmentally aware by increasing its own forest area, but on the other hand it is stimulating deforestation in other regions while becoming the world's largest exporter of timber products and supporting its own economic development.

According to Laurance (2008), half the timber traded on international markets goes to China from growing-economy countries; China is the largest consumer of timber from Southeast Asia and Russia. In 2007, it was estimated that 'at least 80 per cent of Chinese timber imports from Brazil, Cambodia, Cameroon, Congo-Brazzaville, Equatorial Guinea, Gabon, Indonesia, Myanmar, Papua New Guinea and the Solomon Islands was illegal ... (50–60 per cent) of China's import from Malaysia and Russia were estimated to be illegal.' (Laurance, 2008). It required only ten years for China to switch from being a net importer of wood products to becoming the leading exporter of 'furniture, plywood and wood flooring' (Lovett, 2007) using these timber supplies. Today, China is attempting to reduce this reliance on imported timber from all these countries and to ensure that smuggled logs are not consumed by its industries producing these export products (Wang et al, 2008). However, the supply chains are so long and varied that it is difficult to verify the origin of most timber (Lovett, 2007) to ensure that the supply sources are being collected sustainably.

The lesson learnt from the Chinese example is that Indonesia should not develop large export markets that require the importation of forest materials from other parts of the world, but should use its abundant forests to produce products that provide economic return within the country (e.g. biofuels) and can be consumed locally. It seems paradoxical to suggest that Indonesia should use its forests to produce energy when unsustainable practices have been occurring in these forests. Forest fires, illegal logging and forest conversion to agriculture and palm-oil plantations for food and to produce bio-diesel have resulted in unsustainable practices. WWF reported that 1.8 million hectares of forest were converted to palm oil plantations in 2007. Most of the new palm oil plantations are being used to satisfy the burgeoning biodiesel industry and most of the oil was exported to the EU before it imposed restrictions in 2007. According to FWI-GFW (2002) the illegal logging has resulted in 47.1 million hectares of Indonesian forests becoming degraded, and revenue losses of IDR30 trillion or over US$3 billion (FWI/GFW, 2002). These unsustainable forest management practices have been driven by the economic opportunities. To deal with them, Indonesia needs to develop products with higher economic value, and to satisfy the energy needs of rural communities with the production of forest products that provide sufficient economic return, while also being environmental. The approach is not to import forest materials from other countries but to become self-sufficient and to produce environmentally friendly products from the abundant forests that still remain in the Indonesian landscape.

References

AFPA (2004) '"Illegal" logging and global wood markets: the competitive impacts on the U.S. wood products industry', American Forest and Paper Association, November 2004

EIA (2009) 'EIA', www.eia.doe.gov/emeu/cabs/China/Oil.html, accessed 20 February 2008

FAO (2000) 'World Soil Resources Report 90. Land Resource Potential and Constraints at Regional and Country Levels', UN FAO, Rome, Italy

FAO (2006) 'Global Forest Resources Assessment 2005', UN FAO, Rome, Italy

Friel, T. (2002) 'Despite surplus, India can't feed growing hungry', *Reuters News Service*, 24 October 2002, accessed 10 March 2009

FWI/GFW (2002) *The State of the Forest: Indonesia*, Forest Watch Indonesia and Global Forest Watch, Bogor, Indonesia and Washington, DC

Goodman, P. S. and Finn, P. (2007) 'Corruption stains timber trade. Forests destroyed in China's race to feed global wood-processing industry', *Washington Post Foreign Service*, 1 April 2007, pA01

IEA (2007) *2007 Key World Energy Statistics*, International Energy Agency, http://tonto.eia.doe.gov/country/country_energy_data.cfm?fips=AO, accessed 1 September 2008

IPCC (2003) 'IPCC meeting current scientific understanding of the processes affecting terrestrial carbon stocks and human influences on them', *IPCC Working Group I Technical Support Unit*, expert meeting report, Geneva, Switzerland, www.ipcc.ch/pub/carbon.pdf, accessed 4 June 2004

Kotra, R. (2008) 'Dealing with disaster debris', *Biomass Magazine*, September 2008

Laurance, W. F. (2008) 'The need to cut China's illegal timber imports', *Science*, vol 319, pp1184

Lovett, J. (2007) 'World must seek change in China timber trade – report', 10 May 2007, *Reuters News Service*, www.planetark.com/dailynewsstory.cfm/newsid/41814/story.htm, accessed 10 January 2009

Mayer, A. L., Kauppi, P. E., Angelstam, P. K., Zhang, Y. and Tikka, P. M. (2006) 'Importing timber, exporting ecological impact', *Science*, vol 308, pp359–360

Mousdale, D. M. (2008) *Biofuels. Biotechnology, Chemistry and Sustainable Development*, CRC Press, Taylor & Francis Group, Boca Raton, FL

Romero, S. (2009) 'As blackouts hit energy-rich Venezuela, the President tells people to cut back', *New York Times*, 11 November 2009, pA5

Suntana, A. S., Vogt, K. A., Turnblom, E. C. and Upadhye, R. (2009) 'Bio-energy potential in Indonesia: forest biomass as a source of biofuels that reduces carbon emissions', *Applied Energy*, vol 86, supplement 1, ppS215–S221

USFS (2003) 'A strategic assessment of forest biomass and fuel reduction treatments in western states', *USDA FS Research & Development in partnership with Western Forestry Coalition*, www.fs.fed.us/research/pdf/Western_final.pdf, accessed 30 June 2006

Vogt, K. A., Vogt, D. J., Patel-Weynand, T., Upadhye, R., Edlund, D., Gordon, C., Suntana, A. S., Edmonds, R. L., Sigurdardottir, R., Roads, P. A. and Andreu, M. G. (2008) 'Why forest derived biofuels can mitigate climate change: the case for C-based energy production', *Renewable Energy*, vol 34, pp233–241

Vogt, D. J., Vogt, K. A., Gordon, J. C., Miller, M. L., Mukumoto, C., Upadhye, R. and Miller M. H. (2009). 'Wood methanol as a renewable energy source in some western states', in B. Solomon and V. A. Luzadis (eds), *Renewable Energy from Forest Resources in the United States*, Routledge Publishing, Taylor & Francis Group, London and New York, NY

Wang, G., Innes, J. L., Wu, S. W., Dai, S. and Lei, J. (2008) 'Response', *Science*, vol 319, pp1184–1185

WHO/UNDP (2004) 'Indoor air pollution – the killer in the kitchen', Joint Statement WHO/UNDP, Geneva, www.who.int/mediacentre/news/statements/2004/statement5/en/index.html, accessed 10 December 2008

WHO (2007) 'Country profiles of environmental burden of disease and country profiles', World Health Organization, Public Health and the Environment, Geneva, Switzerland, www.who.int/countries/ago/en/, accessed 10 December 2008

World Bank (2007) *Growth and CO_2 emissions: How do different countries fare?*, Environment Department, The World Bank, Washington, DC

WRI (2009) 'EarthTrends Searchable Database Results', World Resources Institute http://earthtrends.wri.org, accessed 3 July 2009

Wunder, S. (2003) *Oil wealth and the fate of the forest: a comparative study of eight tropical countries*, Routledge Publishing, Taylor & Francis Group, London and New York

6

The Soil and Water Connection to Food: Adapt, Mitigate or Die

What Constrains Local Food Production?

It is noteworthy that only five of the 34 countries allocated a major portion of their land to grow food crops. The five countries included advanced-economy, emerging-economy as well as growing-economy countries (Bangladesh, China, India, Nigeria and the UK) (Table 6.1). One-third of the countries included in our list use half of their total land area to grow crops. Despite these differences in the amount of land allocated to food production, there is no relationship between the HDI ranking of a country and its allocation of land to agriculture. This noticeable lack of relationship highlights the greater importance of soil characteristics and climates in determining whether or not it is realistic for a country to invest in local agricultural production (see Chapters 7 and 8).

It is informative to examine the soil factors (e.g. the severity of degradation and soil chemistry) that will determine whether or not a country will be able to

Table 6.1 *Country land area in agriculture in 2005*

%	Land area in agriculture, % of total (by country)
> 80–100	22
> 60–80	4, 7, 14, 30
> 40–60	1, 2, 3, 10, 11, 12, 18, 19, 21, 25, 27, 32
> 20–40	5, 15, 17, 20, 31, 33, 34
> 0.1–20	6, 8, 9, 16, 23, 24, 26, 28, 29
0	13

Note: Country numbers in boxes: 1 – Angola; 2 – Argentina; 3 – Australia; 4 – Bangladesh; 5 – Brazil; 6 – Canada; 7 – China; 8 – Congo DR, 9 – Finland; 10 – France; 11 – Germany; 12 – Haiti; 13 – Iceland; 14 – India; 15 – Indonesia; 16 – Japan; 17 – Malaysia; 18 – Mexico; 19 – Namibia; 20 – Nepal; 21 – Netherlands; 22 – Nigeria; 23 – Norway; 24 – Peru; 25 – Philippines; 26 – Russian Federation; 27 – Sudan; 28 – Sweden; 29 – United Arab Emirates; 30 – United Kingdom; 31 – United Republic of Tanzania; 32 – United States; 33 – Venezuela; 34 – Yemen
Source: FAO, 2008; World Bank, 2008

manage its lands to produce food locally. This information is not gleaned from calculations of the agricultural footprint per capita because this does not reflect the constraints that limit crop production.

It is relatively clear that in most lands soil constraints will reduce crop growth (see Chapter 8). Knowing the chemical constraints in soils that will limit crop growth allows one to determine if it will require a considerable amount of financial and resource investment to improve the productivity of an agricultural field. This understanding also informs a country whether or not it should alter its farming practice to reduce the negative environmental externalities.

Soil chemistry – sets the threshold for food production

The soil chemistry will determine what management activities can be implemented to increase crop production or when management will be unable to compensate for the toxic constraints imposed by soil chemistry. When farmers cannot compensate for their soil constraints, it will be more difficult for them to grow food crops locally. The countries in our list (Table 6.2) are categorized into the different factors that constrain agricultural production in each country. In most countries, more than one factor reduces agricultural production; obviously those factors need to be managed if high crop yields are to be expected.

The most difficult soils to manage are those where Al levels are toxic to plant growth; soils with higher Al also tend to have low base cations and are highly acidic (e.g. oxisols). All these factors reduce plant productivities. Out of the 34 countries examined here, five stand out as having major problems with Al toxicity (Table 6.2). These are all found in tropical climatic zones and face serious challenges to increasing their food production. For example, over 60 per cent of arable lands in Brazil, Congo DR and Malaysia have high Al toxicity problems. Venezuela (55 per cent Al toxicity problems) and Peru (43 per cent) also face serious challenges in growing food crops.

Some crops grow well in soils with higher Al levels, but most crops grown today are not tolerant of this element. Many traditional subsistence agriculturalists grow mostly root crops such as cassava and yams instead of cereal crops, because of the Al found in their soils (FAO, 2000). Tea and pineapple are commonly planted in the tropics because they are also tolerant of higher Al levels. Soils high in Al are difficult to manage using fertilizers. These soils could be managed by adding lime but the large amounts needed to change the soil chemistry are generally not economic; these countries typically do not have local supplies of lime which would make this an affordable option (FAO, 2000).

Another soil constraint, mainly in the semi-arid and arid zones, is salinity (FAO, 2000). From our country list, four countries stand out as needing to manage soil salinity levels: Argentina (12 per cent salinity); Bangladesh (7 per cent); India (7 per cent) and Tanzania (13 per cent). Once these soils accumulate salts, it is difficult to restore them to enable crop-growing; mitigating these soils requires expensive irrigation systems or access to non-saline water (FAO, 2000). There are a few salt-tolerant crops that could be grown in these soils, such as date

Table 6.2 *Grouping of countries into soil and climatic constraints to crop growth. A country may appear in more than one category*

Categories	Countries
High potential arable land (> 40% of total land area)	Angola, Argentina, Australia, Bangladesh, China, France, Germany, Haiti, India, Mexico, Namibia, Philippines, Netherlands, Nigeria, Sudan, UK, US
High realistic arable land after removing severely degraded from total (> 40% of total land area)	Australia, Bangladesh, France, Netherlands, UK
No arable land remaining after removing severely degraded lands from the total	Finland, Haiti, Indonesia, Malaysia, Peru, Russia, Sweden, UAE, Yemen
More than half of the arable lands with no degradation	Angola, Canada, Japan, Namibia, Norway, Russia
Agricultural lands degraded due to agriculture (~ 20–25% of arable lands degraded)	Bangladesh, China, Germany, Mexico, Nigeria, Sudan, US, UAE
More than 40% of arable lands severely degraded	Haiti, India, Malaysia, Mexico, Nigeria, Yemen
Agriculture constrained by low CEC (~20–33% of arable lands with low CEC)	Angola, Congo DR, India, Indonesia, Namibia
Agriculture faces constraints of high Al (> 25% of land has Al toxicity)	Brazil, Congo DR, Indonesia, Japan, Malaysia, Nepal, Peru, Philippines, Tanzania, Venezuela
Agriculture faces constraints of high erosion risk (~ 30% or higher erosion risk)	Haiti, India, Indonesia, Japan, Malaysia, Nepal, Peru, Philippines, UK, Venezuela
Desertification risk (> 50% risk)	Argentina, Australia, Canada, China, Finland, India, Mexico, Namibia, Russia, Sudan, Yemen
Drought risk: high and extremely high (< 40% annual renewable water supplies from endogenous precipitation)	Angola, Argentina, Australia, Bangladesh, Brazil, Congo DR, France, Haiti, India, Mexico, Namibia, Netherlands, Nigeria, Sudan, UAE, Tanzania, US, Yemen
Agriculture faces constraints of high climate risk (Germanwatch Global Climate Risk Index)	Angola, Iceland, Norway, Finland, Namibia, United Arab Emirates, Yemen

palm, barley and cotton (FAO, 2000) but society will not survive by eating barley and date palm alone. On the positive side, in areas where secondary salinity is a problem, people will have clothing to wear because cotton plants grow well in soils high in salts.

Even though Al toxicities and soil salinities are difficult to manage, farmers have effectively managed other soil constraints such as nutrient deficiencies and water supplies. The norm is for most countries to irrigate and/or fertilize their lands to alleviate these soil constraints to crop growth (Table 6.3). In the past, some creative approaches were developed by farmers to increase the organic

Table 6.3 *Percentage arable land irrigated (2003) and fertilized (2002)*

Irrigated range (%)	Arable land irrigated, %	Fertilizer consumption (kg/ha fertilizer)	Fertilizer consumption (kg/ha arable land)
> 80–100	—	549–683	17, 29
> 60–80	—	412–548	—
> 40–60	21	275–411	7, 16, 21, 30
> 20–40	4, 7, 14, 16,18, 20, 24, 34	138–274	4, 10, 11, 13,15, 23
> 0.1–20	1, 2, 3, 5, 6, 9, 10,11, 12, 15, 17, 19, 22, 23, 25, 26, 27, 28, 30, 31, 32, 33	137–0.1	2, 3, 5, 6,8, 9, 12, 14, 18, 20, 22, 24, 25, 26, 27, 28, 31, 32, 33, 34
0	8, 13		0 1, 19

Note: Country numbers in boxes: 1 – Angola; 2 – Argentina; 3 – Australia; 4 – Bangladesh; 5 – Brazil; 6 – Canada; 7 – China; 8 – Congo DR, 9 – Finland; 10 – France; 11 – Germany; 12 – Haiti; 13 – Iceland; 14 – India; 15 – Indonesia; 16 – Japan; 17 – Malaysia; 18 – Mexico; 19 – Namibia; 20 – Nepal; 21 – Netherlands; 22 – Nigeria; 23 – Norway; 24 – Peru; 25 – Philippines; 26 – Russian Federation; 27 – Sudan; 28 – Sweden; 29 – United Arab Emirates; 30 – United Kingdom; 31 – United Republic of Tanzania; 32 – United States; 33 – Venezuela; 34 – Yemen
Source: FAO, 2000; FAO, 2006

matter contents (such as the addition of charcoal into soils) and, thereby, soil nutrient levels; these approaches are even being considered for adoption today. Farmers have adapted superbly to most of their local soil constraints.

One might assume that the ability to apply fertilizers and to irrigate is a characteristic of countries that are more highly developed; however, for the 34 countries in our database there is no relationship between these variables. Nigeria uses the highest percentage of its land for food production (81 per cent) but irrigates less than 1 per cent, and applies the lowest level of fertilizers compared to the other countries (Table 6.2). The UK has 70 per cent of its land-use in agriculture but only irrigates 3 per cent of its arable land, yet applies 307kg/ha of fertilizers annually. Both China and India have similar percentages of their total land-base in agricultural production (~ 60 per cent) and irrigate just over one-third of their arable lands; however, China applies almost 2.5 times the amount of fertilizer per hectare of land as India.

Rates of irrigation and fertilizer application reflect a country's priority for increasing productive capacity. Interestingly, the highest levels of fertilizer application occur in Malaysia and the UAE, even though they have a comparatively lower percentage of their land in agriculture (24 per cent in Malaysia, 1 per cent in the UAE) (Table 6.3). These data do not reflect the fact that some countries, such as Iceland, consume relatively high levels of fertilizers but have little of their land in agriculture; most of the fertilizers are used to grow grain for horses and sheep. For the 34 countries included here, the country that irrigates the highest percentage of its lands (60 per cent) is the Netherlands. Because agriculture there is an important economic activity, with 57 per cent of the land used for agricultural activities, these high irrigation rates are logical.

Severely degraded lands and food production

Despite the lack of any clear patterns between the HDI of a country and how much of its economy is dependent on agriculture, the higher HDI-ranked countries appear to have less of their land classified as severely degraded. Therefore, if the severely degraded land became unavailable for agriculture, these countries would not significantly reduce their agricultural land-base. Germany, Sweden, the UK and the US are exceptions to this pattern because their arable land-base would be reduced by 25–32 per cent if this were to occur. Australia, Canada, Japan, the Netherlands and Norway stand out from the group as most of their arable lands are quite healthy. In these countries, removing degraded lands from agricultural production does not significantly change the total land area that could be used to grow crops.

Many of the emerging-economy and growing-economy countries will lose from 11 per cent to 83 per cent of their arable land for crop production if they are unable to use their severely degraded lands for agriculture. At one extreme, if Malaysia is unable to grow crops on its degraded lands, it will have no agricultural land-base left to grow crops. Another outlier in this group of HDI countries is the Philippines. The agricultural land-base of the Philippines will not vary significantly if they cannot grow food crops on their severely degraded lands.

One of the low HDI-ranked countries, Nigeria, will face severe difficulties in growing sufficient food for its people if the severely degraded lands cannot be used for agricultural production. Nigeria stands out from these countries because its arable land area reduces from 91 per cent to 36 per cent when the severely degraded lands are not included in the total arable land count. It is also the only country in this HDI-ranking group that will face climate-risk impacts on its agricultural production.

In contrast to Nigeria, the other three low HDI-ranked countries (Angola, Congo DR and Tanzania) have less severely degraded lands; therefore, removing these lands from the total agricultural land area will not limit their crop production. These data do not include the other constraints that the FAO has identified as having an impact on agricultural production. Further, the data do not show the impact of having to use a significant portion of annual water withdrawals for agriculture; this ranges from 31 per cent in Nigeria to 89 per cent in Tanzania.

Because the productive capacity of soils is based on several factors, being able to manage only one aspect of a soil's physical, biological, and/or chemical characteristics will not convert a degraded land into a productive farm. Soil fertility, for example, cannot be just managed by applying fertilizers to improve the site quality for plant growth. Soil fertility is influenced by the soil's organic-matter content, its acidity, texture and depth (Gruhn et al, 2000). The same factors determining the fertility levels of a soil also control its water-holding capacity. This means that it may be difficult to grow food in some locations if sustainable production is the goal.

Water Security and Soils

There are many ways to calculate whether a country has secure water supplies. It is useful to know how much of the total renewable water resources originate outside the country boundaries. It is also revealing to know what quantity are recharged by endogenous precipitation (Table 6.4). Both metrics indicate whether a country might be vulnerable in maintaining its water supplies. Several countries – Argentina, Bangladesh, Namibia, the Netherlands and Sudan – are ranked as being highly dependent on water supplies originating outside their borders, by having less than 40 per cent of their annual renewable water supplies renewed by endogenous precipitation. These countries will be especially vulnerable to changes in their water supplies due to climate change if the frequency of drought cycles increases. Argentina has already encountered several years of severe droughts that have reduced its economic growth. Despite the rainfall data and water supplies in rivers, which indicate the vulnerability of these countries to drought, soil data suggest that Argentina, Bangladesh and the Netherlands have an extremely low desertification risk, and Namibia has a medium desertification risk. These different data suggest very different country vulnerabilities to reductions in water supplies due to climate change.

These data also suggest that there are several countries that have a low risk of water insecurities because they obtain very little or none of their water outside the country borders and have more than 80 per cent of the renewable water supplies recharged by endogenous precipitation. Iceland, Japan, Malaysia, Norway, Peru, Philippines, Nepal and Sweden are included in this low-risk group. The high number of Scandinavian countries in this group is noteworthy. Also noteworthy in this group is the inclusion of four tropical countries that have high levels of precipitation. All of these countries have a low risk of desertification.

It becomes notable that only a few countries in our list have high-dependency ratios, i.e. reliance on a significant portion of their water resources originating outside their borders (Table 6.4). Almost all of the countries have an extremely low dependency for water supplies that originates outside their borders. Therefore, there is no relationship between the human development ranking of a country and its dependency on acquiring water supplies outside of its borders. For example, the Netherlands, with 88 per cent of its water supplies originating outside its borders, is an extreme example of a country highly dependent on outside water sources. Similarly, Bangladesh obtains 91 per cent of its water outside its boundaries, followed by Sudan with a 77 per cent dependency ratio and Argentina and Namibia both with a 66 per cent dependency ratio.

The risk of desertification also is not related to the HDI ranking of a country (Table 6.5). These data suggest that the highest HDI-ranked countries potentially face the same risk for desertification as the lowest HDI-ranked countries.

None of the countries ranked as having a high or extremely high desertification risk is dependent on water supplies originating outside of the country borders. Only Angola has a high desertification risk; it obtains most of its annual water supplies from endogenous precipitation. Except for the Netherlands, this

Table 6.4 *Water dependency and drought risk rankings*

HDI		Dependency ratio (%)	Drought risk rank	HDI		Dependency ratio (%)	Drought risk rank
1	Iceland	Extremely low	Extremely low	3	Venezuela	Medium	Medium
	Norway	Extremely low	Extremely low		China	Extremely low	Medium
	Australia	Extremely low	Extremely high		Peru	Extremely low	Low
	Canada	Extremely low	Medium		Philippines	Extremely low	Low
	Sweden	Extremely low	Low		Indonesia	Extremely low	Medium
	Japan	Extremely low	Low	4	Namibia	High	Extremely high
	Netherlands	Extremely high	High		India	Low	High
	France	Extremely low	High	5	Bangladesh	Extremely high	High
	Finland	Extremely low	Medium		Nepal	Extremely low	Extremely low
	US	Extremely low	High		Haiti	Extremely low	High
	UK	Extremely low	Medium		Sudan	High	Extremely high
	Germany	Low	Medium		Yemen	Extremely low	Extremely high
2	Argentina	High	Extremely high	6	Nigeria	Low	High
	UAE	Extremely low	Extremely high		Tanzania	Extremely low	Extremely high
	Mexico	Extremely low	High		Angola	Extremely low	Extremely high
	Malaysia	Extremely low	Low		Congo DR	Low	High
	Russia	Extremely low	Medium				
	Brazil	Low	High				

Note: HDI = Human Development Index [Group 1 = HDI > 0.9; Group 2 = > 0.8–0.9; Group 3 = > 0.7–0.8; Group 4 = > 0.6–0.7; Group 5 = > 0.5–0.6; Group 6 = 0.4–0.5]
Risk rankings or dependencies of a country separated into 5 quartiles (based on per cent renewable water supplies from endogenous precipitation): Extremely low risk or no risk = 81–100 per cent; Low risk = 61–80 per cent; Medium risk = 41–60 per cent; High risk = 21–40 per cent; Extremely high risk = < 20 per cent
Source: FAO, 2000; FAO, 2006

dependency on water supplies originating outside of the country appears less important for a country than its risk for droughts. The Netherlands has an extremely high risk of being impacted by droughts because so much of the total renewable waters originate outside the country borders and it is dependent on endogenous precipitation for most of its renewable water supplies.

Except for Japan, countries with a high desertification risk do not irrigate their arable lands (Table 6.6). Japan was classified as having an extremely high desertification risk, but still irrigates 54 per cent of its arable lands. For the 34 countries examined here, four countries irrigate half or higher portions of their arable lands (e.g. Japan, the Netherlands, Bangladesh and Nepal). Bangladesh and the Netherlands are outliers because they irrigate more than half of their arable land; they have a high drought risk and need to acquire an extremely high portion of their total renewable water resources from outside their borders. Both Bangladesh and the Netherlands will need to consider carefully the choices they make related to water use because they are dependent on water supplies which they will be less able to control.

A few countries are ranked as facing extremely high drought risk because so much of their renewable water supplies originate from precipitation. The

Table 6.5 *Desertification risk by HDI country ranking groups*

HDI ranking group	Desertification risk (%), range
Group 1 = HDI >0.9	0–99
Group 2 = HDI 0.8–0.9	0–97
Group 3 = HDI 0.7–0.8	0–57
Group 4 = HDI 0.6–0.7	72–99
Group 5 = HDI 0.5–0.6	0–90
Group 6 = HDI 0.4–0.5	0–44

Note: Country groups by HDI rank: Group 1 = Australia, Canada, Finland, France, Germany, Iceland, Japan, Netherlands, Norway, Sweden, UK, US; Group 2 = Argentina, Brazil, Malaysia, Mexico, Russia, UAE; Group 3 = China, Indonesia, Peru, Philippines, Venezuela; Group 4 = India, Namibia; Group 5 = Bangladesh, Haiti, Nepal, Sudan, Yemen; Group 6 = Angola, Congo DR, Nigeria, Tanzania

countries that will be especially impacted by climate-change scenarios that alter average rainfall timing and intensity are: Angola, Argentina, Australia, Namibia, Sudan, Tanzania, UAE and Yemen. Several of these countries institutionalized water rationing programmes several times during the last ten years due to recurring droughts that have significantly impacted their economic growth.

Some countries (e.g. Yemen) have historically been successful in managing their water supplies. Today, they face considerable challenges as these traditional systems are not being maintained and there are competing demands for the limited water supplies. For example, the conflict between water uses for food or narcotic plants is a significant problem for Yemen (Worth, 2009). Even though water scarcity is a looming problem, it is estimated that more than half of Yemen's water supplies are diverted to growing qat – a plant with a mild narcotic effect when chewed. It has been difficult for Yemen to deal with these water shortages because of the internal civil conflicts and rising population densities. Worth (2009) reported that the Yemeni government has to truck water supplies to urban areas. Also most of the countryside does not have sufficient water supplies; many people are dependent upon drinking from the same cisterns used by their grazing

Table 6.6 *Percentage arable land irrigated by HDI country ranking groups*

HDI ranking group	Arable land irrigated (%), 2003
Group 1 = HDI > 0.9	0–60
Group 2 = HDI 0.8–0.9	4–23
Group 3 = HDI 0.7–0.8	13–37
Group 4 = HDI 0.6–0.7	1–33
Group 5 = HDI 0.5–0.6	11–56
Group 6 = HDI 0.4–0.5	0–4

Note: Country groups by HDI rank: Group 1 = Australia, Canada, Finland, France, Germany, Iceland, Japan, Netherlands, Norway, Sweden, UK, US; Group 2 = Argentina, Brazil, Malaysia, Mexico, Russia, UAE; Group 3 = China, Indonesia, Peru, Philippines, Venezuela; Group 4 = India, Namibia; Group 5 = Bangladesh, Haiti, Nepal, Sudan, Yemen; Group 6 = Angola, Congo DR, Nigeria, Tanzania animals. This situation is unfortunate, for Yemen has a long history of managing its water supplies using dams, which have persisted for more than 1,000 years, to collect rainfall. They also had effective traditional agricultural production practices which diminished in importance as grains began to be imported to Yemen in the 1960s. The current rates of water consumption are not sustainable in a country where droughts are common and where climate change will probably further aggravate water scarcities.

References

FAO (2000) 'World Soil Resources Report 90. Land Resource Potential and Constraints at Regional and Country Levels', UN FAO, Rome, Italy

FAO (2006) 'Global Forest Resources Assessment 2005', UN FAO, Rome, Italy

FAO (2008) 'FAO Statistics Household Survey Database', International Labour Organization and country publications, www.fao.org/docrep/011/ai476e/ai476e01.htm, 22 July 2009

Gruhn P., Goletti, F. and Yudelman, M. (2000) 'Integrated nutrient management, soil fertility and sustainable agriculture: current issues and future challenges', Food, Agriculture and the Environment Discussion Paper 32, International Food Policy Research Institute, Washington, DC

World Bank (2008) 'World Development Indicators database', April 2008, Washington, DC

Worth R. F. (2009) 'Thirsty plant steals water in dry Yemen. Farmers grow narcotics; drought fuels conflicts', *New York Times*, 1 November 2009, p9

Part 4

CLIMATE AND SOILS: UNAVOIDABLE CONSTRAINTS TO SOLAR CAPITAL

Today the challenges of being sustainable are global and are not unique to a group of countries and their human development ranking. Even countries ranked high by HDI face significant challenges in maintaining their historic development levels without degrading their environments. Of the 34 countries we studied, none of the 12 countries ranked the highest by HDI had a low environmental vulnerability (see Table 3.1). For this HDI group, Canada had the lowest environmental vulnerability rank but is still indexed as being environmentally 'at risk'. Except for France and Germany (both ranked as 'highly vulnerable') and Japan (ranked as 'extremely vulnerable'), the remaining countries in this HDI group are all ranked as being 'vulnerable'. Therefore, except for Canada, none of the countries ranked high by HDI can avoid the problem of having to manage and make choices related to their environments and bio-resources that factor-in what makes them environmentally vulnerable.

Unfortunately, the six emerging economies included in our list (especially China, India and Indonesia) are generally ranked as having environments that are 'high' to 'extreme' in their vulnerability to resource decisions. If this is a correct reflection of their situations, maintaining their bio-resource acquisition at current levels will be challenging, if the environments are not to be degraded. Similarly, Congo DR, Angola, Nigeria and Tanzania are ranked low by HDI and none are resilient to the resource choices they need to make. Angola, Congo DR and Tanzania are in better positions than most of the other countries examined here because they had low environmental vulnerabilities, being ranked as being 'at risk'. These countries are in sharp contrast to Nigeria, which is characterized as being 'highly at risk' and having both vulnerable environments with low bio-resource acquisition potentials. Knowing the vulnerabilities or environmental risks that a country faces does not provide it with an ability to determine the 'trigger points' that it needs to manage for making sustainable choices. Despite knowing a country's environmental vulnerability grade, using this information is still problematic when a country has to make resource choices while not degrading the environment.

This environmental vulnerability includes climate risk but not the constraints of the soils on a country's productive capacity. We suggest that focusing on a country's climate and soil constraints will make it easier to understand what its resource endowment is and how difficult sustainability will be. Knowing that a country is vulnerable environmentally is a first filter that can identify which countries are at risk for degrading their environments while making their resource choices. This information is inadequate by itself to make sustainable choices, unless climate and soil constraints are simultaneously factored in. Using the climate and soils filters will provide the next layer of filters because they provide the thresholds and inherent capacity of any land to provide resources.

Climate change is a common predicament all countries confront, because our resource consumption decisions can alter climates, which then feedback to impact our future ability to acquire our basic survival needs. Climates, especially when they impact available water supplies, constrain the productive capacity possible from a given plot of land. Climate change is superimposed on top of what is already an avoidable constraint: the soil's productive capacity. Unavoidable constraints are the topic of the next two chapters of this book; they determine how difficult it will be for a country to make sustainable choices, and overlie all the other indicators used to examine whether sustainable choices are being made, or how a country develops a profile of sustainability.

7

The FUTURE: Climate Change as a Global Driver Impacting Sustainability

In the past, when the soil environments and/or climates changed sufficiently to decrease a land's productive capacity, a common response of society was not to mitigate or adapt to the changes but to migrate or flee to other regions of the world in search of food or for lands to grow their food (see Chapters 1 and 10). This 4000–10,000-year history of human migration has been the norm, and an effective approach that allowed humans repeatedly to deal with periods of resource scarcity. When people migrated more than a thousand years ago from the Mediterranean region, they were producing food in areas that were more suitable to grow crops for consumption by family members who remained living in the home country (Wild, 1993). By migrating, humans improved their chances for surviving and probably increased their human development potential. For example, European colonialists who emigrated to North America, especially during the 17th century, were able to increase their socioeconomic status, something that would have been less likely if they had remained in Europe.

Today, it is much more difficult to migrate and improve your economic status with other people's resources or to use their land-base to grow your bio-resources. Unoccupied lands are difficult to find; in most cases someone already owns or controls access to the lands and their resources. Either permanent agricultural fields are established or resources are cyclically collected from lands where people have not built perm anent infrastructures because the local environment is not conducive for their continuous survival (see Chapter 2). In both situations, the productive capacity of the lands is managed. The norm is for most land areas to be closely monitored and for resources to be collected as they become available. Despite this lack of infrastructure development or the presence of a low human population density, someone still controls the collection of resources, such as oil or water, from these lands. Competition is fiercer for these limited resources and for the land's productive capacity. This situation means that it is more difficult for a group of people to migrate or flee to another area when the environment becomes less able to provide their survival needs. Consequently, people need to adapt to local environmental constraints, and humans have been very adaptable (see Chapter 11).

Generally, climate change appears to impact societies negatively because it reduces the bio-resource supply capacity of their lands. At other times, climate change may increase societal sustainability as resource supplies become more available. For example, in 2009 climate change began to reveal resource deposits that had not been readily accessible prior to this time. The melting of the glaciers at the North Pole revealed untapped mineral resource deposits at a time when technology exists to extract them. Immediately after it became clear that rich mineral deposits were being revealed, several countries (Canada, Denmark, Norway, Russia and the US) have worked at acquiring documentation to support their ownership of these newly exposed areas. They began to measure their territorial boundaries by declaring that their borders extended onto previously unclaimed portions of the continental shelf. A few countries, for example the Russian Federation, went so far as to use submarines to place a country flag on the ocean floor as an attempt to symbolize their ownership of these resources.

In the past, regional climatic conditions determined which societies were capable of consuming resources and being socially and environmentally resilient (de Blij, 2005; Fagan, 2008). Today and in the future, climates will control which options are available for a country to increase its human development potential using local resources and how much of the bio-resources consumed will have to be imported from countries better suited to provide them. For example, climate change is impacting farmland productivity in parts of India. Farmers in eastern India are currently facing severe problems with their food production because the monsoon rains have not delivered the rainfall they need to grow their crops. Majumbar (2009) wrote that 'India this year suffered its worst start to the vital monsoon rains in eight decades, causing drought in some states'. Joshi and Hadi (2009) also wrote that Citigroup has shown that there is a strong 'correlation between monsoons and private consumption'. If farmers are unable to plant their crops because of the lack of the monsoon rains, the economic repercussions are dire because stock investors have bought shares in companies that sell products to these affluent farmers (Joshi and Hadi, 2009). Being unable to grow food crops reduces the options India has available to develop its human capital.

Until climate change – which history tells us is inevitable (de Blij, 2005) – alters the biotic and abiotic environment at any given location, we can identify what opportunities exist today for a country to use its own resources for social and economic development. We need to recognize the constraints that climates impose on our ability to make sustainable choices. For example, an examination of the world climate map shows how countries such as Russia face obstacles to social development that are a result of most of their contiguous lands being located at latitudes greater than 40 degrees (de Blij, 2005). These obstacles are real despite the fact that Russia is the largest country in the world and has a significant land-base that could be used to grow and extract bio-resources. However, Russia has most of its land-base located in climatically restrictive environments where it is more difficult to increase the land's productive capacity. This demonstrates that the total land area is not a very useful metric to determine what choices a country has to develop its resource capital. A large land-base does not provide food security if most of it is located in areas where temperature limits plant growth. In Russia, the overriding climate control of a land's productive capacity is clearly evident.

Understanding the variable impacts of climate change across the diversity of biomes is fundamental to decoding sustainability and human survival. Humans have a long history of dealing with the impacts of climate change in environments that are either conducive for their survival or where human survival is mostly at the subsistence level. Furthermore, because climate change is not going to be uniformly layered across the globe, understanding the interplay between climates and the provision of bio-resources is crucial for society. Thus, climate change will strongly influence human development and wellbeing, as well as determining where it will be easier for humans to survive.

Even though climate is a great social equalizer because it does not selectively impact just the poor or the rich, people across the entire human development spectrum are forced to adapt. All members of human society have to adapt to the changing climate or any other constraints that have been introduced into their environment. However, rich people, with more mechanisms in place to adapt to an altered environment, are less susceptible to climate change.

Why People Migrate: Geography and Climate Influences on Humans

Past human responses to changing climates: Become a foreigner

It is not new for humans to migrate and expand their resource footprint at the same time. History has shown that humans pursued ephemeral and seasonal resources like many other animals. Humans have a history of being 'foreigners'. This has been a successful strategy that necessitated humans following the food source, such as Laplanders migrating with reindeer, or travelling to areas with higher pulses of abundant food supplies, such as Mongols travelling to grassland steppes where plants were most actively growing at the time (Fagan, 2008). At times human migration was driven by the need to search for new lands because population densities had become too high to feed the entire population from the existing land-base. This was a strong driver for the peoples who later became Norwegians and Danes to travel and colonize Greenland and Iceland (Diamond, 2005).

Animal migration is 'a spectacularly successful strategy among animals, providing access to a richness of ephemeral and seasonal resources that can sustain large populations' (Alerstam, 2008). In the past, migration served humans well, for it functioned as a safety valve for society. It allowed people to pursue resources elsewhere and to be resilient in the face of dynamic and pulsed availabilities of limiting bio-resources.

Historically, changes in local climates have also caused humans to migrate because of their impact, on increasing or decreasing the security of bio-resource supplies. Because climate change does not uniformly impact the globe, the benefits of global warming are not distributed equally. During periods of global warming, some regions of the world will become less suitable for human habitation, whereas another region may become more suitable for their survival. For example, medieval global warming made conditions in Europe very favourable for the humans living there (Fagan, 2008). During this period, Europe enjoyed years of prosperity because the longer and warmer growing season meant that more food could be grown. Human population densities increased and people began to live in cities because sufficient food could be produced by those remaining on the farms (de Blij, 2005).

The positive impacts of climate change in Europe were contrasted by other regions of the world where human survival potential decreased and societies collapsed. For example, 'catastrophic rainfall and intense droughts' severely reduced the survival of clusters of higher-population densities of people living in parts of India, western North America, margins of the deserts and the Eurasian steppes (Fagan, 2008). Civilizations, such as those of the Maya and the Anasazi, collapsed when intense droughts reduced their food supply capacities (Fagan, 2008). The differential impact of climate change on the local bio-resource supply capacity determined when and where people would migrate.

At other times, humans migrated in their search to replenish the bio-resource supplies they had already over-exploited on their own lands. Many historical documents have described how a group of people exploited someone else's bio-resources when they had over-consumed their own. Examples include the Romans harvesting cedar trees in what is the present-day Lebanon, and the British harvesting teak from India and pine from the Caribbean (Winters, 1974; Williams, 1989). Many countries became powerful because they were successful in invading and exploiting bio-resources owned by someone else. If these countries had been restricted to their own land-bases, they probably would not have become the global imperial powers that large bio-resource footprints made possible.

Industrialization also stimulated periods of human migration because new supplies of resources were needed to fuel this growth. This need for new resource supplies stimulated periods of conquest and war against countries uninterested in becoming the 'supplier' to these emerging industrial economies. Humans travelled over great distances and under difficult circumstances to search for new resources, and many lives were lost during these travels.

The Europeans who colonized present-day North America, Africa and Asia crossed large bodies of water (the Atlantic and Pacific Oceans) without knowing what they would find at the end of their journeys. The search for resources, however, was a powerful incentive to make these ocean voyages. The successful return of explorers with ships loaded with valuable resources, such as gold or spices, supported the idea that there were riches available and that they only needed to be harvested by an enterprising group.

Unfortunately, much of the acquisition of these resource riches resulted in the conquered people having unsustainable resource supplies. Their lifestyles were

Table 7.1 *Climatic variables correlated to HDI and energy*

Y variable	X variable	R^2
Human Development Index ranking	Annual minimum temperature	0.47
	Annual maximum temperature	0.56
Gross National Income	Annual minimum temperature	0.56
	Annual maximum temperature	0.63
Energy use (kg of oil equivalent per capita)	Precipitation	0.18
	Average minimum temperature, C	0.40
	Average maximum temperature, C	0.42

reduced as the resources on which they were dependent for their survival were shipped to the lands of the conquerors. These activities stimulated land-use changes that societies are still attempting to mitigate today.

When over-exploitation of resources degraded or altered human habitats, it also reduced the survival capacity of animals dependent on these same exploited habitats. Fragmentation also decreased animal migrations and their adaptation to their environment, for migratory animals consume higher pulses of ephemeral and seasonal bio-resources.

Climate Change and Humans

Climate directly impacts where people live. In the past it was the driver for people to migrate to other parts of the world to search for more suitable habitats capable of providing for their needs (see Chapter 2). Climate change has been implicated in the collapse of several societies when the environment no longer provided the bio-resources needed for survival in that area (Diamond, 2005). Today, climate change is becoming a major driver creating 'climate refugees'.

It is worth exploring how the components of climate, such as rainfall and temperature, influence the human development potential. Temperature indicators correlate well with several aspects of human development (Table 7.1).

In contrast to temperature, precipitation does not explain much of the variance in any of the factors included in our 34-country database. The only correlation with precipitation is that annual precipitation explains 30 per cent of the variance in how much of a country's land area is used for agriculture. Annual precipitation not explaining patterns of human habitation or the lands' bio-resource supply capacity is not unexpected. The seasonal timing of rainfall and its occurrence during periods of crop growth (Wild, 1993) are more important than measures of annual precipitation. Unfortunately, data are not readily available on the seasonal timing of rainfall for most countries.

Approximately half of the variance in the HDI ranking of a country is explained by its minimum or maximum annual temperatures. What these relationships suggest is that people living in hotter climates have a reduced capacity to develop their human capital. This relationship may also reflect the fact that the metrics used to evaluate the human development potential of a country were developed by people living in areas where the annual minimum temperatures are lower (Figure 7.1).

Scientific research suggests that merit can be found in the relationship between temperature and human development potential, if it is studied more closely. For example, some of the hotter and wetter regions of the world have a lower soil productive capacity because they have experienced higher rates of soil weathering due to their predominant climate: in other words, it rains frequently and intensively. This lower soil productive capacity has resulted from a thousand-year history of high rainfall that has eroded and leached essential soil nutrients needed by growing plants (Sanchez, 1976; this volume, Chapter 8). These reduced crop yields require people to expend more time and energy to grow the crops they need to survive. This reduces the time available for them to pursue activities that would increase their development potential. Today, these hot and wet regions of the world are the same locations where more people live in rural environments and need to survive by extracting local bio-resources.

Temperature appears effective in indexing a land's productive capacity and in determining the human survival needs that can be obtained from it. It is also a good index to the economic development potential of a country. For example, temperature indices explain more than half of the country-level variance in the

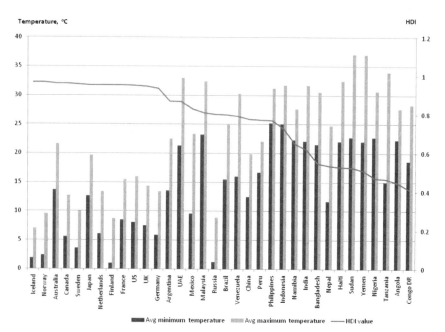

Figure 7.1 *The HDI values of countries plotted against the average annual minimum temperature and average annual maximum temperature*

Source: UN, 2007; WHO, 2007

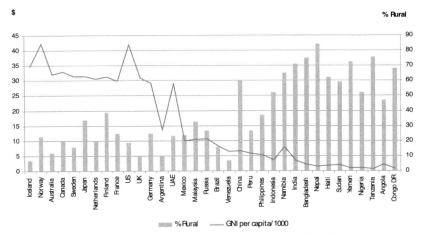

Figure 7.2 *GNI/capita and rural population (%)*

Source: UN, 2007; WHO, 2007

Gross National Income (GNI); as the maximum annual temperatures increase, the capacity of a country to achieve a high GNI decreases (Figure 4.2). This relationship appears logical, for it will be extremely difficult for a country to develop its economic potential if its people's basic survival needs are not being met. Our data comparisons show the links between insufficient food production and the need to have a larger proportion of the population involved in growing food when it is scarce. They also show that a country with a lower GNI has severe hunger problems, a greater proportion of the population living in rural areas and a greater proportion of the workforce producing food (Figure 7.2).

The link between living in colder regions of the world and achieving a higher HDI value is more difficult to explain. Our data do show that as the mean annual temperatures become colder, but still above freezing, the populations have higher income levels, are better educated and are healthier. It would be easy to state that these countries have slower rates of soil development and therefore, the soils are more productive for food production. Although this statement at first glance appears logical, soils are highly variable and humans have managed their soils for a long time to decrease constraints to food production. Therefore, countries with higher HDI are not those that have less weathered soils and, therefore, more secure food production. The unavoidable constraints that soils impose on human survival will be discussed in considerably more detail in Chapter 8. Even though the soil productive capacity may be less useful in explaining patterns of human development when temperatures are colder, it may explain the relationships that are found in the hotter regions of the world.

A superficial examination of temperature and human development relationships would suggest that having a higher annual mean temperature would be advantageous for a country because it would have a lower annual energy demand. Less energy is consumed to heat homes during the winter months because the temperatures are already comfortable; nor do people living in hotter climates cool their homes to the same degree as people living in colder climates heat their homes. This perspective explained the results of the assessment conducted by the National Geographic Society when it ranked countries as to whether they were making 'green' resource consumption decisions. It was found that countries with the highest maximum annual temperatures were ranked more highly as making 'green decisions' (National Geographic, 2008). In the National Geographic assessment, the amount of energy consumed for heating is an important criterion that explains the results of the rankings. Therefore, this evaluation results in a false sense that the 'right' decisions or choices are being made by these countries. In fact, the results of this ranking really reflect the fact that energy for heating is not a trade-off that needs to be made in countries with higher mean maximum annual temperatures.

Making green choices does not equate to how well a country has developed its human capital or how much its climate constrains development. Our data show that countries ranked high in the human development index consume more fossil-based energy per capita while adjusting to living with colder mean annual temperatures. The HDI rankings give a higher ranking to countries where more energy is consumed for heating purposes. The EPI rankings also give a higher environmental ranking to countries that consume higher levels of fossil-based energy for heating. Therefore, the need to consume fossil-based energy for heating does not appear to be a constraint to human development or a determining factor of whether a country can be highly ranked as being environmental.

Equating high human development to favourable environmental indices shows the influence of what data are selected for inclusion in an evaluation. For example, most of the high human development countries are also the largest emitters of CO_2, mainly due to high fossil fuel consumption and need for more energy per capita to keep warm. Our analysis suggests that the amount of CO_2 emitted is less relevant for evaluating whether a country is making environmental choices. An environmental ranking is more sensitive to the amount of land being converted from forests to other uses; if a country has had little land conversion, it is ranked higher in the environmental indices. The higher degree of ongoing land-use conversions in countries ranked lower in the HDI rankings explains why they are ranked as being less environmental. These same countries, mainly located in hotter regions of the world, do not consume a significant amount of fossil-based energy for cooling and most of their CO_2 emissions are derived from land-use changes instead of the consumption of fossil-based fuels (see Chapters 4 and 5). If CO_2 emissions are used as the sensitive metric to measure whether a country is environmental, these lower human development countries would probably be ranked higher and not lower by the environmental indices.

These comparisons made with temperature and human development indices do not explicitly consider that people may not always adapt well or migrate due to climate change. When people do not have an option to migrate, yet need to survive under the constraints imposed by their local climate, societies can become dysfunctional. This social dysfunction is frequently the result of a lack of knowledge of the scientific-based drivers of climate change, or unwillingness to accept that their high consumptive behaviour may have environmental consequences. When societies lack this knowledge or are unwilling to accept the repercussions of their actions, it reduces their ability to adapt. In these circumstances, climate change is attributed to inappropriate behaviour or beliefs held by members of a social group, which means there is no need to adapt. Packaging climate change as a social problem, that is, a belief or value, means that solutions become more 'cosmetic' than 'real'. Such an approach obtains short-term solutions to a climate problem and does not deal with the underlying causes that may make it more difficult for humans to survive.

Climate change and social dysfunctions

Humans have a long history of dealing ineffectively with climate change. These social vulnerabilities are only mentioned infrequently, for scientific assessments have focused on deciphering the direct biological impacts of climate change. Direct impacts of climate change (e.g. sea-level rise and a higher frequency of more severe hurricanes) have appeared to be easier to document or model, even though there is considerable uncertainty in these analyses. These unpredictable and inexplicable changes in climate are internalized by some societies unable to deal with their reduced access to resources.

History has documented how societies have attempted to either appease 'gods' with human sacrifices (as was practised by the Maya civilization), or to search for scapegoats (typically the marginalized people in a society), who can be held responsible for causing the unwanted impacts resulting from climate change. These reactions to climate change were driven by the expectation that killing or sacrificing an individual or groups of people responsible for the bad weather events would result in a return to the more desirable climatic conditions.

In the late 1500s, Europe experienced a 'little ice age', a sharp cooling that directly reduced the productive capacity of the lands and thereby people's access to bio-resources they needed to survive. This same time period coincided with a renewal in witchcraft trials (Kristof, 2008). Burning 'witches' was a simple solution, implemented in order to return climates to 'normal' so that bio-resources that people had previously enjoyed would become available again. These unusually colder climatic events occurred several times during the 250-year time period 1520–1770, and each colder climatic event coincided with an increase in witch burnings. Kristof (2008) accounted how a 'brutally cold May in 1626 led outraged peasants to call for punishment of witches thought responsible'. Because climates are normally cyclic and dynamic, it may have appeared to those involved in witch-burnings that their actions were justified, for climates did seem to return to some semblance of normality. During this several hundred-year period, there were no scientifically credible explanations for the unusual weather events that occurred in Europe. Blaming supernatural factors for the colder climates appeared to provide some control to a population that did not understand what was triggering these climatic events.

Dysfunctional responses by society to climate change are not just part of our history. They still happen today, when a society feels vulnerable to events it cannot explain or control. For example, Tanzania experienced severe drought in 2008 that resulted in poor crop growth. The droughts coincided with a doubling in the number of elderly women accused of being witches and executed with machetes (Kristof, 2008).

Unfortunately, some of the poorest countries in the world are those most impacted by climate change, and these are the same countries facing civil war and unrest (Smith and Barchiesis, 2009). Droughts are linked to increased risk that a civil war may erupt in socially less resilient environments. Kristof (2008) reported on research conducted by Professor Edward Miguel, an economist at the University of California at Berkeley, which 'suggests that a drought one year increases by 50 per cent the risk that an African country will slip into civil war the next year'. Diamond (2005) attributed the brutal killings that occurred in Rwanda to competition for agricultural lands to grow food crops, and the high population density of people attempting to live on the same small tracts of land. He did blame droughts, but it is clear that droughts will increase the competition for agricultural lands as food security decreases.

Recently, wars have occurred at a higher frequency in tropical countries compared to those located in the temperate climatic zones (Price, 2003). This is an unfortunate situation as many of these tropical countries already face severe challenges to growing abundant food because of the limitations of their soil chemistry (Chapter 8). Some of these countries, for example Nigeria, also have highly degraded soils. When agricultural lands are severely degraded, the ability of local people to acquire the bio-resources they need to survive is further reduced (Payne et al, 2002). Therefore, wars or civil conflicts are taking place in an environment that may already have a reduced productive capacity. Under these circumstances, climate change will further reduce the ability of people living in these areas to adapt to another disturbance.

The link between social stability and people's adaptation to the constraints of their climate, disturbances and soil environments has been increasingly recognized as an important attribute of sustainability (MEA, 2005). There are many global examples of a group of people becoming socially dysfunctional when it was evicted from its lands or had restricted access to the bio-resources that had traditionally been essential for its survival (Balmford et al, 2001; Dowie, 2005). When people are unable to adapt by migrating to new landscapes and have lost their traditional lands to harvest bio-resources, environmental degradation is a strong possibility. Dowie (2005) documented the many global examples of the loss of social and environmental sustainability due to people becoming 'conservation refugees'.

Climate change and human health

Climate change can impact human health in several ways but its main impact is through its modification of local temperatures and rainfall amounts. These climatic changes can increase the incidence and spread of disease vectors and the causal organisms of disease. We tend to focus on some diseases spread by mosquitoes (e.g. malaria) because a preponderance of evidence links climate change to mosquito-population fluctuations. When night-time temperatures are higher and there is more rainfall, the number of mosquitoes will increase significantly and malaria outbreaks will increase. Insects are very sensitive to small changes in climate. In fact, the minimum air temperature for the development of the malaria parasite is 15–18°C which is not an uncommon temperature in many parts of the world. Average room temperature is 20°C – a very comfortable and desirable temperature for most humans. This is also a good temperature for the spread of malaria.

The global weather patterns have increased the risk that people living in many of the tropical areas will be exposed to mosquitoes and will contract malaria. These climatic changes have been especially prevalent during El Niño events. For example, the El Niño of 1987 increased malaria outbreaks significantly in Rwanda. The El Niño of 1997–98 resulted in torrential rains in East Africa followed by epidemics of malaria in Uganda. All these changes will cause humans and wildlife to become more vulnerable to diseases.

Climate change, such as droughts, also impacts human health when it reduces food production. Because climates control the productive capacity of any land to produce food, it directly connects to human health. If climate change reduces the rainfall in an area, it will decrease the land's capacity to supply food. Less food means that malnutrition rates will increase, decreasing human resistance to diseases. The link between where one lives (e.g. hot or cold environments), and food supplies and nutrition, will be discussed in Chapter 8.

The impacts of climate change and the spread of disease organisms are not felt simultaneously worldwide. As summarized by Fagan (2008), some parts of the world will have higher rainfall events which will make them more susceptible to disease outbreaks, while other parts will become drier and less susceptible to diseases stimulated by higher rainfall. As noted above, some of the African countries are currently especially susceptible to disease outbreaks transmitted by mosquitoes, because climate change has produced the ideal conditions for their reproduction. The temperate and the more northern boreal climatic regions of the world have not been climatically ideal for the spread of disease vectors and disease organisms; however, climate change that results in higher temperatures and more rainfall will cause these disease organisms to spread, and become more common even in these temperate climatic zones.

In the tropical climatic zones, the spread of diseases has been aggravated by a lack of sanitary conditions, lack of control of the disease vectors such as mosquitoes, poor nutrition and malnutrition, and wars and civil conflicts. For example, Zimbabwe faced a major cholera epidemic in December 2008, but international aid workers were unable to help to control the epidemic because the government was unwilling to let international health workers into the country because of the political conflicts. On 6 January 2009, Angola closed its border with Congo DR in an attempt to avoid the spread of the ebola virus into Angola. At this time, this very contagious virus had already been implicated in the death of 13 people since the outbreak started in the Congo DR (Almeida, 2009). These are human health problems that could be managed if detected early and properly treated. This, of course, does not happen very often.

Water and Resources

Water supplies and human development

It is clear that climates are dynamic and that the history of human development has closely tracked climatically induced changes in regional renewable water supplies. Even though well-documented historical accounts link the development potential of the human capital to their access to clean water, water indicators (e.g. changes in water supplies and/or its availability, and water dependency) at the country level are not very useful in explaining the HDI patterns observed for the 34 countries (Table 7.2). Only the consumptive uses of water explain some of the variance in the human development ranking of a country; this trend exists only for the highest and the lowest HDI-ranked countries, but not for the remaining countries.

Most of the countries ranked higher in the HDI rankings use a higher percentage of their total water withdrawal for industrial purposes, while the countries ranked in the middle to the low end of the HDI rankings allocate most of their water to food production. When food production competes with water for drinking, farmers have been more successful in acquiring the limited water supplies as depicted in Figure 7.3. Most of the growing-economy countries have been unable to provide for all of the clean water needs of their citizens, since food production has priority for water supplies. In these water comparisons, the highest correlation is with the amount of total water withdrawals used in agriculture ($R^2 = 0.45$) and by the industrial sector ($R^2 = 0.44$). The highest HDI-ranked countries on average consume 23 per cent of their total water withdrawal in agriculture; 57 per cent is consumed by their industrial sectors.

The lack of many strong correlations with human development indicators and any water indicators may also reflect the fact that most societies have effectively

Table 7.2 *Correlations between HDI and water indicators*

Y variable	X variable	R^2
HDI ranking	Water footprint/capita [POSITIVE]	0.35
	% total water used in agriculture [NEGATIVE]	0.39
	% total water use in industry [POSITIVE]	0.44
	Water use in agriculture as % of total withdrawal [NEGATIVE]	0.45
	Virtual water export	0.18
	Virtual water import	0.24
	Resupply of aquifers from endogenous sources	0.18

Note: Variable [direction of relationship]
Source: FAO Water Resources Development and Management Service, 2003; FAO, 2005

Figure 7.3 *Caricature of competition for the same water supply by agriculture and for drinking*

adapted to water shortages by acquiring water for their people. This adaptation is suggested by the fact that most countries, except for the lower HDI-ranked countries, are able to provide sufficient access to clean water supplies for their people (Table 7.3). Whether this pattern can be maintained into the future is not clear, for acquiring renewable and chemical-free water is becoming more challenging.

More highly advanced-economy countries do not have their high ranking because of having better access to renewable water from endogenous precipitation (Table 7.3); resupply of aquifers from endogenous sources only explains 18 per cent of the variance in the HDI ranking of a country. This lack of a strong relationship is explained by the wide variation in how much of the resupply of aquifers is from endogenous rainfall within each of our HDI groups.

Table 7.3 *Water information by HDI country ranking groups*

HDI ranking	Annual flow from precipitation (%)	Dependency ratio (%)	Water use in agriculture (% total withdrawal)	Industrial water withdrawal (% total withdrawal)	2003 Arable land irrigated (%)	2006 Population with access to water source (%)
Group 1	52 [12–85]	12 [0–88]	23 [0–75]	57 [18–83]	15 [0–60]	100 [99–100]
Group 2	33 [3–61]	19 [0–66]	63 [18–83]	17 [2–63]	8 [4–23]	96 [91–100]
Group 3	57 [42–68]	12 [0–41]	72 [47–91]	11 [1–26]	22 [13–37]	86 [80–93]
Group 4	19 [3–35]	50 [34–66]	79 [71–87]	5 [5]	17 [1–33]	91 [89–93]
Group 5	32 [3–90]	36 [0–91]	95 [94–96]	2 [1–4]	31 [8–56]	73 [66–89]
Group 6	17 [8–25]	17 [0–30]	62 [31–89]	11 [1–17]	2 [0–4]	50 [46–55]

Notes: a) Grouping and their HDI ranking: Group 1 = HDI > 0.9; Group 2 = > 0.8–0.9; Group 3 = > 0.7–0.8; Group 4 = > 0.6–0.7; Group 5 = > 0.5–0.6; Group 6 = 0.4–0.5
b) % annual flow from precipitation = % annual flow into rivers and the recharge of aquifers generated from endogenous precipitation; Dependency ratio (%) = part of total renewable water resources originating outside country. Mean [range]
c) All data for 2000 unless noted otherwise
Source: FAO, 2000; FAO Water Resources Development and Management Service, 2003; FAO, 2008; World Bank, 2007

In the highest HDI-ranking group (Group 1), several countries stand out as having endogenous precipitation providing over 80 per cent of the renewable water consumed in-country (e.g. Iceland and Norway). However, it is the norm for most of these higher HDI countries to receive about half of their renewable water supplies from rainfall (e.g. Canada, Finland, Japan, Sweden and the UK). Australia is an outlier in this group, by obtaining only 12 per cent of its annual renewable water supplies from precipitation.

It is notable that countries in HDI Groups 4–6 receive little of their water supplies from rainfall. If one excludes Nepal (receiving 90 per cent of its renewable water from rainfall), the countries ranked in the middle to the lower end of HDI rankings have less than 33 per cent of their water resupplied from endogenous precipitation.

These data reflect how most countries have adapted to the water supply scenario they face. A country does not base its decision of how much water to use in agriculture, or how much to irrigate, on its endogenous supplies of water. The Netherlands exemplifies this well. It acquires 34 per cent of its renewable water supplies from annual endogenous precipitation; 88 per cent of its total renewable water resources originates from outside their country borders and it irrigates the largest proportion of its arable lands (60 per cent). Out of the 34 countries, only Bangladesh follows a similar trajectory of water acquisition and consumption as found in the Netherlands.

These data also indicate how much of our water consumption is derived from fossil sources. In many parts of the world, water sources are mainly from the subsurface. Our fresh renewable water sources comprise only 0.3 per cent of the total water found on and in the earth; most of that water is salty and not potable. The most disconcerting point about fossil-water supplies is that in most areas they are being depleted at a faster rate than they are being recharged. For example, the aquifers of Australian Great Artesian Basin should be able to provide much of eastern Australia renewable water for over 1500 years, according to Perry (2008). However, this water source supply is being threatened by excess extraction of water in four of the Australian states for mining, tourism and grazing (Perry, 2008). Most of the water that is currently extracted is being used to maintain some of Australia's most productive agricultural lands. Therefore, Australia is rapidly consuming its fossil water because it does not have adequate surface fresh water, and the pace of water extraction does not appear to be slowing. Also, in 2009, Australia had to ration water consumption because of drought conditions. It was reported in the Australian media in 2009 that the country is entering a ten-year drought cycle similar to others already experienced in the past.

Droughts and bio-resource securities

We are just beginning to understand the impacts of climate change at the local level and to realize how difficult it is to mitigate the negative impacts of climate change. Prior to 800 CE, 80–90 per cent of the people struggled to survive as subsistence farmers, and famines were not uncommon. After this period, summer temperatures increased by 1.0°C to 1.4°C which was sufficient to increase the land's agricultural productivity. Once agricultural productivity increased, cities began to be built in Europe because fewer people could now produce sufficient food to feed those who had moved to live in cities. This small temperature difference was sufficient to allow vineyards to be planted in England. 'England's climate was so temperate that her merchants exported large quantities of wine to France much to the consternation of French growers, who complained loudly' (Fagan, 2008). This example highlights how the human potential for survival in any landscape is strongly linked to climatic events that alter the productive potential of a land and its water-supply capacity.

Cyclic periods of drought make it difficult to have secure supplies of food. This was demonstrated well for the African Sahel. Meteorological data collected between 1901 and 1987 clearly show cycles of rainfall where conditions for crop production were good in some years, but then were followed by large-scale droughts (Wild, 1993). The data from the African Sahel show how this region began to experience lower total rainfalls starting in the 1950s and again in the latter part of the 1960s to 1987. The early 1930s and early 1950s, however, were periods of higher rainfall in this region. This encouraged farmers to plant different crops needing more water and to plant in regions normally receiving less rainfall (Wild, 1993). When droughts followed years of more plentiful rainfall, starvation was common. Low rainfall, therefore, directly impacts the security of bio-resource supplies at the local level.

Our 34-country database also provides examples of how countries adapt to climatically driven changes in renewable water supplies. Of the 34 countries, three countries are outliers because they provide access to water for only around half of their populations: Angola (53 per cent), Congo DR (58 per cent) and Nigeria (48 per cent). These countries are geographically located in a region of the world where droughts are already a common problem, suggesting that this situation will become even worse. Except for Angola, both the Congo DR and Nigeria already have to transport about a quarter of their water from outside their borders, and precipitation is inadequate to recharge their existing water sources. In contrast, Namibia, located on the same continent, has been able to provide for the water needs of a much larger fraction of its population. However, Namibia has to import water from outside its borders to provide for its domestic water demands.

Droughts are recurring phenomena in countries that are more dependent on rainfall to replenish their renewable water supplies. According to the drought-risk assessment (based on how much endogenous precipitation contributes toward annual supplies of renewable water), four African countries (Angola, Congo DR, Nigeria and Tanzania) are ranked as either having a high or extremely high drought risk. This means that their food production will be insecure because droughts may periodically reduce crop productivity. Also, these four countries are already utilizing most of their annual water withdrawals in agriculture. The figures for 2000 were: Angola (60 per cent); Congo DR (30 per cent); Nigeria (69 per cent); and Tanzania (89 per cent).

A few countries are even more vulnerable to water shortages, for they are dependent on renewable water resources that originate outside their borders. For example, Bangladesh (91 per cent dependency ratio), the Netherlands (88 per cent), Sudan (77 per cent) and Argentina and Namibia (66 per cent) are all highly dependent on water supplies that originate outside of their borders. These countries are vulnerable to droughts that produce water scarcities, because these time periods will result in competition for the limited available water supplies. These five countries also have a smaller fraction of their annual renewable water supplies from endogenous precipitation (< 33 per cent) so that they are less able to annually increase their water-storage capacity.

Most of the countries that import little renewable water today are fortunate that annual rainfall events are sufficient to replenish and recharge more than half of the groundwater each year. The only exceptions to this pattern are found for the US and Mexico that do not import water from outside their borders, but have rainfall replenishing only about one-third of the water needed to recharge rivers and the groundwater each year. Both the US and Mexico are using fossil water at high rates and this consumption will probably not be sustainable under a climate-change scenario (or even without a climate-change, for groundwater is being mined in a number of areas). The western, more arid regions of the US, are already facing severe water shortages and competition for water for agriculture and for returning dammed reservoirs back into free flowing rivers, by removing dams, to restore salmon populations. These water shortages will only continue to worsen and will result in much conflict over who has access rights to renewable water supplies.

Two countries in our database are outliers because a significant portion of their renewable water supplies originate from outside the country borders; Argentina needs to import 66 per cent of its water and Namibia 65.7 per cent. Both countries already face severe challenges to acquire sufficient renewable water resources and they will be more severely impacted under a climate-change scenario that includes droughts. In Argentina and Namibia, precipitation only replenishes a small fraction of their renewable water supplies today (less than 17 per cent). Argentina is currently able to provide for all its citizens' water needs, while Namibia is able to satisfy most of this demand (87 per cent access to water). Even though Argentina has been able to provide water to its entire population, droughts during the last decade have already severely impacted its agricultural production. Because agricultural production is important economically for Argentina, these water shortages have impacted its economy; Argentina went bankrupt in early 2000 and has still not totally recovered from this.

Several other countries may experience difficulties in acquiring sufficient renewable water sources in the future. These countries (e.g. Brazil, Congo DR, Germany, Nigeria and Venezuela) are currently obtaining about one-third of their water from outside country borders. The link between the human development potential of a country and its need to import water is not strong. This is due mainly to the fact that several countries have many choices that allow them to adapt to their water shortages. Despite having to import significant portions of their water, some countries (e.g. Argentina and Venezuela) are making choices that allow them to develop their human capital, while others (e.g. Namibia and Congo DR) have been less capable of dealing with water shortages. When countries have to import from over 30 per cent to over 60 per cent of their renewable water resources, they become more vulnerable to climate change because of competing demands for the same water supplies. If one uses the amount of renewable water supplies obtained from endogenous precipitation to rank countries as to their drought risk, it provides the first filter for determining which countries are at risk for not being able to provide adequate water to their people and to meet the water demands of their industries (Table 7.4). This approach identifies those countries with low annual rainfall, and which can be more vulnerable to climate change that increases drought risk.

Today, countries located on the African continent are experiencing droughts that are severely reducing their human development potential. A noticeable trend in the HDI ranking is that most of the countries listed as having a 'low human development' potential are located on the African continent. This is a paradox because this is also a region of the world with perceived abundant natural resources, with the potential of growing food crops. It was recently reported that several oil-rich Persian Gulf countries are buying farmlands in the deserts of Sudan and Ethiopia to grow food for the Persian Gulf countries and 'to turn the global epicentre of malnutrition into a breadbasket for themselves' (Sanders, 2008). In 2008, it was reported that farmers from China were moving to parts of Africa to live and farm these lands. Therefore, these Persian Gulf countries, as well as China, are extending their food footprint into a region where the land has been unable to provide sufficient nourishment and food security for local people.

Table 7.4 *Countries' drought risk rankings and electricity production by hydropower (2000)*

Countries	Drought risk ranking	% hydro in total domestic electricity generation
Angola, Congo DR, Namibia	Extremely high risk	> 90–100
Nepal, Norway	Extremely low risk	
Brazil	High risk	> 80–90
Venezuela	Medium risk	> 70–80
Iceland, Peru	Extremely low or Low risk	
Tanzania	Extremely high risk	> 50–60
Canada	Medium risk	
Haiti	High risk	> 40–50
Sweden	Low risk	
Argentina, Nigeria, Sudan	High to Extremely high risk	> 30–40

Notes: Risk rankings of a country based on the percentage endogenous precipitation that contributed to annual renewable water supplies in 2006. Extremely low risk of droughts = 81–100 per cent of annual renewable water supplies from endogenous precipitation; Low risk = 61–80 per cent; Medium risk = 41–60 per cent; High risk = 21–40 per cent; Extremely high risk = < 20 per cent
Source: IEA, 2007; IEA, 2009

These are also the same African countries that have experienced a history of famine, droughts and political conflicts.

In order to avoid the potential collapse of civilizations in drought-prone areas and to avoid history repeating itself, countries that pursue 'rich natural resources' in other regions of the world need to factor-in the impacts of droughts on the region where they want to grow their agricultural crops. Even if a drought is not currently impacting agricultural productivity, the presence of people surviving at a subsistence level in the same landscapes where these large-scale agricultural projects are being introduced, has the potential to create significant local conflict. In such cases, a historical perspective is relevant, for the resource harvesting may appear to be sustainable in the current landscape, but decadal droughts or other climate change events may push the system to a threshold of unsustainability.

Today, most countries included in our database are able to obtain sufficient water from precipitation recharge of rivers and groundwater. A few countries will be more susceptible to climate change that results in reduced rainfall because more than one-half of their annual precipitation is needed to recharge country water supplies. All the Scandinavian countries face significant problems if precipitation levels decrease, because Finland, Norway and Sweden are all dependent on annual rainfall to resupply more than half of their renewable water supplies; Iceland is also in the same situation and vulnerable to climate change. The impact of reduced rainfall has already been felt in Norway, where more than 90 per cent of the primary energy is generated using hydroelectric power. A few emerging economies (China, Indonesia, Malaysia, Peru and Russia) also are dependent on annual rainfall to replenish more than half of their renewable water supplies.

Water and electricity production

Today, renewable energy production competes for water formerly only used to grow food crops. Angola, Congo DR, Nigeria and Tanzania produce a significant proportion of their domestic total electricity production from hydropower (90.1 per cent in Angola, 99.7 per cent in the Congo DR, 33.4 per cent in Nigeria and 51.7 per cent in Tanzania). Not only is there more competition for water, but electricity production will be severely limited during droughts. In our database, several countries produce more than 90 per cent of their electricity from hydropower, thereby being especially vulnerable to droughts. Half of the countries in our list produce more than 30 per cent of their electricity from hydropower and will also be impacted by droughts.

Data on how much endogenous precipitation contributes to annual renewable water supplies do not completely address the drought risk a country may face due to climate change. Most of the Scandinavian countries are ranked as having a low drought risk, so their electricity generation should be minimally impacted by droughts. Despite this, Norway has experienced droughts that impacted electricity production, but not food production; in 1994, Norway was less able to generate its electricity using hydropower because of severe droughts. Climate change has increased the frequency of droughts in Norway despite the fact that annual precipitation is capable of resupplying most of the annual renewable water supplies.

Norway is especially vulnerable to water shortages because 98 per cent of its electricity production is generated from hydropower. Droughts, therefore, directly impact Norway's ability to continue to produce electricity using more carbon-friendly approaches (hydropower emits little CO_2), compared to using fossil fuels.

A drought, therefore, can reduce the capacity of a country to continue to produce electricity using its hydroelectric dams, especially when much of the annual renewable water is derived from endogenous rainfall that is needed to replenish the aquifers. The data provided in Table 7.4 show how countries are making choices concerning the amount of their electricity to produce from hydropower, despite the fact that they may confront an extremely high drought risk.

Hydroelectric plants in both Namibia and Angola produce more than 90 per cent of the electricity consumed domestically. For Namibia this is a very logical choice because few other options exist for this country to acquire or produce electricity. It is dependent upon electricity imports from South Africa to satisfy what is not produced domestically. In 2005, Namibia imported 55 per cent of its electricity. The need to import over half of one's electricity demand can pose a high risk, however, when the exporting country encounters scarcities that require it to stop its exports on short notice. This will disrupt a country's electricity supply and provide few options for securing supplies elsewhere. In 2008, for example, South Africa ceased exporting electricity to Namibia for several weeks because it was unable to satisfy its own domestic demand. Therefore, Namibia does not have secure supplies of electricity and it also lacks domestic supplies of fossil fuels. Consequently, using hydropower is a logical trade-off that has been made in that country. Namibia has made this decision despite its extremely high risk for droughts that can disrupt domestic electricity production, and the need to import 66 per cent of its total renewable water resources from outside country borders. Other sources of electricity are more costly and do not provide greater security for Namibia.

In contrast to Namibia, Angola does have significant reserves of oil, which could be used to generate the power needed in-country if it has to manage energy production during a drought. Angola, however, has made the choice to export most of its oil and not to provide a higher level of energy security for its residents. Because Angola faces an extremely high risk of droughts, it will be unable to provide more secure energy supplies domestically during these times because of its current oil-export policy.

In our group of 34 countries, three stand out (Australia, the UAE and Yemen) because they generated none or less than 10 per cent of their electric power using hydroelectric dams. All three also are ranked as having extremely high risk of droughts. Whether these countries considered drought risk when deciding whether or not to produce electricity using hydropower is not known, but it is not a logical option for them to adopt because of their high drought risk and the high amount of desert each country has.

Climate is the ultimate global driver determining whether societies can sustain-ably consume resources and develop their human capital. However, sustainability is not just based on how resources are consumed, but whether humans can manage the 'solar income' to produce the resources needed to survive in the first place. In addition to climate, the other unavoidable constraint that has to be better connected and integrated into our sustainability choices is soils.

Despite the importance of soils to society, they are frequently ignored when assessing whether a society is making sustainable choices related to its resource consumption. Even if society ignores soils, scientists trained in the soil sciences do not ignore soils when evaluating the threshold for resource production. They have developed a deep understanding of the local constraints and opportunities that soils provide; this understanding has developed over the more than 4000-year history of agriculture. Policy makers, however, do ignore soils because soil science is locally based and policy decisions are typically being made for larger scales. The benefits of soils to society, and how soils control or are controlled by, the four essential human needs, will be discussed next.

References

Alerstam, T. (2008) 'Give way to the migrants', *Science*, vol 319, p572

Almeida H. (2009) 'Angola shuts off border with Congo to avoid Ebola', Reuters News Service, 6 January 2009, p2

Balmford, A., Moore J. L., Brooks T., Burgess N., Hansen L. A., Williams P. and Rahbek, C. (2001) 'Conservation conflicts across Africa', *Science*, vol 291, pp2616–2619

de Blij, H. (2005) *Why Geography Matters. Three Challenges Facing America. Climate Change, The Rise of China and Global Terrorism*, Oxford University Press, Oxford

Diamond, J. (2005) *Collapse: How Societies Choose to Fail or Survive*, Penguin, New York, NY

Dowie, M. (2005) 'Conservation refugees: when protecting nature means kicking people out', *Orion* Magazine, www.orionmagazine.org/index.php/articles/article/161, accessed 30 May 2008

Fagan, B. (2008) *The Great Warming. Climate Change and the Rise and Fall of Civilizations*, Bloomsbury Press, New York, NY

FAO (2000) 'World Soil Resources Report 90. Land Resource Potential and Constraints at Regional and Country Levels', UN FAO, Rome, Italy

FAO (2005) 'Global Forest Resources Assessment 2005', UN FAO, Rome, Italy

FAO (2008) 'World Resources Report, www.fao.org/docrep/011/ai476e/ai476e01.htm, accessed 22 July 2009

FAO Water Resources Development and Management Service (2003) 'AQUASTAT Information System on Water and Agriculture: Review of World Water Resources by Country', Rome, www.fao.org/waicent/faoinfo/agricult/agl/aglw/aquastat/water_res/index.htm, accessed 23 July 2009

IEA (2007) *2007 Key World Energy Statistics*, International Energy Agency, www.iea.org/Textbase/stats/electricitydata.asp?COUNTRY_CODE=, accessed 1 September 2008

IEA (2009) *IEA Energy Statistics, 2007 Key World Energy Statistics*, International Energy Agency, www.iea.org/Textbase/stats/electricitydata.asp?COUNTRY_CODE=, accessed 2 June 2009

Joshi, H. and Hadi, M. (2009) 'Monsoon rains on India's parade', *The Wall Street Journal*, 25–26 July 2009, pB10

Kristof, N. D. (2008) 'Extended forecast: Bloodshed', *New York Times*, 13 April 2008

Majumbar, B. (2009) 'Naked girls plow fields for rain', Reuters News Service, 23 July 2009, www.reuters.com/article/idUSTRE56M3G020090723, accessed 24 July 2009

MEA (2005) *Millennium Ecosystem Assessment: Ecosystems and Human Well-Being Synthesis. Findings of the Condition and Trends Working Group of the Millennium Ecosystem Assessment*, Island Press, Washington, DC

National Geographic (2008) 'Greendex 2008; Consumer Choice and the Environment – a Worldwide Tracking Survey', pp1–103

Payne, K., Warrington, S. and Bennett, O. (2002) 'High stakes: the future of mountain societies', Panos Report no 44, in N. van der Gaag (ed.), Panos Institute, London

Perry, M. (2008) 'Ancient water source vital for Australia', Reuters News Service, 29 December 2008, http://planetark.org/wen/51028, accessed 3 January 2009

Price, S. V. (2003) *War and Tropical Forests. Conservation in Areas of Armed Conflict*, Food Products Press, The Haworth Press, Inc, New York, NY and London

Sanchez, P. A. (1976) *Properties and Management of Soils in the Tropics*, Wiley, New York, NY

Sanders, E. (2008) 'Will Africa feed rich nations?' World Report, *The Seattle Times News*, 1 October 2008, pA7

Smith, D. M. and Barchiesi, S. (2009) 'Environment as infrastructure: resilience to climate change impacts on water through investment in nature', Perspectives on Water and Climate Change Adaptation, IUCN, Gland, Switzerland, www.iucn.org/about/work/programmes/water/resources/wp_resources_reports, accessed 20 September 2009

UN (2007) *The 2004 Energy Statistics Yearbook*, United Nations Department of Economic and Social Affairs, Statistics Division, New York, NY

WHO (2007) 'Country profiles of environmental burden of disease and country profiles', World Health Organization, Public Health and the Environment, Geneva 2007, www.who.int/countries/ago/en, accessed 10 December 2008

Wild, A. (1993) *Soils and the Environment. An Introduction*, Cambridge University Press, Cambridge

Williams, M. (1989) *Americans and Their Forests. A Historical Geography*, Cambridge University Press, Cambridge

Winters, R. K. (1974) *The Forest and Man*, Vantage Press, New York, NY

World Bank (2007) *Growth and CO_2 emissions: How do different countries fare?*, Environment Department, The World Bank, Washington, DC

WRI (2009) 'EarthTrends searchable database results', World Resources Institute, http://earthtrends.wri.org, accessed 3 July 2009

8

WHERE the PAST and FUTURE Meet: Soils or the Unseen Earth That Nurtures Societies

While climate change is unpredictable, a strong and rich scientific history can inform us on what will make a soil degrade, and what practices are unsustainable. This scientific knowledge has evolved over at least 4000 years of growing crops for food. Despite this, the general public in the industrialized world has little understanding of what practices will degrade soils or how farmers should compensate for their soil deficiencies. This is similar to the caricature shown in Figure 8.1, where food is delivered to a customer at a restaurant, but where the patron does not have a clue what weather events or soil deficiencies might have altered the final food product brought to the table by the waiter. Not everyone, of course, is ignorant of agricultural land-use practices and their repercussions on soil health. For example, the horticultural community and garden club members are actively applying soil-science principles to maintain the health of the soils in their ornamental gardens. This knowledge is mainly being practised in gardens that are not essential for providing local food security, but the gardeners are, however, aware of the climatic influences on their plant growth and the need to manage the soil to maintain its productive capacity.

The understanding of soil constraints is much more highly developed in the countries where a greater proportion of the population is involved in growing food and lives in rural areas. In these areas, the survival of these people depends on their understanding of how to mitigate soil and climate constraints to plant growth. They are mostly impacted by climate, which they cannot control. Past societies effectively adapted to the constraints posed by their soils, and some practices worked so well that they are being considered for adoption today.

Soils are the surfaces that humans walk, trample and build their homes on without thinking about their roles in providing for a multitude of societal survival needs. Therefore, it is surprising that none of the soil characteristics included in our database are connected to the indices that evaluate the vulnerability or environmental risk of a country (see Chapter 3). In fact, the only indicator that is relevant

Figure 8.1 *Caricature of how people do not know what problems a cook faces in producing the food that they eat*

for characterizing soil quality is the *hunger risk* of a country. However, just knowing a country's *hunger index* is not enough to explain the causal factors contributing to this hunger. We contend that if soils could be characterized sufficiently, the *causality* of hunger will emerge, for soils generally reflect the legacy of past human activities as well as determining what type of constraints will impede the land's productive capacity. These 'human derived soil legacies' will influence how difficult it will be for a community to implement 'sustainable' land-use practices.

Soils are essential for almost every facet of human and ecosystem survival. Soils set the upper limits for the amount of bio-resources humans will be able to collect and how difficult it will be to maintain the provision of ecosystem services. Soils maintain the memory or 'legacy' of the good and bad decisions that society has made and may not always be forgiving of past management errors. Fortunately, we have learned how to manage soils so that they retain their health and productive capacity. However, they can only be managed or restored to the thresholds that are inherent to each soil. For example, it may be almost impossible to manage and remove chemical contaminants from soils. The solution today has been to dig up the soil and cart it to a landfill for storage; this is not ideal, for we are also running out of land area that can be used to store contaminated materials.

A core element of estuarine and coastal restoration is the management of 'sediments' and chemical contaminants introduced by industries, in order to restore healthy aquatic and soil ecosystems (see Box 8.1). 'Sediment' is another word for soils that *lack viable biotic communities*: they are biologically 'dead'. Managing sediments to convert them back to being soil is expensive and requires considerable mitigation, as described in Box 8.1. Society is better off if choices are made that do not require sediment mitigation. We will next attempt to summarize the multiple ways that soils or the unseen earth nurture societies, and which society is mostly unaware of because humans have been so effective at mitigating soil constraints.

Box 8.1 Aquatic Infrastructure of Hudson River Estuary, New York and New Jersey, USA

Gene Peck

Watershed-level management is an essential tool to maintain the health of estuaries. Watershed management really means managing the sediments, since these are an essential dynamic component of watersheds. Estuaries and ports are areas of sediment and pollutant accumulation, the latter commonly at levels that damage aquatic biota. Sediments may originate from contaminated areas or become tainted by pollutants contributed by point and non-point sources from all parts of the watershed. Found within the Hudson River Estuary is the Port of New York/New Jersey, the largest port on the east coast of the US, and one which demonstrates well the challenges faced in mitigating and restoring estuaries while also supporting the important economic activities that are essential to a port. This port creates more than 230,000 jobs and brings in over US$20 billion in economic activity to the region.

To facilitate port activities, many areas were deepened from the naturally-occurring 6m depth to 15m, and the natural shorelines and gentle slopes were replaced by vertical bulkheads and deep berths. To maintain these berths and the 380km of shipping channels is a major problem and expense to the port and requires ongoing dredging of an estimated 1.87 million m^3 of sediment. In fact contaminant levels in sediment often require the dredged material to be processed and disposed upland, increasing the costs from approximately US$40 to well over US$100 per m^3. To avoid this and other problems, the Harbor Estuary Program was created to protect, conserve and restore the estuary. It recommended consistent regulatory coordination, sediment-quality mapping, action to address the impacts of contaminated sediments, identification of upstream watersheds with excessive sediment loads and development of plans to reduce those loads.

The objectives of the NJ Transit project are to: expand the rail yard area, increase public access and improve water quality and the estuary. To overcome regulatory hurdles for the extension plan an ecosystems approach was used to design measures to create environmental benefits. The project involves: *dredged material disposal* to provide new land, *point source control* to remove sediments and floatables, *public access waterfront walkway* and a *new and restored aquatic habitat*. Specifically, the planned restoration requires consideration of: *accumulation of sediments*, including those in sewerage discharge and Combined Sewer Overflow (CSO), with 10–40 per cent organic matter and undesirable-to-toxic accessory elements; *water circulation*, which is nearly stagnant; *water-quality conditions*, now highly degraded; and *aquatic species* that are now restricted to impoverished forms. This proposal is even linked with a water-quality model to a regional framework developed for a 42km stretch of the Hudson River that contains the canal.

Soil Management Essential for
Human Development

The challenge we face today is that, as the human capital is developed, people have less direct involvement in agriculture and their food production. With this decreasing direct connection to agriculture, there is a decline in understanding the role of soils in setting the limits to global productivity; i.e. feeding the people and maintaining human and ecosystem health. As human development increases, fewer people work in agriculture and forestry; 85 per cent of the variance in the HDI value is negatively explained by the percentage of the labour force that works in agriculture and forestry (see Chapter 11).

Soils link the past with the future! This linkage or 'legacy stage' is expressed in indicators of soil quality and health and it generally affects the sustainability options that exist for any society in a given landscape. Soils are the medium used to grow our food and they provide the essential nutrients needed by growing plants. They are also the sites where renewable energy supplies (e.g. woodfuel) can be grown. If human actions degraded local soils, it may be difficult to mitigate this degradation using existing farming practices, and consequently human capacity to collect the land's bio-resources may be reduced for decades. When people do not have a choice to migrate to more productive lands, they may need to continue managing these degraded soils to grow their bio-resources. The ultimate impact of needing to use degraded soils to produce food means that these lands are unable to support the larger population densities that have become dependent upon them. In the past, these changes contributed to the eventual collapse of human communities (Hillel, 1991).

Societies may not immediately collapse just because soils have become degraded, but historical accounts have documented how a climate event pushes a community towards being unsustainable. The most common disturbance that affects soils (and humans) is droughts. With the exacerbation of droughts by today's climate change, the potential for a soil's productive capacity to be reduced is a serious problem that some regions of the world will need to manage (Fagan, 2008). Many countries with a high proportion of people involved in agriculture are also those that face a high or extremely high drought risk (Table 6.4). Some, like France, the Netherlands and the US will be better adapted to dealing with climate change. But many others (e.g. Bangladesh, Congo DR, Haiti, India and Nigeria) will be less capable of adjusting to climate change because they are more dependent upon collecting bio-resources that are controlled by the unavoidable constraints of soils and climate.

The link between food and population growth is obvious, for humans are not adapted to capture energy from the sun, as plants do – contrary to a vision espoused by some science fiction authors. Even though the public frequently does not make the explicit link between sufficient food supplies and soil quality, or how its land-use activities impact the soil, it has been concerned about the need to produce sufficient food. Nutrition and whether the world will have enough food to feed itself have been recurring discussions throughout history. In the late 18th and early 19th centuries, the British scholar Thomas Malthus developed his theories about the limits to human population growth. In 1798 he wrote 'An Essay on the Principle of Population' that suggested there are limits to growth, and that continued population growth will result in poverty, human suffering and environmental degradation (Malthus, 1798). The rationale behind his ideas is that human population growth occurs exponentially but food production only increases slowly or is linear. Despite these dire predictions, food production has kept up with population growth. Increasing food production, however, has direct impacts on soils and their health and, therefore, on their productive capacity to produce 'solar income', that is, crop biomass.

In many cases we have implemented practices that increase food production beyond the nutrient-supply capacity of many soils, just to produce sufficient food to feed our growing populations. Unmanaged soils are able to provide sufficient nutrients to plants if plant-growth rates are equivalent to the soil's supply capacity. If farmers want to obtain a higher crop biomass than what is possible based on each soil's nutrient-delivery capacity, plants will have to be fertilized with nutrients that limit their growth rates. Pushing plant growth beyond a soil's nutrient delivery capacity to increase food production has to be implemented carefully because there are potential negative environmental externalities associated with these practices (e.g. excessive application of fertilizers in the mistaken belief that more is better). When humans recognized these negative impacts, they modified practices to reduce them while still attempting to maintain plant growth rates at these higher levels.

In the process of trying to grow more food, society has applied chemicals that were not normally present at such high levels in soils. Several chemicals are applied in agriculture to increase plant growth rates and/or to eliminate the pests and pathogens that reduce crop yields. For example, fertilizers are applied to increase plant growth rates so more food is produced, and herbicides are applied to eliminate competition from other plants trying to grow on the same plot of arable land. These other plants – weeds – compete for nutrients and water needed by our food crops. Of course, pesticides are applied to keep herbivores and others (e.g. insects) from eating the food that we have grown for our own consumption.

Some practices had more negative impacts than others. For example, the application of nitrogen (N) fertilizers have had a greater impact on ecosystem health than many of the other practices implemented, especially when N is not in its organic form. Nitrogen is an integral part of the enzymes that fix carbon during photosynthesis but it also determines how much of the plant tissues are eaten by animals (its herbivory rates) and microbial growth rates. Excessive N in ecosystems tends to impair the health of soil ecosystems and increases the growth rates of weedy or exotic plant species that are better adapted to higher N levels. It also stimulates higher herbivory rates as the food becomes more nutritious to herbivores.

Chemicals applied to agricultural fields to increase crop yields have also been causally linked to human health problems. In the 1940s and 1950s, massive quantities of synthetic N fertilizers were applied to agricultural fields to increase crop growth rates. These N-based fertilizers entered into the aquatic and terrestrial ecosystems at a rate not recorded previously in human history. Higher N levels began to be detected in humans, especially in the form of nitrates in babies. For example, in the 1940s groundwater contamination by nitrates was observed following the application of excessive amounts of fertilizers (Wild, 1993). When this problem was identified, steps were taken to reduce or control fertilizer applications. The last recorded death from excess nitrates in the groundwater occurred in 1950, but the legacy of excessive N applications still persists in the soil. Consequently, in those areas, N fertilizers no longer need to be applied to agricultural fields to increase plant growth rates. These higher N applications have indirectly altered the availability of other nutrients in soils, because nitrate-N can increase soil acidification rates and thereby cause the leaching of basic nutrients, such as calcium, from soils (Wild, 1993). Furthermore, some agricultural soils no longer need phosphorus (P) applications because soils have retained this element after excess quantities were applied in the past.

Over-fertilization is still occurring in all countries regardless of their human development ranking. Eutrophication of streams and large bodies of water due to fertilizer applications is commonly reported in the media, as well as being documented in the global literature. Interestingly, food production was one of the main drivers causing the over-application of fertilizers in the past, but today the biofuels industry (e.g. ethanol produced from agricultural crops and palm oil to produce the oils for biodiesel) is contributing to many of the eutrophication events reported in the media. In the midwestern states in the US, corn is increasingly being planted and fertilized for the production of ethanol. The excess fertilizers have been transported into the Mississippi River and finally into the Gulf of Mexico, where anoxic zones are killing fish (Rabalais, 2002).

Even though we recognize the problems associated with excessive applications of fertilizers, these applications will continue as countries struggle to feed their populations and to produce cheaper transportation fuels. Agriculture has evolved to a science of 'sustainable agriculture' where crops can be efficiently grown with minimum negative environmental externalities. These principles, however, are not always applied effectively, especially when society faces many other more urgent problems, such as feeding people.

There are many direct human health impacts from the application of chemicals to soils to increase our food production (e.g. leaching of nitrates into the human drinking water); however, the nutritious quality of our food is also affected by these applications. A plant's nutrition is only as good as the soil it grows in, and a faster growing plant (used to produce more food or more biomass for energy production) may not provide the nutritious meal we need to be healthy. It is important to briefly discuss why soils are so variable and why some food crops grow better in some areas but not in others.

Soils are Not Equally Good for Food Production

Soils are quite diverse and only some are good for growing crops

Soil development can be described using an equation. This is a useful approach, for it identifies the major factors important in describing how a soil develops and why it has its particular chemical, physical, and/or biological attributes. It also explains why there is a high variability in the capacity of a soil at any given location to provide a good growth medium for plants, and identifies what soil factors will constrain a land's productive capacity. The soil-forming equation includes:

- Climate.
- Relief or topography.
- Parent material.
- Organisms.
- Time.

Soils are very diverse and can be excessively moist or well-drained, shallow or deep to the bedrock, have low to high fertility, and/or have low to high water-holding capacity. All these characteristics will affect its erosion potential; which plants can grow well in it; which plants will successfully out-compete others growing in the same environment; and whether grazing animals (including humans) will derive sufficient nutrients from eating plant materials.

United States soil scientists have classified soils into 12 taxonomic groups or orders that describe their unique physical and chemical properties. Each taxonomic group is further subdivided into several more groups. These soil taxonomic groups describe the tremendous variability in soils that are found around the world. They also describe where plants will or will not grow well because of chemical toxicities or high salinities. Out of the 12 taxonomic groups, only a few are ideally suitable for the productive growth of agricultural crops without considerable additional inputs or mitigation.

Climate has had a significant influence on the depth and intensity of weathering and, therefore, the nutrient status of a soil (Brady, 1990). Tropical wet regions have the greatest depth of weathering of their parent material mainly due to the high precipitation rates that have been common in these ecosystems. In these regions, most of the original essential plant nutrients that existed in the parent material have been weathered and leached below the rooting zone of most plants. Trees have developed several unique adaptations to acquire and store these nutrients. In some Brazilian rainforests, tree roots and their symbiotic associations grow at depths as great as 30m, where the soil nutrient concentrations are higher. The wet tropical forests have also adapted to recycle nutrients within the vegetative biomass itself, for instance where mats of roots and symbionts grow 40cm deep on the surface of the soils and collect minerals leached from senescing plant tissues. This strategy, of efficiently recycling nutrients within vegetative biomass itself, can almost isolate the plant from needing to acquire soil nutrients.

FAO (2000) identified eight soil characteristics that can constrain plant productivity or plant 'solar capital'. These constraints are those that are most likely to result in low soil productivity; either plants will grow slowly on these soils or only those plants adapted to mitigate the soil constraint are able to grow. These eight soil constraints are:

1 Hydromorphy – poor soil drainage.
2 Low cation exchange capacity (CEC) – low capacity to retain added nutrients.
3 Aluminum (Al) toxicity – elemental toxicity and strong acidity.
4 High phosphorus (P) fixation – high levels of ferric and aluminum oxides (in acidic environments) or calcium oxides and hydroxides (in alkaline environments) complex with phosphorus and make it unavailable to plants.
5 Vertic properties – clays that contract and expand with moisture changes.
6 Salinity and sodicity – presence of salts and sodium (Na) in solution.
7 Shallowness – shallow soil depth and the growing medium with rock near the surface (less rooting volume available).
8 Erosion hazard – high risk of soil erosion due to steep slopes or moderate slopes, but also erosion-prone soils due to texture, mineralogy, organic matter, climate, hydrology, etc.

A comparison of the country-level constraints that agriculture faces suggests that farmers have to consider, or adapt to, several constraints simultaneously. It becomes clear from Table 8.1 that each of the 34 countries faces several major soil problems simultaneously, requiring some type of management mediation to increase crop productivity.

The data in Table 8.1 clearly show how every country faces several soil constraints, but generally countries only have one dominant constraint that reduces their soil's productive capacity. For example, Indonesia has 75 per cent of its land area affected by 'low CEC', but it does not have to deal with salinity constraints. Malaysia has 76 per cent of its lands characterized as having a 'high erosion risk', but none of them has a 'low CEC'. Similarly, the Philippines has 62 per cent of its lands characterized as having 'high erosion risk' but no 'low CEC' or 'salinity' problems; more than half of its lands have no soil constraints. China, Mexico and the US have a similar percentage of land degradation being caused by agricultural activities (22 per cent) and they also have similar percentages of the total land area without major soil constraints. Therefore, it is difficult to generalize what a country's soil degradation risk will be, because of the multiple factors that can limit productivity at any given location. Assessments of soils should, therefore, be conducted at the local level to identify their constraints.

Table 8.1 *Soil constraint characteristics by country (2000) by HDI*

HDI group		Low CEC (%)	Erosion risk (%)	Al toxicity (%)	Salinity (%)
1	Iceland	1	22	0	0
	Norway	0	9	7	0
	Australia	12	13	4	3
	Canada	0	15	4	0
	Sweden	0	2	4	0
	Japan	0	34	27	0
	Netherlands	3	1	1	0
	France	0	24	8	0
	Finland	0	2	11	0
	US	0	24	19	0
	UK	7	29	30	2
	Germany	1	14	21	0
2	Argentina	0	10	0	12
	UAE	2	13	14	1
	Mexico	0	26	2	1
	Malaysia	0	76	62	3
	Russia	0	19	5	..
	Brazil	10	16	63	0
3	Venezuela	2	30	55	1
	China	0	16	11	8
	Peru	2	30	43	1
	Philippines	1	62	26	1
	Indonesia	75	47	30	1
4	Namibia	23	9	0	4
	India	44	29	5	7
5	Bangladesh	0	15	16	7
	Nepal	0	31	30	0
	Haiti	0	38	5	0
	Sudan	9	10	5	1
	Yemen	0	9	0	4
6	Nigeria	13	26	8	2
	Tanzania	9	5	0	13
	Angola	31	12	27	0
	Congo DR	26	5	60	0

Note: HDI = Human Development Index [Group 1 = HDI > 0.9; Group 2 = > 0.8–0.9; Group 3 = > 0.7–0.8; Group 4 = > 0.6–0.7; Group 5 = > 0.5–0.6; Group 6 = 0.4–0.5]. Aluminum = Al; Cation Exchange Capacity = CEC
Source: FAO, 2000, 2006

Good soils, good crops and good food security

People may not want to restrict their food consumption to crops that can be grown in a local soil because of the local soil constraints; this could mean having a diet mainly of potatoes, with their limited protein value. If a local soil has a low availability of essential plant nutrients, plants growing in these soils will be low in these nutrients and may not provide humans the essential minerals they need to be healthy. To obtain these basic essential nutrients, people would have to eat large quantities of that food, a lifestyle that is unrealistic. Food production is also reduced when the wrong crops are grown in each soil. The impact of growing one crop over large landscapes in Baduy Land, southwest Java, is described in Box 8.2. There, conversion of forests to potato production is triggering soil degradation and therefore decreasing crop productivity.

In other locations around the world, mainly tropical, the soil chemistry (e.g. Al concentrations) may restrict which plants can be grown in a soil, for many plants are not tolerant of higher Al levels. This restricts food production to a few root crops, such as cassava or manioc, or tea, which grow well despite the higher soil Al levels. Because Al complexes with other macronutrients (e.g. P and Ca), higher Al levels also decrease the nutrient value of a plant. Furthermore, if people are mainly restricted to consuming root crops, they will not be ingesting a balanced nutritional regime and will have to supplement their diet with other minerals and protein to be healthy. Many root crops are high in carbohydrates, and farmers have also selected varieties with higher sugar contents because they can feed more people. Under these soil-constraint scenarios, a healthy diet would require the importation of food from other regions of the world better able to grow a diversity of nutritious foods.

The likelihood of soil degradation is quite high where food is being grown on soils that are in the later stages of development. In this situation, it will be difficult to manage lands so that their carrying capacity is not exceeded. It may be more sustainable to have farmers growing crops on lands better suited for farming, rather than on the lands that are poorly suited for this purpose. The question that needs to be asked at every local level is whether it is even possible for the local or regional soils to support the plant growth and production levels needed to satisfy local food demand. If the answer is 'no,' then the next question is whether the soils should be restored to a higher level of productivity, using practices already developed by farmers in other regions of the world.

The soil chemistry tells us what type of food crops and how much food can be produced in any given land area. The Green Revolution and technology have increased our crop productivity, but soils and local climates dictate what management practices can be implemented to increase food production. If the soil is low in nutrients or naturally contains toxic chemicals, the capacity of humans to produce abundant crops will be severely limited. Our country analyses have shown that soil fertility is not bounded by the human development status of a country; because a country is a highly advanced-economy, this does not mean that it has to irrigate or use more fertilizers to produce its food compared to the growing-economy countries. The analyses have shown that the management

Box 8.2 Indonesian Communities and Decisions Related to the Social and Environmental Functions of Forests

Asep Sugih Suntana and Mia Siscawati

Indonesia consists of 18,110 islands and islets, with five major islands and 30 groups of smaller islands; the land area totals almost two million square kilometres. It has the fourth largest population in the world, and 62 per cent of its people live on Java. With 500 ethnic groups and additional hundreds of sub-ethnic groups, it has a history of rich cultural diversity. Approximately 20 million people in Indonesia live around forest land and 30 per cent of these are highly dependent on forest resources for their livelihoods. Yet farming is the main activity in most forest-edge communities. Strategies adopted by several rural communities are presented here to demonstrate how local decision-making processes vary by community and are related to what each defines as being acceptable social and environmental functions of forests.

The Baduy People: Baduy Land is one of very few remaining areas of southwest Java covered by pristine mountainous tropical rainforest (138ha). It is inhabited by an indigenous people who manage and preserve forests using traditional knowledge and methods. They divide their forest into sacred forests, protected forests and managed complex agro-forests. The people themselves are divided into two groups: Inner Baduy (with strong traditional values) and Outer Baduy (which maintains outside communication by selling forest products, e.g. wild honey and handmade products). Baduy has chosen to use preventive measures to ensure the sustainability of their natural resources and livelihoods. They will disturb a natural setting only as a last resort when all other options are exhausted.

The Dieng People: In the mountains of Central Java, Dieng Plateau is a densely farmed agricultural area in an active hydrothermal landscape. Currently, farmers face water scarcity, soil erosion and a reduction in soil/land quality. Other problems have been created by illegal timber cutting and firewood gathering for household needs and commercial purposes, and conversion (both legal and illegal) of forested lands into potato fields. This conversion causes the drying up of natural springs, biodiversity loss and other environmental and social problems. Although the rate of production has been reduced by 30 per cent, the community of Dieng still thinks that growing potato is the appropriate choice to support their livelihoods. In practice, there is no type of land that is not being used as a potato plantation, even though long-term effects are a threat to sustainability. The Dieng people utilize a natural setting to gain its economic benefits without totally considering either the social or the ecological implications.

practices that need to be used to produce sufficient and nutritious crops are dictated in part by which soils are present locally. This analysis also suggests that humans have mitigated the constraints of their soils and adopted other modes of acquiring food (e.g. animal husbandry, hunting wildlife, etc.) where the soils are unable to allow productive crop growth.

Soil Degradation and Food Security

Soil degradation and global soils

The health and productive capacity of a soil is a critical factor for all countries to assess. Soils develop through time and their physical and chemical characteristics change in a way that determines the types of plants that can be grown at any location, and the capacity of the land to grow food crops. The typical feature of a soil changing with time (as the soil becomes older) is that it becomes more nutrient-poor and contains more chemicals toxic to humans and plants. This is the situation in the wet tropics where soils have lost much of their available nutrients over a several thousand-year span of heavy rainstorms (Sanchez, 1976). The result is that many tropical areas have limitations on which crops can be grown, and shifting agriculture has to be practised to allow the soils to renew themselves. The prevalence of soils with low-nutrient concentrations have made integrated nutrient management a goal for these lands. The fertility of a soil is an important challenge facing those pursuing sustainable agricultural practices in lands that are already severely degraded or where the soils are 'old' (Gruhn et al, 2000).

According to FAO (2000), only one-quarter of the world's land area has soils lacking only one of the eight major constraints critical for defining a soil's fertility class. FAO (2000) identified parts of North Asia (east of the Urals), the Asia–Pacific region and North America as having the highest amount of soils without major constraints. This assessment suggests that those regions that have the highest 'total area of soils without major constraints coincide with regions that are the world's leading grain-producing and exporting countries', that is, parts of Europe, Russia, the US, Canada, China, Australia, India and Argentina (countries are listed in order of highest absolute area) (FAO, 2000).

Of the 34 selected countries, two – Iceland and the UAE – have major constraints on all of their soils that limit crop growth (Table 8.2). In response to its severe erosion problems, Iceland is implementing many soil restoration projects, including the aerial seeding of exotic lupins across large areas of severely degraded soils. These N-fixing plants are effectively stabilizing these soils because they grow well where other plants are less able to grow. There have been many debates in Iceland on the use of exotic plants to manage these severely degraded soils, but there are few other options that can be used to restore these lands.

These data also show that one-half of the selected countries (17 of the 34 countries) have less than 20 per cent of their land area without some major soil constraint (or in other words, > 80 per cent of their arable land has some soil constraints) (Table 8.2). The important take-home message from this table is that all 34 countries have soil constraints that decrease crop productivity on at least 50 per cent or more of their arable land! Normally a country has to ameliorate some soil constraint because it reduces crop production; these data support that need (Figure 8.2).

Table 8.2 *Arable lands without any soil constraints, by country for 2000*

Arable land without major soil constraints (%)	Country codes
> 80–100	—
> 60–80	—
> 40–60	10, 12, 14, 16, 25, 26
> 20–40	2, 4, 6, 15, 18, 20, 22, 30, 31, 32, 33
> 0.1–20	1, 3, 5, 7, 8, 9, 11, 17, 19, 21, 23, 24, 27, 28, 34
0	13, 29

Note: Country codes: 1 = Angola; 2 = Argentina; 3 = Australia; 4 = Bangladesh; 5 = Brazil; 6 = Canada; 7 = China; 8 = Congo DR, 9 = Finland; 10 = France; 11 = Germany; 12 = Haiti; 13 = Iceland; 14 = India; 15 = Indonesia; 16 = Japan; 17 = Malaysia; 18 = Mexico; 19 = Namibia; 20 = Nepal; 21 = Netherlands; 22 = Nigeria; 23 – Norway; 24 = Peru; 25 = Philippines; 26 = Russian Federation; 27 = Sudan; 28 = Sweden; 29 = United Arab Emirates; 30 = United Kingdom; 31 = United Republic of Tanzania; 32 = United States; 33 = Venezuela; 34 = Yemen
Source: FAO, 2000

Linking soil degradation to societal sustainability

Society has been working at improving agriculture ever since humans began to grow and manage plants to produce food (Hillel, 1991). Humans have become amazingly skilled in adapting crop growth to the constraints of the local soil and climate, and the capacity to adapt land-use practices to soil constraints is probably why soil indicators are not reflective of a soil's productive capacity. This includes nutrient delivery (its CEC), how much fertilizer needs to be applied, how severely degraded a land is, how many people need to be employed in the production of food, and so on. Furthermore, soil indicators do not explain how environmentally vulnerable a country will be to disturbances.

Compared to the other five HDI groups, HDI group 6 has twice as much of its total area classified as potential arable lands, and available for growing crops

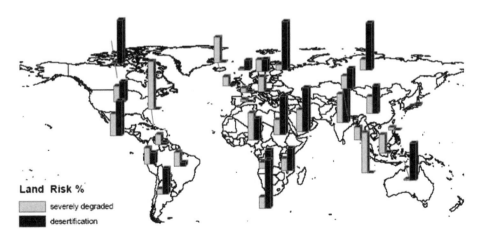

Figure 8.2 *Country plots of the severity of soil degradation and desertification risk*

(Table 8.3). Despite this, these countries were not using their total potential land area (67–73 per cent of the total land area used to grow crops) for agriculture in 1994 (Table 8.3). These data reflect the mid-1990s timing of the data collection, when civil unrest was common in these countries. During these times, farmers were not planting their fields because of concerns about being killed or having their crops stolen or confiscated by soldiers; this contributed, as well, to the higher hunger index rankings published for these countries. With the exception of Nigeria, these countries have a lower proportion of their arable lands degraded. These lower degradation rates may also reflect the fact that less land is being farmed. In the future, increased rates of soil degradation are highly likely, for these countries need to increase their food production. In 2005, these countries were still importing a significant amount of their food. Soil degradation is inevitable unless sustainable agricultural practices can be implemented, and the traditional soil management practices adopted that are effective in reducing soil fertility (Gruhn et al, 2000). Whether sustainable agriculture can be practised in these countries is unclear because it is urgent that more people are fed.

Another trend suggested by these data is that many countries, irrespective of their HDI ranking, are using a greater portion of their land-base for agriculture than the total arable land estimated to exist in that country (Table 8.3). In the highest HDI and the high HDI-ranked emerging-economy countries (Australia, Canada, Japan, Mexico, Norway, Russia, the UAE and the US), this pattern of using more land to produce food is common. All of these countries have a low hunger index; therefore, they are making decisions that have not reduced their country-level food security. Three (Australia, Canada and the US) exported more agricultural products than they imported, suggesting that they are able to grow excess food. Three others (Norway, Russia and the UAE) are also using more of their arable lands to grow crops, but they are still unable to produce enough food to feed their own people; these three countries have to import 4–6 times more food than they export.

Table 8.3 *Arable land characteristics for countries grouped by HDI in 2000, unless given otherwise*

HDI Rank	Potential arable land of total land area (%)	Potentially arable/land 1994 actually in use (%)	Land degradation due to agricultural activities (% of total land area)
1	37 [0–79]	62 [19–289]	8 [0–23]
2	30 [0–64]	673 [30–3900]	8 [0–22]
3	33 [12–60]	49 [7–98]	8 [0–22]
4	41 [15–67]	44 [6–82]	4 [0–8]
5	30 [0–67]	86 [15–108]	6 [0–16]
6	71 [67–73]	15 [1–49]	9 [0–26]

Note: Groupings and their HDI rankings: Group 1 = HDI > 0.9; Group 2 = > 0.8–0.9; Group 3 = > 0.7–0.8; Group 4 = > 0.6–0.7; Group 5 = > 0.5–0.6; Group 6 = 0.4–0.5; Mean [range]
Source: FAO, 2000

Japan is also an interesting outlier in this group of higher HDI-ranked countries; it utilizes eight times more land area for agriculture than it potentially has available. In 2005 Japan had to import 40 times more agricultural products than they were capable of exporting. From a soil's perspective, Japan has the potential to increase its land's productive capacity, for it has the highest percentage of total land-base (57 per cent) with no major soil constraints.

Several of the middle and lower HDI-ranked countries also utilize more land for food production than they potentially have available (e.g. Bangladesh, China, Haiti, India, Nepal, Philippines and Yemen); these countries are also ranked in the middle to high end of the hunger-index ranking. Of these, only Yemen is utilizing less of its land for agriculture than the area potentially available. Utilizing a higher proportion of the total land for food production does not provide food security for these countries. Except for India, they need to import food or manage their soil constraints.

What is noteworthy is the fact that only three countries are not under- or over-utilizing their potential arable land-base. Argentina, Indonesia and the Netherlands utilize exactly the same percentage of land to produce agricultural crops as has been estimated to be their potential arable land-base. All three produce enough agricultural crops to feed their people, and so have food security. They are also able to export more than twice the amount of agricultural products they import; this shows the importance of agricultural commodities for economic growth.

The amount of land area used to grow crops compared to what is potentially available as arable land provides the first filter for characterizing the food security of a country. It does not, however, address the soil constraints that each country faces, nor does it acknowledge whether lands are being degraded during food production. Humans have been effective in adjusting their agricultural practices to the specific constraints of each soil, so that these constraints are not a common topic of discussion in media outlets. For the countries in our list, the role of agriculture in contributing to land degradation is amazingly consistent: 8 per cent of the total land area. This trend also suggests that agriculturalists have generally evolved practices to minimize the degradation of their lands. Even though we know that soils set the threshold for food security, human adaptability to different soil conditions makes it difficult to link food security to soil-quality indicators. Humans have been extremely successful at adopting different agricultural practices to compensate for the soil-nutrient deficiencies that exist on their lands. They have also become effective at increasing the food value of crops using breeding, genetic selection and fertilizer applications.

Correcting soil-nutrient imbalances was one of the core tenets of the Green Revolution, and extensive fertilizer applications were used to increase crop yields of new, improved varieties of plants. The fertilizers used in the Green Revolution were produced from petroleum-based products, demonstrating the link between oil, and food production. Even though humans grew more food and were able to feed global populations, it also resulted in significant environmental problems, such as the contamination of groundwater and soil with chemicals. When these environmental problems occurred, farmers had fewer choices in ameliorating the constraints of their land-base as they grew food crops. In industrialized countries, these practices resulted in the contamination of water supplies and soils, and they have necessitated the restoration of arable lands. Although the Green Revolution was extremely successful, it also highlighted the environmental externalities that can result from increasing food production beyond the land's capacity to realistically produce food at this level of growth.

Recently, new constraints and indicators have been introduced that farmers have to consider during agricultural production. The carbon-storage role of soils has emerged as an important topic because half of the terrestrial carbon is found in soils (Vogt et al, 2007). During the last few hundred years, mechanization and the use of agricultural practices that increase plant growth rates have already resulted in the loss of almost half of the organic carbon that was previously stored in soils. This has forced changes in agricultural practices (e.g. no-till agriculture) to reduce the loss of carbon in the form of organic matter from soils being used to grow food crops. Because agricultural practices can impact global climate change and can be used to mitigate CO_2 emissions, farmers have to include new constraints to their farming practices. Agriculture, as in the past, remains very much an essential practice that continues to evolve in response to dynamic environments and climate, as well as new societal demands.

Except in a few cases (e.g. Chinese farmers moving to parts of Africa), farmers do not have the luxury of moving to a different area to farm if they mismanage their soils. They need to grow crops on the only soil available to them. Therefore, if they use poor farming practices, it is they who will have to deal with the repercussions of the additional new soil constraints that will reduce their soil's productive capacity.

Focusing on whether soils will degrade due to some agricultural practice is probably not very useful, because farmers have been extremely efficient at developing agricultural practices to compensate for their soil deficiencies and to farm-degraded soils. Because humans have been so adaptive in their food production, it is difficult to identify indicators at the country level that would suggest whether soils are going to degrade further, or what practices should be avoided. A more useful approach to understand soils, and the constraints they introduce for making sustainable bio-resource decisions, might be to focus on the direct links between soils and human health.

Your Health Is Dictated by Where Your Food Is Grown

Nutrient deficiencies in food and human health problems

It almost seems trite to state that human health starts in the soil, but this is a statement that is generally correct and overlooked. It is not the soil *per se*, but the macronutrients and trace elements that are found in the soil, that are important for human health. There are many examples of the soil–plant nutrient link to human health. Even though the iron (Fe) contents of soils are normal, some regions of the world have low availabilities of soluble Fe that can be taken up by plants. In fact iron-deficiency anaemia is the most commonly observed mineral deficiency recorded in humans.

Since nutrient deficiencies are directly linked to soil-nutrient-supply capacity, human health problems due to mineral deficiencies are very much controlled by soil quality and how we manage soils. Humans need over 20 macronutrients and trace elements to maintain their health.

A conceptual depiction of how some human diseases are more impacted by nutrients, while others are more influenced by one's genetic make-up, is shown in Figure 8.3. The most common nutrition-related impact on human health is that people are more vulnerable to diseases when they are unable to maintain a balanced and nutritious diet.

Some of the important functions of minerals for humans and plants are summarized in Table 8.4. If these minerals are limiting, they can disrupt the growth of plants and the normal functioning of the human body. What is clearly evident from this table is how many minerals are essential for both plants and animals, even if only in trace amounts.

Several elements – iodine (I), sodium (Na) and selenium (Se) – are needed by humans but not by plants (Table 8.4). There is a greater risk that humans and animals will have deficiencies of these elements in their diets because plants are not actively transporting them into their tissues from the soil. Elements required by animals are generally the same minerals that are essential for plant growth, with the notable exception of sodium (Na).

A newly emerging field of 'medical geology' is beginning to shed light on the many different ways that soils are impacting human health (Keller, 2000). Because human health is complex and it is difficult to identify a single disease-

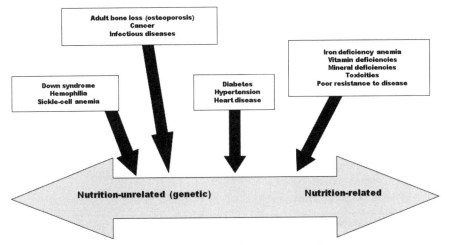

Figure 8.3 *Conceptual depiction of some human diseases resulting from nutrient deficiencies*

Table 8.4 *Minerals in plants and human health*

Minerals	Human health link	Role in plants
Nitrogen	Important component of proteins, amino acids, hormones	Essential component of protoplasm & enzymes (proteins), important component of chlorophyll (photosynthesis); typically the most limiting nutrient for plant & microbes
Phosphorus	Essential for energy transfer in biochemical pathways (e.g. ADP, ATP)	Essential for energy transfer in biochemical pathways (e.g. ADP, ATP); critical for root growth
Potassium	Helps prevent heart, kidney diseases & diabetes; deficiencies cause heart disease	Helps maintain cell turgor, selective ion uptake across root membranes, regulates water absorption through leaf pores; stomatal control; enzyme activation (photosynthesis)
Calcium	Essential for building bones; deficiencies cause bone deformities	Essential for building cell walls of plants; regulation of hydration; enzyme activator
Magnesium	Deficiencies cause asthma, chronic bronchitis, heart disease & bone deformities	Regulation of hydration; basal metabolism (photosynthesis)
Manganese	Important for bone formation & in immune system	Essential for photosynthesis & nitrogen metabolism; controls leaf & root diseases
Zinc	Needed for healthy skin, maintains immune system, aids sight, taste & smell; deficiencies cause chronic bronchitis	Important in pollination, formation of growth regulators, protein breakdown, & seed germination; enzyme activator
Copper	Deficiencies cause chronic bronchitis, heart disease & bone deformities	Photosynthesis, nitrogen metabolism
Sodium	Deficiencies cause poor nervous system development	Not required by plants
Iodine	Deficiencies cause goitres or enlargement of the thyroid gland	Not required by plants
Selenium	Deficiencies cause chronic bronchitis & heart disease; small amounts essential for animals & human health	Not required by plants

Source: Larcher, 1975; Ensminger and Konlande, 1993

> ## Box 8.3 Examples of human health links to soil nutrients
>
> - Schistosomiasis, snail fever, is not commonly found in the Amazon even though the environments are optimal for it. Low calcium (Ca) levels in water, due to the highly leached soils and soil acidity, means that it is not common in the Amazon.
> - Iodine deficiencies in the drinking water leading to goitre.
> - Heart disease (coronary heart disease and cardiovascular disease) linked to drinking water with low concentrations of Ca and Magnesium (Mg) – 'soft' water. Where rivers flow through sedimentary rocks, low in sulphates and high in bicarbonates, the drinking water is hard and there are fewer deaths from strokes.

causing factor, the link between soil chemistry and human health is still evolving and there will never be a one-indicator link to health. Despite this, many studies have shown links between human health and soil/water deficiencies or imbalances in mineral supplies (see Keller, 2000). A few examples of human health links to soil nutrients are summarized in Box 8.3.

Excessive consumption of some minerals, as well as nutrient deficiencies, can cause human health problems. Local geochemical anomalies resulting from a lack of, or toxic concentrations of, particular trace minerals in the human diet have been noted throughout human history (Aggett, 1988). They have been mostly caused by three trace elements, fluorine, selenium and iodine. Aggett (1988) described the extensive occurrence of Se in higher concentrations in people living in particular regions of China where Se levels are toxic, and have triggered cardiomyopathy. The high concentrations of water-soluble Se are taken up by the cereal food crops which then introduce it into the human diet. The primary source of selenium is volcanic activity.

In the past, people's health was strongly impacted by nutrient deficiencies because they had limited food options due to the necessity of consuming locally grown food. These food supplies were as nutritious as the soil quality found on the farms. This was more of an issue in some regions of the world because of local soil constraints such as low nutrient availabilities, high Al, salinity and sand contents.

Human health, agriculture and nutrient deficiencies: the soil connection

Many of our minerals are derived from the weathering of parent material. The primary source for sodium is weathering from minerals and organic materials, whereas the secondary sources are atmospheric inputs which originate from the sea or salt beds. Calcium mainly becomes available during soil weathering, but some recent studies have shown that atmospheric inputs occur with air pollution. Historically, higher inputs of Ca into forests of the northeastern US (i.e. New England) were attributed to Native American burning of grasslands in the US Midwest. More recently, cement-manufacturing plants, also located in the

Midwest US, have been linked to Ca inputs into these same New England forests.

Some of these weathered minerals can negatively impact health. For example, arsenic is toxic and becomes available for human and plant uptake following the weathering of some metamorphic rocks. Chromium too, released from the weathering of basic igneous rocks, is toxic when present in large amounts.

All these elements become available during the weathering of parent material. Because the available amounts of some macronutrients and trace elements are typically low, farmers have experimented with their lands to increase their nutrient-delivery capacity or to add nutrients back into the soil. Early societies had already recognized the link between managing soils well and crop yields. According to Hillel (1991), by 'the time of Cato the Censor (234–139 BCE), the Romans were aware of the need to boost soil fertility by means of fallowing, as well as by crop rotation, liming acid soils and adding manure.' It was not until the 18th century, however, that the technological developments arising from industrialization contributed towards significant increases in farm yields. During this time, the technology to manufacture fertilizers and pesticides using chemicals flourished; the first artificial fertilizer was invented in 1842 (Hillel, 1991). This allowed farmers to specialize in crops based on local climate and the soils, while achieving 'a high degree of self-sufficiency' that had not been possible prior to these technological developments (Hillel, 1991).

Now it has become easy to apply fertilizers to alleviate mineral deficiencies for any soil that has experienced reduced crop growth. Some fertilizers (K and P) were applied to increase the yields of our food crops and not *just* their nutrient quality (Ensminger and Konlande, 1993). These mineral applications have been very effective in correcting soil-mineral deficiencies at the local level of a farm.

When soils are deficient in certain trace elements, fertilizing agricultural fields is not always the preferred option to alleviate mineral deficiencies in the human diet. For example, iodine and fluoride deficiencies in the human diet are not effectively alleviated by applying fertilizers to soils to increase their concentrations in food crops. The iodine deficiencies are a result of soils having low iodine concentrations so that human dietary requirements cannot be satisfied by eating plants growing in these soils. Iodine deficiency has to be managed since it causes goitres (enlargement of the thyroid gland) in humans. The reason that fertilizing soils does not work in increasing iodine concentrations in food is because it is not an essential plant element, so plants will not actively take it up from the soil. This problem was resolved by adding iodine to table salt, taking advantage of a common practice for people to 'salt' their food during a meal. Unfortunately, despite the addition of iodine to salt, iodine deficiencies have not been eliminated from the human population (Aggett, 1988). Fluoride deficiencies have also been mitigated by adding fluoride into our drinking water because fertilizing crops with fluoride was less effective. Fluoride is needed in small amounts for human teeth and bone development (Ensminger and Konlande, 1993).

Human societies also improve food quality when processing and packaging food products to sell in markets. One only has to look at the writing on materials used to package our foods to see what nutrients or vitamins have been added into each food product. These additions were not always due to food producers wanting to contribute to a balanced diet for people. Heavily-processed foods have been shown to have lower trace-element contents, necessitating food processors to replace them into the food product during its processing. For example, Aggett (1988) mentioned the loss of manganese, iron and zinc from flour being milled.

In the industrialized world, some humans also supplement their diets with daily dosages of multi-vitamins and minerals in a 'pill' form instead of eating foods that are higher in these minerals. This trend is especially common today because people are opting to eat foods that do not provide the essential nutrients they need to be healthy. In the US, consuming daily doses of multi-vitamins and minerals has almost become the norm and a way to offset the nutrients or trace elements missing from diets.

Wildlife and nutrient deficiencies: eating soils

Other animals also face the problem of their food supplies being deficient in some minerals. Since animals are more dependent upon eating the plants found in their habitat, any deficiency in the soil will immediately translate into a deficiency of that mineral in plants growing on these soils. When animals have to eat these mineral-deficient plants, they too become deficient in these same minerals. There are significant repercussions to animal-based human food supplies if the soil has a poor capacity to provide any one of the limiting minerals. Some parts of Australia were unable to develop a profitable livestock industry, for example, until copper fertilizers were applied to the pastures.

Wild animals go to extraordinary lengths to obtain the nutrients that they lack in their diets. Because plants do not accumulate sodium (Na), animals have adapted to acquire the Na that is essential in the mammalian diet for development of the nervous system. A common animal response to low Na concentrations in plant tissues is for them to eat mushrooms (which accumulate Na even though the fungi do not need it) or the ingestion of sodium-rich soils (salt licks).

Klaus et al (1998) suggested that dominance of geophagy (licking or eating soil) by elephants and other mammalian species in the rainforest regions of Africa is correlated to the poor nutrient status of these highly leached soils. Holda et al (2002) studied how African elephants practise geophagy to obtain Na when its levels in the plant tissues they eat, or in their natural water supplies, are too low.

Holda et al (2002) noted that elephants do not lick or eat soil in those regions of Africa where the water supplies have higher Na concentrations. Even the seasonal distribution of elephants has been linked to Na availabilies in the environment. Several generations of elephants have been recorded travelling into dark caves in western Kenya to find clay deposits that they ate to acquire nutrients missing in their diets (Burne, 2002). The bones of numerous elephants that died during these trips into the caves attest to the dangers that these elephants are willing to face due to the need to acquire the nutrients missing in their normal food supplies.

Soils, therefore, are important habitats or growth media for the animals and plants that co-inhabit this world with humans. Because soils determine the pool of nutrient supplies available, they strongly influence the nutrient status of plants and the resulting nutrient deficiencies or toxicities in animals. As many animals eat plants for food, soils will ultimately determine whether animals will be able to acquire sufficient nutrients from eating plants for food. Soils are an important and integral part of the ecosystem within which humans live and share with many other plants and animals. This makes it more critical that we understand the implication of soil-management decisions at an ecosystem level, for soil chemical deficiencies or toxicities impact the entire ecosystem.

Forests Buffer Societies Living on Nutrient-Poor Soils

Forests grow well on poor soils

When the US Soil Conservation Service (SCS) – now known as Natural Resource Conservation Service (NRCS) – classified soils as to their appropriateness for agricultural uses, soils with severe limitations were restricted to pastures for grazing animals, or for the growth of trees. Classification as unsuitable for cultivation was founded on:

- slopes being too steep;
- a high erosion potential;
- the presence of rocks (i.e. too stony);
- the risk of droughts because of soils having lower water-holding capacity (related to the amount of organic matter in the soil and soil texture, as sandy soils have a low water-holding capacity).

It is notable that productive forests are found growing in the locations where agriculture is more difficult to practise.

It is also informative to note what percentage of the land area is in agricultural production globally. According to the FAO, about one-tenth of the global terrestrial area is used for growing crops (Table 2.1). This suggests that a smaller fraction of our terrestrial land-base is ideally suited to growing crops and that productive agricultural lands are mainly being used for this purpose. Globally, one-third of the terrestrial land area is covered by forests, mostly in land areas that are not ideal for or conducive to intensive agriculture. Therefore, humans need to recognize the constraints that soils impose on land-uses, and identify where a forest area should not be converted to other uses, such as land-use practices that require more highly productive soils.

Besides the climate, soil-nutrient status determines which tree species and forest types grow at any location. For example, hardwood or deciduous species are commonly found growing in deeper soils with higher concentrations of organic matter and more available nutrients. These soils also have higher moisture contents. The productive agricultural lands in the midwestern US are a result of

Table 2.1 *Land area distribution types for the US and the world*

	United States	World
Forests, woodlands	29	33
Pastures, rangelands	26	23
Agriculture	20	10
Desert	14	32
Built land	7	2

Note: Units = percentage of total in 1999 for the world data; 2005 for the US (except for built land which are 2001 data). The high variance in the published numbers means that the totals do not equal 100 per cent. *Source:* FAO, 2008; Alig et al, 2009

the high level of organic matter in the soil and the continual input of wind-blown soil (i.e. loess) adding non-weathered materials. The high productivity of the American prairies and the Argentine pampas is due to the high amount of organic matter found in these soils. These grasslands have soil characteristics that make them more amenable to being converted to agricultural uses.

In contrast, forests dominated by coniferous and evergreen species are less suitable for agriculture. These forests are found growing on rocky, more drought-prone and nutrient-poor soils. If these forest types were converted into agricultural production, crop yields would be quite poor. Agricultural production would not be efficient and would require the expenditure of considerable funds to alleviate the existing soil constraints using chemical fertilizers and irrigation.

It is important to retain forests in our landscapes because they are so well adapted to grow under the extreme conditions imposed by soil and climatic constraints. Trees are adapted to grow in nutrient-poor soils and under a variety of moisture conditions (e.g. conditions of excessive moisture, and in saline water dominated by mangroves). In contrast to agricultural crops, trees have adapted to grow well where nutrient levels are low, soil depths are shallow, soils are rocky and where toxic chemicals (e.g. Al) are present in higher concentrations. Because trees and their symbionts are tolerant of toxic heavy metals, trees are planted in mine spoil wastes to restore the productive capacity of these lands and are being used in phytoremediation, to remove toxic chemicals from water or soils. Trees are amazingly adapted to different environmental conditions and in fact they are found growing in almost every biome type globally except the tundra. Most environments have at least one or two tree species able to grow under the constraints posed by the soil and climate. Only humans have adapted to their environments as well as trees, although insects, and of course microbes, are also extremely well adapted to their environments. In fact, today there is no terrestrial landscape that does not have the 'human footprint' imprint or legacy that is not connected to a tree in some way.

Trees are better adapted than humans to the environment and climates

Humans can be found living in every region of the world. They live in areas that experience extreme cycles of disturbance (e.g. volcanic eruptions in Iceland, earthquakes in China and Indonesia, typhoons in the Philippines and hurricanes in the Caribbean) that can decimate their population densities. Humans have been remarkably adaptive to their environments and altered them when they were less suitable for their survival by being too cold, too hot, too dry or too wet. Today, a small fraction of the global terrestrial landscape has been turned into built environments (i.e. large cities), but bio-resources are utilized or harvested from over 60 per cent of the terrestrial land area (Vogt et al, 2007; see this volume, Chapter 6). This means that humans have successfully utilized or managed most of the terrestrial landscape. The history of humans living on this earth, however, is short (the modern *Homo sapiens* arrived about 200,000 years ago) compared to trees (i.e. gymnosperms) that have been on this world for more than 220 million years.

Despite the fact that humans live in every biome in the world, they have not been as adaptable as trees because there are some environments (e.g. hyper-arid deserts or tundra) that humans have to migrate from seasonally to survive. Trees cannot migrate like humans and have to tolerate all of the climatic and anthropogenic disturbances of their local environment; the distributions of trees do change in response to changes in the environment but these species changes occur at longer time-scales.

Tree species are adapted to grow in the multitude of different climatic and soil zones. There is a diversity of tree species that is uniquely adapted to particular environmental conditions. Although climatic conditions may be particularly harsh for humans, the growth cycles of trees adjust to take advantage of the time periods when conditions are suitable for their growth. For example, humans are not very tolerant of cloudy, overcast days or having to experience cycles of low daylight found at northern latitudes during the winter; these conditions have been linked to depression, higher suicide rates and high rates of alcohol consumption. In contrast, trees grow during conducive conditions, and their tissues are maintained from stored carbon stored in their tissues during the time when the environment is less favourable to support tree growth. Trees grow very well on very rocky soils, even when it appears that there are insufficient nutrients for them to grow. Figure 8.4 presents a caricature of how a tree can be found growing on rocks and adapted to acquire the nutrients it needs to grow; it may be hundreds of years old and growing slowly each year, but is able to persist in this environment.

Trees are finely adapted to their local environments. They have survived because they have evolved to be relatively resistant to pests and shorter-term climate changes; they are the survivors who have lived for hundreds of years in the face of adverse climatic conditions and attacks by fungal and pest pathogens. In the Pacific Northwest US, the large and magnificent old-growth Douglas fir trees

Figure 8.4 *Depiction of tree adapted to growing on rock alone*

are adapted to survive for hundreds of years (over 1000 years for some individual trees) of environmental change – an amazing feat considering what they have experienced. These long-lived trees have survived there because they grow slowly, are resistant to pests and pathogens and are adapted to multiple climate changes. These survival characteristics are, by necessity, the opposite of what agricultural crops are bred to tolerate. The latter are selected to grow fast and produce high yields; chemicals are used to control pests and pathogens so plants do not have to be adapted to protect themselves.

When humans see large and old trees, they assume that the site is nutrient-rich. A highly productive forest, or one with a large amount of biomass, does not have soils that are nutrient-rich. When European colonialists first travelled to the South American tropics (such as the Amazon) and saw the dense and luxuriant forests that grew there, they thought that these lands would be highly productive for agriculture. When they cleared them to plant crops, they found crop growth was dismal. What they did not originally recognize was that the soils are extremely nutrient-poor. The forests were a legacy of efficient nutrient cycling by the vegetation that had developed over timescales of several hundred years. In this case, the soils did not determine the productive capacity of the forests but the efficiency at which a forest was able to keep the nutrients from leaching into the soils. Trees forged symbiotic associations with fungi and bacteria that increased their successin competing for nutrients, the lack of which would limit their growth.

These symbiotic associations expand the adaptive mechanisms available for trees and increase their competitiveness in face of the natural soil constraints that exist at any location; symbionts also function as selective membranes at the root level that allow trees to avoid taking up toxic minerals from soils that could affect their growth, and to fend off root pathogens that would produce enzymes to attack tree tissues for food. Another amazing adaptation of trees is their ability to allocate more of the biomass to roots in order to acquire nutrients more efficiently from soils when nutrient availabilities are low (Vogt et al, 1996). When soil nutrient levels are higher, these same trees allocate more carbon into above-ground tissues involved in fixing CO_2 (leaves as well as the stems and branches that support the leaves) and less into roots. These adaptations are what allow trees to grow in environments where nutrient levels are low or where chemical toxins are present in the soil.

Trees are extremely well adapted to compete for and acquire scarce nutrients. Studies conducted in the Amazon region documented how apogeotropic roots grew out of the soil and up the stems of other plants to hotspots (higher concentrations) of nutrients that were flowing along their stems; roots were recorded growing some 13m up the stem of another tree (Sanford, 1987). Roots growing up the stems of neighbouring trees are unusual because they mainly grow into the soil. In cloud forests, plants are adapted to grow roots from stems located in the canopy of a tree to take advantage of the nutrients that are carried by clouds. Trees are supremely adapted to grow in low-nutrient soils or even in a soilless medium.

Shifting agriculture is practised by indigenous communities in areas where the soil nutrient supply capacity is low. As part of shifting agriculture, communities take advantage of the efficiency with which trees compete for scarce nutrients by using trees to provide a pulse of nutrients for their growing crops. Shifting agriculturalists collect trees from the land area to be converted into crop production and then burn them to produce a 'fertilizer' (the ash). This practice takes advantage of the greater efficiency of trees to acquire limiting nutrients from the soil and then to store them in their tissues while they are growing. Without this shifting agriculture practice, crops would not grow well in these areas because the soil nutrient supply capacity is too low.

Shifting agriculture today is becoming less sustainable, as indigenous communities are decreasing the time interval between agricultural production and allowing trees to grow back to replenish soil nutrients. In the Indian Himalaya, the shifting agriculture is no longer being practised at five year intervals but after a year or two, as described in Box 8.4. When population pressures and the need to grow food change the cycles of shifting agriculture, the benefits that accrue from allowing forests to restore soil nutrients over a longer timescale are eliminated. What is happening in the Indian Himalaya is also being repeated in the Brazilian Amazon and other tropical forests.

When practised appropriately for a site, shifting agriculture is a practice that takes advantage of the natural supply capacity of the lands, and works because trees are able to maintain symbiotic associations that allow them to acquire limiting nutrients. If these lands are managed as intensive agricultural production units, crops will need to be fertilized, since the natural supply capac-

Box 8.4 Environmental and Social Resiliency in the Indian Himalaya

Rajesh Thadani

The Himalaya mountain range forms an arc 2400km long that separates the Indian subcontinent from the Tibetan Plateau. This range is very important to the Indian subcontinent both ecologically and socially, and is home to almost one-fourth of the world's population. It forms a barrier that feeds soil- and rainfall-derived water supplies into the numerous rivers that are essential for boosting the agricultural productivity of the region. Over 70 per cent of the Indian Himalaya contains 'hills' less than 2500m in height; this is the same location where population densities are high compared to other mountainous areas. Rainfall varies considerably from rain-shadow areas of the Western Himalaya, represented by the area west of Nepal, to rain-forest-like conditions in the Eastern Himalaya, with over 2500mm of annual rainfall. In the outer ranges in the west, 1000mm of rainfall per annum is not uncommon, and irrigated fields are carved into the mountainside. As populations have grown, degradation of the Himalayan forests and natural systems has occurred; this also impacts the heavily populated Indo-Gangetic plains. While the people of the Western Himalaya have been well-connected to those plains, the Eastern Himalaya, represented by Nagaland and Arunachal, has remained more isolated and fragmented culturally, as well as maintaining their animistic societies and more 'primitive' agricultural systems. Different practices have evolved in both landscapes to respond to the local constraints of each environment. These will be further described next.

The state of Uttarakhand in the west, with the headwaters of the Ganga and Yamuna rivers, is characterized by settled agriculture and a history of social and cultural practices dating back well over a thousand years. Although agriculture is closely tied to animal husbandry, forests are essential to the sustenance of the agricultural systems – green fodder for draft and milk animals, and leaf litter, which is part of compost fertilizer. In addition, firewood collected from forests is the main energy for cooking and heating; and medicinal plants, lichens and mosses supplement the incomes of the poorest people. An oak–pine-dominated ecosystem is common from around 1400 to 2200m in elevation, the zone that has the highest population density. The more desirable oak forests have been partially replaced by pine forests due to unsustainable practices by the people, resulting in inferior woodfuel, useless fodder for cattle, poor compost fertilizer, less retention of water and increase in fire risk. These in turn have resulted in increased rates of out-migration, in particular of able-bodied and more enterprising males, some agricultural abandonment and weakening of village institutions. This leads to a further downward spiral.

The states of Nagaland and Arunachal on the eastern periphery of the Himalaya form part of the catchment of the mighty Brahmaputra River. Inhabitants of these regions practise swidden or shifting agriculture; in this practice the vegetation is slashed and burned on the slopes, which are then are cultivated for only a year or two before being abandoned for approximately five years, until the swidden cycle is repeated. However, rotations of five years are not sustainable, either ecologically or economically. The flatter, irrigated fields, with rice as the dominant crop, compose less than one-tenth of the total land. While too much of Nagaland practices swidden farming, replacing it can be done only at the cost of damage to the traditions and social resilience of the system. However, a change in focus from worrying about the cycle length to introducing tree crops and enhancing conservation measures to reduce soil erosion and increase moisture conservation has borne fruit, in the form of various horticultural and cash crops. Effective conservation needs to be compatible with the social needs and constraints of the local people.

ity of the soils will not be adequate to maintain agricultural production. There are several repercussions of applying high amounts of fertilizer: (1) native plants in the forest are not adapted to these higher nutrient levels and will be out-competed by faster-growing exotic plant species, which means a shift in plant species dominance to non-native species; and (2) the symbiotic fungi that have formed mutualistic relationships with native plants are also not adapted to high nutrient levels and will not remain in these forests; this will decrease the native fungal diversity as well as provide less protection to plants against toxic chemicals naturally present in these soils. There will also be a loss of a traditional practice that was developed to allow farming to occur in soils with low nutrient levels. Furthermore, since agricultural plants are less able to adapt to their soils, farmers will have to expend more energy and time in ameliorating the soil environment to grow crops.

Because trees are so well adapted to so many extreme environmental conditions, they provide a buffer to human societies, as well as maintaining ecosystem resiliency. Trees are a valuable bio-resource for humans throughout the world and not just in a few niche locations, and can facilitate human survival across a broad range of ecosystem types. Forests also provide many other ecosystem services valuable to humans (see Chapter 11). Even if agriculture cannot be practised in all forestlands because of the nutrient-poor soils, forests can still provide food to humans because of the animals that live in them (Yamagiwa, 2003). In the African and American tropics, hunting in forests may provide the only protein consumed by people surviving at the subsistence level.

Many forests are also the source of the renewable water supplies. The cloud forests in Mexico and many other regions of the world capture moisture from the atmosphere that eventually flows into rivers and provides the water supplies consumed by the lowland communities (Box 8.5). The cloud forest area is shrinking rapidly in many places because of competitive demands on the land that has seen these forests converted to other uses. It has been extremely difficult to balance the demand for resource supplies, the economic opportunities and the conservation goals of the various stakeholders, who in one way or another expect to derive benefits from these forests or the land itself, for instance by converting forests into cattle ranches. These uses compete against the lowland communities who want the water that originates in these forests. The challenges in balancing the multiple products and ecosystem services are described in Box 8.5.

Forests are closely linked to the water cycle and can be lost from our landscape if less precipitation falls in an area or if there are severe droughts. Therefore, climate change will determine where forests will grow. Trees are not immune to climate change that decreases the amount of rainfall in an area. If less rain falls in the semi-arid regions, it will jeopardize the growth of forests which need a minimum amount of precipitation to survive. When rainfall falls below the minimum level needed by forests, these ecosystems will revert into grasslands. These shifts from grassland to forest and back to grassland have been repeatedly recorded in the savanna–forest ecosystems of South America (Mann, 2002).

Box 8.5 Linking Water and Forest Conservation in the Mountains of Mexico

Jason Scullion

In the cities and towns of Mexico's arid Tehuacán-Cuicatlán region, southeast of Mexico City, trees are few, water is scarce and both are continuing to decline. In Mexico, 40 per cent of all groundwater has been pumped beyond its natural recharge rate. Additionally, 73 per cent of the water is unfit to drink, including water found in 95 per cent of the rivers. To address some of these problems, the government developed the Payment for Environmental Service (PES) hydrological programme (PSAH), in which direct cash payments are made to selected forest owners to conserve their forests. Much of the water supplies in rivers originate in forests, so maintaining intact forests should increase water supplies. Mexico's PSAH programme rewards forest owners, who receive payments to protect their forests, and provides benefits to downstream communities who are assured greater water security. The PSAH programme started in 2003 with 127,000ha of forest receiving cash payments and grew to cover 546,000ha by 2007. Additionally, the Global Environmental Facility (GEF) and the World Bank agreed to provide a grant of US$15 million and a loan of US$45 million, to assist Mexico's PES programmes.

The majority of Mexico's forests are owned by individuals and communities inhabiting the forests; many owners, who are poor and marginalized, often decide to cut the forests, rather than conserve them. As a result, half of Mexico's forest cover has been lost in the last 50 years. Furthermore, since 1976, over 350,000ha of the nation's forests have been lost each year, placing Mexico in the top tier of countries with high deforestation rates worldwide. The causes of deforestation are most closely associated with the relative profitability of agriculture and pastoral activities versus the collection of forest products. However, some forests, especially cloud forests, provide other ecosystem services (e.g. water). The PSAH programme is attempting to provide an economic return from conserving cloud forests, to reduce their conversion to other uses.

Cloud forests play an important role in the provision of water for downstream communities. In central Veracruz, just beyond the arid plains of the Tehuacán-Cuicatlán, lies the rugged Sierra Madre Oriental mountain range. Tucked in it is the municipality of Coatepec, the coffee capital in Mexico, which as a downstream community is dependent on upland sources of water. In 2003 it established Fidecoagua, a trust fund and Mexico's first PSAH programme, as a direct response to drought, as well as a recognition that loss of the region's cloud forests was a likely factor contributing to water shortages. The hydrological effects of 'cloud stripping' by these forests can add the equivalent of 5–20 per cent of the water delivered by local rainfall; in some locations this value approaches 60 per cent. The programme also aims to protect the other ecosystem services generated by cloud forests; 30 per cent of Mexico's endemic species are restricted to these forests. Cloud forests cover less than 1 per cent of the country but contain about 12 per cent of its species diversity.

Even with the PES programme, it will be challenging to retain cloud forests because they are located in economically depressed areas. In one of two watersheds in Coatepec, 16 per cent of the people have electricity, 30 per cent have piped water, 30 per cent are literate and 90 per cent rely on firewood for fuel; the main causes of regional forest loss are illegal wood cutting and the expansion of crops and pastures. The two programmes cover an estimated 17 per cent of the municipality's forests. Although compliance is near 100 per cent, 30 per cent of the participants indicate they would convert their forests to pasture or agriculture once the payments stop.

Their reversion to grassland will reduce the ability of people living in these landscapes to use the forests as a safety valve for energy production or to practise shifting agriculture based on burning trees to produce ash as a crop fertilizer. Loss of forests also reduces the amount of renewable water sources available. In the US, it has been estimated that 80 per cent of renewable water supplies originate in forests.

References

Aggett, P. J. (1988) 'Trace element status of the human diet', Proceedings of the Nutrition Society, vol 47, pp21–25

Brady N. C. (1990) *The Nature and Properties of Soils*, 10th edition, Macmillan Publishing, New York, NY

Burne J. (2002) 'Animal instinct', *The Guardian*, 17 January 2002, www.primates.com/misc/index.html, accessed 7 July 2009

Ensminger, A. H. and Konlande, J. E. (1993) *Foods & Nutrition Encyclopedia*, 2nd edition, CRC Press, Boca Raton, FL

Fagan, B. (2008) *The Great Warming. Climate Change and the Rise and Fall of Civilizations*, Bloomsbury Press, New York, NY

FAO (2000) 'World Soil Resources Report 90. Land Resource Potential and Constraints at Regional and Country Levels', UN FAO, Rome, Italy

FAO (2006) 'Global Forest Resources Assessment 2005', UN FAO, Rome, Italy

Gruhn P., Goletti, F. and Yudelman, M. (2000) 'Integrated nutrient management, soil fertility and sustainable agriculture: current issues and future challenges', Food, Agriculture and the Environment Discussion Paper 32, International Food Policy Research Institute, Washington, DC

Hillel, D. J. (1991) *Out of the Earth. Civilization and the Life of the Soil*, The Free Press, New York, NY

Holda, R. M., Dudley, J. P. and McDowell, L. R. (2002) 'Geophagy in the African elephant in relation to availability of dietary sodium', *Journal of Mammalogy*, vol 83, pp652–664

Keller, E. A. (2000) *Environmental Geology*, 8th edition, Prentice-Hall, NJ

Klaus G., Klaus-Húgi, C. and Schmid, B. (1998) 'Geophagy by large mammals at natural licks in the rain forest of the Dzanga National Park, Central African Republic', *Journal of Tropical Ecology*, vol 14, pp829–839

Larcher, W. (1975) *Physiological Plant Ecology*, Springer-Verlag, Berlin, Germany

Mann, C. C. (2002) '1491', *The Atlantic Monthly*, March 2002

Malthus, T. R. (1798) *An Essay On The Principle Of Population. As It Affects the Future Improvement of Society*, 1st ed., Penguin Classics, www.econlib.org/library/Malthus/malPop.html, accessed 30 May 2009

Rabalais, N. N. (2002) 'Nitrogen in aquatic ecosystems', *Ambio*, vol 31, pp102–112

Sanchez, P. A. (1976) *Properties and Management of Soils in the Tropics*, Wiley, New York. NY

Sanford, R. L. Jr (1987) 'Apogeotropic roots in an Amazon rain forest', *Science*, vol 235, pp1062–1064

Vogt, K. A., Vogt, D. J., Palmiotto, P., Boon, P., O'Hara, J. and Asbjornsen, H. (1996) 'Review of root dynamics in forest ecosystems grouped by climate, climatic forest type and species', *Plant and Soil*, vol 187, pp159–219

Vogt, K. A., Honea, J. M., Vogt, D. J., Edmonds, R. L., Patel-Weynand, T., Sigurdardottir, R. and Andreu, M. G. (2007) *Forests and Society. Sustainability and Life Cycles of Forests in Human Landscapes*, CAB International, Wallingford, UK
Wild, A. (1993) *Soils and the Environment. An Introduction*, Cambridge University Press, Cambridge
Yamagiwa, J. (2003) 'Bushmeat poaching and the conservation crisis in Kahuzi-Biega National Park, Democratic Republic of the Congo', in S. V. Price (ed.), *War and Tropical Forests. Conservation in Areas of Armed Conflict*, Food Products Press, The Haworth Press, Inc, New York and London

9

The Ultimate Constraint to Human Sustainability: Solar Income

We will make the case that the ultimate constraint to human sustainability will be determined by the amount of available 'solar income' held by a group of people. Solar income translates into the land's productive capacity, and we contend that to be sustainable we need to shift towards managing and using mostly current solar income (Box 9.1). This would move us to the idea of living within our 'solar income' rather than the 'solar capital' (Box 9.1). Our current approach to assessing sustainability of resource uses mainly measures our solar capital – the area of a natural resource or the quantity of fossil fuel supply that exists. Using this approach, it is easy to calculate that we have hundreds of years of resource supplies and reserves, so there is less concern about consuming resources. If the focus centred on identifying the productive capacity thresholds or the 'income' available from lands being used to consume resources, it would become easier to make decisions that were more sustainable, because climate

---

Box 9.1

Solar capital is defined as the total amount of fixed carbon available for human use. In energy terms this is coal, oil and their relatives (tar sands, etc.), and natural gas. Forests contain a lot of fixed carbon too, and their current mass is also solar capital. Solar income is the annual increment of fixed carbon captured in agriculture and forestry (or other solar energy captured such as PV, wind or hydro). The analogy with financial capital is that capital should only be invested (used) to enhance income, and only income should be used for expenses. Thus we should use fossil fuels to enhance our ability to capture solar energy. We do this when we use fossil fuels to enhance forestry, agriculture, and the non-carbon sources above. We don't do it when we use fossil carbon for transportation fuel, direct home heating, and for other reasons. To fully accept this analogy, we must assume that the goal is to move to using only current solar income at some future time. That is probably unrealistic, but defines an upper limit.

and soils would be factored into decisions. This approach also provides us a way to measure thresholds so that we do not continue to over-consume our solar capital unsustainably.

Productive Capacity Potentials and Human Survival

One of the difficulties in measuring sustainability has been that of detecting when an activity will shift some land-use choice towards becoming 'unsustainable'; less resilient or less capable of recovering after a disturbance. Several assessments have been conducted to determine the sustainability of land-use activities and whether humans are extracting too much of the earth's productive capacity. The ecological footprint index for countries is a useful tool to determine whether countries have an ecological deficit or reserve (Ecological Footprint and Biocapacity, 2006). It can be an initial filter to determine whether new land-use activities should be considered for adoption. However, this index neither addresses the quality of the soil and how that controls the level of plant growth possible at any location, nor how much the productive capacity can be increased without causing soil degradation. Nor does it indicate when increasing or even decreasing a footprint will result in irreparable damage to the lands or reduce social and/or environmental resiliency. This index should, therefore, be used as a first filter when examining a country's land-use capacity, but it should not be used as the only tool to make decisions.

Ecosystem ecology has developed a tool – productive capacity or Net Primary Production (NPP) – that can be ascertained and used to determine whether resource-consumptive behaviours or ecosystems are sustainable in the face of dynamically changing environments. Productive capacity is typically measured as changes in biomass for a given land area during a one year time period. Productive capacity 'has been defined as the ability of the ecosystem to do work (i.e. whether it be to produce human desired products or adapt to natural variations within the ecosystem)' (Vogt et al, 1997). It is a useful measure to examine the sustainability of human consumptive behaviour or the ability of an ecosystem to continue to maintain the biodiversity that directly (e.g. herbivore eating grass) or indirectly (e.g. predator eating the herbivore) consumes this productivity to survive. Agriculture and forestry are managed to optimize the productive capacity of their respective products; management attempts to optimize the conversion of photosynthate into marketable products. The utility of this measure is why several attempts have been made to determine whether human consumption of ecosystem productive capacity is sustainable.

Energetics is a fancy name for solar income, or a land's productive capacity, and is the basis of ecosystem ecology. Beginning in the 1960s, ecosystem ecologists began to use the energetic focus to compare ecosystems using a common metric (Vogt et al, 1996). Since the magnitude of this metric changes with the unavoidable constraints that are found in our environment (climates and soils), it is useful in allowing us to articulate how difficult it will be to make sustainable decisions while consuming 'solar income'.

Other researchers have used the productivity of ecosystems to examine how much of the global productivity is harvested by humans. In 2007, Haberl and colleagues published a paper that calculated how much of the global NPP created in the year 2000 was appropriated by humans. This type of information can help society to determine whether humans are changing the level of NPP they are appropriating. The assessment used data on land use, land cover and soil degradation to calculate how much of the annual growth was being removed or altered by humans. Based on the Haberl et al (2007) analysis, it appears that globally humans are using or taking 23.8 per cent of the annual growth that is produced – globally half of this harvest of NPP is from crop lands for food production. This value is lower than the intermediate value calculated by Vitousek et al (1986), who estimated that humans appropriated 30.7 per cent of global productivity. Both these authors calculated a range of values for the percentage of 'terrestrial co-opted' NPP, with the intermediate calculation including 'material that human beings use directly or that is used in human dominated ecosystems by communities of organisms different from those in corresponding natural ecosystems'. This estimate also included organic material killed and burned during land clearing or conversion.' Vitousek et al (1986) also calculated a high estimate of how much NPP is co-opted by humans that included the potential NPP lost due to human activities. This higher value (38.8 per cent) is the one most commonly reported in the literature.

At first impressions, the calculation made by Haberl et al (2007) appears a useful basis on which to make sustainable decisions. However upon further reflection about what such a value means and how it can be used to change human behaviour and reduce the human bio-resource footprint, it is difficult to take these data and determine how to alter human consumption of global NPP. A component of this problem is that we really do not know what the threshold of 'no return' is, where the human appropriation of resources is going to reduce human choices and increase societal vulnerability. Neither do these data address the adaptability or mitigation efforts that have been the cornerstone of human survival, nor the natural ability for landscapes and soils to recover from negative impacts. How much of the available resources humans can appropriate without negatively impacting the environmental and social resiliency will vary, depending on several factors: where one is located geographically, what the soil constraints are and which locations face significant climate risk or are environmentally vulnerable. Such analyses also have to be site-specific because of the significant regional variation in the productive capacity of soils.

The study by Haberl et al (2007) also provided data to show that the percentage of NPP that was appropriated by humans varied considerably by region. Again, these data are interesting to look at but are difficult to use to make policy decisions on how to increase the resilience of societies and environments in the regions of interest. In the data, the highest percentage of NPP removed by humans annually was found in northern Africa and western Asia (42 per cent appropriated), southern Asia (63 per cent), western Europe (40 per cent) and eastern and southeastern Europe (52 per cent). According to Haberl et al (2007), Sub-Saharan Africa, eastern Asia, Latin America, the Caribbean, Oceania and Australia appropriated the lowest levels of their annual production. So the questions that one must ask are: 'Are human appropriations of NPP too high to be sustainable when the levels are above 40 per cent? Are the countries with less than 40 per cent appropriation of NPP the models that other countries should mimic, or are they the locations where the land productive capacity cannot provide any more NPP without the collapse of the agricultural or forest production in that area?' We know that landscape constraints have a strong influence on where crops can be grown, where there are suitable grazing lands and where forests are dominant. In fact the authors explain that the variations they recorded for western Europe reflect the extensive use of 'high yielding, intensive agricultural systems' that are not used elsewhere. In Central Asia and Russia, the percentage appropriation of NPP reflects the reduced productivity in these locations (Haberl et al, 2007).

At the end of their paper, Haberl et al (2007) cautioned against promoting the use of biomass to produce energy in order to reduce our fossil fuel-related carbon emissions. Their caution resulted from concerns that too much land is being used globally to grow bio-resources for human consumption, and that extensive areas of land have been altered by humans in the pursuit of these activities. These are valid concerns, but we suggest that biomass is part of the resource endowment and can provide humans with the ability to adapt to their environment (see Chapter 12). It is an essential energy supply for societies living in several growing-economy countries that have few other choices. Our caveat for how much biomass to collect is that it should not surpass annual growth or NPP, and that biomass should be efficiently converted to fossil fuel substitutes using second- and third-generation technologies. Historical data on local farm practices should also be used to derive thresholds for certain management activities and their impact on soil production (such as those held by the Rothamsted Experimental Station in southern England). Until we begin to derive thresholds beyond which human appropriation of global NPP becomes detrimental to the environment, we cannot credibly make decisions on what are sustainable practices. These thresholds will also need to be modified to include climatic factors and past land-use legacies that either increase or decrease the growth of plants.

Solar Income Equates to Sustainable Choices

To be able to determine the sustainable bio-resource provision capacity of any given site requires that a 'reference' condition can be calculated for comparison purposes. If a 'reference' condition cannot be calculated, it will be extremely difficult to determine whether a management activity has the potential to degrade a site, since the site might already be highly degraded and so especially susceptible to being further degraded, that is, moving to a less resilient state. If so, its productive capacity – its solar income – may still be limited because the land exists in a matrix of soil and climatic conditions that may constrain the land's 'realistic' productive potential.

The NPP of global forests is informative in demonstrating the variations that soils and climates impose on forest growth (Vogt et al, 1996). High NPP for forests is not the norm, and may not reflect site constraints to tree growth, because trees are well adapted to growing under the soil and climatic conditions that exist at any location (see Chapter 5). Boreal forests are limited by cold temperatures which reduce physiological activity and therefore a tree's productive capacity, while temperate forests tend to have the highest NPP. The link between NPP, climates and soils is apparent from the fact that the total living biomass greater than $300Mg\ ha^{-1}$ was not found in warm boreal, temperate and subtropical climatic zones, while the tropical and cold temperate climatic zones consistently had biomass values over $300Mg\ ha^{-1}$. It is an interesting fact that humans have primarily lived in those areas where forests have higher productive capacities.

The utility of measuring an ecosystem's productive capacity is apparent from comparing how much and where humans have collected forest resources (Table 9.1). For forests, there is a pattern showing that the more productive forest types are those that have been significantly altered by humans. The range of total NPP within a forest biome type reflects the soils where forests grow. The temperate broadleaf forests produce sufficient annual productivity to maintain a diversity of wildlife species as well as humans. In addition, these are the forests that also have more nutrient-rich soils and higher water-holding capacity, which means that they have been historically converted into agricultural lands.

Soil chemistry controls the maximum productive capacity possible at any site. In a ten-year study of tropical forests in Puerto Rico, land-use legacies have significantly modified the soil chemistry and its water-holding capacity, and therefore the productive capacity of these forests (Beard et al, 2005). For example, the highest tree growth rates were found in sites with the highest soil moisture contents and where soil nitrate levels were also higher. The higher soil N levels

Table 9.1 *Total forest productivity and how much forests have been altered by humans*

Forest biome	Total NPP (Mg/ha/yr)	Human intensity of use and degree to which it has been altered (%)
Temperate broadleaf deciduous	13.5–18.7	82
Tropical (dry, deciduous)	17.5	46
Tropical (rainforests, evergreen)	11.4	25
Temperate coniferous	11.2–14.9	12
Boreal evergreen	1.9–7.0	< 1

Note: The higher the percentage of human-altered, the greater the number of products that have been available for human survival and the more altered it is. Total NPP = above ground + below ground NPP
Source: Vogt et al, 1996

were a legacy of planting N-fixing trees as overstorey cover to provide shade for coffee plants. Due to historical land uses, calculating average soil moisture and nitrate concentrations for the forest stand would have missed the significant differences that existed at the local level of the watershed. Furthermore, these forests responded differently to five hurricanes that impacted them during this ten-year period. The trees growing in the higher soil moisture conditions and with higher nitrate levels were more resilient and recovered faster after each hurricane. It appeared that forest productivities were not only affected by the hurricanes, but also responded differentially to each hurricane, depending upon local soil conditions and legacies. These forests are highly resilient to the common climatic events for this region. This adaptation to disturbances has made these forests amazingly resilient to human activities and suggests that their 'solar income' can be sustainably managed by humans.

Similar local variations in soil chemistry and physical properties have been recorded in many other forests globally. Since these differences occur at small scales within a forest, it is important to understand this variance because it determines which tree species are found growing at any location and how resilient each species is to drought or changes in soil chemistry (Palmiotto et al, 2004; Kulmatiski et al, 2007).

Being able to measure the 'solar income' of a landscape will allow us to use green plants as the metric to measure whether our bio-resource consumption choices will maintain the productive capacity of a landscape or degrade it (see Box 9.1). It is important to be able to detect when an ecosystem has a significant risk of being degraded, even when there are no visible symptoms. We propose to use 'solar income' to document how well an ecosystem recovers when it is disturbed by human activities or by natural disturbance cycles. Focusing on the 'solar income' – tree growth rates – was effective in determining the resiliency of tropical forests to land uses and disturbances in Puerto Rico (Beard et al, 2005). It is important that we do not focus on what the productivity is today but begin to estimate what the future productivity will be, subsequent to our land-use decisions. The past productivity only reflects what was possible in the past, based on the climate and soil conditions that existed at that time. It will not reflect the changes that are occurring in the climate and soils that may impact future growth rate potentials.

It is also important to estimate how much land productivity is 'realistically' available and not to assume that all forests are equivalent to one another. We have already seen how differences in soils and land-use legacies alter NPP and forest resilience after a disturbance. The generalized values that are published in the literature do not reflect the local or regional variability in NPP and therefore how much of a resource can be collected at any location. Therefore, we tend to overestimate the amount that can be collected. If a more realistic estimate was developed, it would reduce the risk that choices are unrealistic. For heuristic purposes only, we are calculating a realistic forest area to collect forest products by removing the forest area under protected status from the total forest area. There is a greater likelihood that the data of forest area in protected status provide a more realistic estimate for most countries, even if some clearly are only 'paper' protected areas, which is why we will examine the repercussions of not being able to collect forest products from protected forests next. Similar calculations can be used to determine the 'solar income' that needs to be managed because the forest is impacted by disease, insects or by fire.

Losses From and Unavailable Solar Income: A Forest Lens

Calculating the 'potential' and 'realistic' forest cover highlights the options forests can provide for each country. If disturbances were factored into these calculations, it would identify the 'realistic' options for using or not using forests. Disturbances typically result in the loss of forest cover so that a forest provides fewer options for a community dependent upon it. The realistic forest area would calculate a solar income from forests that would not overestimate a forest's potential to provide ecosystem services and products. Ultimately, a 'realistic' value for how much forest materials to sustainably collect from a forest should be based on local or regional measures of forest NPP since this varies by local climate and soils. The solar income will ultimately determine the frequency at which forest resources are available for collection at each location (Vogt et al, 1997).

Several places in the world are notable for the amount of forest that is being impacted negatively by disturbances that reduce the 'potential' forest cover (Table 9.2). If these data realistically represent forest conditions, it suggests that several countries face severe challenges in maintaining their forest cover and NPP. For example, forests in the US are regrowing after agricultural abandonment and therefore the US is ideally positioned to use forests to sequester carbon. However, these assessments are based on 'potential' and not 'realistic' values of forest cover. Forests in the western US are unhealthy due to past land-use activities such as fire control. These forests need urgently to be managed to reduce their continuing losses to insects and fires, and not to be more protected. In fact, the percentage of forest area annually impacted by insects, disease or fire in the US is equivalent to half of the total forest area being protected (Table 9.2). This is a significant annual loss of forest cover that reduces the capacity of US forests to provide ecosystem services.

Several other countries face similar problems to the US. Canada, India and Nepal are also losing more of their forest area to insects, diseases or fire than the area that is protected. Canada protects 5 per cent of its forest lands but has the same amount of forest area impacted annually by insects, diseases or fire. Under such circumstances, the amount of land in forests will continue to decrease because of these disturbance agents.

Those countries that are losing as much forests to insects, diseases or fire as they are protecting, are losing the ability to use forests as a tool to adapt to their environments. Nepal has 8 per cent of its forests under protected status, but 10 per cent is impacted annually by disease, insects or fire. India has 19 per cent of

Table 9.2 *Forest area protected or lost each year due to disturbances by a country's HDI ranking*

HDI group		Protected areas (IUCN categories I–V) (% of total land)	Deforestation: average annual change 1990–2005 (%)	Forest area impacted annually by insects, disease, fire (% of total)	Forest production in wood fuel (% of total forest products) [Biomass % of total primary energy consumed]
			Annual forest area losses due to disturbances or harvested for energy		
I	Iceland	5	6	0	0 [0]
	Norway	6	0	2	14 [4]
	Australia	7	0	..	17 [4]
	Canada	5	0	5	1 [4]
	Sweden	10	0	1	9 [17]
	Japan	8	0	0	1 [1]
	Netherlands	5	0	0	4 [3]
	France	3	1	2	7 [4]
	Finland	3	0	0	8 [20]
	US	16	0	8	10 [3]
	UK	15	1	0	1 [2]
	Germany	29	0	0	11 [4]
2	Argentina	2	0	2	29 [4]
	UAE	0	2	0	0 [0]
	Mexico	1	−1	0	85 [5]
	Malaysia	4	0	0	12 [5]
	Russia	5	0	1	26 [1]
	Brazil	4	−1	0	55 [27]
3	Venezuela	34	−1	0	71 [1]
	China	11	2	4	67 [13]
	Peru	3	0	0	82 [16]
	Philippines	5	−2	0	72 [24]
	Indonesia	5	−2	0	70 [29]
4	Namibia	4	−1	6	0 [14]
	India	5	0	19	94 [29]
5	Bangladesh	0	−1	0	97 [34]
	Nepal	8	−2	10	87 [86]
	Haiti	0	−1	..	89 [76]
	Sudan	4	−1	..	88 [80]
	Yemen	0	0	..	100 [1]
6	Nigeria	4	−2	..	87 [78]
	Tanzania	15	−1	..	90 [92]
	Angola	4	0	0	76 [64]
	Congo DR	8	0	..	95 [93]

Note: Data are from 2000, 2004 and 2005. HDI = Human Development Index [Group 1 = HDI > 0.9; Group 2 = 0.8–0.9; Group 3 = 0.7–0.8; Group 4 = 0.6–0.7; Group 5 = 0.5–0.6; Group 6 = 0.4–0.5]; .. = no data

Source: UNEP-WCMC, 2004; FAO, 2006; HDI, 2007/2008

its forest area impacted annually by these disturbance agents and protects 5 per cent of its forest area. In 2005, India used 94 per cent of its forest production as woodfuel; biomass and wastes accounted for 29 per cent of the primary energy consumed. India cannot continue to utilize its forests using traditional approaches or practices especially since the 'realistic' forest area is considerably smaller than the 'potential' estimate suggests.

The UK has also lost the use of its forests to provide resource options because of setting aside most of its forests into protected zones. This means that if in the future the UK decided to use its forests for other purposes, this could be hindered unless the protected status of its forests is changed. The UK has been fortunate that its forests have been minimally impacted by insects, disease or fires.

From our list of 34 countries, those with high potential for utilizing their forests and woodlands for socioeconomic development are: Australia, Finland, Japan, Malaysia and Sweden. These countries could increase the development potential from their forests and woodlands because they have significant land area in these categories, are also not as dependent on combusting woodfuel for energy and do not annually lose much of their forests to insects, diseases or fire.

Most of the countries where the 'potential' forest areas are exactly equivalent to their 'realistic' forest area are those that have little total forest area (4 per cent or less). Countries with little forest area (Haiti, Iceland and Yemen) are in a situation where they will not be able to use their forests to develop economic opportunities for their people. The only exception to this pattern was found for Mexico where the 'realistic' and 'potential' forest areas are equal: 43 per cent of Mexico's land area is in forests, which means that forests can be used to provide ecosystem services.

Most of the growing-economy countries do not collect data on how much of their forest area is impacted by insects, disease or fire. Therefore, it is impossible to determine how much is at risk to being lost because they are unhealthy. These are also the same countries that produce 76–93 per cent of their primary energy from wood: Angola, Congo DR, Haiti, Nepal, Nigeria, Sudan and Tanzania (Table 5.2). This high dependence on woodfuel for energy suggests an urgency to calculate a realistic forest cover when deciding how to use these forests. It may be that these forests should be candidates for large-scale forest restoration efforts and more efficient conversion of wood into energy.

Is Local Food Production Sustainable?
The Solar Income Factor

Whether or not locally grown food is the most sustainable choice to make will also be determined by the land's productive capacity. Again, productive capacity indexes the soils and climate found at any location and how they constrain the potential productivity. All areas are not equally productive and this should inform choices about where food should optimally be grown, to minimize land degradation. In the industrialized countries, environmental concerns encourage people to call for the opportunity to buy only locally grown food, with the idea that it is more environmentally beneficial. This raises the interesting question of whether people can or should live on food grown locally.

This simple question of where to grow food in the most environmentally beneficial way does not consider the fact that growing crops on some lands is more efficient than growing the same crop where climate and soils constrain soil productive capacity (see Chapters 7–8). If crops can be grown more efficiently in one area, it will reduce the emissions of CO_2 that result from growing that crop. Evans (2009) quoted a University of Toronto professor who stated that 'Highly efficient farms in California produce roughly 17 times as many strawberries as a typical Ontario "farm" using the same amount of land and resources'. Such an approach to considering where to grow certain crops optimally would include the climatic and soil constraints when making decisions on the best uses of land. The idea of optimizing land uses to reflect the inherent constraints of the land itself is also being employed to make decisions when water security is an issue; the virtual water footprint is also being used to determine if infrastructures should be adopted for delivering water to grow crops, or to buy food crops from other countries more suitable for growing them.

Today, local food production is being touted as a way to become more 'environmental' without considering the local constraints and impacts of soil physical or chemical properties on crop growth and nutrient value. The idea of local food production being a 'green' choice is derived from the idea that each person's environmental or carbon footprint will be lower, because less fossil fuel is consumed during the transportation of food to the local markets. A superficial analysis suggests that this idea is sound because the transportation sector does contribute one-quarter of the total CO_2 emitted globally. However, this approach does not factor-in the point that all soils are not equal, because of the factors included in the soil development equation. The soils that develop in one area may allow plants to grow quickly and still produce food crops that are nutritionally well-balanced. On the other hand, another soil may be in a developmental stage where it is difficult to grow sufficient food crops, or what is grown may not be very nutritious. Most soils have probably developed to stages that are somewhere in between these two scenarios.

Whether food production is environmental is being evaluated using the 'food miles,' in other words the total distance that food travels from its production to its consumption (Evans, 2009). Food miles are linked to CO_2 emissions because transporting food utilizes fossil-based energies. As summarized by Evans (2009), the food mile is flawed because it attributes higher levels of energy consumption with food growth and distribution.

Many countries are facing the fact that they are less capable of producing all of the bio-resources that their societies demand, and are searching for creative solutions to the unavoidable constraints of their climate or plant and soil productive capacities (FAO, 2003; MEA, 2005; Schmidhuher and Tublello, 2007). Today, one of the choices available to a country is to import a resource from a country that is better positioned to produce it. Hoekstra and Chapagain (2007) mentioned that this is an approach that currently is not broadly recognized as a viable option, but it is one in which a country can shift its production of food from those areas with low water-productivity to those with higher water-productivity relationships. This would decrease the whole global water footprint and increase the efficiency of global water use. Hoekstra and Chapagain (2007) cited how this is the approach taken by Jordan as it 'externalized its water footprint by importing wheat and rice products from the USA, which has higher water productivity than Jordan'.

This recognition of constraints to a land's productive capacity also explains the decisions being made by countries to grow their food supplies somewhere else in the world. Some of the Persian Gulf countries are beginning to grow their food in northern Africa. How this will play out in the future is not clear, because so many of the African countries have been unable to provide sufficient food for their own people (Wiesmann, 2006). These same African countries have also been experiencing severe droughts and cycles of famine. According to Below et al (2007), half of the 22 million deaths that resulted from natural disasters between 1900 and 2004 were due to droughts; droughts therefore killed more people than other extreme weather events or earthquakes. Societies have historically been and continue to be especially vulnerable to droughts.

In other situations, countries are investing in technology to increase the supply of a limiting resource, such as desalination to acquire clean water or importing bio-resources. For example, the UAE is allocating resources to import food and also desalinate water. The UAE imports two to three times more food per capita than the other countries included in our database and has also been desalinating water to satisfy its freshwater needs. The UAE produced 385 million m^3 of desalinated water between 1992 and 2000; this compares to Yemen that produced 10 million m^3, and Sudan, which produced 0.4 million m^3 of desalinated water during the same time period (FAO Water Resources Development and Management Service, 2003). None of the other countries included in our list produced desalinated water during this period.

Climatic limitations (e.g. temperature and moisture) and soil-quality differences (see Table 8.1) determine whether locally grown food will be nutritionally adequate to maintain human health. In the past, poor human health was generally connected with people who settled in larger communities and were dependent on local sources of foods (Steckel and Rose, 2002). Even today, if the extreme north of northern European countries only ate locally grown foods, their food choices would be quite limited throughout most of the year. They would eat a lot of potatoes because these root crops grow well at those latitudes and also store well; they would only have a variety of green, leafy vegetables during a three- to four-month period each year. They would also have to acquire year-round supplies of berries or other food sources high in vitamin C or in vitamin D in order to avoid vitamin deficiencies. Today with the global commerce in food items, these extreme northern Europeans have access to fruits high in vitamin C at any time of the year; these foods are grown in the more tropical and/or hotter climatic regions of the world. If these foods ceased to be imported to these extreme northern regions of Europe, they could ingest their vitamin C or vitamin D from synthetic supplements (e.g. pills) to compensate for what they lack in their diet from locally grown food. This daily ingestion of a 'pill' to acquire vitamins is not a preferred solution.

Some countries (e.g. Japan) have also opted to support local agricultural production to have better control of their food supplies (i.e. food security). Japan has placed high tariffs on food imports to reduce how much food is brought into Japan and as a way to support its farmers. There are limits to how much food Japan can grow locally, however, because only 13 per cent of Japan's total land area is suitable for agricultural production (FAO, 2006). This goal of producing food locally has resulted in Japan having the highest level of conversion of other lands into agricultural production of the 34 countries included in this study. Agricultural production is being forced to expand onto lands that are less suitable for these purposes. Japan also faces severe soil constraints (34 per cent erosion risk; 27 per cent Al toxicity) because its soils are relatively homogeneous and formed mostly from volcanic parent materials. Even though the climate in Japan may be conducive to growing a diversity of crops, the relatively homogeneous soils place a restriction on and limit the diversity of agricultural crops that can be grown.

Global production of food is not the only answer to food security because food safety is an issue when food becomes contaminated by microbes or chemicals during its processing and transport over longer distances. It has been estimated that 5000 people die annually in the US because of microbial contamination of food. Food can become contaminated in several ways: through chemicals used to increase animal or plant growth rates (e.g. antibiotics and hormones), during fertilization of plants or by microbes during food processing and transportation. These concerns, valid or not, have been used by governments to restrict the importation of food from other countries to support their own agricultural industries. Food contamination, however, is not just confined to food produced for global consumption, but also can occur at local or regional scales when industrial quantities of food need to be processed. Therefore, only eating local foods may not free one from having to deal with food-safety problems.

Human health issues linked to food security will remain ongoing, for so much of our food production is global. Locally grown food, especially organic food, has become quite popular recently as one solution to increasing food safety. Local food production, however, has been successful in satisfying the food needs of only a small proportion of the population. It has become a 'niche' market for those able to pay a higher price for foods that are less chemically stimulated or contaminated. If the general public is to be better fed and obtain a more nutritious diet, globalization of food production is a logical choice. Geography already tells us that we cannot grow the diversity and amount of nutritious food crops needed to feed people on every piece of land that is available for crop production.

Societies are focusing on acquiring resources from within their own boundaries as a means of securing their resource supplies. This is similar to the ecosphere or small glass globe that people use to represent a sustainable ecosystem; the ecosphere is an enclosed system containing photosynthetic algae and shrimp. These enclosed systems can maintain viable populations of algae and shrimp for several years, but give a false impression to the observer, for they appear to be 'sustainable' without any human input. Of course, this ecosphere has no climate or soils that might constrain the life it holds. They are very simple systems that cannot mimic the complexity of ecosystems and are poor models for humans to attempt to simulate. They have very defined borders within which the two organisms continue to live. Humans need to recognize that most borders are political human artefacts, just as the glass globe is an artificial constraint constructed by humans.

Globalization has historically contributed to human adaptation and allowed us to extend beyond the artificial boundaries that we commonly use to define our territories. We need to think about globalization as an antidote for the local constraints that climates and soils impose on a land. For example, it is probably not a good idea to expect some of the African countries facing severe droughts to produce most of their food locally. This suggests not that country boundaries should be broken, but that the area of the footprint should be expanded in order to be sustainable. Country boundaries are artificial political constructs that were commonly made by people who conquered these lands. For example, De Blij's (2005) *Africa* summarized how the European powers divided the ownership of the African continent for themselves and created political boundaries on paper. Our discussion supports the fact that political boundaries do not mean much when determining one's resource footprint. The reality is that political boundaries are critical, but we should recognize that making decisions within a political boundary can bias the decision to the point that the best decision is not made.

References

Beard, K. H., Vogt, K. A., Vogt, D. J., Scatena, F. N., Covich, A., Sigurdardottir, R., Siccama, T. C. and Crowl, T. A. (2005) 'Structural and functional responses of a subtropical forest to 10 years of hurricanes and droughts', *Ecological Monographs*, vol 75, no 3, pp345–361

Below, R., Grover-Kopec, E. and Dilley, M. (2007) 'Documenting drought-related disasters: a global reassessment', *The Journal of Environmental Development*, vol 16, pp328–345

de Blij, H. (2005) *Why Geography Matters. Three Challenges Facing America. Climate Change, The Rise of China and Global Terrorism*, Oxford University Press, Oxford

Ecological Footprint and Biocapacity (2006) 'Edition', Global Footprint Network 2006, www.footprintnetwork.org/gfn_sub.php?content=national_footprints, accessed 20 February 2008

Evans, P. (2009) 'Local food no green panacea: professor', *CBC News*, 22 July 2009, www.cbc.ca/consumer/story/2009/07/22/consumer-local-food.html?ref=rss, accessed 23 July 2009

FAO (2003) 'The State of Food Insecurity in the World 2003', UN FAO, Rome, Italy

FAO Water Resources Development and Management Service (2003) 'AQUASTAT Information system on Water and Agriculture: Review of World Water Resources by

Country', Rome, www.fao.org/waicent/faoinfo/agricult/agl/aglw/aquastat/
water_res/index.htm, accessed 23 July 2009

FAO (2006) 'State of the World's Forests 2005', UN FAO's Global Forest Resources
Assessment, Rome, Italy

FAO (2008) 'World Resources Report, www.fao.org/docrep/011/ai476e/ai476e01.htm,
accessed 22 July 2009

Haberl, H., Erb, K. H., Krausmann, F., Gaube, V., Bondeau, A., Plutzar, C., Gingrich, S.,
Lucht, W. and Fisher-Kowalski, M. (2007) 'Quantifying and mapping the human
appropriation of net primary production in earth's terrestrial ecosystems', *PNAS*,
vol 104, pp12942–12947

HDI (2007/2008) 'Human Development Index', http://hDrundp.org/en/statistics/,
accessed 1 October 2008

Hoekstra, A. Y. and Chapagain, A. K. (2007) 'Water footprints of nations: water use by
people as a function of their consumption patterns', *Water Resource Management*,
vol 21, pp35–48

Kulmatiski, A., Vogt, K. A., Vogt, D. J., Wargo, P. M., Tilley, J. P., Siccama, T. G.,
Sigurdardottir, R. and Ludwig, D. (2007) 'Northeastern US forest response to cation
remediation', *Canadian Journal of Forest Research*, vol 37, pp1574–1585

MEA (2005) *Millennium Ecosystem Assessment: Ecosystems and Human Well-Being
Synthesis. Findings of the Condition and Trends Working Group of the Millennium
Ecosystem Assessment*, Island Press, Washington, DC

Palmiotto, P. A., Davies, S. J., Vogt, K. A., Ashton, P. M. S., Vogt, D. J. and Ashton, P. S.
(2004) 'Soil-related habitat specialization in dipterocarp rain forest tree species in
Borneo', *J of Ecology*, vol 92, pp609–623

Schmidhuber, J. and Tubiello, F. (2007) 'Global food security under climate change',
PNAS, vol 104, no 50, pp19703–19708

Steckel, R. H. and Rose, J. C. (2002) *The Backbone of History. Health and Nutrition in the
Western Hemisphere*, Cambridge University Press, Cambridge

UNEP–WCMC (2004) *World Database of Protected Areas, Protected Areas, Plant and
Animal Biodiversity*, United Nations Environment Programme, World Conservation
Monitoring Centre Consortium, Cambridge, UK, www.unep-wcmc.org, accessed 20
February 2009

Vitousek, P. M., Ehrlich, P. R., Ehrlich, A. H. and Matson, P. A. (1986) 'Human
appropriation of the products of photosynthesis', *BioScience*, vol 36, pp363–373

Vogt, K. A., Vogt, D. J., Palmiotto, P., Boon, P., O'Hara, J. and Asbjornsen, H. (1996)
'Review of root dynamics in forest ecosystems grouped by climate, climatic forest type
and species', *Plant and Soil*, vol 187, pp159–219

Vogt, K. A, Gordon, J., Wargo, J., Vogt, D., Asbjornsen, H., Palmiotto, P. A., Clark, H.,
O'Hara, J., Keeton, W. S., Patel-Weynand, T. and Witten, E. (1997) *Ecosystems:
Balancing Science with Management*, Springer-Verlag, New York, NY

Wiesmann, D. (2006) 'A global hunger index: Measurement concept, ranking of countries
and trends', FCND Discussion Paper 212, International Food Policy Research
Institute, Sustainable solutions for ending hunger and poverty, December 2006,
www.ifpri.org/divs/fcnd/dp/papers/fcndp212.pdf, accessed 9 January 2009

Part 5

SOCIETIES ADAPT TO A QUAGMIRE OF RESOURCE CHOICES

10

Debunking Sustainability Myths

Making sustainable choices is not just a matter of either understanding how society adapted in the past, or deciphering the volumes of accumulated data that are available globally. The human factor must also be considered. Humans have biases and values that influence what data we select to include in our decision-making processes. Humans have a tendency to include their biases or values as part of the database used to make assessments. This is similar to addressing the simple problem of needing to water a plant so it does not wilt by adding information on ocean temperatures because it is one's specialty (Figure 10.1). These biases are typically not explicitly stated in our assessments, or may not be very clear to a decision-maker. They generally revolve around where people live, such as whether they are urban or rural residents, and the assumption that high

'I like it, but it needs to be more complicated'

Figure 10.1 *Depiction of how human values complicate the development of solutions*

population densities equate to lower global-carrying capacity as resources become over-exploited. These 'facts' do not take into consideration the long history humans have of being able to adapt to their environment or in some cases of adapting their environment to suit their needs. People do not just 'flee' conditions that reduce their survival potential, but adjust their behaviour to compensate for the limits of each environment.

We have developed anecdotal evidence or *facts* that we use to support our views. These biases also become part of our decision-making process. For example, people living in rural and rural-urban interfaces (RUI) settings are not considered to be as environmentally or culturally aware by those living in cities (Vogt et al, 2000; Korner and Ohsawa, 2005). In Washington state, the conflicts between farmers and ranchers and non-land based industries erupt frequently over conservation and resource extraction values especially when there is an economic downturn. The higher population density of a city means that they have more political power to write the regulations controlling land-use activities in the rural and RUI settings.For example, in King County in Washington State (US), the growth management act requires over half of the land to be left untouched (e.g. not converting forests into pastures for horses or no cutting of trees). These laws also impact city dwellers but because their house lot sizes are so small, with perhaps one or two trees growing on a lot, these regulations are less restrictive compared to what is experienced by people living in rural and RUI settings who might own 20 or more hectares of forestland. In King County, the growth-management policy was designed to achieve environmental and conservation goals but triggered high deforestation rates instead, especially in the RUI. When land owners were unable to make money from their forest ownership, these lands were sold to land developers to build houses. In this case, the view that rural and RUI communities are less environmental and their activities need to be restricted resulted in unacceptable negative repercussions on conservation efficacy due to the loss of forest lands. A similar perception also emerged from the indices introduced in Chapter 3.

Another topic that is hotly debated and prominent in our social consciousness is the role of *population density* in causing unsustainable resource exploitation and societal collapse. Typically, large population densities are assumed to create environmental problems, because they trigger changes in land uses as more people compete for a limited resource base. Society automatically equates a large population density to environmental degradation. This does not take into consideration the fact that many of the European countries which ranked high on the HDI also have some of the highest population densities found on the globe. So why are these countries not degrading their environments? Why are high population densities in the lower HDI countries equated with environmental degradation? Are these lower HDI countries more dependent on local bio-resources? Are the higher HDI countries practising good environmental stewardship locally but causing environmental degradation elsewhere?

It is interesting to note that society has created 'facts' about where people live, and derived implications of population density on our environment that are not necessarily based on reality. The rationale used to justify one fact may be counter to the actual reality. For example, the population density of rural communities is lower than that of cities; this should result in a positive interpretation of rural areas. Because cities are centres of higher population density, they should be the causes of resource exploitation that results in environmental degradation. People living in cities, therefore, should be more regulated than people living in rural areas since resources will be less over-exploited. We know that this does not happen, for the resources consumed by people who live in cities come from rural areas. Cities are the hotspots of resource consumption that are primarily satisfied by the production which occurs in the rural areas. These 'perception' stories should not be used to define how environmentally aware a group of people happens to be. However, they do tell a story about how well societies have been able to adapt under some very harsh living conditions.

In fact, rural people are probably more adaptable than urbanites to a changing climate or environment. People living in rural areas have been forced to recognize and make better use of their viable resource choices because traditionally they have higher unemployment rates and there are fewer alternative job options because employment is primarily bio-resource based. They have fewer choices to develop their human capital. The farmers in India waiting for monsoon rains so that they can grow their crops are an example of the limited choices that rural communities can face. Even though these farmers are highly adapted to their environment, climate change in the form of droughts is making their livelihoods less sustainable. In contrast, rural residents can usually satisfy or perhaps partially satisfy one necessity – food – since they probably have sufficient land area to grow food crops. Urbanites are more distant from the resources they use and from an understanding of what triggers resource-supply insecurities. If you live in a city, it is easy to drive to a store and buy whatever product you want from what is available on a store shelf. Most consumers in cities do not think about droughts that might have forced a store owner to buy tomatoes from Mexico instead of California.

We will begin this chapter with a discussion of how societies have adjusted to their climates. We have developed a number of myths that are climate-based; for example, many in the advanced-economy countries long for the hot, wet tropics, and the thought of sitting under a palm tree without recognizing how difficult it may be to live here.

Temperature and Where You Live Do Matter

Humans are able to tolerate a wide range of environmental conditions which might make you think that it does not matter where you live. People travel easily from cold to hot environments. Most do not recognize the constraints that temperature imposes on human survival, for it is so easy to travel between these different climatic zones. Even if humans are not comfortable living in some extremes, this has not deterred them from migrating to these areas in recent times.

Table 10.1 *Climatic variables correlated to human development indicators*

Y variable	X variable	R^2
Human Development Index ranking	Annual minimum temperature, °C	0.47
	Annual maximum temperature, °C	0.56
Gross National Income (GNI)	Annual minimum temperature, °C	0.53
	Annual maximum temperature, °C	0.59
Energy use (kg of oil equivalent per capita)	Average minimum temperature, °C	0.40
	Average maximum temperature, °C	0.42

Except for personal preferences, climate is not given much thought when people are deciding where they want to live. Nevertheless, despite human adaptation to extreme climates, these do impact the bio-resource supply capacity of each environment and where it will be easier for humans to live and develop their human capital (see Chapter 2). Typically we would not consider colder climates to be more conducive for developing our human capital.

Our data suggest that if you want to be a high HDI-ranked country then you need to relocate to the colder and not to the hotter temperature regions of the world (Table 10.1). Half of the variance in the HDI ranking of a country and its GNI is explained by a temperature metric. However, if the relationship was this straightforward, it would be easy for society to pursue the goal of being highly developed simply by moving to the colder parts of the world. Unfortunately, this solution would result in very crowded living conditions in these colder places because no one would want to live in the hot tropics. This is especially interesting in view of the fact that humans evolved originally in the equatorial area(s) of the world.

The fact that temperature reflects the human development potential and the GNI of a country is interesting, because humans are now able to adapt to extremes of temperature by altering their environments. When the temperature is uncomfortable, humans have learned how to engineer their environment to increase their comfort level by wearing more clothing, or by removing some clothing, depending on the weather. This adaptation is commonly used by other animals that either grow a thicker fur coat during the winter months or forage during the night-time when temperatures are cooler. However, humans are more sophisticated in regulating their temperatures because they build artificial structures that can be heated or cooled. This means that humans can wear fewer clothes indoors, even when the outside temperature is below freezing. By controlling the temperature of their environment through using artificial structures, humans have been able to adapt to multiple temperature regimes and live on every piece of land or water on this globe, and have not been reduced to living in a few comfortable environments. Other animals have adapted to their localized environment while humans adapt the environment to meet their requirements.

Altering the temperatures of one's environment, however, takes energy. In fact, the temperature extremes explained about 40 per cent of the variance in how

Table 10.2 *Energy use and climatic variables ranked by HDI value*
(from highest to lowest)

	Energy use (kg of oil equivalent/capita)	Average minimum temperature (°C)	Average maximum temperature (°C)	Precipitation (mm)
Iceland	12,219	1.9	7	798
Norway	6948	2.4	9.6	763
Australia	5978	13.7	21.6	1222
Canada	8417	5.6	12.7	834
Sweden	5782	3.6	10	539
Japan	4152	12.6	19.7	1467
Netherlands	5015	6.1	13.4	780
Finland	6664	1	8.7	650
France	4534	8.5	15.5	650
US	7893	8.1	16	1056
UK	3884	7.5	14.4	611
Germany	4180	5.9	13.4	571
Argentina	1644	13.5	22.5	1215
UAE	11,436	21.3	33	94
Mexico	1713	9.6	23.4	816
Malaysia	2389	23.2	32.4	2427
Russia	4517	1.2	8.9	691
Brazil	1122	15.5	24.9	1455
Venezuela	2293	16	30.3	913
China	1316	12.5	19.9	1112
Peru	506	16.7	22.1	1014
Philippines	516	25.2	31.2	2201
Indonesia	814	25	31.8	1655
Namibia	683	22.3	27.7	360
India	491	22.1	31.7	2401
Bangladesh	158	21.5	30.6	2154
Nepal	339	11.7	24.8	1425
Haiti	269	22	32.5	1226
Sudan	469	22.7	37.1	162
Yemen	328	22	37	231
Nigeria	734	22.7	30.7	1538
Tanzania	499	15	34	1148
Angola	615	22.3	27.7	1250
Congo DR	289	18.6	28.4	1700

Note: Data from 2005 except precipitation data which are from 2007
Source: HDI, 2007/2008; World Bank, 2008; FAO, 2008; UN, 2009

much energy was consumed per capita for our 34 countries (Table 10.1). People living in the tropical countries are not expending the energy to cool their environments, while those living in colder climates are required to heat their environments (Table 10.2). If the people living in the tropics chose to expend energy to cool their environments, they would need to consume more energy to lower temperatures than people living in the colder climates who heat their buildings. Twelve of the tropical countries in our database have high annual maximum temperatures (ranging from 22 to 34°C) and consume a low amount of energy (269–814kg of oil equivalent per capita). This level of energy consumption compares to the 4180–8417kg of oil equivalent per capita consumed by people living in the temperate climatic zones. These tropical countries also ranked lower in the HDI, suggesting that using energy to cool one's environment has a lower priority when one's basic survival needs cannot be satisfied – for instance, when it is necessary to burn wood to cook food instead of generating electricity. People living in the boreal or cold temperate climatic zones are less able to survive without artificial heat, as evidenced by the high amount of energy they consume.

It is informative to examine, from a somewhat different perspective than was used in the previous discussion, two outlier countries from our database – Iceland and the UAE. Both countries consume a higher level of energy when compared to others located in similar geographic and climatic zones. The context for each country will be further discussed because it reveals the choices and the trade-offs each country has made.

The level of energy consumption in Iceland initially appears to be logical, for this country experiences even colder climates than the other Scandinavian countries, and colder temperatures equate to the consumption of more energy for heating. When the outside temperature is at freezing point, it will take more energy to keep humans comfortable in their built environment. This is the situation found in Iceland. Iceland has a low average minimum temperature (1.0–3.6°C) and the highest level of energy consumption compared to the 34 countries selected for our study (12,219kg of oil equivalent per capita) (Table 10.2). Iceland's minimum and maximum temperatures are the lowest for any of our 34 countries; it is also 2–3°C colder than the other Scandinavian countries.

Therefore, one might speculate that the quantity of energy consumed in Iceland is very high, but logical based on its cold temperatures. However, is this explanation logical for Iceland? Are cold temperature regimes an unavoidable constraint that will force people to use more energy to heat their homes? This explanation does not make sense because Iceland has a low population density. Therefore, its energy consumption per capita is too high for its population density. This amount of energy would convert each house in Iceland into experiencing 'sauna-like conditions' during the entire year. Of course, this is not the situation. Iceland's high energy consumption has another explanation, and the high use of energy is not related to what each Icelander consumes. It results from the previous Icelandic government deciding to attract to Iceland industries (e.g. Al smelting) that require large supplies of inexpensive electricity. This decision was made to stimulate economic development activities and to create employment

Box 10.1 Description of the United Arab Emirates

Seven sheikhdoms on the Arabian Peninsula combined to form a federation after Britain pulled out of this barren coastal region in 1971. The United Arab Emirates comprises Abu Dhabi, seat of the federal government and the oil capital; Dubayy (Dubai), the main port and commercial industrial hub; Ajman; Umm al Qaywayn; Ras al Khaymah; Al Fujayrah; and Sharjah. Oil, discovered in 1958, is the major income-earner. Oil wealth brought foreign workers, who now make up about three-quarters of the population. A favourite destination for tourists, the country has a liberal attitude towards other cultures and beliefs (National Geographic, 2009).

opportunities in Iceland. Unfortunately, this strategy did not help Iceland when the global banking system began to fail in 2008. Partly because of this economic downturn, the previous Icelandic government was voted out of office by Icelanders in 2009.

Another outlier is the UAE (Box 10.1). The UAE experiences temperatures that are at the extreme end of the temperature range (maximum temperatures = 40°C) and it also has a high energy demand (11,436kg of oil equivalent per capita). The UAE consumed almost the same amount of energy per capita as Iceland, but in this case energy was consumed to build the infrastructure to develop its human capital potential (Table 10.2).

The population density of the UAE is low and similar to Iceland; this suggests that there are other factors responsible for the high level of energy consumption. For the UAE, high energy consumption is linked to development of its human capital, because its bio-resource capital is inadequate to develop the economy. The UAE has built an 'artificial' infrastructure to support its economic growth. It stands out from the other countries within the same HDI ranking group because it is consuming almost ten times more energy. One could assume that the UAE has abundant supplies of oil so that it does not worry about how much oil it consumes to produce energy. The UAE made a strategic decision to use its oil revenues to convert a 'drowsy fishing village to a tax-free business haven, attracting more tourists than the whole of India' (National Geographic, 2009). The UAE has built its human infrastructure capacity (e.g. the tourism industry and banking), and *human capital*.

So, what did the oil revenue build in the UAE? It built the world's largest artificial and manufactured infrastructures. For example, the business centre of the UAE, Dubai, has built a luxury hotel on an artificial island. The UAE boasts building some of the tallest and largest infrastructures in the world, including the world's tallest skyscraper and largest shopping centre and airport. Indoor ski slopes allow tourists to ski at any time of the year. One of the world's first unique engineering feats also became a reality in Dubai: the first rotating tower, an entire building moving and turning on its base. This houses four penthouses and a villa. In 2006, Dubai announced that it was building a rotating tower powered by solar cells. This tower is an 80,000-tonne building that would be rotated once every week, designed to be a residence for 200 families (Hanlon, 2009). These manufactured structures have made the UAE the global leader in artificially altering an environment to build an economy. Its human development potential is not bio-resource-based, and bio-resources do not allow the UAE to adapt to climate change.

The UAE can only stimulate economic growth by developing its only resource, fossil fuel. The landscape is a desert and the country faces all the constraints that are particular to living in a desert (see Chapter 2):

1   no forest cover nor, therefore, the resources and services that forests can provide;
2   the inability to grow food to ensure food security;
3   no access to the abundant renewable water supplies needed to sustain a 'solar economy'.

The UAE has a 'fossil capital' that makes it dependent on oil revenues for its socioeconomic development. It has plenty of oil and its revenues can be used to import its essential human needs. Oil, however, does not grow food or cause rain. This dependence on one resource to provide those options has been especially apparent during 2009 when oil prices decreased in the global markets. The economy of the UAE and the continued development of its artificial infrastructure have been severely impacted, and many projects have been put on hold. Developing its human capital was a successful strategy for the UAE during periods of global economic growth, but the country has been vulnerable to the global economic downturns 2009. Because of its poor resource options, it will be difficult for the UAE to make sustainable decisions since it is at the mercy of the fluctuating global oil markets. Despite the problem of local sustainability, even during times of low energy prices, this region has continued to exert significant influence on the economies and political decisions being made in all other parts of the globe.

This brief discussion about temperature and how society has adapted to different temperatures begins to reveal some lessons from the decisions that countries have made. The two outlier examples just discussed suggested that a focus on mainly developing human capital, at the expense of developing the bio-resource capital, can in hindsight be unsustainable. Before examining more closely how societies have adapted to develop their human and resource capitals, the roles of population density and of living in rural environments will be examined. These indicators tell us how societies have adapted superbly to living in larger population centres and to live in rural areas with bio-resource rich environments.

Do High Population Densities Equate to Unsustainable Choices?

There is no connection for our countries between population density and the HDI ranking. Population density explains 3 per cent of the variance ($R^2 = 0.03$)

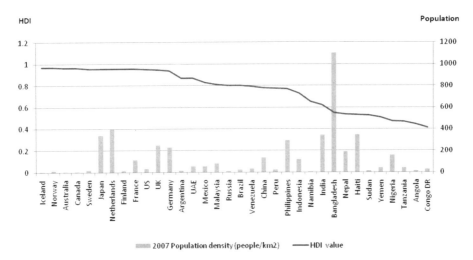

Figure 10.2 *HDI value plotted against population density (number of people/km²)*

in HDI (Figure 10.2; HDI ranking of 1 is best). High population densities do not equate to a country making unsustainable resource consumption choices, nor its ability to develop its human capital. This lack of correlation between population density and a country's HDI rank suggests that population density by itself is not important, but that how humans adapt to the unavoidable constraints they face in their environment is more relevant (Figure 10.2).

High population densities do not prevent a country from developing its human capital. For example, Japan was ranked in the top HDI group (out of 177 countries) but also had one of the highest population densities in our 34 country list. In contrast, Nigeria had a high population density but ranked at the bottom of the HDI rankings. This does not mean that a country need not decrease its population densities but it does suggest that a focus on managing population densities will not change a country's access to bio-resources and its ability to sustainably consume them. The fact that Japan is ranked so high in the HDI is due to its efficient use of resources. For example, Japan has a high population density but also practises one of the highest rates of recycling in the world. This means that Japan does not have to expend as much energy on producing new products and therefore in acquiring new resources.

On the flip side, if a country has a low population density does not mean that it is able to develop its human capital to a greater extent then if it had higher population densities. There is no link between population density and a country's human development potential even when population density is low (3–20 people/km²). If one only includes the Scandinavian countries in such a comparison, the conclusion would be that low population densities equate to a high HDI rank. The Scandinavian countries generally had low population densities and high HDI rankings. However, the Scandinavians share this population ranking with several countries that rank at the bottom end of the HDI rankings (e.g. Angola,

Table 10.3 *Population density (people/km²) plotted to food indicators*

Y variable	X variable	R^2
Population density	Arable (agriculture, pastures) land per cent of total land area	0.66
	Share home budget spent on food	0.07
	Proportion of population undernourished	0.004
	Water dependency ratio	0.19

Argentina and Sudan). This fact supports the idea that population density by itself does not constrain a country's capacity to develop its human capital.

When population density was regressed against all the variables in our database, few significant relationships were found (Table 10.3). Out of all of these indicators, only the amount of arable land as a percentage of the total land area is correlated to population density. Even though population density could be predicted by knowing how much of a country's land is used for growing crops and as pastures to feed domestic animals, the human development potential of a country is not related to these factors. Because the percentage of a country's land area in agriculture and pastures explains a significant proportion of a country's population density, it suggests that having a higher percentage of one's lands in agriculture does allow a country to support a larger population, even if it has no influence on how well a country develops its human capital. Of course, this relationship does not account for the fact that many of the advanced-economy countries import a significant amount of food, and the total arable land is probably less important in driving their human development capacity.

Population density was not related to how much of the home budget was spent on food or the proportion of the population that was undernourished, either. If a country has a large proportion of its people employed in agriculture, their population densities need not increase to produce sufficient food. In contrast to population density, the HDI rank of a country was correlated to how much of the home budget is spent on food purchases, i.e. the higher the HDI rank of a country, a lower propertion of the home budget was spent on buying food. The pattern produced by these data showed that the advanced-economy countries are having to spend a smaller fraction of their income on food costs, while the growing-economy countries are having to use most of the family income on food purchases. The main point here is that we cannot use population density as a means to determine the choices that a country makes to achieve food security. Ultimately, the choices that societies make to adapt to the unavoidable constraints and lack of resource supplies will determine how much they can develop their human capital.

As would be expected, population density is not correlated to how much energy production, such as woodfuel, is derived from forests (Table 10.3). Because several countries with higher population densities are also very dependent upon woodfuel for energy (see Chapters 4 and 5), we expected to see stronger relationships between population density and woodfuel consumption. Our data did not show any relationship between population density and how dependent communities were on woodfuel.

The link between population density and lack of access to bio-resources is frequently mentioned as a causal factor for wars and civil conflicts. Diamond (2005) suggested that the civil wars that erupted in Rwanda during the 1990s were caused by too many people competing to own the small plots of farmlands available. Based on our country analysis, we could not make the case that having a large population density would eventually result in social conflict and environmental degradation.

In our database, several countries highly ranked by HDI also had very high population densities, but these countries are not experiencing social conflict or degrading their lands. For example, the Netherlands has the second highest population density with 396 people/km^2, followed by Japan with 338 people/km^2, 249 people/km^2 in the UK and 230 people/km^2 in Germany. All four countries have successfully adapted to the climatic and soil constraints that can reduce their access to resources, and they have continued to build their human capital. This suggests that socioeconomic development is compatible with large population densities as long as the trade-offs in bio-resource consumption can be made sustainably.

Rural Landscapes: Rich in Resources and Rich People?

Today, the global trend is for more than half of the global population to live in cities. This is not, however, practised in countries that have not been able to develop their human capital. Most of the lower HDI-ranked countries in our database have higher proportions of their populations living in rural areas and are dependent on bio-resources found in their local environments for their survival. This trend is in sharp contrasts to the advanced-economy countries, where the populations primarily live in urban settings but are dependent upon bio-resources from the rural landscapes.

Our 34-country data results:

- In the advanced-economy countries, on average *21 per cent* of their population live in the rural areas (range: 7–39 per cent);
- Emerging-economy countries have similar patterns of population distribution as highly industrialized countries; *29 per cent* of people live in rural areas (range: 7–60 per cent);
- In the growing-economy countries, *66 per cent* of the population live in rural areas (range: 47–84 per cent).

Table 10.4 *Private ownership of forests by country*

Private ownership of total forest area, %	Countries
81–100	Norway, Sweden
61–80	Finland, France, UK, Yemen
41–60	Germany, Iceland, Japan, Netherlands, US
21–40	Australia
0–20	Angola, Bangladesh, Canada, China, India, Indonesia, Malaysia, Mexico, Nepal, Nigeria, Peru, Philippines, Russia, Sudan, UAE, Tanzania

Note: Private ownership of forests in 2000; no available data for Argentina, Brazil, Congo DR, Haiti, Namibia or Venezuela
Source: FAO, 2006

The trend for people to migrate to cities from the rural agricultural areas continues as a country becomes more industrialized. The other trend is that fewer people are involved in agriculture or other bio-resource employment activities. Furthermore, urban societies place less value on jobs in rural areas even though they are dependent upon resources from these environments.

Intuitively it makes sense that, if resources are abundantly available, societies should be better able to develop their human capital and their economic potential. Therefore, the abundant availability of resources in the rural landscapes should be able to satisfy the survival needs of people who live in these environments, and allow people to adapt to a changing climate. Since this is not what is found for people living in rural landscapes, alternative explanations must be examined.

Because most rural people do not own the lands on which they live, they are unable to control access to existing resources in their neighbourhood. This lack of land tenure means that rural people have little input regarding the decisions on how to use the land, or they lack the security that they can continue to access these resources in the near future.

The amount of private forest ownership is revealing (Table 10.4). In most of the growing- and emerging-economy countries, governments own a majority of the forests. These are the countries where a greater proportion of the people live in rural areas and where forests comprise a larger proportion of the total land area. This means that rural people are unable to determine what they will do with forests because the rules for forest uses are established by governments. Even when indigenous people have user rights to the forests, and community forests have been established, the final decision maker on forest use is still the government.

The advanced-economy countries or those that are highly ranked by HDI are notable for having the highest percentage of their forests owned by private individuals or corporations. Individuals, not governments, obtain the economic benefits from the collection of forest materials. In this group of countries, Australia and Canada are outliers to this general pattern because in both cases governments own more than half (and in the case of Canada, most) of their forestlands.

Table 10.5 *HDI ranking compared to labour and population statistics*

Y variable	X variable	R^2
HDI ranking	% population living in rural area [NEGATIVE]	0.70
	% labour force in agriculture/forests [NEGATIVE]	0.85
	Share of home budget spent on food [NEGATIVE]	0.86
	Proportion of population undernourished [NEGATIVE]	0.58
	DALY [NEGATIVE]	0.84
	Malnutrition (% stunting) [NEGATIVE]	0.78
	% labour force in industry [POSITIVE]	0.54
	% labour force in services [POSITIVE]	0.83
	Agricultural imports in US$/capita [POSITIVE]	0.62

Note: variable [direction of relationship]; DALY: Disability Adjusted Life Years

The disjunct between the development of human capital in rural areas and the benefits or the economic rewards of resource extraction is apparent from our database. Countries that have been less able to develop their human capital; i.e. lower HDI-ranked countries, have a large proportion of their population living in rural areas and are dependent on extracting local bio-resources. In fact, there is a strong inverse relationship ($R^2 = 0.70$) between a country's HDI ranking and what proportion of the population lives in rural areas – the higher the HDI ranking of a country, the fewer people living in rural areas (Table 10.5). These are the same countries where resources are owned by governments and not by private individuals or corporations. Furthermore, living in rural areas does not translate into higher incomes for most rural people; the proportion of the population living in rural areas explained 48 per cent of the variance in income (i.e. GNI).

Over half of the HDI ranking of a country is explained by a few simple indicators that indirectly evaluate a country's food security status (e.g. how much of the home budget is spent on food, and human health relationships) (Table 10.5; Figure 10.3). For example, the people living in growing-economy countries spend a greater share of their home budget on food but still have lower life expectancies and poor nutrition; the share of the home budget spent on food explains 86 per cent of the HDI ranking. These data also show that the advanced-economy countries are paying significantly more to import food than other countries (see Chapter 11). In fact, 62 per cent of the HDI ranking is explained by whether a country has to import agricultural crops. Therefore, food security is a more relevant factor explaining the socioeconomic status of a country, and a lack of food security appears to relegate a country to being unable to develop its human capital. The advanced-economy countries have successfully acquired food security by having the capacity to import the food supplies they need.

The percentage of the population employed in forestry and agriculture versus the industrial or services sectors is also connected to the HDI ranking of a country (Figure 10.3). The growing-economy countries, that is, those ranked lower by HDI, have fewer people working in the service and industrial sectors and most people are employed in agriculture and forestry. Over 80 per cent of the variance

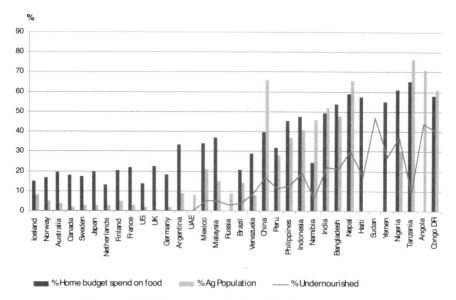

Figure 10.3 *Country agricultural indicators by HDI*

Source: FAO, 2006; HDI, 2007/2008; WHO, 2008

in the HDI ranking is explained by what percentage of the labour force works in bio-resource-based industries or in service industries. These trends do not reveal the fact that advanced-economy countries are still consuming many resources from the emerging- and growing-economy countries.

Unfortunately, employment in bio-resource-related professions have not been a healthy choice for people. When a larger proportion of the total population has been dependent on jobs in agriculture, people tend to be less healthy, are more under-nourished, experience higher rates of malnutrition and have shorter life spans (Table 10.6). This suggests that if countries ranked lower in the HDI ranking want to make decisions that would move them up the scale, they need to have a smaller portion of their population involved in food production and shift employment into the service sector. Of course, this does not deal with the fact that the continuing demand for bio-resources has been increasing and not decreasing, so there will be a demand for someone to continue to be the supplier of these bio-resources.

Table 10.6 *Proportion of the population involved in agriculture plotted against human health indicators*

Y variable	X variable	R2
Agricultural population, % of total	DALY [POSITIVE]	0.70
	Life expectancy [POSITIVE]	0.65
	Malnutrition (per cent stunting) [POSITIVE]	0.65
	Proportion population undernourished [POSITIVE]	0.60

Note: variable [direction of relationship]; DALY: Disability Adjusted Life Years

Therefore, the take-home messages from our data analysis are that when a larger portion of the population lives in rural areas there was a greater than 50 per cent chance that people: (1) are less healthy; (2) have higher malnutrition rates; and (3) have shorter life-spans (see summary below). These relationships suggest that living in the rural environment of a country is unhealthy for humans. These lower HDI-ranked countries are the same ones that have had extremely alarming rates of hunger, according to the Global Hunger Index (Chapter 3; Wiesmann, 2006).

The following health relationships resulted from our data analysis:

- The Health Index Disability Adjusted Life Years (DALY) due to environmental burden of disease per year (per cent) was positively linked to the percentage of the population living in rural areas ($R^2 = 0.52$);
- Life expectancy at birth was negatively linked to percentage of the population living in rural areas ($R^2 = 0.54$);
- Malnutrition (percentage stunting) was positively linked to the percentage of the population living in rural areas ($R^2 = 0.68$).

How well a country has developed its human capital is also related to what materials are predominantly used to produce energy. For example, most of the growing-economy countries are very dependent on wood biomass and wastes to produce their energy (see Figure 7.4); the HDI ranking of a country and the amount of wood biomass and wastes consumed as the primary energy supply explain 61 per cent of the variance between these two factors ($R^2 = 0.61$). Comparison of the amount of wood biomass and wastes used as the primary energy supply to the total amount of fossil fuels consumed as the primary energy supply produces $R^2 = 0.74$. In general, emerging-economy countries do not consume fossil fuels for energy even though several of them are major oil producers. For example, Angola became the largest source of crude oil imports to China in 2006 (EIA, 2007). These oil-producing and lower HDI-ranked countries export most of their oil and little is used for domestic consumption. People living in these countries are primarily burning wood, which they collect from their forests, or they convert trees into charcoal to sell to industrial projects.

There is also an inverse relationship between the amount of money spent on food and how much fossil fuel is the primary-energy supply. Fifty-eight per cent of the variance in the consumption of fossil fuels is explained by how much of the household budget is spent on food (Figure 10.4). If a greater proportion of the budget is spent on food purchases, less money is available to buy and consume oil.

These data further suggest that when a country has greater than 50 per cent of its population living in rural areas, it will be extremely difficult for that country to be environmentally friendly or to develop its human capital. The three lowest HDI-ranked countries in our list are all located in Africa: Angola, Congo DR and Nigeria. Despite the fact that these three are all significant exporters of oil to other countries (in 2005 Angola exported 94 per cent of its crude oil production,

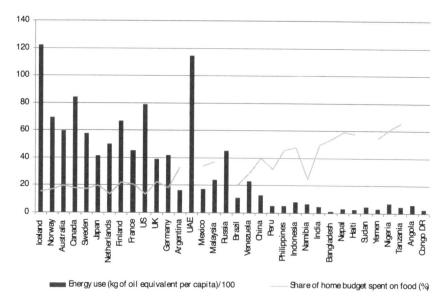

Figure 10.4 *Amount of energy consumed per capita plotted against the amount of family income spent on food purchases, $R^2 = 0.58$*

Source: World Bank, 2007; FAO, 2008

Congo DR 100 per cent and Nigeria 92 per cent), forests still provide most of the energy consumed by residents of these countries. The governments of these three countries are not shifting to becoming fossil-carbon-based economies and their people are still over-exploiting forests for woodfuel. In contrast to these three countries, Namibia does not have oil reserves and has to import much of its energy. Although it does not have secure energy supplies, Namibia has managed to be ranked higher by HDI and the EPI rankings than the other Western African countries analysed. Further, it has not experienced the political instability that is driving unsustainable bio-resource uses by the countries to the north.

There are a few exceptions to the general trend of a large rural population decreasing the development of a country's human capital. A few emerging-economy countries (e.g. India, China and Indonesia) have high rural populations, but have developed their human capital sufficiently to be ranked in the middle or higher by HDI. Despite these exceptions, rural-based economies are generally not ranked highly by environmental indices. This conclusion reflects the fact that the environmental-sustainability rankings are driven by conservation values and not the choices made by societies in response to the climatic and soil constraints imposed on them by their rural environments.

Some countries will find it more difficult to be environmentally friendly because they face so many more constraints compared to other countries. For example, Nigeria is very environmentally vulnerable and a high proportion of its land is severely degraded. It also faces an intermediate risk to climatic events. This means that Nigeria will have more difficulty in using its land to develop and satisfy food, energy and water needs because of a greater susceptibility to stochastic climatic events and inability to use the land to buffer resource demands. In contrast to Nigeria, Angola and Congo DR have a lower proportion of their lands that are degraded and are less vulnerable environmentally. Even when comparing these last two countries, Angola is better positioned than the Congo DR to deal with climate change, for it has a lower risk of climatic events disrupting its development activities. This highlights the importance of characterizing countries by all the constraints that make it difficult for them to make sustainable choices.

Since rural people are more dependent on collecting their bio-resources for socioeconomic development, a common view held by urbanites is that when a higher proportion of the population lives in rural areas, deforestation rates will be higher. Our data did not support this assumption. A large rural population does not automatically result in the loss of forest cover and higher rates of forest exploitation. In countries where over 50 per cent of the people live in rural areas (e.g. India, China and Nigeria), the high population densities have translated into significant loss of forest cover. However, this pattern is not repeated in Congo DR and Indonesia, where over 40 per cent of the lands are still in forests despite having over 50 per cent of the population living in rural areas.

It is also found that the degree of land degradation is not related to a higher proportion of the people living in rural areas. As expected, there is no relationship for how many people live in rural areas and the climate risk of a country. This raises interesting questions about what the environmental ranking of a country means, because it is not related to how much the land has been degraded due to land uses, or the climatic risk faced by a country – all factors that should reduce the capacity of a society to adapt to change and to survive.

These data suggest that knowing how many people live in rural areas cannot be used to conclude whether a country will be able to make sustainable choices. The comparisons made above suggest the importance of political stability and land tenure to develop a country's human capital as it develops its resource capital.

High resource capital and low human capital	High resource capital and high human capital
Low gross national income	High national income
High proportion of population living in rural areas	Small portion of population living in rural areas
Workforce mostly in agriculture and forestry	Workforce mainly in service and industry sectors
Low import of agricultural products	High import of agricultural products
Most of the home budget is spent on food	Only-third of home budget is spent on food
Population is unhealthy, undernourished, experiencing malnutrition	Population is healthy, over-nourished
Forest biomass, wastes primary energy	Fossil fuels primary energy

These data do separate countries into two different worlds based on how they rank, relative to their resource capital and human capital (see below). Half of the world has access to the productive capacity provided by our natural landscapes and the other half is less able to access them. These patterns are summarized below and show how the resource capital directly determines the social or human capital potential of a group of people.

To decode sustainability we need to understand the implications of one sector of society being totally dependent on obtaining resources from landscapes over which it has less control; this sector is also less knowledgeable about the factors that constrain these resource supplies. As urban areas are the political centres in a country, resource-use decisions are frequently made without a good understanding of the repercussions on the survival of people living in the rural areas. It is an imperative for the urban centres to maintain the flow of goods and services to them from the rural areas or city life, as we know it, will collapse (Grimm et al, 2008). This flow results in a geo-political inequality where trade and policy are used to ensure that goods and services continue to transfer to the cities (Korner and Ohsawa, 2005).

One of the distinctive characteristics of a society split into two worlds is the need to transport resources between them. Fossil carbon has been the 'pipeline' between the rural and urban areas. If fossil carbon supplies diminish, it will become more difficult for urban communities to maintain their current lifestyles. Societal dependence on fossil-carbon supplies will continue and now the emerging-economy countries are rapidly moving towards becoming fossil carbon-based economies. At the same time, countries are attempting to mitigate their CO_2 emissions, which means that difficult choices need to be made regarding our fossil carbon economies.

Another myth is that global societies can shift to a non-carbon world and maintain their socioeconomic status. The advanced-economy countries also appear to expect the emerging- and growing-economy countries to deliver the solutions to the difficult choices that need to be made to mitigate CO_2 emissions by changing their land-use practices. This shifts the burden away from advanced-economy countries having to make the difficult choices that will impact their industrialization activities.

Is it Realistic to Expect a Low Carbon-use World to Reduce CO_2 Emissions?

Economic development and fossil carbon

The links between socioeconomic development and fossil fuels suggest that it will be difficult to mitigate climate change by weaning countries from the use of fossil carbon. This dependency is attested to by the cyclic fluctuations between the prices for a barrel of oil, use of vehicles and the ease with which people return to driving when oil prices decrease, especially followed by lower gasoline prices.

When oil prices are higher, media discussions resume on whether we have reached 'peak oil'. Despite these concerns, few people are willing to make the difficult choices that would transition societies towards a low-carbon world. Fossil fuels have become an integral part of most human development activities in every country. Growing- and emerging-economy countries exhibit beliefs that they are entitled to enjoy the benefits that were possible because of fossil carbon. Climate change is making these choices even more difficult to implement and is raising the spectre of a country needing to reduce its fossil fuel consumption in order to decrease its CO_2 emissions.

There is no relationship between how a country is ranked for its emission of total CO_2 and how that country has altered its CO_2 emissions over a ten-year period (Figure 10.5). Noteworthy is the prominent ranking of the emerging-economy countries as the ones that have experienced significant increases in CO_2 emissions (e.g. China with a 68 per cent increase, India 53 per cent, Indonesia 48 per cent and Malaysia 73 per cent). These countries are rapidly emerging in the global economic scene. This trajectory of change in CO_2 emissions is ominous because it suggests that emissions will only continue to rise.

Many studies have documented the fossil fuel link to CO_2 emissions (see Chapter 4). It is also clear that countries which historically have been low CO_2 emitters (e.g. Angola ranked 70th, Norway ranked 53rd in 2005) have been dramatically increasing their emissions. Between the years 1994 and 2004, there was a 169 per cent increase in CO_2 emissions by Angola and a 43 per cent increase by Norway – both oil-producing countries. The increase by Angola occurred while Angola was exporting 94 per cent of its crude oil production.

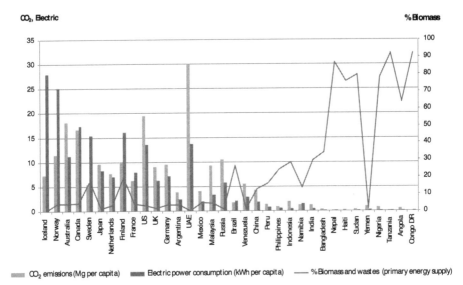

Figure 10.5 *Comparison of CO_2 emissions per capita against electric power consumption and against biomass wastes as a % of total primary energy*

Other than Sweden and Germany, all countries in our list experienced increases in their CO_2 emissions even if these increases were less than 30 per cent. The only growing-economy country that has decreased its CO_2 emissions is Nigeria. Most countries are unable to make the choices that will result in lowering their CO_2 emissions.

The unavoidable constraints of climate change and a land's productive capacity (Chapters 7 and 8) have been major factors that have not allowed countries to reduce their carbon emissions. For example, the 43 per cent increase in CO_2 emissions in Norway can be attributed to droughts, which forced the production of electricity to switch from hydroelectric dams to fossil fuels.

The challenges faced by countries wanting to decrease their CO_2 emissions is apparent from the trade-offs that Angola has needed to make. Angola has become the major exporter of oil to China, but forests continue to provide Angola with the majority of the energy consumed domestically. The high poverty and malnutrition rates found there also make it difficult for the government to manage CO_2 emissions while still developing economically. The land's productive capacity also constrains Angola's ability to obtain secure bio-resource supplies and allow its people to begin to develop their human capital. However, despite its increased emissions of CO_2, it is important to remember that Angola still has much lower total emissions compared to the advanced-economy countries.

The carbon backbone of society

Because of the concerns raised about human consumption of energy and its potential to alter climate in a way which causes society to become more vulnerable to disturbances, some have called for society to move from its current dependence on carbon to produce energy, in other words to move beyond a 'carbon world'. This call for a shift to another 'element' other than carbon has been difficult to achieve. Today, no material exists that would be capable of replacing carbon while continuing to provide society the resources and products that they are accustomed to having. Carbon is ubiquitous – it is the backbone and fabric of almost everything on this globe, including human bodies. If it were removed from all the products in which it is found, humans would not have upright forms, trees would not exist and food as we know it could not be grown. Autotrophic plants take energy from the sun and CO_2 to build their biomass; about 50 per cent of a tree's biomass is carbon. It is the biomass that herbivores eat to live. The human body contains 18 per cent carbon by mass. Our fossil fuels are carbon-based compounds that formed from biomass materials that grew millions of years ago; biomass was buried under high temperature conditions and converted to the fossil fuels of today. When society burns this material to obtain energy, this causes CO_2 to be emitted. The energy we obtain from combusting fossil fuels results from the splitting of the chemical bonds that plants originally built when forming their biomass. Therefore, this carbon is essential for maintaining the web of life. Until society develops some novel technology to replace carbon as an energy source, it will remain the backbone and fabric of our society.

In people's minds, our fossil fuel or carbon economy is synonymous with oil. When we debate whether we want to continue to be a carbon-based economy, the discussion revolves around oil. This focus on oil happens despite the fact that coal contributes as much global CO_2 emissions as oil. In 2005, of the 27,136 Metric Tons (Mt) of CO_2 emitted globally, coal combustion contributed 40.5 per cent of the total while oil contributed 39.5 per cent (IEA, 2007). Natural gas contributed 19.7 per cent of the total global emissions during the same period. These values help to explain why there is such global interest in converting from coal and oil to natural gas, which is considered to be a less 'dirty' fossil fuel. Natural gas as a transportation fuel would be a big boost to the security(ies) of alternative sources of energy and would help mitigate some of the CO_2 emissions. There is currently adequate natural gas in the US to handle the conversion in that country; this would have drastic global effects by substantially diminishing the political influence of the current major oil-producing countries. Further improvements in technology may even increase supplies of natural gas to levels higher than those suggested by the people holding the most optimistic view of natural gas abundance.

Currently there are debates on whether global oil supplies have peaked and whether society should switch to alternative sources of fuel. Reaching peak oil will not mean an immediate shortage of oil; it only means that we are on the later half of a bell curve, as far as production is concerned. However, technology has changed the timing of the peak a number of times. If tar sands and oil shales are included as possible resources that become proven reserves (these are currently political and/or environmental decisions), then oil may have a very long future. King Hubbert, who came up with the concept of peak oil, indicated that his projections were based on existing technology at the time he made the projections 50 years ago. Depending upon what is included as part of global oil supplies, peak oil may not be a supply problem but more of a political or environmental decision.

Oil companies appear confident that they will continue to provide all the oil needed by consumers. They also assume that society will continue to rely primarily on hydrocarbons for their energy consumption. This forecast was made by the chief executive of Exxon Mobil, the largest corporation in the western world (Saudi Aramco and other national oil companies are larger) and ranked as the 26th largest economy in the world despite the fact that 'oil reserves are harder to find, resource-rich governments have become more assertive and global warming concerns have spurred forceful calls to action on environmental matters' (Mouawad, 2008).

Unlike the oil shortages that occurred in the 1970s, today the western, industrialized countries no longer dominate or control oil supplies. When compared to the 1970s, industrialized countries that power their economies with oil have less control or influence over the acquisition of oil supplies. A look at the statistics on who controls oil supplies and who are the consumers of oil is informative. Mouawad (2008) summarized this as the 'new oil order'. According to Mouawad (2008), in the 1960s more than half of the world's oil production was controlled by the following companies – Exxon Mobil, BP, Royal Dutch Shell, Chevron,

ConocoPhillips, Total of France and Eni of Italy. The home-base of these companies was located in either the US or Europe. However, today these same companies produce only 13 per cent of oil globally. Another change is that the '10 largest holders of petroleum reserves are state-owned companies, such as Russia's Gazprom and Iran's national oil company' (Mouawad, 2008). These state-owned companies are deciding who will acquire the petroleum supplies as they become available on the global markets. China has been especially effective and competitive in accessing these petroleum resources.

The question that one should ask is, 'Given the uncertainty of their oil supplies, either due to hostile producers or to environmental or other political problems, will western industrialized countries move away from being carbon-based economies?' The answer is, 'Probably not – unless there is an unexpected breakthrough in technology, or a crisis that drives a very strong urgency'. According to Mouawad (2008), oil security is not just a supply issue, for we are not facing a geological peak in oil – the world is not running out of oil – but rather a 'geopolitical peak oil'.

So even if one accepts the fact that there is sufficient oil to supply global needs, several other issues will determine whether oil supplies are available to power the economies of industrialized countries:

- Will the economies of western countries be able to depend on these state-owned companies to supply their oil needs?
- Many of the oil-rich countries are more assertive, wishing to control their resource supplies and who has access to them. Oil-rich countries will make the decision about whether to supply the industrialized countries.
- The emission of CO_2 during the combustion of fossil fuels and the need to mitigate climate change.

The repercussions of a shift from oil as being the dominant hydrocarbon used to power our economies, and moving away from a carbon economy, are not understood by many. Scientists accept the link between CO_2 emissions and fossil-energy sources (IPCC, 2000), but there has not as yet been agreement about whether global warming mitigation is possible by shifting away from a carbon-based economy. The considerable debate about the efficacy of adopting *carbon-based* biofuels as substitutes for fossil fuel attests to the lack of consensus on what mitigation efforts should be adopted (see Chapter 5).

When the negative reactions to the use of food crops to produce biofuels arose because of their environmental and social impacts, woody biomass and grasses were introduced as alternative feedstock. The suggestions that trees and grasses should become the future feedstock of biofuels has been disputed for several reasons: environmental issues; values that do not condone felling any trees; the still-developing technology of converting biomass efficiently into alcohols; the competition between producers of food crops and forests for research funding; traditional forest producers who have not shown interest in developing alternative uses for forest; and, of course, a healthy mix of politics.

Box 10.2 Woodfuels as Bioenergy: Snapshots from Cebu, Philippines

Elizabeth Remedio and Terrence Bensel

For the year 2000, the total Philippine energy consumption was equivalent to 249.47 million barrels of fuel oil. Of that total, 49 per cent was obtained from indigenous sources and 51 per cent was imported. Biofuels are currently a major energy resource for both households and industries in the Philippines. Estimates suggest that approximately 10 per cent of all rural households in the Philippines receive income from selling woodfuels. Furthermore, it is estimated that, on average, the sales of woodfuels is 40 per cent of the total income for these households. Using indigenous resources, instead of imported fossil-based fuels, also translates into foreign exchange savings estimated to be worth millions of US dollars.

Despite the rapid urbanization of Cebu, the second largest city in Central Philippines, thousands of households in the city and province of Cebu continue to depend upon biomass resources as their primary or secondary source of household cooking fuel. Cebu is a microcosm of the overall income trend for the Philippines, where 40 per cent of the population falls below poverty levels; it also represents a small-scale replica of other national trends regarding the materials used to produce energy. Fossil fuels are increasingly being used because of their perceived convenience, safety and cleanliness. Even commercial and industrial establishments that prepare (native) food-related products are shifting away from their historical use of woodfuel because of smoke problems. Combining household and commercial/industrial woodfuel consumption data show that aggregate woodfuel use in Cebu City declined by ~ 12 per cent from 1992 to 2002; the use of biomass residues also decreased by 4 per cent, while charcoal consumption dramatically increased by 58 per cent. As urbanization continues in Cebu City, both households and businesses are shifting away from using woodfuel and biomass residues to produce energy; these energy sources require more storage space and generate too much smoke.

Despite these trends towards using fossil fuels, cultural taste, personal preferences and economic considerations are the most important reasons why bioenergy will continue to be a significant portion of the total energy mix in Philippine markets. Consumption and production of biofuels have generated incomes and jobs for thousands of families who are involved in the intricate, multi-level woodfuel trades. There has been an informal trading and distribution network from Cebu's rural area to its urban area that has been a thriving and sustainable industry for the past five decades (e.g. generating US$4 million revenues in 2002).

Many countries still expect that forests will allow them to mitigate their CO_2 emissions. The vision of how forests can mitigate climate change varies depending on the socioeconomic status of a country. Advanced-economy countries look at forests in other parts of the world to be the solution to climate change, by using them to sequester the carbon those countries emit. Most of the advanced-economy countries do not have more forest lands that they can set aside to mitigate global CO_2 emissions because their lands have other priority uses (see Chapter 5). As articulated in Box 10.2, most of the domestic energy production in the Philippines comes from forests. There are no other alternatives to energy from forests (e.g. woodfuel and charcoal production) so setting aside forests to sequester carbon is not a realistic option there.

Forests can be used to sequester carbon in many ways. They sequester carbon in their biomass, and liquid fuels can be produced that can be substituted for fossil-carbon supplies. Alternative uses of trees, other than as timber, are grossly under-developed. Trees grow and are carbon-fixing structures that are effective sequesters of carbon at decadal to century timescales. These timescales mean that trees used for energy can mitigate carbon emissions. Trees also sequester carbon in a growing forest. Therefore, trees or plants can contribute to mitigating global warming in several different ways (Vogt et al, 2005).

Achieving a sustainable carbon society that provides energy security at the local level is a complicated and tricky problem that requires many trade-offs. Even if addressing one of society's needs (e.g. energy supplies) appears logical, it may not be the preferred choice because of the many trade-offs that a decision introduces and the need to factor in the unavoidable constraints of the local environment. Energy use should not diminish the supply of available clean water, nor should it compete with food production. Bio-resources are a locally available resource that have the potential to provide choices for rural communities and are 'climate friendly' because they are carbon neutral. Despite this potential, rural communities have been struggling with becoming part of the energy future.

The reluctance to move beyond a fossil fuel economy is due to the negative impacts that this decision would have on the economy of every country in the world. There is good reason for this reluctance. Carbon, in the form of fossil fuels, has become the backbone and fabric of our societies and it will be extremely difficult to pluck carbon from our development activities without countries 'collapsing'.

Therefore, to accurately decode sustainability, there is a need to be able to identify the constraints for each resource and to understand how decisions made for one of the resources needed for human survival feeds back to impact the sustainability of another human need. This concept refers back to the Sustainability Web that was described in Chapter 1. There will not be one single answer to any problem, but a portfolio of options where the trade-offs that will be required are spelled out so that the decision makers can fully access information regarding which plan will have the best chance of being sustainable. This portfolio of options needs to consider both the regional context where the products are consumed, and the possible adverse effects to the sustainability of the location that produced the product. This is similar to the LCA approach, except that social capital and resource capital are inadequately measured during a life-cycle assessment. However, a life-cycle approach would be quite cumbersome if it needed to simultaneously include all four of the human survival needs. Also, the data required for an LCA do not exist at the scale where this analysis needs to be conducted (Vogt et al, 2010).

Country level assessments need to produce a suite of tools to resolve the many factors introduced in the *Millennium Ecosystem Assessment: ecosystems and human well-being* report (MEA, 2005). Unfortunately, these assessments cannot be narrowly focused since that would over-simplify them to the point where they were almost useless. In addition, the current indices and indicators are not very effective at reflecting the vulnerability of societies to the decisions being made. Any assessment should be able to answer the following questions when exploring the potential of a country to make decisions that moves it towards being more sustainable:

- How vulnerable are people living in an area?
- How do the decisions impact people who are the producers and/or the consumers of a product or ecosystem service?
- How are people adapting or not adapting to the effects of the decisions?
- How can people mitigate the impacts or repercussions of the decisions?

To decode sustainability will require the development of multiple models of sustainability. We need to study countries that have learned how to be adaptive and to consider how applicable their situation is in another location. Sustainability means that we 'need to keep a suite of tools available that can be used to adapt for an unknown future'. We need to develop adaptability tools, and not tools for assessing fixed conditions. Part of being adaptive is maintaining options. When we focus on resolving one human need at a time, we end up ruling out potential options and in some cases create problems elsewhere, since all four of the human needs are completely interconnected. We also need to determine how countries can turn their 'potential' into 'realistic' capacities to provide for their societies' current and future needs. This last goal will be possible when there is an understanding of the constraints that each country faces, and when we are able realistically to evaluate the productive capacity of their environments.

Food Security Solution: Do We Need Another Green Revolution?

Food security has been a problem that appears to have a solution – the Green Revolution. The Green Revolution was a period of large increases in agricultural production that began in Mexico and expanded to India and China (see Box 10.3). Dams and other engineered infrastructure harnessed lakes, river and groundwater for farming and energy production. Increased trade enabled food to be transported from surplus countries and regions to countries and regions which did not have enough food production capacity, chose to allocate land and water resources to other productive uses, desired to obtain seasonal foods, and/or purchased imported food for lower prices.

Box 10.3 History of the Green Revolution

The Green Revolution began in Mexico in the early 1950s through the work of an Iowa plant breeder named Norman Borlaug. In 1999 the *Atlantic Monthly* estimated that Borlaug's revolution saved more than one billion people. The transfer of Western technological methods of farming to less developed countries was a brainchild of US Vice President Wallace that began to be implemented during the Second World War, the research project was funded by the Rockefeller Foundation. Borlaug began his painstaking work of developing a rust-resistant strain of wheat in Mexico in 1943. By the early 1950s Mexico's wheat shortage was over and wheat farms were so productive that farmers were able to buy synthetic fertilizer for the first time, and wheat plants were so heavy with grain that plant breeding to develop a stronger stem had to be undertaken so they would not fall over. By 1960, farmers in Mexico were reaping 50–75 bushels/acre (3.4–5.0Mg/ha), compared to 11 (0.7Mg/ha) when Borlaug arrived in the country.

At the same time most of the developing world was starving. Borlaug's wheat came to the rescue, and high-yield seeds were shipped to India and Pakistan. India's wheat harvest doubled in four years. Borlaug won the Nobel Peace Prize in 1970 for his work in ending the Pakistan and Indian food shortage in the 1960s. These methods were also taken to Africa, but record harvests led to surpluses, leading to collapsing prices. It appears that the lack of the infrastructure to move the food, commodity markets for price stability, and other supports for farmers are critical factors in African hunger. The Green Revolution is criticized for the extensive use of pesticides and fertilizers, the frequent depletion of marginal lands, increasing CO_2 levels, loss of biodiversity and the extensive use of water that this type of farming requires. There is a second Green Revolution beginning that is being funded by the Gates Foundation's Global Development Program, and which focuses on genetically engineered seeds.

Today, it seems that with all the advancements made in increasing the productivity of food crops (i.e. the Green Revolution), food security should be assured. Our advances in agricultural production should mean that a pattern of low food security is broken. However, food riots occurred in 2008 because the cost of buying food had risen to unaffordable levels, following the diversion of food crops to the production of biofuels. These riots would not have occurred if there were adequate food supplies at affordable prices. A rise in malnutrition (estimated at 40 million people in 2008) can be attributed to rising food prices.

Even though some countries have reported high rates of famine and malnutrition, global food production appears to have matched population growth over the last century. Or has it? Food production, especially the high-yield agriculture that resulted from the Green Revolution, has been sufficient to sustain the globe's 6.5 billion people (Box 10.3). This view is supported by several indicators. One tracks the ratio of global cereal stocks to its utilization, and this indicator has been declining, suggesting that adequate global cereal stocks exist. This indicator, however, hides the fact that the increase in cereal production in 2008 was accomplished by the advanced-economy countries, which were able to increase their cereal production rapidly in response to increasing global prices (FAO, 2008). In contrast, the growing-economy countries only recorded an increase of 1.1 per cent in their cereal production; if China, India and Brazil are excluded from these calculations, cereal production decreased by 0.8 per cent globally. Cereal imports by advanced-economy countries increased by 127 per cent between 2005 and 2008. Therefore, the cereal production of advanced-economies is masking the reduced crop yields that have been occurring in growing-economy countries; the major wheat and coarse grain exporters are Argentina, Australia, Canada, the EU countries and the US.

Historically, farming practices have been adaptive and opportunistic. Humans responded to environmental changes and their needs using whatever technology, natural resources, institutions and market mechanisms were available at the time. Water was always one of the essential ingredients allowing farming to occur, and farmers adapted their practices to changing climates. In addition, fertilizers, pesticides, labour, mechanization, storage and marketing have all influenced food production and availability. Increases in agricultural output in the 20th century can be attributed to horizontal expansion of arable land and the capacity to intensify production through the application of seed, fertilizer and pesticide technologies, and the ability to store, deliver and pump surface and groundwater.

Recently, international organizations are attempting to understand the impact of climate on agriculture and food security because societies are becoming increasingly vulnerable to climate change. The FAO (2003) defines food security as: 'a situation that exists when all people, at all times, have physical, social and economic access to sufficient, safe and nutritious food that meets their dietary needs and food preferences for an active and healthy life'. FAO (2008) suggests that all four components of food security (availability, stability, accessibility, and utilization) must be adequate to achieve food security. Until recently, climate-change simulation studies only included one of these four factors – food availability – nor did these simulations include climate-change impacts on fisheries or forestry (Schmidhuber and Tubiello, 2007).

The recent volatility in food commodity prices, however, is a warning that the globe's food supply systems are not infinitely elastic. There have been changes in normal demand due to the unintended consequence of bio-fuel policies that were diverting the use of food crops for energy. This illustrates how sensitive both subsistence and intensive farming systems can be to external shocks. It also highlights the fact that global food supplies are not secure even today, despite the increased growth benefits that resulted from the Green Revolution.

Despite all the increases in the growth of food production, global food security has not been achieved. In growing-economy countries, the number of chronically hungry people started to increase from the late 1990s, and by 2001–2003 the total number of undernourished people worldwide was 854 million (FAO, 2008). The GHI 'captures three dimensions of hunger: insufficient availability of food, shortfalls in the nutritional status of children and child mortality' (Wiesmann, 2006). It also reflects well whether a country is capable of maintaining its food production. This ranking includes 97 growing-economy countries and 22 that are in transition to becoming industrialized countries. The 'hot spots' of hunger were found in South Asia and Sub-Saharan Africa; the GHI shows that in the latter region food security has decreased, while in South Asia food security has improved. In southern and eastern Africa, the population of food-insecure people has doubled over the last 25 years while per capita cropped area has declined by 3 per cent (FAO, 2006).

Another factor that contributed to a country having a high GHI score was the prevalence of disease, which further weakens the human population (Wiesmann, 2006). The spread of HIV and AIDS directly impacts food security, as the adults involved in agricultural production become ill or die prematurely. The link between poor health and not getting enough food is already known (see Chapter 2) and is evident in these countries where civil unrest continues today.

The most alarming and the worst hunger-index rankings are found in Sub-Saharan countries engaged in wars and civil conflict. Out of the 12 countries that were ranked as having the worst GHI in 2003, nine had fighting and civil unrest decreasing their food security (Wiesmann, 2006). Out of the countries included in our analysis, the Congo DR and Angola were ranked among the 12 countries as having the worst GHI score. Congo DR received its GHI score in the 1990s when violent conflicts were common; a comparison between 1982 and 2003 showed that Congo DR's GHI score became twice as bad during this time period. Warfare decreases food security and increases malnutrition because farming stops during violent outbreaks. Therefore, food shortages are common. People living in urban areas had even less food and competed for the same food supplies as those living in rural areas.

Unfortunately, a high GHI score reflects the 'history of political crises, violence and bad governance ...' (Wiesmann, 2006). Unless these political and military conditions alter, very little change can be expected in the health of these people. Both Angola (with a history of political conflict and warfare) and Congo DR (experiencing continuing warfare and political conflict) have a significant portion of their population who are malnourished.

Even if political conflict ceased in Angola and Congo DR, food security would be an unreachable goal. Something similar to the Green Revolution needs to happen, for the productive potential of these lands is not being reached today. Much of the land is already being used for agriculture or grazing animals, and putting more land into agriculture is not possible. The implications of this malnourishment are huge because many people have no social resiliency, are less capable of contributing towards increasing the human development potential of their country and are dying prematurely. There are several reasons why agricultural production has been decreasing in the growing-economy countries, and soil moisture deficits and weather-related crop damage have been the predominant factors limiting agricultural productivity.

Poverty, political strife and lack of investments in human and financial resources are contributing to food insecurities. In these countries, insufficient infrastructure for irrigation, storage and transportation of water also contributed to a lack of food security. Higher food prices are driven by higher costs for energy and other inputs, increased competition for grains, market and trade failures, and market speculation. Higher food prices can lead to increased hunger even if food is available. The inter-action with socioeconomic drivers, such as populations and income growth, has the potential to exacerbate or counteract the direct impacts of climate change. Climate change is in general expected to exacerbate water stress and this may have severe impacts in regions already under stress from population growth, rapid economic development, land-use changes, pollution and urbanization.

The Millennium Ecosystem Assessment reported that in the last 50 years humans have changed ecosystems more rapidly and extensively than ever before, in order to meet our growing demands for food, fresh water, timber and fuel (MEA, 2005). In Africa 75–250 million people are projected to be exposed to increased water stress, and yields from agriculture are expected to decrease as much as 50 per cent in some countries. The areas of semi-arid and arid land will increase. Land areas classified as very dry have already doubled since the 1970s. These land areas constrain local food production.

References

Diamond, J. (2005) *Collapse: How Societies Choose to Fail or Survive*, Penguin, New York, NY

EIA (2007) 'Energy profile of China', *Encyclopedia of Earth*, http://eoearth.org/article/Energy_profile_of_China, accessed 9 July 2009

FAO (2003) 'The State of Food Insecurity in the World 2003', UN FAO, Rome, Italy

FAO (2006) 'Global Forest Resources Assessment 2005', UN FAO, Rome, Italy

FAO (2008) 'World Resources Report', www.fao.org/docrep/011/ai476e/ai476e01.htm, 22 July 2009

Grimm, N. B., Faeth, S. H., Bolubiewski, N. E., Redman, C. L., Wu, J., Bai, X. and Briggs, J. M. (2008) 'Global change and the ecology of cities', *Science*, vol 319, pp756–760

Hanlon, M. (2009) 'The solar-powered rotating skyscraper', *Gizmag*, www.gizmag.com/go/6648, accessed 5 September 2009

HDI (2007/2008) 'Human Development Index', http://hDrundp.org/en/statistics, accessed 1 October 2008

IEA (2007) *2007 Key World Energy Statistics*, International Energy Agency, http://tonto.eia.doe.gov/country/country_energy_data.cfm?fips=AO, accessed 1 September 2008

IPCC (2000) *Land Use, Land Use Change and Forestry – a special report of the IPCC*, Cambridge University Press, Cambridge

Korner, C. and Ohsawa, M. (2005) 'Mountain systems', in B. Fitzharris and Shrestha, K. (eds), *Ecosystems and Human Well-Being: Conditions and Trends*, Millenium Ecosystem Assessment 2005

MEA (2005) *Millennium Ecosystem Assessment: Ecosystems and Human Well-Being Synthesis. Findings of the Condition and Trends Working Group of the Millennium Ecosystem Assessment*, Island Press, Washington, DC

Mouawad, J. (2008) 'At Exxon, making the case for oil', *New York Times*, 15 November 2008, www.nytimes.com/2008/11/16/business/16exxon.html?th&emc=th, accessed 10 June 2009

National Geographic (2009) 'United Arab Emirates', National Geographic Atlas of the World, 8th edn., 2004 http://travel.nationalgeographic.com/places/countries/country_unitedarabemirates.html, accessed 5 Sept 2009

UN (2009) *World Statistics Pocketbook*, United Nations Statistics Division, http://data.un.org/CountryProfile, accessed 20 March 2009

Vogt, K. A., Larson, B. C., Gordon, J. C., Vogt, D. J. and Fanzeres A. (2000) *Forest Certification. Roots, Issues, Challenges, and Benefits*, CRC Press, Boca Raton, FL

Vogt, K. A., Andreu, M., Vogt, D. J., Sigurdardottir, R., Edmonds, R., Schiess, P. and Hodgson, K. (2005) 'Enhancing sustainability of forests in human landscapes by adding non-traditional values to younger forests', *Journal of Forestry*, vol 103, no 1, pp21–27

Vogt, K. A., Vogt, D. J., Shelton, M., Colonnese, T., Stefan, L., Cawston, R., Scullion, J., Marchand, M., Hagmann, R. K., Tulee, M., Nackley, L., Geary, T. C., House, T. A., Candelaria, S., Nwaneshiudu, I., Lee, A. M., Kahn, E., James, L. L., Rigdon, S. J., Theobald, R. M. and Lai, L. X. (2010) 'Bio-resource based energy for sustainable societies', in W. H. Lee and V. G. Cho (eds), *Handbook of Sustainable Energy*, Nova Science Publishers Inc, Hauppauge, NY

WHO (2007) 'Country Profiles of Environmental Burden of Disease and Country Profiles', World Health Organization, Public Health and the Environment, Geneva 2007, www.who.int/countries/ago/en, accessed 10 December 2008

Wiesmann, D. (2006) 'A global hunger index: Measurement concept, ranking of countries and trends', FCND Discussion Paper 212, International Food Policy Research Institute, Sustainable solutions for ending hunger and poverty, December 2006, www.ifpri.org/divs/fcnd/dp/papers/fcndp212.pdf, accessed 9 January 2009

World Bank (2008) 'World Development Indicators database', Washington, DC

11

Portfolio for Managing Natural and Human Capital

Many countries that may appear to be well endowed with resources, are ranked correspondingly high in the HDI and environmental rankings. However, it is not just the availability of in-country resources that makes a country sustainable, but whether the people living there are able to adapt to environmental or social changes. A case in point is the Netherlands. Adaptation is a highly developed skill that is embraced by the entire Dutch population. The Netherlands faces many resource limitations that it has managed to overcome. A major bio-resource exporter, it has developed its human capital despite having only one-half of its land capable of producing crops, 60 per cent of the crops exported needing to be irrigated and 88 per cent of its renewable water originating from outside its borders. Despite not having an abundance of resources, the Netherlands has been making decisions that are adaptive to its landscape and that have not increased its socioeconomic vulnerability to disturbances. The Netherlands devotes a consider-able portion of its economic activities to agriculture, but has degraded less than 5 per cent of its total land area while pursuing this goal. This is in sharp contrast to countries such as the Congo DR that have an abundance of fossil and renewable resources but have not been able to provide for their basic human needs. Because human development is linked to adaptability, the Netherlands is ranked high by HDI while the Congo DR is ranked very low by this same index.

Unfortunately, the decision to become socially and environmentally resilient is not a simple process, where the same set of tools can be utilized for every location or situation. It would be much easier if humans could consider just a few factors or indices when making these decisions, and once the decision is made then the process would work anywhere in the world. This would be similar to an exhibit that the senior author saw in a museum in Dover, UK in the summer of 2007. An interpretative display had been set up where the public could play a game on a computer to determine what resources early voyagers needed to successfully travel by boat to other lands. In this computer game, the person needed to deter-mine the number of people, the number of boats and the amount of supplies and animals needed to be placed on a boat to emigrate successfully. The solution was simple: either you did not take enough boats, people and supplies or you took too many. In this computer game, you failed if your boat sank and you did not obtain the rewards of colonizing new lands. Perhaps a few boats would sink because of 'bad' decisions, but the game could be restarted and no one would be hurt. If real-life decisions were this simple, it would be easier to pursue sustainability goals. However, this interpretative display in Dover is simply a game and not real life. In real life, 'bad' decisions cannot simply be deleted, and people do get hurt. Unfortunately, we are not playing simple computer games and the decisions made in one part of the world may adversely affect those living in what appears to be a totally unconnected region.

The other problem society faces is the difficulty of determining what to include in a sustainability assessment, because ecosystems are complex and solutions to environmental problems require a long time to resolve (Gordon and Berry, 2006; Palmer and Filoso, 2009). To expedite problem-solving, we tend to focus on economic instead of environmental or social metrics. This is primarily because economic metrics can be measured over shorter timescales, while environmental and social metrics are controversial, reflect individual or group values, are hotly debated by scientists and play out over longer timescales. Indicators that play out over longer timescales are difficult to build societal consensus upon, because there is too much uncertainty associated with the decision. It is much easier to make decisions at the shorter timescales even when these are based on fragmented information. But does the economic solution provide a bandage, or a 'real' solution to the complex mix of factors that need to be considered when pursuing a model of sustainability? It may be simpler, but does it reduce or increase the risk that wrong decisions will be made? Nordhaus and Shellenberger (2007) suggest that an economic solution is the primary approach to deal effectively with environmental problems. Is this correct?

Our global history is replete with examples where an economic approach appeared to simplify resource consumptive decisions and the choices made were considered on hindsight to be 'good' decisions. Despite these successes, much of the discussion that has already occurred in our book suggests that this is a 'tunnel' vision way of evaluating success, and cannot adequately measure whether a sustainable choice was made. For example, European colonization of Asia and North America were economically driven, and these colonizers were able to increase their socioeconomic status in these newly conquered lands. However, no consideration was given to the environmental impacts or social consequences in the colonized lands. We contend that economics is an important component of a sustainability assessment, but that it needs to include social and environmental externalities so that societies do not collapse in the future.

Civilizations that collapsed tell us stories of how societies did not or were unable to adapt. We have used these stories to understand what makes a society unsustainable, but they are fragmentary snapshots of what really happened. Historical records may not include critical clues needed to really understand the conditions. They are static dialogues, and historical chronologies, and it is not clear if the circumstances that caused these collapses are in play today.

Even though we may be able to monitor many facts about society and its use of resources, this information may be less useful in determining whether we are making sustainable choices. What we track may be based on the potential and not the realistic or constrained choices. If we shifted the focus to determining how societies adapt, it will be easier to decode the principles of sustainability. Since society is continually adapting to the constraints imposed by local and global factors, this should be a more fruitful approach. Historically, humans have been very effective at utilizing each landscape for what it was best suited, and selecting new options when needed.

Humans adapt in several ways and the following four are especially critical in increasing a society's adaptability to an unpredictable future environment:

1   Communication technologies that allow a person to know what is happening in the global markets or monitor changes in product demand;
2   Education which allows a person to acquire the new skills needed to switch to a new profession and which educates the entire population, including women, so that everyone can be adaptive;
3   Importing resources that are not readily available locally, or have negative local environmental externalities that are unacceptable because they increase societal vulnerability to climate change;
4   Valuing labour involved in resource management.

The utility of each type of adaptation will vary depending on the local context and the land's productive capacity, as well as the cultural traditions of a group. The next section will examine these further, since each increases a society's ability to adapt to its environment and to climate change.

Developing Human Capital

Communication technologies

The fact that much of the variance in HDI rankings can be explained by two variables (computers and mobile phone subscriptions) describes how important communication has become to the human development potential of any society today. Communication is an important vehicle that allows societies to adapt, for knowledge or 'knowing the facts' prepares people to make better choices. It allows us to examine the full range of options available when decisions need to be made. For our data, 84 per cent of the variance in the HDI ranking of a country is explained by the number of mobile telephone subscriptions found in the population. The higher the number of mobile phone subscribers in the population, the higher a country's HDI ranking. The number of internet users in the population explains 72 per cent of the variance in the HDI ranking; the more people connected to the internet, the higher the HDI rank.

These communication tools are no longer just available in industrialized countries. They are transforming how business is conducted all over the world and have allowed greater participation by people previously excluded from the global markets. The US was once called the land of opportunity, where poor people could strive to become millionaires as long as they were willing to work hard and diligently. Today, communication technology is creating new opportunities for people to move up in the social strata regardless of where they live.

These tools have become essential in rural areas, where they are facilitating and developing economic opportunities. The report of farmers in India using mobile phones to call the markets to determine what to plant in the fields is a good example of the liberating influence of this technology. In India, having mobile phones means the farmer no longer has to take a day-long bus trip to the city to obtain the information on what crops to plant, and instead can concentrate on farming rather than spending time acquiring market information or even planting the wrong crop. In Haiti, mobile phones are the lifeline of businesses in an environment where there are no electrical grids to power land-based communication technologies. Mobile phones liberate people from waiting for the infrastructure to be developed in order to allow them to be part of the global communication network. Prior to mobile phones, people in growing-economy countries might wait years to have a landline phone installed in their homes. Even when these landlines had been installed, power outages still meant frequent interruptions in their ability to communicate.

Thomas Friedman (2009) summarized how during economic downturns, society becomes more innovative, and groups begin to invent new approaches to conducting business in order to survive. He wrote 'the country that uses this crisis [recession] to make its population smarter and more innovative – and endows its people with more tools and basic research to invent new goods and services – is the one that will not just survive but thrive down the road.' He goes on to write that Russia and China are wasting the opportunities that can arise from a recession, because Russia is not diversifying its economy and China is blocking the internet, which begins to restrict the ability of its population to innovate and explore new ideas.

The core ideas espoused by Friedman are those that we think are essential for a society to make sustainable choices. Adaptation is a key element, and works when it increases the choices available. These choices have to be able to weather the inevitable downturns that normally occur in any industry. They have to buffer society from unpredictable and inevitable changes. Change is inevitable. We cannot stop change, but we can increase society's ability to adapt to it by strengthening the formal institutions (such as universities or technical programmes) and informal educational processes (e.g. communication tools) that include all members of society.

Make the whole society adaptable: Educate females

Education is directly correlated to the economic status of a country and its human development potential. If a country does not emphasize the education of its population, it will have to accept that it will be unable to fully develop its human capital. Education is also one of the major ways that societies maintain their ability

Table 11.1 *Correlations between socioeconomic indicators and girls in education*

	Ratio of girls to boys in primary & secondary education (%)	Combined gross enrolment ratio for primary, secondary & tertiary education (female, %)
Population density (n/km^2)	0.00	0.00
GNI per capita, Atlas method (current US$)	0.09	0.51
% rural	0.40	0.61
Life expectancy at birth, total (years)	0.29	0.76
1998 or 2003 population below poverty line (% = making < US$1/day)	0.14	0.51
2001–2003 Undernourished population, of the total (%)	0.39	0.58
Adult illiteracy rate (% aged 15 and older 1995–2005)	0.64	0.47
Human Development Index value	0.47	0.88

Note: Data from 2005, unless noted otherwise
Source: FAO, 2006; HDI, 2007/2008; WHO, 2007; FAO, 2008; Mongabay, 2008; World Bank, 2008

to adapt. It provides the skill sets essential for managing the globe's resource capital and income, and gives the workforce the ability to make choices to increase its survival when societies and environments are dynamic and unpredictable. It allows the workforce to adapt and pursue alternative employment opportunities when there is a need.

However, this means educating the entire population and not just a portion of the population (i.e. males). If females are excluded from pursuing educational opportunities, half of the members of any society will not have the skills to adapt. This situation does not bode well for a country's pursuit of its sustainable livelihood goals.

The relationships between several socioeconomic indicators and the participation of girls in education are provided in Table 11.1. These data show several trends. There is no relationship between a country's population density and whether females are allowed to become educated. Another way of stating this is: just because there are more mouths to feed does not mean that fewer females are educated.

Educating female children is highly correlated to the socioeconomic status of a country; when most female children are educated, a country had a higher HDI ranking and a higher GNI per capita (Figure 11.1). Because these are the same factors that were strongly connected to the proportion of the population who live in rural areas, the same relationships are formed between the proportion of females who are educated and these factors. Countries ranked high by HDI overwhelmingly provide equal educational opportunities for both male and female children; they also have a higher proportion of their population pursuing an educational degree beyond the primary education level.

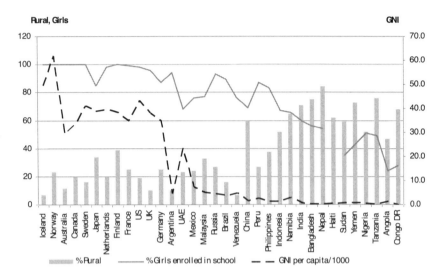

Figure 11.1 *Female children educated plotted against the proportion of the population in rural areas and their GNI*

Source: HDI, 2007/2008; WHO, 2007; World Bank, 2008

When a larger portion of the population lives in the rural areas and is employed in agriculture/forestry, there are fewer educational opportunities and a larger portion of the population is illiterate. Dependence on employment in bio-resource-based industries commonly found in rural landscapes has many negative

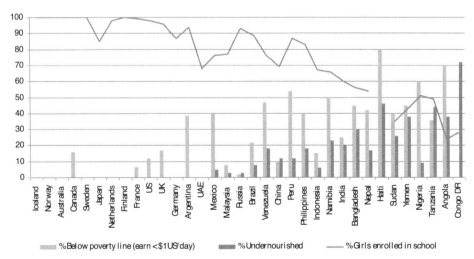

Figure 11.2 *Relationships between female education, poverty and being undernourished*

Source: FAO, 2008; HDI, 2007/2008; Mongabay, 2008; World Bank, 2008

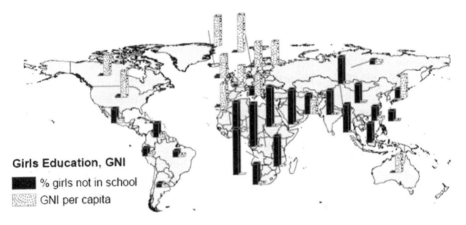

Figure 11.3 *Percentage of girls not in school plotted against GNI per capita*

aspects. Female, as well as many male, children have fewer educational opportunities because they enter the labour pool when young; they are less able to take advantage of educational opportunities and are relegated to lives of poverty and poor health (Figure 11.2). When this happens, it decreases the ability of society to adapt to changing climates or environments, since the energy of most people is expended in growing food on a land-base that probably has many constraints, or may already be severely degraded.

One cannot identify the cause-and-effect relationships for the data included in the above figures, but the correlations suggest that all these parameters are closely linked. Therefore, if you resolve one of the problems, there is a strong likelihood of resolving others. For example, when fewer females are educated and subsistence survival is the norm, the following conditions pertain: life expectancy is shorter, more people live below the poverty level and a higher percentage of the population is undernourished. It makes sense that, by not educating this half of the population, females are effectively removed from being involved in developing new economic opportunities in a country (Figure 11.3).

Being Adaptive Means Being Global and Importing Bio-resources

More than a thousand years ago, people began to hone their trading skills and were importing resources not locally available; there is a suggestion that tobacco was transported from South America to the land that is present-day Egypt to use in preserving mummies. Bartering and trading for resources have thus long historical roots and are practices towards which humans seem to be attracted. Probably the first person who cut down a tree to build a boat and then travelled to some distant land was a trader. If it had been a long sea voyage, food options would have become very limited in a matter of days. Bartering and trading for resources were necessary upon arriving in foreign lands because the voyagers would have been unfamiliar with their new environments and which plants were edible. It is well documented that the first European colonialists arriving in North America would not have survived without the help provided by Native Americans. It might have been a different history if the Native Americans had not provided this knowledge. Prior to the arrival of the Europeans, Native Americans had developed sophisticated plant propagation programmes. European colonialists traded for their knowledge and transported the plants back to Europe to feed their growing populations.

The building of cities also required food to be transported between regions or watersheds, even if only a few kilometres. When humans built cities in Europe after 800 CE, people became more dependent on one another. Those living in cities were no longer able to produce their own food; this started the process of people needing to transport large quantities of food products into their cities. In Europe, this probably formalized the process for bartering, trading and the importation of goods from the surrounding communities and adjacent countrysides. The need to acquire resources from the surrounding countryside still exists today, even though it generates considerable conflict as urbanites attempt to control resource-supply chains in rural landscapes.

We have already described the long history of societies improving their economic status, and adapting to limitations in resource supplies in their own backyards, by consuming someone else's resources (see Chapter 2). Human history has recorded how few societies were able to survive solely on resources located within their own territorial boundaries. If they did manage to do this, people were not always very healthy (Steckel and Rose, 2002). When societies (such as that on Easter Island) did collapse, it was because they were unable to pursue resource supplies elsewhere. It has not been the norm for societies to shrink their energy, forest, water and food footprints when supplies began to limit their economic development potential. Societies innately recognize that they will need either to shrink their resource-use footprint or acquire the resources elsewhere. Few societies have intentionally chosen to shrink their resource-use footprints. Most of the time, they have expanded their resource footprints by importing items they need or want, or by acquiring them through some other means.

Obtaining resources grown on someone else's land continues today. The recent purchase of agricultural lands in Sudan and Ethiopia by the oil-rich Persian Gulf countries shows that the latter recognize the unavoidable constraints pertaining to their own lands. They are not acquiring these lands to grow food for the African countries where the crops will be grown, but to grow food for themselves. The Persian Gulf region is a desert where water scarcities reduce crop production. They are adapting to their own land's constraints by either importing food from elsewhere or managing someone else's land productivity for their own benefit. For the Persian Gulf countries, this is a sustainable decision, but it is not one that addresses whether the increased sustainability of the Persian Gulf countries will decrease the survival choices of the people living in Sudan and Ethiopia.

Today, many countries do not have a choice to increase their land's productive capacity, which means that controlling access to and competing for resource supplies produced elsewhere is an important political strategy. Unless major technological breakthroughs occur, agricultural practices have already optimized plant growth rates and it will be difficult to increase a land's productive capacity. Climates and soils are unavoidable constraints that have set the limit for a land's productive capacity. These constraints force us to conclude that we cannot sustainably grow food, collect forest materials, obtain clean water and get energy from each piece of land. After hundreds of years of growing crops, we know that many lands have some constraint that makes it difficult to produce sufficient food (see Chapter 8). Therefore, open trade routes are essential for societies to access secure supplies of resources.

Today, the importation of goods and services continues to be an important part of the adaptation of societies to resource scarcities. Many essential (and at times non-essential or luxury) goods and services are traded because they are not available locally. When a country is less able to import or to compensate for its lack of a resource, its human development potential can be severely curtailed. These links between a country's ability to import resources and its human development potential will be explored next.

Agriculture and forests: important import products

The capacity to import agricultural and forest products helps countries to develop socioeconomically and to maintain the engines of their economies. For our 34 countries, the capacity to import agricultural crops explains 73 per cent of the variance in the HDI ranking of a country during 2004–2005 (Table 11.2); the more agricultural crops imported, the higher the HDI rank. These data also suggest that most of the growing-economy countries have little capacity to import food.

Food importation can be expensive, and many growing-economy countries do not have the financial resources to buy food in global markets. The advanced-economy and emerging-economy countries annually spend a significant amount of money to import food – from US$20,268 to US$176,117 per capita on agricultural imports. These costs compare to the US$1078–8164 per capita spent on average by growing-economy countries to import food. Because growing-economy countries have high malnutrition rates and high poverty levels (see Chapter 3), they are unable to feed their people from local resources grown on their agricultural lands. Under such conditions, growing-economy countries need

Table 11.2 *HDI plotted against forest and agriculture imports*

Y variable	X variable	R^2
HDI ranking	Forest imports in US$/capita	0.50
	Agricultural imports in US$/capita	0.73

to make choices to import highly nutritious foods or their high malnutrition rates will not change.

Compared to the other countries included in our study, Iceland and the Netherlands are outlier countries because they spend a significantly higher amount annually per capita to import food. Iceland spent US$100,000 per capita on food imports and the Netherlands spent US$176,117 per capita. Not only does Iceland import a large amount of food, it also holds the record for consuming more energy per capita than most other countries. For Iceland, consuming high amounts of energy and buying large quantities of food on the global markets make sense because of the unavoidable constraints imposed by their geography. It does not have the soils and climates that will yield abundant food crops or grow vast forests to provide them with energy.

Geography, however, cannot be invoked as the direct causal factor explaining the higher rates of food importation by the Netherlands. However, geography may indirectly explain why it has decided to import so much food. Because of its central and strategic geographic location in Europe, the Dutch have been world-class traders and travellers throughout their history. Therefore, importing food, which is then exported all over the world, is part of their economic development strategy.

Several other countries also stand out because of the larger amount they have spent per capita on importing food when compared to countries within the same HDI-ranking group. The UAE (US$117,568 per capita), Malaysia (US$23,468 per capita) and Namibia (US$13,937 per capita). Interestingly, the UAE and Iceland have pursued similar strategies in relation to energy and food (see Chapter 3). The UAE spends more money per capita on food imports compared to many other countries, but they also consumed more energy per capita. Because three-quarters of the population of the UAE are foreign guest workers brought in to help build the infrastructures for its tourism and banking centres, one could assume that much of the imported food is destined not to feed its own citizens, but to feed these workers and tourists. In addition, the UAE is also a major food exporter and appears to be pursuing a similar strategy to the Netherlands, i.e. a global trade economy.

Our data verify the significant trade (export and import) routes in agricultural products that exist globally. The average net food imports per capita are significantly lower than the total food imports per capita, suggesting that countries are exporting portions of what they import. Although some countries like the Netherlands export much of what they originally imported, these export products have been converted to another form and repackaged (Table 11.3).

Of the three countries that spend more than US$100,000 per capita on importing food, only Iceland ends up being a net importer of agricultural crops. The Netherlands and the UAE export more food crops than they import. However, these data also show that most countries are net importers of food; only seven out of the 34 countries are net food exporters, and two (China and Nigeria) balanced their imports with their exports.

The import of forest products is also important in explaining a significant portion of the variance in the HDI ranking of a country. Even though forest and

Table 11.3 *Countries grouped by whether they have net food imports or exports*

	Countries
Net food imports US$/capita	Angola, Argentina, Australia, Bangladesh, Brazil, Canada, Congo DR, Iceland, Finland, France, Germany, Haiti, India, Indonesia, Malaysia, Mexico, Namibia, Nepal, Peru, Philippines, Russia, Sudan, UK, Venezuela, Yemen
Net food exports US$/capita	Japan, Netherlands, Norway, Sweden, Tanzania, UAE, US
Net food imports and exports balance one another	China, Nigeria

food imports explain a similar proportion of the HDI ranking of a country, they have very different constraints (see Chapters 5 and 8). The amount of forest materials imported per capita explains 50 per cent of the variance in the HDI ranking of a country ($R^2 = 0.50$); the higher HDI-ranked countries imported a considerable amount of forest products per capita. These countries spent on an annual average from US$91 to US$304 per capita to import forest products. This amount compares to the average US$1 per capita spent on forest imports by the medium to low HDI-ranked countries.

A few countries not ranked as advanced-economy are unusual in that they import a higher level of forest products than the average within their HDI group. The UAE expended US$151 per capita for forest imports; Yemen US$70 per capita; Malaysia US$57 per capita; and Mexico US$32 per capita. The fact that the UAE appears again as an outlier is interesting. The UAE has fewer resource options in-country and is more dependent on maintaining its global economic status by importing its resources.

Because there is no relationship between the HDI ranking of a country and the percentage of the GDP spent on importing goods and services, just importing goods and services is not a sensitive indicator of where a country will rank in the HDI-ranking system (Table 11.4). Even though the advanced-economy countries

Table 11.4 *Country HDI ranking groups and the percentage of GDP represented by import of goods and services*

Country HDI ranking group	Imports of goods and services (per cent of GDP); Mean [range]
Group 1	33 [13–30]
Group 2	43 [12–100]
Group 3	30 [3–71]
Group 4	37 [23–51]
Group 5	32 [23–42]
Group 6	37 [27–49]

Note: HDI = Human Development Index [Group 1 = HDI > 0.9; Group 2 = 0.8–0.9; Group 3 = 0.7–0.8; Group 4 = 0.6–0.7; Group 5 = 0.5–0.6; Group 6 = 0.4–0.5]

Table 11.5 *Energy use correlated to forest and agricultural imports*

Y variable	X variable	R^2
Energy use (kg of oil equivalent per capita)	Forest imports in US$/capita	0.57
	Agricultural imports in US$/capita	0.52

are importing a larger amount of goods and services compared to the other HDI-ranked countries, all countries are spending a similar portion of their GDP to import goods and services.

This lack of explanatory power for the import of goods and services as a percentage of the GDP suggests that agricultural and forestry imports are particularly sensitive and better indicators of the HDI ranking of a country; 50 per cent and 73 per cent of the HDI ranking of a country is explained by forest imports and agricultural imports in US$ per capita, respectively. This highlights the importance of the type of goods and services being imported in explaining a country's HDI ranking. This is further supported by the fact that agriculture (including forestry), as a percentage of the GDP, explains 74 per cent of the variance in the HDI-ranking value of a country.

Another interesting relationship highlighted by these data is that the amount of forest and agricultural imports is highly correlated to the amount of energy consumed per capita (kg of oil equivalent per capita) (Table 11.5). Over half of the energy use per capita is explained by how much is spent on forest and agricultural imports per capita. This suggests that transporting forest and agricultural materials globally is an energy-intensive endeavour. This link between energy consumption and the amount of agricultural/forests imports per capita is especially apparent for two countries in our database – Iceland and the UAE. Both countries are outliers from the other countries because of their high consumption levels of both resources.

A diverse fossil fuel importation imperative for development

The need to import all three of the fossil fuels used to produce energy is a common characteristic of the advanced-economy countries (Table 11.6); fossil fuels also provided most (75–100 per cent) of the energy consumed in these countries. For example, Japan has over 80 per cent of its primary energy derived from oil, coal and natural gas and has to import almost all of these supplies. Five of the advanced-economy countries in our group (e.g. Australia, Canada, Germany, the UK and the US) have fossil fuels providing three-quarters of their primary energy, but only oil was imported; each of these five countries has its own local supplies of coal or natural gas. Australia, Germany and the US have their own coal deposits while Canada and the UK have sizeable natural gas fields as well as coal reserves.

The Scandinavian countries have a diversified energy portfolio that consists of fossil fuels and renewable energy resources, and one energy material does not dominate their energy production (Table 11.6). Fossil fuels provide a smaller

Table 11.6 *Energy characteristics of our 34 countries and how much needed to be imported, by HDI groups*

HDI group	Electricity % imported	Crude Oil % imported	% total primary energy	Coal % imported	% total primary energy	Natural gas % imported	% total primary energy
Group 1							
Iceland	0.0	0	25	100	3	0	0
Norway	8.0	3	44	91	2	0	16
Australia	0	87	31	1	63	5	19
Canada	4.0	44	36	42	10	10	30
Sweden	11.7	104	29	95	5	100	2
Japan	0.0	100	47	101	21	96	13
Netherlands	22.8	3	40	100	10	53	43
France	1.7	98	33	98	5	102	15
Finland	15.1	98	31	68	14	100	10
US	1.0	66	41	4	24	20	22
UK	2.5	77	36	77	18	23	35
Germany	7.8	97	36	32	24	91	23
Group 2							
Argentina	6.3	1	37	100	1	4	50
UAE	0	0	28	0	0	0	72
Mexico	0.2	0	59	43	5	17	25
Malaysia	0.0	30	43	96	10	0	42
Russia	0.5	1	21	12	16	2	54
Brazil	9.0	20	42	82	7	45	8
Group 3							
Venezuela	0.0	0	50	0	0	0	38
China	0.2	42	19	1	63	0	2
Peru	0.0	51	54	88	7	0	11
Philippines	0.0	101	35	80	13	0	6
Indonesia	0.0	41	37	0	14	0	17
Group 4							
Namibia	55.4	0	67	100	0	0	0
India	0.4	73	24	12	39	17	5
Group 5							
Bangladesh	0.0	100	19	100	1	0	29
Nepal	7.5	0	9	98	3	0	0
Haiti	0.0	0	23	0	0	0	0
Sudan	0.0	0	20	0	0	0	0
Yemen	0.0	0	99	0	0	0	0
Group 6							
Nigeria	0.0	0	14	0	0	0	7
Tanzania	4.2	0	6	0	0	0	2
Angola	0.0	0	29	0	0	0	6
Congo DR	0.1	0	3	71	1	0	0

Note: All data are from 2005; b) HDI = Human Development Index [Group 1 = HDI > 0.9; Group 2 = 0.8–0.9; Group 3 = 0.7–0.8; Group 4 = 0.6–0.7; Group 5 = 0.5–0.6; Group 6 = 0.4–0.5]
Source: IEA, 2007; HDI, 2007/2008; OECD/IEA, 2009; UN, 2007

fraction of the total primary energy consumed in these countries (range of 28 to 62 per cent); with the highest amount of fossil fuel consumption in Norway (62 per cent), followed by Finland (55 per cent), Sweden (36 per cent) and Iceland (28 per cent) (Table 11.6). The Scandinavian countries stand out from the other advanced-economy countries in that they are using a higher portion of 'solar income' (i.e. renewable resources such as geothermal, water power and energy from forests) in their energy mix. Norway and Iceland import few if any fossil fuels, but Sweden and Finland import all the fossil fuels that they consume. Finland derives almost half of its energy from coal and natural gas while Sweden derives about 7 per cent of its energy from these fossil fuels.

The patterns of fossil fuel consumption found within the advanced-economy countries are less apparent for countries ranked lower by HDI. For example, many of the emerging-economy countries (e.g. Brazil, China, India, Malaysia, Mexico, Peru and Russia) preferentially consume one or more of the fossil fuels, but none of the three fossil fuels is imported at any significant level. Even though oil appears to be the preferred fossil fuel consumed by these countries, several countries consume higher amounts of coal and natural gas than oil. For example, coal is the dominant fossil fuel consumed in China and India; coal accounts for 63 per cent of China's primary energy and 39 per cent in India. Similarly, natural gas accounts for 50 per cent of the primary energy consumed in Argentina, 42 per cent in Malaysia, 54 per cent in Russia and 54 per cent in Brazil.

The countries ranked the lowest by HDI consume almost no fossil fuels and, therefore, are not importing these resources (Table 11.6). These countries use their 'solar income' (i.e. woodfuel) and not fossil fuels to build and develop their economies. However, this focus on energy production from 'solar income' using local resources is not a sustainable choice for these countries. FAO has already predicted that woodfuel supplies are inadequate to provide for their future energy demands. It is ironical that several of these countries are also major producers of oil but are not using it to develop their own human capital.

For the two lowest HDI-ranked countries in our list (Angola and Nigeria), the small amount of fossil fuels consumed in-country is not a decision made by residents of these countries. Both Nigeria and Angola face energy shortages that have been driven by political factors or warfare; in Nigeria less than 20 per cent of the primary energy consumed is from fossil fuels and in Congo DR the amount consumed is less than 5 per cent. Most of the oil supplies in Nigeria and Angola are used to generate export dollars for the country and not to provide energy for domestic consumption.

When looking at the need to import a fossil fuel compared to the percentage that each fossil fuel contributes to the total primary energy, oil appears to be unique in that most of it, or a significant proportion, needs to be imported. This need to import oil occurs even when oil accounts for less than half (from 31–41 per cent in Finland, France, Germany, Japan and Sweden) of the total primary energy consumed. In China, crude oil accounts for the next to the largest percentage of the total primary energy consumed and 42 per cent of that has to be imported. Oil is the second most important fossil fuel to be consumed in India after coal. Three-quarters of Indian oil supplies have to be imported. It should be noted that the dependency of Brazil, with its recent oil discoveries in 2009, have substantially changed.

When countries consume natural gas and/or coal, they appear to be more self-sufficient in these two fossil fuels and need to import little of what they consume. India is similar to China, in that 39 per cent of the total primary energy consumed in India comes from coal, and little of this (12 per cent) has to be imported. It is also noteworthy that coal provided 63 per cent of the total primary energy consumed in China in 2005 and China does not need to import coal. When a country such as Japan needs to import most of the coal it consumes, coal tends to be a small fraction (< 10 per cent) of the total primary energy consumed. This contrasts with the oil situation.

Unlike oil, the need to import electricity did not appear to be related to a country's HDI rank. In 2005 Namibia had to import the highest level of electricity (55.4 per cent) compared to the other countries (Table 11.6). Three of the advanced-economy countries included in our country list also imported electricity; the Netherlands imported 22.8 per cent, Finland 15.1 per cent and Sweden 11.0 per cent. These are the same three countries already identified as outliers because of the high amount of food per capita that they also import.

The dependency of a country on importing part of its energy is complicated by the fact that countries export, as well as import, energy even when they are ranked as one of the largest producers of energy (IEA, 2007). For example, the US produces the largest percentage of the world's electricity (23.4 per cent or 4268TWh) and exports 20TWh, but at the same time it imports 45TWh. Similarly, Germany produces 3.4 per cent of the world's total electricity (613TWh), but it exports 61TWh and imports 57TWh. A similar story exists for Canada.

Importing fossil fuels has not been considered a positive decision for a country to make. A common view espoused in the global media is that resource securities can only be achieved from local production of a resource. For example, Ediger et al (2007) developed a fossil fuel sustainability index that is based on how dependent a country is on foreign sources of energy, how much domestic sources have been depleted and the environmental degradation resulting from its consumption (e.g. based on the amount of C emissions). This fossil fuel sustainability index suggests that 'countries supporting oil as the one and only major player for consumption without adequate local reserves are condemned to suffer due to incompetent energy policies' (Ediger et al, 2007). The need for diversifying the energy choices is an important one, but how much of it should be locally produced is less clear.

In summary, these data also demonstrate that advanced-economy countries have a diverse fossil fuel portfolio composed of all three fossil fuels (Table 11.6), and several also consume renewable energy supplies (Chapter 5). In most cases, none of the three fossil fuels dominates as the preferred fossil fuel to consume. When the three fossil fuels are consumed by those living in the highest HDI-country group, many of the supplies have to be imported. Several of the emerging-economy countries are following a similar pattern to this group of countries. In contrast, most of the lower HDI-ranked countries are dependent on one or, at most, two fossil fuels. They also import little of their fossil fuels and only consume them when they were domestically available.

Valuing Labour as a Resource

The link between the degree of human development and the distribution of labour in bio-resource versus service industries suggests that society values certain types of labour over others (Table 11.7). The type and the number of employment sectors a country has becomes an important metric defining how that country will be ranked in the HDI. We tend not to value rural jobs or bio-resource-based jobs. For example, 85 per cent of the variance in the HDI ranking is explained by whether people work in agriculture/forestry – the higher the HDI ranking, the fewer people who work in agriculture or forestry. The relationship between the percentage of the labour force working in the service sector also explains a large portion of the variance in the HDI ranking ($R^2 = 0.83$); the higher the HDI ranking, the greater the population working in the service industries.

As we become more industrialized, we tend to place less value on the agricultural and forestry sectors of society and place a higher value on industrial jobs. This can be seen in the strong relationships between the HDI ranking of a country and where people are employed (Figure 11.4). Thus, even though we value food and the need to feed people, few people are engaged in food production in the advanced-economy countries. For the 34 selected countries, the highest HDI-ranked countries have less than 4 per cent of their labour force in agriculture/forestry and 72 per cent work in the service industries. In contrast, the growing-economy countries have 68–73 per cent of the labour force engaged in agriculture or forestry work and 20 per cent of the people work in the service industries. Therefore, the major difference in the HDI rankings of a country is found in how many people work in the agriculture/forestry and in the service industries.

Table 11.7 *HDI rankings correlated to development and labour variables*

Y variable	X variable	R^2
HDI ranking	% labour force in agriculture, forests	0.85
	% labour force in industry	0.54
	% labour force in services	0.83
	% of GDP in agriculture	0.74
	% of GDP in industry	0.02
	% of GDP in services	0.67
	Export of goods/services as % GDP	0.00
	Import of goods/services as % GDP	0.00
	Technology export as % of GDP	0.24

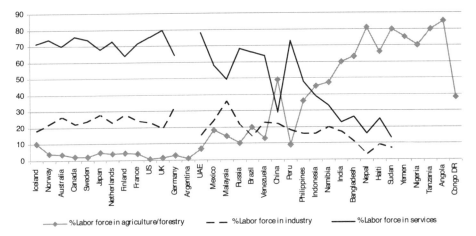

Figure 11.4 *Country labour statistics for 2008*

Source: Nation Master, 2009; World Bank, 2008

The proportion of the labour force in the industrial sector is less important in determining where a country is ranked by HDI. This could be an artefact of the smaller workforce involved in industrial jobs; the proportion of the population engaged in industrial jobs ranges from 24 per cent to 19 per cent in the advanced-economy and the emerging-economy countries, while the growing-economy countries have 8–10 per cent of their labour force working in industries. Even though the proportion of people working in the industry sector is lower than that found in the agricultural and services sectors, industry does comprise a large portion of the GDP in all of the countries. The proportion of the labour force working in industry ranges from 8 to 24 per cent for the 34 countries, while the industry value added as a percentage of GDP ranges from 24 to 42 per cent. This suggests that as more people are employed in agriculture/forestry and in the service sectors, fewer people will be employed in industry itself. If a country has a goal of increasing the employment of its people, these data would suggest that more jobs will need to be created in the agriculture/forestry and services industries than in the industrial sector.

The lack of value for employment in the agricultural/forestry sectors is probably explained by the quality of life experienced by those living in rural areas. When a large portion of the population is engaged in agricultural activities, these individuals have shorter life-spans, are more undernourished and have a lower GNI (see Chapter 10). These are not commendable goals for any growing country. Also, the youth in the growing- and emerging-economy countries do not want to pursue the professions of their grandparents (i.e. farmers) because they have seen how hard it is to work in these sectors. They aspire to become lawyers, doctors and professors.

References

Ediger V. fi., Hoşgőr, E., Sűrmeli, A. N. and Tathdil, H. (2007) 'Fossil fuel sustainability index: an application of resource management', *Energy Policy*, vol 35, pp2969–2977

FAO (2006) 'Global Forest Resources Assessment 2005', UN FAO, Rome, Italy

FAO (2008) 'World Resources Report, www.fao.org/docrep/011/ai476e/ai476e01.htm, accessed 22 July 2009

Friedman, T. L. (2009) 'Invent, Invent, Invent', *The New York Times*, 28 June 2009, p8

Gordon, J. C. and Berry, J. K. (2006) *Environmental Leadership Equals Essential Leadership. Redefining Who Leads and How*, Yale University Press, New Haven, CT

HDI (2007/2008) 'Human Development Index', http://hDrundp.org/en/statistics, accessed 1 October 2008

IEA (2007) *2007 Key World Energy Statistics*, International Energy Agency, http://tonto.eia.doe.gov/country/country_energy_data.cfm?fips=AO, accessed 1 September 2008

Mongabay (2008) 'Country data', http://rainforests.mongabay.com/deforestation/2000/Australia.htm, accessed 30 March 2009

Nation Master (2009) 'Country labor statistics', www.nationmaster.com/statistics/stats&all=1, accessed 21 February 2009

Nordhaus, T. and Shellenberger, M. (2007) *Break Through. From the Death of Environmentalism to the Politics of Possibility*, Houghton Mifflin Company, Boston, MA and New York, NY

OECD/IEA (2009) *Climate Change Information by Country*, www.oecd.org/infobycountry/0,3380,en_2649_34361_1_1_1_1_1,00.html, accessed 21 February 2009

Palmer, M. A. and Filoso, S. (2009) 'Restoration of ecosystem services for environmental markets', *Science*, vol 325, pp575–576

Steckel, R. H. and Rose, J. C. (2002) *The Backbone of History. Health and Nutrition in the Western Hemisphere*, Cambridge University Press, Cambridge

UN (2007) *The 2004 Energy Statistics Yearbook*, United Nations Department of Economic and Social Affairs, Statistics Division, New York, NY

WHO (2007) 'Country profiles of Environmental Burden of Disease and Country Profiles', World Health Organization, Public Health and the Environment, Geneva 2007, www.who.int/countries/ago/en, accessed 10 December 2008

World Bank (2008) 'World Development Indicators database', April 2008, Washington, DC

12

Sustainable Ecosystems: Investments in Human and Natural Capital

At one particular level, sustainability cannot be perfectly decoded or quantified, just as love, hope and charity cannot. Sustainability in its largest sense will remain a goal in which many believe and to which many aspire, but there will be as many definitions as there are aspirants. This does not mean that it is a bad goal, but rather that it must include a large array of human and natural conditions and that these will vary in time, place and the eye of the beholder. However, it is important for several reasons to try to establish some grounds for agreement on what is desirable and possible to do in its pursuit. First, as globalization of human activities and biota proceed, rules are being made that can contribute to, or inhibit, global sustainability. Next, decisions are being made about which nations, regions and locales need the most attention in the pursuit of sustainability. Stalled economic development is seen by some to preclude the 'bottom billion' people in the world from looking forward to a sustainable future (Collier, 2008). Others see a need for the greatest carbon emitters to come under strict limits for carbon emissions if the worst consequences of human-caused climate change are to be avoided. Many believe that, although forest destruction and degradation in the tropics and subtropics are contained in a relatively few nation states, they pose a severe threat that is global in scope. Our purpose in this final chapter is to suggest a simple classification system and land- and water-based approach to determining (1) those countries with the most to teach others – albeit in different social and environmental settings – with regard to sustainability, and (2) how to begin to quantify sustainable behaviour.

How do we move away from making snapshot decisions? A snapshot approach to decoding sustainability is unwise because you may conclude that a decision is sustainable when, in fact, you have not adequately characterized the context for the decision. Do you have enough information to draw a conclusion? A good way to visualize the problem of using snapshots of sustainability as models for making far-reaching decisions, is by considering the reliability of descriptions of an elephant made by blindfolded people, each of whom is touching a different part of the animal. Another example of the difficulty of using snapshots (or tunnel

Figure 12.1 *Analogy of determining how many beds are in a house from looking through one window of the house*

vision) of sustainability to make decisions is exemplified by the notion of a person peering through one open window to look into a house (Figure 12.1). This view only reveals one room and may suggest that there are no beds in the house despite every other room having a bed in it. You cannot describe the entire house by the view that you have of that one room.

The difficulty of understanding the context of a real-world decision is characterized by a situation experienced by two of the authors in the Brazilian Amazon. Two villages on opposite sides of a major Amazon tributary seemed, at a quick glance – in other words, in a snapshot – to have similar forests, and both negotiated to sell their timber to an international buyer. However, one of the village's forests was growing on a coarser-textured, sandy soil deposited by the meandering river, whereas the other forest was on a finer-textured soil containing higher amounts of clay, thereby increasing the soil's nutrient exchange capacity. A 'snapshot' decision to sell timber owned by the village located on the higher nutrient-quality soil would probably have no future surprises as their forests quickly regenerate. They can begin to re-appropriate the ecosystem services derived from their growing forests after very little delay. However, the 'snapshot' timber sale by the village located on the more nutrient-poor soil could produce an unexpectedly long wait to harvest any future ecosystem services or economic returns while waiting for the slower-growing forest to mature.

These examples demonstrate the need to make sure that one is *not* making an ill-informed snapshot decision. The current emphasis of the international community is to strive to build capacity in communities and to understand when a decision makes a society more vulnerable to disturbances, such as climate change (IPCC, 2007). This approach is ideal, for it exemplifies how countries have been able to develop their human capital while facing scarcities of bio-resources. These countries, which have been highly adaptable, provide us many lessons which can be used in making sustainable decisions.

Positioning countries in a cell matrix is one possible approach to help decrease the risk of making snapshot decisions. It identifies the choices being made by each country when facing similar problems or unavoidable constraints. Outliers, found at both extremes of the scale for each resource, are useful in identifying countries that will be able to make sustainable choices relatively easily. The other outliers are countries where it will be extremely difficult to make the trade-offs required to consume resources. This is discussed in more detail in the following section.

Cell Matrix of Resource Endowments and Human Adaptability

By understanding a country's natural resource supply capacity and how adaptable or resilient its societies are, one can begin to determine how far that country is from making sustainable decisions (see the box that follows for some examples). We propose that resource supplies could be separated into (1) resource endowments (renewable and fossil resources), and (2) social resilience, or how societies adapt to their dynamic natural and social environments (see Chapter 11). The ideal scenario would be for a country to be positioned in the 'More adaptable' and 'High resource endowment' box (see Chapters 9 and 11).

		Adaptability	
		More adaptable	Less adaptable
Resource	High	XX	
endowment	Low		XX

We propose that a cell matrix be initially produced for each of the four resources discussed in Chapters 4–6. In our example, we assume that HDI is a valid estimate of social, political and intellectual resilience. Actual non-index parameters, such as university graduates per capita, female literacy, patents per capita and others, could also be used to estimate resilience.

Even countries that are currently ranked as having a high resource endowment and high adaptability or social resilience, could still benefit and gain insights from this process of producing cell matrices. For example, there is no guarantee that these countries will continue to be ranked as high or as fortunate in the future. They need to make choices that do not reduce their ability to consume or to produce resources under a climate-change scenario. If they have a higher risk to climatic events or their choices reduce supplies in the countries providing their bio-resources (see Chapters 4–6), they are at risk of lowering their development potentials.

On the vertical column of this resource capacity/human capacity matrix we provide any one of or an aggregate estimate of, the 'raw materials' of sustainability (water, energy, food and forests) per capita for the specific nation in question. On the horizontal row we provide an estimate of the nation's ability to meet change. This row is best seen as human capacity for ingenuity and resilience, and is estimated by educational level, research capability, human health and institutional strength (discussed in Chapter 11). At the aggregated level, nations to be compared are separated into low, medium and high groups for each row and column. The implication of the matrix is that achieving sustainability should be relatively easy for those countries in the upper left quadrant, more difficult for those in the lower left as well as in the upper right quadrant, and very difficult for those in the lower right quadrant relative to the others.

To illustrate our approach further, we constructed matrices that plotted nations as to their resource endowment and social resilience using the following parameters:

*   Food production endowment – amount of agricultural land per capita;
*   Fossil energy endowment – oil resources;
*   Forest/woodland endowment – forest area per capita;
*   Water endowment – the percentage of a country's water demand resupplied by endogenous precipitation.

The utility of this approach is demonstrated for each of the four resources that we introduced earlier in the book. This is followed by a cell matrix for climate and soil constraints to show how both constraints relate to the ability of a country to adapt to change. This type of exercise can be conducted at the country level as we describe next, or it can be used to evaluate the resource and social heterogeneity of a regional landscape. This approach clarifies the choices that need to be included and how difficult it will be to make sustainable choices.

Agricultural land endowment and social resilience

Based on the agricultural endowment/social resilience matrix below, it appears to be the exception for a country to have a high amount of agricultural land available per person to grow food. Only three out of our 34 countries rank high in respect of their agricultural land endowment. However, the social resilience of these three (Angola, Australia and Namibia) varies from low to high. Our data suggest that the norm is for most countries to have a low amount of agricultural land per capita, but that this low natural endowment does not impact on whether a country has a low or high social resilience. Therefore, food security can be achieved from a smaller land-base but climate and soil constraints (discussed in Chapters 7 and 8) should be factored into the analysis. Humans have been very good in acquiring higher plant productivities from a smaller land-base.

This matrix suggests that eight of the 34 countries (Bangladesh, Congo DR, Haiti, Nepal, Nigeria, Sudan, Tanzania and Yemen) will have a difficult time in providing food security for their people using their own lands, because they have

		Social resilience		
		High	Medium	Low
NATURAL ENDOWMENT (agricultural land in ha/capita)	High (> 2 ha/cap)	Australia	Namibia	Angola
	Medium (1–2 ha/cap)	Canada, US	Brazil, Mexico, Russia	- -
	Low (< 1 ha/cap)	Finland, France, Germany, Iceland, Japan, Netherlands, Norway, Sweden, UK	Argentina, China, India, Indonesia, Malaysia, Peru, Philippines, Venezuela, UAE	Bangladesh, Congo DR, Haiti, Nepal, Nigeria, Sudan, Tanzania, Yemen

not developed their social resilience. These countries are ranked low in their land endowment as well as in social resilience. They will therefore find it difficult to make choices to increase food supplies and to decrease hunger. Although some of these countries produce oil, they have not successfully used their oil supplies to increase social resilience. Based on our assessment, the priority for these countries should be to focus on increasing their social resilience and not to increase the amount of agricultural land in crop production.

It appears that the amount of land endowment in agriculture is not related to a country's HDI ranking. Only one country (Australia) is ranked as having a high agricultural land endowment and high social resilience simultaneously. It is interesting that the Scandinavian countries are ranked high in most categories of human development, but have a low natural endowment in agricultural land. The land endowment is decoupled from a country's ability to develop its human capacity, since most of the advanced-economy countries import a significant amount of their food and are not solely dependent upon their agricultural land-base for their food security (Chapter 11). Furthermore, the Netherlands is a major agricultural exporter despite having a low agricultural endowment.

The metric to evaluate food security only uses the land area to measure food production. It does not reflect the soil and climatic constraints each country faces, nor does it address how much food is grown in each country. The reason for this is that farming is a well-developed science and is a summary of the accumulated successes and failures experienced by farmers over the several thousand-year history of agriculture (Chapter 8). Not everyone has profited from this knowledge – Africa did not benefit from the Green Revolution that transformed agricultural production in China and India – but this situation is changing rapidly. Many governments of growing-economy countries recognize the need to acquire this farming knowledge, and have been inviting scientists specializing in soils and crop growth to help increase the productivity of their lands for food production. In other cases, countries such as Ethiopia are allowing foreign farmers to acquire land for food production, in order to obtain the Green Revolution technology to increase their land's productive capacity (see later discussion).

Oil endowment and social resilience

A similar cell matrix can be produced for a country's oil endowment. We are using 'oil endowment' rather than 'fossil fuel endowment' because:

1   oil products are used universally for transportation;
2   crude oil is moved from an exporting country to an importing country with relative ease;
3   there are environmental problems associated with coal production and its use at present.

Resources (estimate of accumulations likely to be commercially available in the future) rather than reserves are used in the matrix, since technology and demand are expected to result in resources becoming reserves. This matrix is similar to that for agricultural endowment, as it suggests that energy from oil does not determine how well a country is able to develop its human capital. For example, many of the high and medium social-resilience countries have low to medium oil endowments. Most countries have been able to make the choices to acquire the oil supplies they need to power their economic growth. For example, oil and gas made the 'modernization' of Malaysia possible.

		Social resilience		
		High	*Medium*	*Low*
OIL ENDOWMENT	High	Brazil, Canada, Norway, Russia	UAE, Venezuela	Angola, Congo DR, Nigeria, Yemen
(oil resources compared to	Medium	UK, US	Malaysia, Mexico	
present demand in country)	Low	Australia, Finland, France, Germany, Iceland, Japan, Netherlands, Sweden	Argentina, China, India, Indonesia, Namibia, Peru	

This oil endowment/social resilience matrix also highlights how countries have adapted to develop their social resilience in the face of low oil security. It should be noted that most of the advanced-economy and emerging-economy countries have a very diverse fossil-energy portfolio (see Chapter 4). China and India consume their own coal supplies to power their economic growth. This matrix also shows that despite some countries having a high oil endowment, this does not necessarily equate to high social resilience. It also emphasizes that countries have many difficult choices to make in relation to the acquisition of oil supplies. For example, even when oil endowments are low, the demand is high. Most of the higher ranked-HDI countries are carbon based economies and have not determined how to replace the various oil products they consumed on a daily basis (see Chapters 2 and 10).

Forest and woodland endowment and social resilience

In contrast to the agricultural and oil endowment patterns, the forest and woodland endowment appears to be more closely linked to how well a country is able to develop its social capital. This forest endowment/social resilience matrix reveals how countries ranked as having high social resilience (e.g. Australia, Canada, Finland and Sweden) also have high forest endowments. Australia is shown as being favoured in this matrix because it has a significant area of woodland (tree canopy cover of 5–10 per cent, FAO, 2006), rather than forest. It is also noteworthy that none of the low resilience-ranked countries have a high forest and woodland endowments. This is unfortunate, because these same countries will be less able to use their forests to enhance their social resilience because they are too dependent upon them today, especially for energy (see Chapter 5). These comparisons support our contention that bio-resource endowments are crucial for countries to be able to make sustainable choices (Chapter 5). Not all of the high social resilience countries are using their forests to build their sustainability capital, since several of the countries that are dependent on fossil energy are also countries that are protecting their forests and have a higher forest and woodland endowment per capita.

| | | Social resilience | | |
		High	Medium	Low
FOREST & WOODLAND ENDOWMENT (ha/capita)	High (> 4 ha/cap)	Australia, Canada, Finland	Namibia, Russia	- -
	Medium (2–4 ha/cap)	Norway, Sweden	Argentina, Brazil, Peru, Venezuela	Angola, Congo DR
	Low (< 2 ha/cap)	France, Germany, Iceland, Japan, Netherlands, UK, US	China, India, Indonesia, Malaysia, Mexico, Philippines, UAE	Bangladesh, Haiti, Nepal, Nigeria, Sudan, Tanzania, Yemen

This matrix comparison does not indicate how much of the forest and woodland is used for energy or other products and how much has protected status. There can be a downside to just protecting forests, because disturbances will continue to impact them. Some are more susceptible to disturbances because of past land-use activities and because of climate change. For example, several countries have not been effectively managing their forests to decrease their annual losses to fire and pest/disease outbreaks. The US protects about 16 per cent of its total forest area but about 8 per cent is impacted by fire and insect/disease problems. Similarly, Nepal, with a low forest endowment, has about 10 per cent of its forests impacted by disturbances, and India has 20 per cent of its forests impacted by fires, disease and insects. Those countries with low forest endowments cannot afford to lose more of their forest area to disturbances.

		Social resilience		
		High	Medium	Low
WATER ENDOWMENT (% annual river discharge & aquifer recharge generated from endogenous precipitation)	High (> 66%)	Iceland, Japan, Norway	Peru, Philippines	- -
	Medium (33–66%)	Canada, Finland, France, Germany, Netherlands, Sweden, UK, US	Brazil, China, India, Indonesia, Malaysia, Russia, Venezuela	- -
	Low (< 33%)	Australia	Peru, Argentina, Mexico, Namibia, UAE	Angola, Bangladesh, Haiti, Nigeria, Sudan, Tanzania, Yemen, Nepal

In contrast to the advanced-economy countries, most of the growing-economy countries are highly dependent upon their forests for energy and for the procurement of other products. These are also the countries (e.g. Bangladesh, Haiti, Nepal, Nigeria, Sudan, Tanzania and Yemen) that will be the least able to use their forests to procure resources and to build their sustainability capital. Nigeria and Yemen could potentially consume fewer forest materials to produce energy because they have oil supplies, but they have not made this trade-off decision.

Water endowment and social resilience

In contrast to the food and fossil energy matrices, the water and forest endowments produce similar trends and appear to be coupled to a country's social resilience. This matrix positions countries ranked with high social resilience as having high to medium levels of their water endowments replenished by endogenous precipitation. In the HDI group 6, only Australia will experience low water security. The other outlier in the advanced-economy country group that may experience water insecurities is the Netherlands. In this case, insecurity is a result of extreme dependence on outside sources of fresh water (88 per cent of total renewable water originates outside the country's borders).

Amazingly, all of our 34 selected countries ranked as having a low social resilience also had a low potential to replenish their river discharge and to recharge of their aquifers from endogenous precipitation. Therefore, it appears that countries ranked as having a low social resilience would find it extremely difficult to secure their water supplies. These countries contrast with the high to medium social resilience countries, where fewer difficult choices will be needed to acquire secure water supplies, since precipitation replenishes about half of their water demand.

A few of the countries with low water endowments also have a significant proportion of their total renewable water resources originating outside of their borders. Thus, not only do Argentina (66 per cent), Bangladesh (91 per cent), Namibia (66 per cent) and Sudan (77 per cent) depend on water supplies that originate outside their borders, but precipitation recharges a minimal amount of their fresh water supplies. These countries will find it especially difficult to provide water security for their people.

Climate and soil constraints to natural and social capital

The resource endowment and social resilience matrices need to include the unavoidable constraints of climates and soils, for they determine how feasible it will be for a group of people to adapt. A good example of this is the dependence of farmers in India on monsoon rains to provide the water they need to irrigate their crops. The farmers are adapted to these rains, but they have no ability to control when the rains arrive or their intensity when it does rain. Yardley (2009) wrote:

> *India's new economy may be based on software, services and high technology, but hundreds of millions of Indians still look to the sky for their livelihoods; more than half the country's 1.1 billion people depend on agriculture for a living even though agriculture represents only about 17 percent of the total economy.*

In general, we know that soil degradation and climate risk decrease social resilience, but our data suggest that no human development group is more or less impacted, or more or less resilient because of its climate risk, or the degree to which its soils are degraded. The absence of a pattern reflects the considerable ability of humans to adapt and to respond to disturbances without decreasing their future ability to make choices. Even though people have adapted quite well to the constraints and disturbances that they face, it is informative to examine how the 34 countries are grouped relative to their climate risk and soil degradation. Both factors will determine how difficult it will be for a country to make choices that contribute towards country-level sustainability.

		Climate risk		
		High	Medium	Low
SOIL DEGRADATION	High	Iceland, UAE,	Malaysia, Nigeria Argentina, Brazil,	Haiti, Peru
	Medium	Yemen	Netherlands, Sudan, Sweden, Tanzania	Bangladesh, China, France, Germany, India, Indonesia, Mexico, Nepal, US
	Low	Angola, Finland, Namibia, Norway	Australia, Canada, Congo DR, Japan, UK	Philippines, Russia, Venezuela

The grouping of only two of our 34 countries, Iceland and the UAE, indicates that they have high levels of soil degradation and also face a high risk of climatic disturbances. These are the countries least able to pursue alternative choices for developing their economies and building their social resilience (see Chapter 11), and are also the same countries that consume more energy per capita and import more food than the others in our list. Additionally, both Iceland and the UAE have fewer resources within their own borders and their landscapes mainly comprise subpolar conditions or hot desert, respectively.

For the UAE, the high climate risk and soil degradation rank will make it more difficult for it to adapt socially to these factors. The country has low bio-resource endowments other than its high fossil-energy stocks; it ranks low in available agricultural land, amount of forest and woodland area, and the amount of its water supplies obtained from precipitation. The UAE is very aware of these constraints as evidenced by its decisions related to energy production coming mainly from natural gas, its need to desalinate large amounts of water and the importation of most of its food. Climate change will only increase the challenge for the UAE to provide secure food and water for its people and to increase its social resilience.

Iceland will also have difficult choices to make in providing secure food, water and energy for its people because of its low natural and fossil endowment. Iceland is fortunate to have a high water endowment and is able to obtain all its renewable water through rainfall. This probably also explains the past interest in attracting industries that could be powered using cheap hydropower. Unlike the other Scandinavian countries, Iceland has little forest area and also has a low agricultural land endowment.

Plotting resources on the cell matrix allows us to categorize countries as to their resource endowments in relationship to their human development rank, and consequently to identify the choices that each country needs to make. Once countries are plotted by their resource endowments and the degree that soils and climates constrain their productive capacity, it is then easier to understand the impact that decisions would have on social resilience, in other words the ability of societies to adapt to their resources and environments. We have developed a 'fulcrum of sustainability' concept to visualize and help determine how all these components are interconnected to, and affected by, one another. By combining the cell matrix approach with the fulcrum of sustainability, it will be easier to tease apart the choices that a country should make by identifying those areas where decisions are most likely to decrease or increase a country's sustainability capital.

The Fulcrum of Sustainability

The classification of countries (or even regions or intra-country areas) by natural endowment and human capital can give us defensible notions about which countries or regions have advantages and disadvantages in the pursuit of a sustainable future. Furthermore, analysis of the reasons for the classification can indicate the most rewarding directions to pursue. Another way of framing the choices countries make is the concept of fulcrum of sustainability (Figure 12.2). This figure shows that the human capital (and adaptation, as discussed in Chapter 11) is the fulcrum that decreases or increases the investments and capital available to a country. Many factors will move the human capital towards the right or the left. Some of the most important factors that move the human capital to the right (increasing sustainability capital) or left (decreasing sustainability capital) are summarized as:

Decreases sustainability capital	Increases sustainability capital
Corruption	Education and health
Resource over-use	Improved socioeconomic conditions
Irreversible resource depletion	Technology
Soil degradation	Solar, geothermal, nuclear and biofuels energy
Lower plant productivity capacity	Retention of forest cover
Climatic disturbances	Organic fertilization of agricultural lands

The fulcrum of sustainability suggests that by not choosing to invest in a country's natural endowment, a country can shift towards a lower sustainability capital. On the reverse side, investments in resources can increase the sustainability capital. We are characterizing human capital as being the fulcrum point that switches the magnitude of the impact of investments and capital. Societal choices and decisions create the balance between investments and capital.

Each country needs to use the cell matrix approach to determine where it is positioned today with respect to the four resource endowments. Once this information is available, a country can position itself on the fulcrum diagram. At this

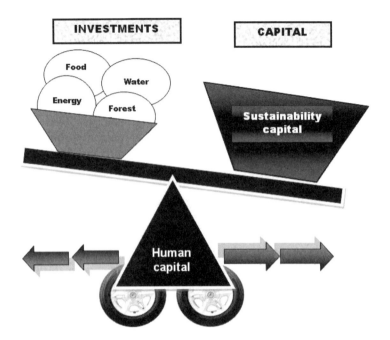

Figure 12.2 *Conceptual fulcrum diagram of sustainability*

point it becomes easier to 'unpack' the choices that are available for each country. A few countries that are ranked as having a high social capital have variable levels of resource endowments. Countries with low resource endowments, but with high human capital, have increased their sustainability capital to higher levels than their resource endowment would have indicated. These countries have been making the right choices for themselves and are maintaining the resilience of their societies. Australia, for example, has a high agricultural, and forest and woodland endowment that it can use to develop its economies, but it should factor-in its low fossil resource endowment and low water endowment. The challenge for Australia will be securing its supplies of fossil energy and water since these resources can shift the fulcrum sufficiently so that their sustainability capital decreases. Similarly, Norway is well endowed with resources, but has a low agricultural land endowment along with a medium forest/woodland endowment. Norway is very aware of its choices related to these two resources; it imports a considerable amount of food, and 30 per cent of its forest products are imported. Norway has been able to maintain its sustainability capital by importing its resources. It is easier for Norway to make a decision that affects its sustainability capital than it would be for Australia, since scarcities of water and fossil resources are more difficult to manage in the latter.

For some countries, to move the fulcrum towards increasing their resource sustainability capital will require that they invest in the development of their social capital. These are the countries currently ranked as having a low social resilience. Many of these now have, or have had, a high resource endowment, but have not been choosing to use their resources to help increase their social capital. When their resource endowment is depleted because of over-exploitation, social resilience will increase when restoring resource endowments and mitigating negative externalities. For example, Bangladesh, Haiti and Sudan are located in the lower right box (low/low) in each of our four resource endowments/social resilience matrices. Similarly, Yemen is located in this low/low position in three of the matrices, but it does rank high in its fossil fuel endowment category. This suggests that it will be especially challenging for these countries to increase their social resiliency, because their natural endowments have become very low. For these countries to pursue sustainable livelihood opportunities, they would need to re-establish their ability to collect 'solar income' and to use it to develop societal resilience. At the same time, they should also factor-in the unavoidable constraints of climates and their local soils, because these will impact their resource productive capacity (see Chapter 7) and, therefore, their ecosystem-supply capacities. These countries in the low/low resource endowments/social resilience categories are especially sensitive to these climate/soil constraints.

We will next examine the utility of the fulcrum of sustainability and the cell matrix approach to clarify the choices that need to be made by countries. We will briefly discuss the choices being made at the country level and by the international communities to mitigate climate change. This will be followed by a brief discussion of how importing resources increases a country's portfolio of choices by mitigating its unfavourable climate and soil constraints.

Climate change mitigation

One of the most prominent issues in the minds of many people today is climate change and how to mitigate and/or reduce societal vulnerability to its impacts. Climate change immediately focuses attention on the carbon cycle, since it is the production and consumption of resources that determine how much GHG is emitted by each country. When mitigating climate change, the most important decisions a country needs to make are centred on its land-use practices and how much and what type of fossil fuels are consumed in energy production. These topics need to be addressed since they are the dominant sources of GHG emissions.

Using the matrix approach to identify which countries are the major contributors to CO_2 emissions per capita and to identify when land conversion is the primary reason for these emissions is revealing. It should be noted here that CO_2 emissions data per capita are being used here, and not total CO_2 emissions. Country emissions rankings vary considerably depending on which data are used. This matrix approach highlights which countries may contribute more towards mitigating CO_2 emissions, and when CO_2 emissions from land conversion may not appreciably mitigate global CO_2 emissions because these contributions are already low.

Simultaneously comparing the data on total CO_2 emissions per capita and the proportion CO_2 emitted during land conversion highlights the challenges facing

| | | Social resilience | | |
		High	Medium	Low
'LOSS OF ENVIRONMENT' Endowment	High	--	UAE	--
		--	Brazil, Indonesia, Peru	Congo DR, Nepal, Tanzania
CO_2 emissions per capita (Mg CO_2/capita) (IEA, 2007)	Medium	Australia, Canada, Finland, Netherlands, US	Russia	--
CO_2 emissions due to land conversion (%)		--	Malaysia, Philippines, Venezuela	Angola, Haiti, Nigeria, Sudan
	Low	France, Germany, Iceland, Japan, Norway, Sweden, UK	Argentina, Brazil, China, India, Indonesia, Malaysia, Mexico, Namibia, Peru, Philippines, Venezuela	Angola, Bangladesh, Congo, Haiti, Nepal, Nigeria, Sudan, Tanzania, Yemen
		Australia, Canada, Finland, France, Germany, Iceland, Japan, Netherlands, Norway, Sweden, UK, US	Argentina, China, India, Mexico, Namibia, Russia, UAE	Yemen

Note: CO_2 emissions per capita: High $=> 20MgCO_2$ emitted per capita; Medium $= 10–20Mg\ CO_2$ emitted per capita; Low $= < 10Mg\ CO_2$ emitted per capita.
% total CO_2 emitted due to land use (e.g. deforestation) in italics and bold face: High $= > 67$ per cent; Medium $= 33–67$ per cent; Low $= < 33$ per cent; no data available for Bangladesh.

climate change mitigation. Who should provide the solutions to a global problem and what other goals should be attached to climate change mitigation efforts? Using the Loss from Environmental Endowment/Social Resilience matrix highlights how much of the media attention is focusing on deriving solutions for climate change from those countries with low to medium social resilience, who have high conservation value in their forests and who are less able to adapt to the proposed choices. For example, though Brazil, Indonesia and Peru are ranked as having high CO_2 emissions due to land conversions (especially from deforestation), these countries are ranked low for the total amount of CO_2 emitted *per capita*. Consequently, the greater benefits to mitigating CO_2 emissions will probably not result from land management decisions made in these countries.

Even if all the forests were protected in these three countries, they would have a negligible impact on global CO_2 emissions.

Countries experiencing significant land conversion from forests are the same countries that will be less capable of making sustainable resources choices. Protecting forests is not a good option in these countries as long as their population continues to be highly dependent on forests for products. These countries with lower social resilience face the loss of part of their sustainability capital if the energy needs of their people cannot be resolved. Congo DR, Nepal and Tanzania are in a similar situation to the three countries discussed above, having high deforestation rates and high CO_2 emissions due to land conversion. Interestingly, they are not receiving as much global media attention because they have fewer species of high conservation value.

The high social resilience-ranked countries have not found it easy to develop consensus on practical solutions to climate change or to alter their consumptive behaviour even though they are the major contributors to global CO_2 emissions. Four countries (China, Japan, Russia and the US) have the greatest potential to mitigate climate change impacts, but pursuing such a policy would have major repercussions on their rate of economic development. The implications of reducing fossil carbon consumption are enormous and will reverberate through a country's economy. As already discussed in Chapter 10, industrialized societies are still trying to work out how to decrease their reliance on carbon, both fossil and non-fossil. Since fossil fuels are responsible for 70 per cent of total global CO_2 emissions, it is logical that managing fossil fuels will need to be part of the solution for decreasing CO_2 emissions. At some point, global societies will have to make the decision to close the loop on the carbon cycle to reduce emissions, managing wastes generated during carbon combustion better, or adopting carbon capture technologies.

Mitigating climate change can be a difficult choice for any country to make, since the global community expects a country to make decisions that mitigate its global impacts, and not to focus solely on other country-level problems. Global expectations can become a narrowly focused approach to the social and environmental problems facing a country, and may not factor-in the four resources that may determine whether a country's choices are sustainable. The global community may therefore subvert country goals or make country-level decisions suboptimal in the local landscape.

Each country is making complex choices that it would normally use to develop its economy, but now it also has to include CO_2 emissions as a critical factor in its decision making, and at the same time consider what the global impacts of its decisions may be. Deciding who pays the costs of the benefits accrued to the global community is controversial and not a choice that has been made easily using consensual approaches. Part of the problem has been the global community focus on biodiversity benefits and not the needs of the local communities living with this biodiversity. Frequently, these assessments do not examine a country as an 'ecosystem' or how choices may decrease a country's social endowment.

This matrix also highlights how several advanced-economy countries have made decisions to lower their total CO_2 emissions. Several high social resilience countries (France, Germany, Iceland, Japan, Norway, Sweden and the UK) emit lower amounts of CO_2 even though they are highly industrialized; this suggests that their resource choices have not resulted in losing part of their environmental endowment. It also suggests which countries need to make decisions that help reduce their CO_2 emissions because their emissions are higher compared to other countries. The UAE was an outlier in our database because of its high level of CO_2 emissions per capita, which indicated a high fossil energy consumption by a smaller population. Even so, the UAE is least able to make constructive choices to reduce its CO_2 emissions per capita even if it wanted to, because of its low *total* resource endowment.

Even though CO_2 can be used to index the loss of some environmental endowment at a country level, it can also highlight how difficult it is to search for global climate change solutions in one's own backyard. Climate change has the potential to increase or decrease a country's natural as well as its social endowment (IPCC, 2007) depending upon which feedback loops come into play. If it decreases a land's productive capacity because of droughts, it will further constrain economic development and the procurement of resources. Therefore, it is imperative to consider the constraints, in order to help determine the best solutions to mitigate global climate-change impacts. There is also the need to ensure that the choices are not made using the narrow 'tunnel vision' approach, in order to ensure a higher probability of producing the expected results.

Climatic disturbances can decrease a country's sustainability capital especially if over-exploiting a resource causes environmental degradation when soils or climates constrain a land's productive capacity. To reverse this trend, a country will need to invest in its natural endowment (e.g. by restoration and mitigation) and consider the adoption of technologies that are environmentally friendly. A country needs to make choices that shift the fulcrum of its society towards a higher sustainability capital. Another approach a country can take to increase its sustainability capital is to import those resources that it is less capable of producing sustainably.

Importing resources

Other features that a matrix can highlight is how global the world has become, and the role of the advanced-economy countries in maintaining their social resilience by being able to import their natural capital to maintain their development efforts. As would be expected, none of the countries ranked as having a medium- to low-social resilience, other than the UAE, import any significant amounts of agricultural or forest materials. Since it is clear that agricultural crops and forest materials are not ideally produced in each landscape, these countries need to be able to make choices that will allow them to begin to import resources to increase their social resilience (see later discussion).

		Social resilience		
		High	Medium	Low
IMPORTING NATURAL CAPITAL Agricultural and forest products imported, (US$/capita)	High (> US$100,000/ capita)	Iceland, Netherlands, Norway	UAE	- -
	Medium (US$50,000– 100,000/ capita)	Canada, Finland, France, Germany, Sweden, UK	- -	- -
	Low (< US$50,000/ capita)	Australia, Japan, US	Argentina, Brazil, China, India, Indonesia, Malaysia, Mexico, Namibia, Peru, Philippines, Russia, Venezuela	Angola, Bangladesh, Congo DR, Haiti, Nepal, Nigeria, Sudan, Tanzania, Yemen

Several of the high social-resilience countries (Iceland, the Netherlands and Norway) have elected to import a significant amount of their natural capital. They have made these choices because one or more of their natural endowments is low and doing this has allowed them to maintain their social resilience. The amount of agricultural and forest products imported is highly correlated to the HDI rank of a country, suggesting that this choice directly feeds back to maintaining social resilience.

		Social resilience		
		High	Medium	Low
IMPORTING FOSSIL CAPITAL % of total primary energy imported as fossil fuels	High (> 67%)	Australia, France, Netherlands, US	Argentina, Brazil, India, Mexico, Namibia, UAE	Angola, Bangladesh, Congo DR, Haiti, Nigeria, Sudan, Tanzania, Yemen
	Medium (3–67%)	Canada, Finland, Germany, UK	China, Indonesia, Russia, Venezuela	- -
	Low (< 33%)	Iceland, Japan, Norway, Sweden	Malaysia, Peru, Philippines	Nepal

Unlike the importation of natural capital, the importation of fossil capital is a less sensitive indicator for how resilient a country's society will be. The fact that this is a 'carbon-molecule dependent world' for energy makes the importation of fossil fuels less of a choice. This contrasts with the importation of natural capital where a country can decide not to import additional supplies, and instead use their financial resource to help develop their social resilience. In contrast, the fossil capital is less able to provide this benefit because it is required, and the fossil capital is an 'imperative' to import until alternative energy choices are developed.

The composition of the fossil capital is also quite diverse for all but the growing-economy countries. Countries that consume little fossil capital today are also those that are mostly dependent upon their forests for energy, and there is therefore a strong need to increase the productive capacity of their natural endowment. Nepal, for example, has low social resilience and a low ability to import fossil capital; it also has a low natural endowment. Nepal is an ideal country to begin restoring its natural endowment, in order to increase its social resilience.

There are also many 'paths' to being sustainable and to 'local sustainability', for the ability to define the carrying capacity of a local environment may not contribute towards 'global sustainability'. There is a balance between investments in resources and the sustainability capital, as shown in the fulcrum diagram. This shows that societies can move the importance of investments versus capital by the decisions they make. The increases of sustainability capital are based on the factors discussed in Chapter 11 that provide adaptive capabilities to societies. Investments in resources decrease when climate changes, corruption, or soil degradation decrease the amount of resource capital. Therefore, a country's choices will move it from making sustainable choices to not making sustainable choices, depending on decisions that it makes.

The matrix approach to sustainability shows the context of the decisions that countries need to make in order to acquire resources. It also presents possible connections that this resource consumption has to a country's social resilience. It does not address the constraints that a country may face in producing its own resource supplies, or the constraints faced by the supplier countries. To address these, countries need to be able to determine their solar capital and solar income if they want to make sustainable choices and adapt to climate change.

Final Thoughts on Sustainability Unpacked

As we have argued previously, we see water, energy, food and forests as the 'natural' keys to sustainable futures for nations, regions and localities. When these are juxtaposed to the aggregated human ability to innovate to meet change, we have a crude estimate, at least, of the probability of realizing a sustainable future. Sustainability, in this sense, is the hope that humans can live indefinitely within the Earth's bounds with dignity and without destroying the systems that ultimately sustain them, often described as environmental and natural resources. As we have tried to demonstrate in the preceding chapters, using a representative sample of nations, the pursuit of sustainability appears at first glance to be hopelessly complex. Nations vary enormously in their endowment of natural resources (forests, arable lands, fossil fuels, temperature and moisture regimes, biological diversity, etc; Chapters 3–6). Similarly, they vary as much or more in their political stability, social resilience and ability to cope with unexpected change.

Thus a first approach to decoding and quantifying sustainability is to compare nations using the idea that a major ingredient of sustainability is the ability to meet change, often unpredicted change, successfully. Failures can be caused by unsustainable consumption of resources, caused, in turn by poor management or overpopulation, or simply by failure to alter human institutions as times change (Brewer, 2007).

Therefore, how does one society or even one country move away from repeating the historical patterns of social and environmental problems created by economic development and industrialization, by using these four resources? It is crucial to begin to address these issues, for growing- and emerging-economy countries are rapidly emulating the historical patterns already followed by the advanced-economy countries. It has become increasingly clear that past approaches to economic growth and industrialization result in social and environmental problems when resource supplies are insecure, and may increase the inability of societies to be resilient in the face of an uncertain and unpredictable future. If the influence of resource choices on social adaptation is understood, it may be possible to avoid repeating these patterns. Today, the competition to acquire resource supplies is intensifying because supplies determine whether countries can be economically more competitive. When they are less competitive for resource supplies, social unrest, and problems relating to the environment, as well as to human health, are possible outcomes.

Many approaches can be used to characterize whether choices in resource consumption are sustainable, and there is no need for another model to confound decision makers. For example, in 2008 Paul Collier clearly articulated the difficulties that confine and marginalize a billion people to poverty: conflict and natural resource traps, land-locked with bad neighbours, and bad governance in a small country. There is tremendous merit in these types of analyses. We propose that there is also a need to make choices that are globally based. *Think Global but Act Local* has been a common bumper sticker on cars in the US. It summarizes well why all the countries on this globe, not just the poor countries, need to determine the risk of their local habits of resource consumption and production and how they impact those living in other countries. Even countries that appear to be making sustainable decisions and have successfully developed their human capital may face repercussions from the choices they make, because of climate-change impacts occurring in other parts of the world, or because they drive decisions being made at a distant location. When our decisions do not factor-in choices being made in other regions of the world, they give us a false sense of security because technology has made us less risk-adverse to some disturbances (Tenner, 1996).

Tenner (1996) described how high tide control in Bangladesh encouraged thousands of people to move into reclaimed areas that are floodplain zones, which resulted in hundreds being killed when these zones were flooded during a cyclone. The capacity of these lands to mitigate the impacts of storms has been reduced because of extensive deforestation in the mountains, which magnified downstream impacts of torrential rainfall by increasing runoff and erosion rates. Therefore, in Bangladesh, forest practices had repercussions on water supplies and food production, subsequent to climatic events which reduced people's ability to adapt to disturbances. People did not make these choices with the knowledge of their negative impacts. These negative impacts are a result of unpredictable factors that were not obvious when the decisions were being made. There is a temporal disjunct between decision making and negative impacts, as a major disturbance may be needed to trigger a resultant disastrous event. The overwhelming negative impacts of these unpredictable events are the reasons that we need to reduce the risk of making wrong choices.

If we are to predict where lands can be sustainably managed, some further analysis is necessary. We base this further synthesis and analysis on the belief that the natural endowment of the earth and of nations is the basis of any and all approaches to sustainable behaviour. The primary feature of this endowment can be viewed as the solar radiation arriving at the outer surface of the Earth's atmosphere.

We further suggest that it will be easier to make more sustainable choices when societies consume from the solar income pool (amount of carbon fixed annually) rather than from the solar capital pool (amount of carbon fixed over geologic time) (see Box 9.1). Using solar income as a factor to understand the difficulties a country will face in making sustainable choices will be more useful.

The need to be able to evaluate the land's productive capacity – its solar income – is highlighted by many emerging-economy countries (such as Saudi Arabia, South Korea and Qatar) which are searching for more productive land in Africa (for example, in Mali, Senegal, Sudan and Ethiopia) to grow and control their own food production, and at the same time to reduce their need to import food grown by others (Rice, 2009). This has been labelled 'agro-imperialism' and is being driven by food shortages concerns in these emerging-economy countries. A recent World Bank and FAO study suggests that the 'last large reserves of underused lands is the billion-acres Guinea Savannah zone, a crescent-shaped swatch that runs across Africa all the way to Ethiopia and southward to Congo and Angola' (Rice, 2009). These countries are introducing Green Revolution technologies into a landscape where small farmers have been eking out a living and famine and droughts are recurring events. Development agencies have suggested that these countries need to increase their land's productive capacity and this is only possible by using Green Revolution technologies and a shift from small farms. This suggestion should be adopted cautiously since the constraints introduced by climate and soils (discussed in Chapters 6–9) will make it difficult to increase agricultural productivity. There is a significant risk of land degradation and reductions in social resilience if degraded lands are placed into intensive agriculture.

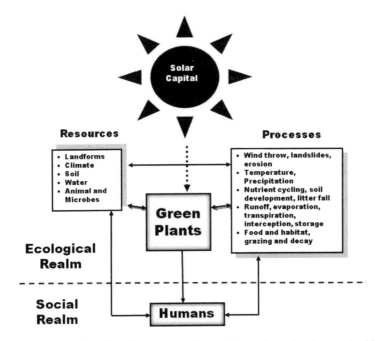

Figure 12.3 *Using the solar-centric view to determine what is sustainable at specific locations*

This 'solar-centric' view of the world and sustainability gives us both a starting point, and a logic to use in modelling what may be sustainable and what may not be, in specific places. The synthesis model is illustrated above in Figure 12.3.

The first step is to compare nations (or regions, or areas within countries) regarding how much of the photosynthetically active solar radiation they receive is converted to stored chemical energy contained in living organisms. The second step is to examine the conversion processes to see if they can continue into the far future, or are clearly temporary and are based on inputs known to be ephemeral. The mining of groundwater, the loss of soil productivity through erosion, the effects of pests and the effects of climate change all are examples of process-limiting agents and are thus sustainability limiting. The third step is to calculate 'ecosystem fit', which is the ratio of incoming photosynthetically active radiation (PAR, visible light) to the amount captured by conversion processes that are not ephemeral (Gordon et al, 1992). Actually these calculations are best attempted in terms of net primary productivity (see Chapter 9), the net rate of capture of carbon through photosynthesis. Thus:

Total current NPP – ephemerally supported NPP / Theoretical maximum NPP = Ecosystem fit

The limited model shown in Figure 12.3 only shows a partial view. In the 'social realm' lie all human endeavours and processes. Our contention is that their scope and sustainability are limited by the processes labelled 'ecological realm' in the diagram; similarly, the 'ecological realm' processes are modified and often limited by human decisions and activities. The separation of the two realms is thus, in that sense, artificial. However, analysis based on this view proceeds best by describing the parts before reconnecting them.

The next step is to trace the allocation of the 'true' NPP in national terms, to calculate how much is in agriculture and in forestry harvests, and to protection purposes, and to examine the implications of the allocation for sustainability. This analysis is not particularly appropriate for countries such as Singapore that get most of their sustenance through trade. Nevertheless, it can be adapted to those countries through an examination of trade patterns: that is, upon an examination of those countries upon whose NPP they live, and the probability of that livelihood being secure and sustainable.

NPP is expressed per unit area and depends on photosynthesis by green plants. Thus, any national comparisons must be weighted by the size and fraction of their area capable of supporting green plants (forests, agricultural and pasture lands, parks and urban forests). Just as importantly, 'fossil' photosynthate (oil, coal, natural gas and peat) and mineral resources available to the compared nation must be accounted for. Finally, in this 'ecological' analysis, water resources will be the third determining factor.

The challenge today is to use large datasets to maintain a diversity of resource choices that also allows humans to continue to adapt to their environment. These should also facilitate making choices, inasmuch as the repercussions of past decisions should be known. Ultimately, decisions are made by people and policy makers. People do not stop adapting, however, while policy makers debate options. Choices are continually being made and need to be made. Each community cannot simply adopt the choices made by a neighbouring community, but it does need to understand its land constraints and opportunities and how best to adapt to them. Despite the need to characterize each country's unique landscape, large datasets can help in understanding the resource options as well as the choices that were made under a particular set of circumstances, so that it becomes possible to make better choices.

The Green Revolution increased the productive capacity of agricultural lands using technology, fertilizers and pesticides. Although the social and environmental costs of the revolution were higher in some locations than in others, it worked! The Green Revolution debunked the myth that high population densities means millions of people will starve. During the 1960s the view was that India would never be able to feed itself. The focus on population size did not factor-in the ability of farmers to produce more food from each unit of land. To address the continuing growth in the country's population and higher demand on its water supplies, Indian farmers were taught how to increase their farm productivities; farmers planted high-yield seeds that were more tolerant of droughts, used chemical fertilizers and irrigated to improve crop yields. Prior to the Green Revolution, farmers in India were subsistence cultivators of rice – a crop that is not very tolerant of droughts. Six years after the Green Revolution introduced high-yield seeds to India, they were self-sufficient in the production of all the cereal crops. Therefore, the Green Revolution increased the adaptability of farmers in India, but the farming practices introduced in the past cannot adapt to the constraints imposed by climate and soils.

In the Green Revolution example, technologies in plant breeding compensated for the large population densities by allowing more food to be grown per unit of land. Sometimes a focus on population size or where people live ignores the fact that humans are great at adapting their behaviour, developing technological breakthroughs or shifting to other resources in periods of scarcity. How well humans will adapt to climate change is unknown at this time, but they have a suite of tools that allows them to adapt. Human history is a series of stories documented, in part, by people who were successful in adapting to their environment. They are the survivors and typically these are the people who write their version of history.

It becomes very apparent from exploring stories from different countries and finding out the reasons why people live in particular parts of the world, that:

1   energy, food, forest materials and water supplies cannot be simultaneously obtained from the same landscape;
2   acquiring one of these four resources has repercussions on the future supply capacity and sustainability of the remaining resources.

This means that if the goal is to allow societies to adapt in order to reduce their vulnerability to climate change, there is a need to manage 'human capital and income' and 'resource capital and income'. Such knowledge would allow a decision maker to determine how difficult it will be for a country to make sustainable choices. An important element of this is NPP, or the natural endowment, since it determines how much energy will be needed to alter the natural productivity of any land. It also clarifies what other resources, such as water supplies, are needed to achieve higher productivities.

If a country's low natural endowments are a result of past land-use activities, there is a need to restore the natural capital in order to reduce societal vulnerability to climate and social change. Investments in nature do not just consist in protecting forests, but in managing them to re-establish their health and perhaps increasing the area of 'managed' forests, especially along the urban–rural interface. Natural endowment is one of the few elements that a country can manage itself, and is effective in contributing towards the development of a country's social resilience. There are many reasons supporting the need for a country to develop or restore its natural endowment. Not only does its restoration increase the acquisition of secure resource supplies for a country, but it also is environmental as it reduces land degradation and also increases social resilience in the face of climate change.

People and the economy are more vulnerable to the potential impacts of climate change, such as droughts, floods and storms, when watersheds and coastal areas are degraded. There is a critical *natural infrastructure* that needs to include the maintenance and restoration of these areas, which include watersheds, wetlands, rivers and deltas. Healthy ecosystems provide the vital services that build the social and economic resilience needed to cope with climate change. Natural and interconnected infrastructures of major river basins, lakes, wetlands, floodplains, natural estuarine and coastal structures and groundwater recharge all reduce the risk from climate change because they create resiliency in the ecosystem.

Resilient ecosystems services also allow humans to become more resilient economically to climate changes. However, there will be hotspots of vulnerability to climate change in these interconnected water systems, to which we should be sensitive. One example is the deltas and coastal mega-cities downstream from the dry lands in some regions and mountains, which are the source(s) of major rivers and associated groundwater regimes. How can the vulnerability of these areas be addressed? Coping with floods, droughts, storms and sea level rise will depend on water storage, flood control and coastal defence. Providing these functions by simply building infrastructure such as dams, reservoirs, dykes and sea walls will not be enough. Engineered infrastructures may not be as inherently flexible as natural systems. They can weaken resilience, especially in a changing climate, where ecosystem adaptation is essential.

Preparing for adaptation now is more cost-effective than waiting until the impacts of climate change are irreversible. The environment provides the necessary 'natural infrastructure' for climate-change adaptation. When watersheds and coastal areas are degraded, people and their economies are more vulnerable to impacts of climate change. All hydrological impacts are of significance to agricultural practices and production, given that agriculture is practised in most parts of the world. For example, changes in precipitation and evaporation have impacts on both river and groundwater systems which could then affect agricultural productivity.

There are many other river basins where investment in the natural infrastructure is reducing its vulnerability to climate change. In 2008, the Worldwide Fund for Nature reported that the following river basins were highly vulnerable to climate change, especially after prior investments had reduced their abilities to provide ecosystem services: the Lower Danube, Eastern Europe; Great Ruaha River, Tanzania; the Yangtze Lakes, China; the Rio Conchos, Mexico; and the Rio São João, Brazil (Palmer et al, 2008). In these instances, restoration of the natural infrastructures was made, as well as involving stakeholders in their management. The capacity to deal with future uncertainties is possible by using a system-based bottom-up approach, utilizing technology and financing and by combining this with capacity building and developing a multi-stakeholder governance structure.

Biological capital can be defined as any resource that can be used to generate economic wealth. The loss of biological capital due to environmental degradation can be compared to a corporation losing its capital; without it, no bank or company can function and will go bankrupt. Given current rates of environmental degradation, we are living beyond our means in terms of natural capital. In his 1939 book *Value and Capital*, Nobel Prize winner and economist John Hicks introduced the notion of the importance of increasing capital stock to increase or maintain the welfare of an economic entity (Hicks, 1939). A company must take care of, and invest in its machinery through capital investments, or it will not be profitable. He spoke about manufacturing capital, but this can also be applied to using our environment.

Costanza et al (1997) valued of the world's ecosystem services and natural capital. Their thesis is that ecological systems and natural capital are critical to the functioning of the earth, and that they contribute directly and indirectly to human wellbeing. They estimated the current economic value of 17 ecosystems services, including climate regulation, water regulation, soil formation, nutrient cycling and 13 more in 16 biomes. They estimated the yearly value to be an average of US$33 trillion per year. Depletion of this natural capital will undermine human welfare, when important systems such as water and soils become degraded.

Ecosystem-value analysis measures what someone is willing to give up in other goods and services in order to obtain a particular good, service or desirable state of an ecosystem. The ecosystem-value analysis, however, may not fully reflect the true cost to ecosystems of decisions made. For example, monetary valuations can be estimated for the disturbance of filling in a wetland, but the ecosystem-value analysis will probably not reflect the full social costs or benefits derived from that decision to fill it in. The 'market' does not usually take these factors into consideration, and it is impossible to truly evaluate the value of an ecosystem, given a cost/benefit and opportunity/cost analysis. In a market-based economy, human actions often result in unintended consequences and side effects. Management and conservation of ecosystems require trade-offs; such trade-offs are based on human values (cultural values of the predominant culture). Before a financial value is placed on a resource, there should be a better understanding of natural systems and their true benefits to society. If ecosystem services cannot be accurately quantified in monetary terms, then they may not be valued appropriately and given the importance they deserve. In addition, our economic system is based on short-term gains, such as corporate profits and stock prices, but it might be more useful to value nature in the long-term rather than short-term.

At times this investment in natural capital means that a country will have to make choices to import resources that they are less capable of producing environmentally at home. This decision, however, has to factor-in the global community as well as the negative repercussions for collecting resources from unproductive or unmanaged lands. Our human history is replete with examples of societies developing their social resilience by taking someone else's resources; this is not an option today. There is a need to shift from the 'one problem' focus that is so common still and to recognize that the consumption of one resource is guaranteed to be linked to, and will affect, some other resource. We can reduce the risk that we are making 'bad' choices if we ensure that societies can remain resilient by using their solar capital that is managed environmentally.

The potential of the NPP analysis presented above lies in finding limits to 'sustainability' and in finding ways to compare areas in sustainability terms. Similar possibilities undoubtedly exist in other frames of reference. Perhaps the most important lesson of the preceding chapters of this book is that we have a long, hard road ahead to define the data required to assess 'sustainability', to systematically gather the data across national and cultural boundaries and to find ways to engage and cooperate to produce databased actions to pursue a sustainable future.

References

Brewer, G. D. (2007) 'Inventing the future: scenarios, imagination, mastery and control', *Sustainability Sciences*, vol 2, pp159–177

Collier, P. (2008) *The Bottom Billion. Why the Poorest Countries are Failing and What Can be Done About it*, Oxford University Press, Oxford and New York, NY

Costanza, R., dArge, R. deGroot, S., Farber, M., Grasso, B., Hannon, K., Limburg, S., Naeem, R., ONeill, V., Paruelo, J., Raskin, R. G., Sutton, P. and vandenBelt, M. (1997) 'The value of the world's ecosystem services and natural capital', *Nature*, 387, pp253–260

FAO (2006) 'Global Forest Resources Assessment 2005', UN FAO, Rome, Italy

Gordon, J. C., Bormann B. T. and Kiester, A. R. (1992) 'The physiology and genetics of ecosystems: a new target or 'Forestry contemplates and entangled bank', Proceedings of the Twelfth North American Forest Biology Workshop, Sault Ste Marie, Ontario, CA, 17–20 August 1992, pp1–14

Hicks, J. (1939) *Value and Capital*, Oxford, Clarendon

IEA (2007) *2007 Key World Energy Statistics*, International Energy Agency, http://tonto.eia.doe.gov/country/country_energy_data.cfm?fips=AO, accessed 1 September 2008

IPCC (2007) 'Summary for Policymakers', in M. L. Parry, O. F. Canziani, J. P. Palutikof, P. J. van der Linden and C. E. Hanson (eds) *Climate Change 2007: Impacts, Adaptation and Vulnerability. Contribution of Working Group II to the Fourth Assessment Report of the Intergovernmental Panel on Climate Change*, Cambridge University Press, Cambridge

Palmer, M. A., Liermann, C. A. R., Nilsson, C., Flörke, M., Alcamo, J., Lake, P. S. and Bond, N. (2008) 'Climate change and the world's river basins: anticipating management options', *Frontiers in Ecology and the Environment*, 6, pp81–89

Rice, A. (2009) 'Agro-imperialism', *The New York Times Magazine*, 22 November 2009, pp46–51

Tenner, E. (1996) *Why Things Bite Back. Technology and the revenge of unintended consequences*, Vintage Books, New York, NY

Yardley, J. (2009) 'Drought puts focus on a side of India untouched by progress', *The New York Times*, vol 158, no 54,789, 5 September 2009, ppA1, A6

Index